What Kinds of Guns Are They Buying for Your Butter?

A BEGINNER'S GUIDE TO DEFENSE, WEAPONRY, AND MILITARY SPENDING

What Kinds of Guns Are They Buying for Your Butter?

A BEGINNER'S GUIDE TO DEFENSE, WEAPONRY, AND MILITARY SPENDING

SHEILA TOBIAS, PETER GOUDINOFF,
STEFAN LEADER, AND SHELAH LEADER

WILLIAM MORROW AND COMPANY, INC.
New York   1982

Library of Congress Cataloging in Publication Data
Main entry under title:

What kinds of guns are they buying for your butter?

Bibliography: p.
Includes index.
1. United States—Armed Forces—Weapons systems.
2. United States—Military policy.   3. United States
—National security.   I. Tobias, Sheila.   II. Title.
UF503.W48   1982   355.8'2'0973   82-12565
ISBN 0-688-01374-0

Printed in the United States of America

First Edition

1 2 3 4 5 6 7 8 9 10

BOOK DESIGN BY BERNARD SCHLEIFER

To our teachers,
past and present

Contents

ONE: THE DYNAMICS OF DEFENSE   15

    The Weapons   18
    Why Nations Arm   23
    The Secular Priests   28

TWO: WEAPONRY AND WARFARE   32

    Sticks and Stones   36
    Science, Weapons, and War   43
    World War II and Beyond   48
    Bombers and Bombs   49
    Nuclear and Thermonuclear Weapons   53
    Nuclear Effects   62
    Missiles   74
    Conclusion   77

LONG ASIDE: BREAKING THE CODE   78

THREE: THE EVOLUTION OF STRATEGIC WEAPONS   86

    Two Kinds of Warfare: Strategic and Tactical   86
    Bombers: The Strategic Air Command (SAC)   89
    Intercontinental Ballistic Missiles: ICBMs   94
    Submarine-Launched Ballistic Missiles: SLBMs   107
    The Triad   114
    Soviet Second-Generation Missiles   116
    Strategic Defense   117
    MIRVing   122
    Catching Up   125
    Cruise Missiles   128
    B-1 Bomber   129
    Trident Submarine   131

MX   133
War in Space   134
Other Countries Heard From   135
Conclusion   135

FOUR: DEADLY LOGIC: THE DETERRENCE OF WAR 137

Capability Analysis   140
Massive Retaliation   141
Flexible Response   146
Thinking About the Unthinkable   150
Arms Limitation   158
The Period After Détente   166
Conclusion   172

FIVE: WEAPONS FOR FIGHTING
        "CONVENTIONAL" WARS   174

Firepower   177
The M-16 Rifle   177
Modern Artillery   179
Surface-to-Surface Missiles   181
Tanks   183
Antitank Weapons   189
Bombs   195
Mobility and Maneuver   195
Cargo Planes   196
Armored Vehicles   199
Helicopters   202
Fighter Aircraft   204
Tactical Missiles   219
AWACS   223
Naval Weapons   225
Conclusion   234

SIX: WHY WE BUY THE WEAPONS WE BUY   236

War vs. Peace: The Bottom Line   242
The Cast of Characters: The Defense Community   245
Profits   248
Cost Overruns   256
DOD: The Department of Defense   260
The Weapons Procurement Process Today   271
Where It All Comes Together: The Defense Budget   280
Conclusion   284

SEVEN: CONTROLLING THE ARMS RACE 286

A Little History 287
Controlling Nuclear Arms 291
SALT I 299
SALT II 304
Verification 316
Détente, Linkage, and Arms Control 321
Future Trends 323

EIGHT: DEFENSE CONTROVERSIES IN THE 1980s 326

The Troubled North Atlantic Alliance 328
The Rapid Deployment Force 334
The Naval Debate 339
Chemical and Biological Warfare 343
The B-1 345
MX—A Missile in Search of a Home 349
ABM, ASAT, and the War in Space 358
The High-Tech Debate 366
What Is Quality? 372
Conclusion 378

AFTERWORD 380

APPENDIX I: MAP OF NUCLEAR WEAPONS
        LOCATIONS IN THE UNITED STATES 385

APPENDIX II: TOP U.S. DEFENSE CONTRACTORS 388

WORKING VOCABULARY 390

FURTHER READING 410

ACKNOWLEDGMENTS 416

INDEX 419

ABOUT THE AUTHORS 431

The greatest danger of war seems to me not to lie in the deliberate actions of wicked men, but in the inability of harassed men to manage events that have run away with them.
                                        —HENRY KISSINGER

What Kinds of Guns
Are They Buying
for Your Butter?

A BEGINNER'S GUIDE TO DEFENSE,
WEAPONRY, AND MILITARY SPENDING

1.

The Dynamics of Defense

MORE THAN ANY OTHER political issue—even more than the economy, which seems to mystify the experts—defense, weaponry, and military spending are subjects that discourage the amateur. Many people, to be sure, feel very strongly about war and peace. For deeply held religious, political, or personal reasons certain people abjure arming at all costs, and they get their point across by refusing to serve in the military or by throwing blood on the Pentagon steps. Others, more selective in their antiwar stance, do not disapprove all wars, just some. And still others are convinced that our nation's security, especially in the face of Soviet military strength, can rest only on military strength of our own and a readiness to use our might—even our nuclear might—to deter war and to defend our interests, wherever they may be.

For most citizens, however, as the pollsters testify again and again, while their feelings may run high, their level of understanding of military policy and their willingness to become informed about its details are very low indeed. As one measure of this, we asked hundreds of people during the period when SALT II was much in the news whether they understood what the S in SALT stood for. To our dismay, more than half did not recognize that S stands for strategic, and very few were conversant with the military meaning of that term.

In fact, strategic weapons (in contrast to tactical or theater weapons) are traditionally only those weapons that can strike at the enemy's heartland. In the context of SALT II, "strategic arms" were to apply only to nuclear weapons of intercontinental range; that is, land-based intercontinental ballistic missiles, submarine-launched ballistic missiles, and long-range bombers. The people we queried were "for" or "against" arms control in a passionate way; but without knowing what kinds of weapons were involved or in what ways they were to be limited, how could these people have effectively debated either side on SALT?

The same level of misunderstanding surfaced when we talked about our nuclear arsenal. Most people were surprised to learn that the nuclear weapons stockpiled today are very much more powerful than the atomic bombs dropped on the Japanese at Hiroshima and Nagasaki at the end of World War II. The fact is, we (and the Russians) have transformed our arsenals during the past twenty-five years from atomic to primarily hydrogen warheads and bombs, and the few atomic devices still produced are small and are meant for battlefield applications or are used as triggering mechanisms for much larger hydrogen bombs. In fact—and this is precisely what is not widely appreciated—a one-megaton hydrogen bomb, a fairly standard size in modern arsenals, has the explosive power of almost 100 Hiroshima bombs and is 100,000 times more destructive than the standard high-explosive aerial bomb used in World War II.

Today a growing number of citizens here and abroad are beginning to protest the continuing arms competition between the United States and the Soviet Union and to worry about the political consequences and the high cost of America's proposed weapons modernization, as well as the scope and pace of Soviet weapons developments. Yet few people have come to grips with their personal level of ignorance about military subjects and with the consequences of that ignorance for the nation as a whole. Why is this? Is it aversion? Anxiety? A sense of powerlessness? Despair? Or is it that we do not know how to begin to ask the questions that will give us the knowledge to make us more confident and more persuasive in the debates about military affairs?

The stuff is certainly complicated. Not just the weapons, but the systems, the politics, the bureaucratic structures, the relations with industries that work for the military, to say nothing of military doctrines themselves. We all know this much: that nuclear energy is the release of the very forces that glue matter together and that the world had to await the genius of Einstein and the ingenuity of Fermi, Oppenheimer, Teller, and the other physicists to break through the limits of dynamite and TNT to unleash the vast explosive power that our weapons now command.

Once upon a time the tools of war were familiar in civilian life as well. Citizen soldiers brought their horses and rifles, their feed and their blankets to battle. But today the majority of our weapons—nuclear and non-nuclear, guns and vehicles—have no other utility than fighting. This means most of us never get to see or feel modern weaponry. We have the barest sense of the relative size of our ships and planes. And unless we make a special effort, we cannot begin to know the difference between an A-10 and F-4 (both airplanes), a Polaris and Poseidon (submarine-launched missiles), not to mention TOW, EMP, CEP, Sidewinders, and the like.

Not that the information is classified. It's available in abundance. There are thousands of books, scientific journals, military magazines, and even popular publications to read. But again, unless we have a background in engineering or military science or are amateur battle buffs, these sources are either not normally at hand or are hard to follow. We have to rely instead, when military matters make the news, on well-done but still complex newspaper and newsmagazine stories which generally focus on what is *new* and not on the older context in which some weapons development or change in doctrine is taking place. Besides, the language is arcane. While terms like *megatonnage, throwweight, deterrence,* and *MIRV* have slowly made their way into the public's vocabulary, like the term *strategic* these words are familiar without being really understood.

Even the Congressmen and -women who have to make judgments about defense, weaponry, and military spending do not always fully comprehend the technical details. One House Foreign Affairs Committee staffer told us—without being as surprised as we—that what his members really need to know are "how many Hiroshimas" a new warhead represents. Like the rest of us, some members of Congress cannot fathom "TNT equivalence" hundreds of times larger than the first atomic bombs. And if our elected leaders find themselves unable to talk turkey with the experts, who can?

In the beginning, we four authors thought this book would deal largely with defense and military spending and that weaponry would be treated in a useful and usable inventory of current instruments of war. But as we have thought more about these matters, we have changed our minds. While questions such as Why do nations arm? or the various nuclear war scenarios are interesting and important for lay people to grasp, we now understand that one reality is the weapons themselves. Their capabilities and the fear that if we do not exploit all the technological possibilities the Russians will do it first are important factors driving military policy and shaping military thinking. (Although, as we shall see in the pages that follow, they are not the only forces at work.)

We began to discover—especially the two women who began this project at about the same level of ignorance as the citizens we queried—that knowledge about the weaponry, including its technical aspects and above all its technical limitations, helps us understand how it is intended to fit into our military planning. Moreover, we realize now that this kind of information is by itself empowering. Without pretending to anything like expertise in these matters, we find that a general familiarity with the weapons gives even those of us who are new to the subject much more credibility in debate and makes us feel far more comfortable thinking about defense, surely one of the most important issues of our day.

THE WEAPONS

If you can forget for a while that they are instruments of destruction, modern weapons are dazzling in terms of their power, their precision, and what they can be programmed to do and girded to withstand. There are airplanes that can be programmed to fly but 50 feet off the ground at 700 miles per hour, literally skipping over hillocks and telephone poles—the terrain being continuously observed and the route adjusted by complex radar; missiles, which are accurate over a 6,000-*mile* projected path (from Tucson, Arizona, to Murmansk, USSR, for instance), and which can score a hit within 500 *feet* of their targets after passing twice through the earth's atmosphere and traveling at 20,000 miles per hour; tanks so massive that they can drive through houses with hardly a bump; guided bombs with television "eyes"; air-launched cruise missiles so effective in finding their targets that they can be aimed and launched from hundreds of miles away; radar able to "see" thousands of miles; air transports bigger than high-rise buildings, capable of hauling hundreds of soldiers and hundreds of thousands of pounds of equipment. Not to mention massive aircraft carriers crewed by 5,000 or more men who operate nearly 100 jet fighters and bombers in almost any weather; and nuclear-powered submarines cruising the world underwater for 60–70 days at a time without surfacing for fuel, air, or supplies.

Indeed, if making things work is an art form, weapons builders have pressed the fields of engineering, design, applied science, and artificial intelligence (that is, computer-operated systems) to their limits. And the implementation of these designs, including testing, production of prototypes and mass assembly, is a marvel of scientific management guiding a collective effort. While the hull of a Trident submarine is being manufactured by one company and its nuclear power plant by another, its missiles will be produced by still a third, and all presumably will come together at the end in more or less perfect engineering harmony.

Certainly, there are civilian structures that have resulted from the same sort of talent and organization. We are reminded of the fitting of the last structural piece of the St. Louis Gateway Arch in 1965. Two construction teams had begun, following a blueprint, each from the opposite ends of the arch to build upward. Then, at the appointed hour, the two teams met with one more space to fill and one more perfectly fitting block. Everyone in St. Louis came out to watch that day and stayed, of course, to cheer.

So it is with the weapons. We cannot but applaud the feats. But of course when we think about their capabilities we are wary and scared.

Nuclear weapons, with their massive release of explosive power, have been around now for almost forty years, but are still being "improved" in the sense of being made more powerful, more tailor-made for certain tasks, and more compact. In the past ten years alone, the efficiency of nuclear weapons has improved substantially. But even as those weapons continue to evolve, a whole new kind of warfare—the harnessing of light by laser, called "directed energy"—is just around the corner. Our children may in their lifetime witness the scrapping of old (and hopefully never used) intercontinental ballistic missiles rendered vulnerable and obsolete by laser beams.

And while the earth is still our primary fighting surface, war in space—attacks and counterattacks on satellites—is already being contemplated by both sides.

The foregoing is not meant to substitute gush for gore but rather to help us understand why even the most advanced weapons often engender counterweapons and why it is that governments seem unable to say Halt! The drive to do and make anything that can be done and made can be explained by our fear that the Russians might do it and put us all in jeopardy. Our leaders, after all, take an oath to protect and defend the nation against domestic and foreign enemies. And as we shall see, the world is a dangerous place. But also at work is the attraction of the new, because like Everest for the mountaineer, the possibilities are there. The point is that so long as the President, the Congress, the military, and many of our fellow citizens want to do what can be done, the military budget has got to grow and the technological complexities of our weapons systems increase.

Besides the engineering possibilities, it is our rivalry and fear of the Soviet Union of course that drive our military spending. Much of what we build is built with the Russians in mind, and they, too, are locked into watching and emulating us and into protecting themselves from us. To wit: the United States was seriously considering the production of a new long-range bomber in the 1950s which was given the designation B-70 (*B* for bomber). For reasons that we shall not go into here, the bomber was never produced in large numbers. Just two prototypes were manufactured. One crashed while on a publicity flight and the other found its way into the Air Force Museum at Wright-Patterson Air Base in Dayton, Ohio. But no matter. The Russians, having some advance warning of the size and capabilities of the plane, went ahead and built a fighter to match its capabilities and shoot it down if necessary. Now the Russians find themselves with MiG-25 fighters specifically designed to attack the B-70 that we long ago decided not to deploy, and they had to find another use for the planes.

Another driving pressure to continue spending for weapons is the numbers of men and women supported directly and indirectly by the industry. Some 70 percent of all engineers are said to be working in one way or another on military hardware. Perhaps as many as 5.8 million workers, out of a total labor force of 90 million, work in defense or defense-related industries. Dozens of cities and towns, all the way from Marietta, Georgia, where Lockheed Aircraft has one manufacturing facility, to Texas, Long Island, Connecticut, Seattle, Boston, California, and Arizona—where we are writing this—thrive because of the military budget. The economic dislocations that closing or reducing production in these factories would mean would be far greater than the impact of the slump in auto production in Michigan. This is not even to calculate in the economic role of the military men and women who are members of or retired from the armed services. And when Congress began to consider reducing the size of the increase in the fiscal 1983 defense budget, Secretary of Defense Caspar Weinberger was quick to note how many jobs would be lost as a result.*

We have, in short, without necessarily pointing a finger at a military-industrial complex, a massive national *commitment* to military spending. What security it provides benefits us all. Moreover, because of the particular benefits to some citizens and their communities, there is a significant inertia in the situation as it has come to be. The outbreak of nuclear war would, of course, benefit no one. (Conventional wars are very costly these days. The British are reported to have spent $1 million *an hour* battling the Argentinians in the 1982 Falklands War; the Israelis, an entire year's GNP in the 1973 war.) But arming to deter such an outbreak can

*The Washington Post, March 9, 1982, page A2.

be said to benefit many, mainly in terms of security, but financially, too.*

In times past, weapons were either offensive (designed to attack the enemy) or defensive (intended to protect us from enemy attack). Nuclear weapons have produced a fundamental change in our strategic thinking. Unlike all previous weapons in history, nuclear weapons (at least the strategic kind) are used mainly as *deterrents*. They can threaten. They can hold populations hostage. They can attack the enemy after he attacks us, in a punitive way, and they can even be used preemptively in anticipation of an attack, but they cannot *shield* us—they cannot defend us in the traditional way that "defense" used to imply. Thus, since the first and only two atomic bombs were used against the Japanese at the end of World War II, nuclear weapons exist not to be used.

Since both the United States and the Soviet Union today have enough thermonuclear weapons to destroy one another, you are probably asking yourself, Why do we keep building more? The answer lies partly in technology and partly in doctrine. To work, deterrence requires several preconditions: The enemy must know, roughly, how much and what kinds of nuclear weapons we have—that is, our capability. And the enemy must believe in our willingness to use our weapons—that is, our credibility. As one expert put it recently, "It's not enough to have enough weapons, you must be *seen* to have enough." If we are to remain "credible," our leaders tell us, we have to be able to retain our technological edge over the Soviet Union. And since we surely do not want to be surprised by some new missile or bomber or radar that the Russians develop (because they are not standing still), we have to continue to work on many new weapons. As a result, nuclear weapons increase in numbers and improve continually.

When our nuclear monopoly ended in the 1950s, our political leaders had two choices (or so they perceived their choices to be): first, to seek nuclear superiority, a costly and perhaps elusive goal; or, second, to seek nuclear parity— rough equality in nuclear power.

---

*Of course, we could also reduce our commitment to military spending, and might, like Japan and West Germany, find the economic results salutary.

Some believe that the Reagan administration, with its renewed interest in expanding our nuclear forces and its refusal to seek ratification of the Strategic Arms Limitation Treaty (SALT II), is seeking nuclear superiority. To accomplish this, there is a projected six-year weapons modernization plan that calls for $78 billion for bombers and cruise missiles, $51 billion for sea-based weapons, $42 billion for intercontinental ballistic weapons (missiles), $29 billion for nuclear defense (air defense and civil defense), $22 billion for command control and communications (C^3); or a total of $222 billion for new weapons to add to and in some cases replace those we have now. Of course, the Reagan administration insists it is merely trying to redress a balance upset by Soviet spending.

What is the context for all of this buying? Why do nations arm?

WHY NATIONS ARM

She was planning to buy a gun. "I'm not going to stand passively by and be mugged," she said. "Someone tries to break into my apartment, I'm going to blow him away." The bravado concealed a certain amount of anxiety. And with good reason. Some parts of our cities are not safe. Everyone knows someone who has been mugged, raped, or burgled. Women feel especially vulnerable since they are often victims of violent crimes and "everyone knows" you cannot find a cop when you need one. Besides, the police cannot be everywhere and a great deal of street crime goes unpunished.

The world, too, seems violent and unsafe. Political kidnappings, assassinations, and bombings occur almost daily. In Lebanon and Northern Ireland, innocent civilians are crushed between warring factions. There is a simmering guerrilla war in Afghanistan which from time to time spills over into Pakistan. There is a war in El Salvador and another in Ethiopia. The North Vietnamese are still fighting, now in Cambodia. The war between Iran and Iraq is no less violent and, indeed, may throw the whole Persian Gulf into chaos. And the war over the Falklands has been costly to both sides.

Elsewhere there is internal strife. The Soviets threatened to intervene in Poland but the Polish security forces did it for them. Communal violence in Lebanon is always in the background, like static from a badly tuned radio. The Arab-Israeli conflict seems endless in spite of the Camp David accords. Palestinian terrorists attack Israel and the Israelis respond. The Israelis bombed an Iraqi nuclear reactor in 1981 because they feared it was being used to develop nuclear weapons. They virtually annexed the Golan Heights (captured from Syria in the 1967 war), and the Syrians, who have refused to negotiate peace with Israel, called it an act of war.

Hostility from past wars simmers as well. The Soviets, for example, still hold four islands seized from the Japanese at the end of World War II. They not only refuse to negotiate their return, but they have fortified them, literally within sight of the Japanese island of Hokkaido. The Japanese, who devote less of their resources to arms than any other major country in the world (less than one percent of their gross national product, compared to nearly 6 percent of ours), fiercely resent the Soviet presence and worry about the growth of Soviet power in Asia. Indeed, the Soviets have probably done more to cause the Japanese to increase their defense spending than American pressure on them.

Why do nations arm? They usually give the same reason as the woman who wants a gun. The world is unsafe. And most people do not expect things to get any better. A 1981 Gallup Poll conducted in twenty-six nations found that most people in all the countries surveyed believed 1982 would be at least as troubled a year as 1981, probably worse, and they were right. Nations—some more than others—face a variety of dangers and feel they need weapons to protect themselves. They worry, first and foremost, about protecting their borders and their independence (sovereignty, in the lingo of lawyers and political scientists). They worry internally about *coups d'état* and revolutionaries. Because of fear, they buy or build guns, tanks, fighter planes, missiles, and other kinds of military equipment and they train people to use them. In 1980 alone, all the nations of the world spent a total of nearly $600 billion on weapons.

National leaders cannot find a cop when they need one, because there are no cops to police the world. True, from time to time the United Nations forms a "police force" to separate antagonists in the Middle East, on Cyprus, or in Africa to secure a truce. A multinational force is currently stationed in the Sinai to assure Egyptian and Israeli compliance with provisions of the Camp David Agreement. The UN sometimes uses its moral and political authority to "condemn" international violence. Sometimes it can even stop wars. But rarely has it been able to prevent war. And it obviously has not been able to prevent terrorism.

As economists say, "There's no free lunch." Everything has a cost, and it is not all monetary. People who arm to protect themselves against crime may cause fear among their neighbors, causing them in turn to arm. And people sometimes go berserk and shoot others for no apparent reason. Sometimes children find firearms and shoot playmates or siblings. People get killed in the heat of arguments or because they are mistaken for burglars. And, of course, some people acquire firearms not so much to protect themselves as to threaten others. There are good reasons to be afraid.

So it is with nations. Some cause anxiety among their neighbors because they have more arms than seem necessary for self-defense. Egypt worries about Libya's large military forces, and lots of countries worry about Libya's public support for terrorists. What are Libyan military forces doing in Chad? What are Cuba's plans in the Caribbean? Will the North Koreans invade South Korea again?

Then there are the Soviets. The CIA estimates that the USSR spends between 12 and 14 percent of its gross national product to produce arms and to maintain large armed forces—four million strong. They cannot produce automobiles in numbers sufficient to satisfy their citizens, but they produced 3,000 tanks in 1980 (compared to 750 produced in the United States). They can't produce enough food to feed their people. Why do they devote such a large proportion of their resources to weaponry?

The Pentagon says, somewhat ominously, that the Soviets spend more than is necessary for legitimate self-defense. Perhaps they do. On the other hand, they have been invaded several times in recent history and have seen much of their country ravaged and their population decimated in World War II. Current Soviet leaders, among the oldest (average age over seventy) of the world, experienced that war firsthand and remember it well. They would rather not repeat the experience and certainly not on Soviet territory. Arguments about Soviet military intentions have raged for years. Since no one can read the minds of Soviet leaders, we cannot be sure of their aims. But one thing is clear: whatever their intentions, the Russians' pursuit of their national security causes us to worry about ours and vice versa.

Is our fear rational? That is hard to answer. At times our fear of communism has been hysterical, as during the Red Scare of the 1920s or in the McCarthy period of the early 1950s. Nevertheless, there are the beginnings of cooperative political and trade relationships. Yet the two countries remain geopolitical and ideological rivals. Not only do the Soviets represent a fundamentally different (and for most Americans dangerous) view of the organization of society, they also have the means to kill 100 million Americans within thirty minutes. It is not necessary to believe that the Soviets are planning such an attack or even that they are likely to launch one without provocation. (The Pentagon acknowledges that a surprise nuclear attack is the least likely of all the contingencies for which it plans.) The fact that they have the means to do it means we dare not ignore them. And our having the same capability makes us, of course, the source of the same kinds of anxiety for them.

The geopolitical rivalry between our two nations can be traced back to the middle of the nineteenth century. A mid-century cartoonist, with amazing foresight, drew a picture of the world with Uncle Sam encompassing one half and Ivan the other, labeling his picture "Two Young Giants." Today our rivalry extends over much of the world because both giants tend to believe that the friendship and security of other parts of the world are vital for their own security. As a consequence, they not only have to be prepared to defend their own territory, but that of their allies as well.

The United States has global interests. Its security depends on countries far from its shores. Oil from the Persian Gulf is vital for the United States and for Europe. We depend on a host of raw materials from other parts of the world. (We import at least half our supplies of more than twenty vitally important materials.) And we sell billions of dollars' worth of goods every year to developing countries as well as to western Europe and Japan. Their freedom and independence and their willingness to buy from us are important to us.

The Soviets, too, see parts of the world beyond their borders as vital for their security. They cultivate and support friendly regimes and liberation movements in Asia, Africa, the Middle East, and Latin America. Obviously they prefer friendly regimes in eastern Europe. Poland is especially vital. For hundreds of years the Poles and Russians were enemies. The Nazis seized Poland in 1939 and, despite their nonaggression pact with the Soviet Union, invaded Russia two years later. So it is not surprising that the Soviets cling so tenaciously to eastern Europe and especially East Germany and Poland. As George Kennan points out, "it was the memory of the grievous injury done the Soviet Union by the Germans while they were fighting in that country that caused the Soviet regime to consider it vital to its security to retain ultimate control of at least the eastern third of Germany and all intervening territory, in order to ensure that Russia would not again be confronted by a rearmed and united Germany, possibly allied—this time—with the United States."[*]

The cost of this security is high. The Soviets have to maintain large military forces in or near eastern Europe at all times and periodically use or threaten to use them to keep acceptable regimes in those countries. The principal cost, however, is borne by the eastern Europeans themselves. They pay with their freedom and independence.

Collectively, NATO (the North Atlantic Treaty Organization) spends more on armaments than do the Warsaw Pact nations (including the Soviet Union). And overall, NATO armed forces are about equal in terms of numbers of men under arms to those of the Warsaw Pact.[†] (Of course not all NATO troops are located where they would do the most good, and the Soviets could probably achieve local superiority by concentrating their forces and attacking at a time and place of their own choosing.) Furthermore, the Soviets have few real friends among the world's nations. In some parts of eastern Europe they are tolerated. Elsewhere they are hated. The 1981 imposition of martial law in Poland will certainly not make the Soviets more popular. And to the east there are the Chinese, who, since the Sino-Soviet split, can-

[*] "As the Kremlin Sees It," *The New York Times,* January 6, 1982, page A19.
[†] International Institute of Strategic Studies, *The Military Balance, 1981–82* (London, 1982), page 124.

not be trusted by the Russians. The Soviets keep about one-fourth of all their military forces in the Far East because of this potential threat.

There is also a psychological reason why the Soviets maintain the kinds of military forces they do. They want to be treated as a superpower and they cannot equal or rival the West in any area other than in arms. They cannot do it in agriculture. They cannot create a comparable standard of living for their citizens. Nor can they match us, Japan, or western Europe in advanced technology for civilian production. The Soviets have acquired a rough parity with our nuclear arsenal. By some measures they surpass us; by other measures we surpass them. We both have the capacity to inflict devastating damage on the other.

But as we have seen, all these nuclear weapons cannot shield us from attack. For the past thirty years we have used our nuclear weapons to deter an attack by threatening to retaliate if we are attacked. The resulting stalemate has created an uneasy peace. And this, by itself, has fundamentally changed the issues of defense, weaponry, and military spending. It is also one reason why there probably cannot be any real security without arms control.

THE SECULAR PRIESTS

Early in 1982, then Secretary of State Alexander M. Haig, Jr., said that the government was not going to follow the lowest common denominator of public opinion in selecting a policy on El Salvador. The public "mood," he said, was too unreliable. We did not have the facts or the understanding of foreign affairs to play a role.

But who does? How do the people who make those decisions about national security *know* and what do they know that makes them so different from the rest of us?

Writing more than a century ago, John Stuart Mill noted that by the nineteenth century all the traditional sources of authority had been discredited. Previously the masses had been led, taught what to think and whether to think, either by divinely ordained or noble leaders. While Mill celebrated the end of that period, he noted with amazing prescience that people could not long tolerate an absence of that kind of authority and predicted (though he did not use the term, John Kenneth Galbraith in our own time was to name them) that soon we would be serving a new kind of authority—the "secular priests."* Mill thought that these people would be scientists. The power of the new priesthood would rest on their specialized knowledge.

Most decisions about weapons, strategy, and national security—although they may be formally promulgated by the President and dutifully voted on by the Congress—are born in the heads of our new secular priests. There is a defense community made up both of people in high positions in the Department of Defense and the Department of State and of those who have held or will hold these positions again when the administration changes. In many instances, the incoming President does not know the men (very few women are part of this community) he will select to advise him on military policy before he has been elected. He relies on recommendations by other experts and trusted political allies.

What were these people doing, one often wonders, in the months before they were nominated to these top posts?

Many were in waiting, in a sort of "government in exile." Think tanks provide the support they need between administrations. The Democrats, for example, rely heavily on the Brookings Institution. The Republicans for the past few years have been relying on several institutions: the Georgetown University Center for Strategic and International Studies, the Hoover Institute of Stanford University, and the American Enterprise Institute. Some Presidents raid Harvard, others the California Institute of Technology or the Rand Corporation. Business is of course another important source.

There is, then, a professional defense community that numbers in the few hundreds at the highest levels, the thousands at the middle-management stratum. Whether in or out of government, they stay in communication with one another and with political leaders who might in the future be

*John Stuart Mill, "The Spirit of the Age," Gertrude Himmelfarb, ed., *Essays on Politics and Culture* (New York: Doubleday, 1962), pages 3–50, especially pages 12–13; John K. Galbraith, *A Life in Our Times: Memoirs* (Boston: Houghton Mifflin Company, 1981), *passim.*

looking for experts. While waiting they continue to study national security and military questions and write analytic articles for such journals as *Foreign Affairs, Foreign Policy, International Security, Commentary, The Public Interest, Aviation Week & Space Technology,* the American Enterprise Institute's *Defense Review, Armed Forces Journal, Survival,* and the like.

Most local newspapers cover defense sporadically and certainly not in depth. They report the "news," that is, decisions after the fact. The national newspapers do a better job. In fact, one military affairs writer, Leslie Gelb of *The New York Times,* was considered so well informed on defense matters that he was recruited for a position in the Carter administration as director of the State Department's Bureau of Political-Military Affairs. His successor at the *Times,* Richard Burt, was recruited for the same post by the Reagan administration. The *Times, The Washington Post, The Wall Street Journal, Time, Newsweek,* and *U.S. News and World Report* surely deserve prizes for their efforts to clarify the esoteric nature of the debates on weaponry, for their helpful diagrams and insightful reporting. But even where defense is thoughtfully covered, it is out of context. What we beginners need to know is how we got to where we are. And what are the fundamental assumptions our leaders are making about the weapons and about the Russians that lead them to these decisions?

Most people never had a course in college called "Strategic Studies" or "National Security." Yet the subject has become an important field of study with headquarters in several key universities in this country and abroad. In addition to providing the government with available experts for high positions, centers for research on strategic studies, together with weapons laboratories manned by scientists and engineers, give our leaders the data they rely on in making their decisions. The way the military "knows" that a certain number of A-10 airplanes are going to be needed to stop a massive Soviet tank assault on Europe—there are no dress rehearsals in war—is by modeling; that is, simulating with the use of computers what so much firepower mounted against so many armored vehicles is likely to produce. When the computer crunches out its solutions to the problems presented to it, the weapons analysts tell the military that our forces are "adequate" or unlikely to have the desired effect.

No one, not even the President, can easily challenge this level of expertise. Nor can he easily challenge the "strategy experts" who assure him that given everything they know about Russian interests in Europe and Russian military capabilities, the Russians might mount a massive tank assault if certain developments were to take place. Oh, yes, the experts are aware of the glitches in the system. They tend to report their conclusions with a "plus" or "minus" confidence level, and carefully hedge their predictions (they may be wrong but only by this much or that much). But those computer print-outs and those reams of analyses can be hard to withstand. And if the President is unwilling to accept the data, there are other political figures who will be happy to use the experts' conclusions to support their views.

George Kennan, writing in 1982, is so dismayed at the failure of our leaders to wrest a bigger and different picture from all of this information that he predicts the "peoples of America and Europe" will soon insist on taking on the job of deciding on their own national security irrespective of the experts' advice. But until then—if that day actually occurs— the ordinary citizen ends up not being listened to because the experts, with some justice, say he does not know what he is talking about.

Maybe it is possible to learn.

2.

Weaponry and Warfare

LET'S IMAGINE YOU have become interested in defense policy. You are concerned about the military budget and want to take a meaningful part in debates on the issues involved. But you have never owned a firearm, you don't know the difference between a musket and a bayonet, you never played with toy soldiers, and when you read *War and Peace* you skipped the battles. You are not an engineer or scientist. Otherwise you might happen upon articles on weaponry in professional magazines like *Science* or *Tech News*. You've never seen *Aviation Week & Space Technology*—a weekly newsmagazine—on any of your friends' coffee tables, or *Military Enthusiast,* and no one in your family, as far as you know, is a member of the Military Book Club. Yet you have questions about defense spending and nuclear weapons, and you want to be able to talk to knowledgeable people about these issues. Where do you begin?

Well, if it's thermonuclear war you care about, you might start with deterrence theory and strategic doctrine (see Chapter Four). Or if it's the expensive weapons we've got or are talking about buying, you might try to get up to speed with some current weapons inventories (see Chapters Three and Five). But the technology of weapons and the assumptions and scenarios behind them rest so much on what has gone before that you might just find yourself even more confused, even intimidated. Besides, how do you know what you need to know if you do not know anything at all?

Perhaps it is best, then, to start at the beginning, both because the tools of war in earlier times were simpler and because the rate at which tactics and weaponry changed was considerably slower. The history of war is the story of attempts by groups of men and nations to gain control over other people. To do this, since the dawn of recorded history men have invented tools of war that kill or wound (or threaten to kill and wound) their enemies, destroy their fortifications, and consume the resources they need to continue fighting.

This is not to imply that killing, injuring, and destroying are the only objectives of war; or that they are the only means of keeping score. In the Middle Ages, knights were usually not killed but captured and held for ransom. In some primitive tribes, even to this day wars "end" as soon as one person on either side is hurt. But since war as we know it is characterized by inflicting or threatening to inflict so much damage that the enemy agrees not to continue fighting, a history of weaponry will give us much insight into war.

What happened in history seems to have been inevitable. With every new weapon in time (though sometimes a great deal of time had to elapse) came a defense against that weapon. And with every successful defense came some new means to overcome it. Walled fortresses and cities provided protection against men armed with pikes, swords, and crossbows. These walls in turn were brought down by bombards—massive siege weapons that hurled stones, iron balls, burning pitch, and even primitive explosives—and once the walls were down, of course, foot soldiers moved on in. Yet, fortifications notwithstanding, the tough, professional, and disciplined Roman infantry, armed with short swords, spears, and shields, was invincible for centuries. It expanded the Empire and protected its borders, until internal disorder permitted hordes from the East on foot and mounted on horseback (and aided by the invention of the harness and bridle) to defeat them. As Roman roads decayed during the Middle Ages, armored knights on horseback became the principal offensive and defensive weapons system. Protected by chain mail armor (a flexible iron mesh), iron helmet and shield, equipped with sword and lance, the knight and his fast-moving horse were more than a match for the infantry of the time. When English longbowmen (not of noble blood)

bombards

chain mail armor

longbow

demonstrated in the fourteenth century that their arrows could bring down mounted knights, they set in motion diverse changes in warfare. Knights had to add plates of armor and clothe their horses in armor, too. By the seventeenth century their armor had become so heavy and awkward that it prompted James I of England to quip: "Armor provides double protection. It keeps the knight from being injured, and it keeps him from injuring others as well."

There is no question that advances in weapons technology tend to render previous offensive and defensive systems obsolete, and to give advantage to the side that is first with the new technology. Perhaps the most graphic example of this is given by Bernard and Fawn Brodie, authors of one of the best and most readable histories of weapons, in describing the arrival on the scene of battle of the English longbow.* The war was the Hundred Years' War between England and France. The battle was the Battle of Crécy, in northern France, and the year was 1346. The English won, we are told, because their longbows could shoot farther, with greater accuracy at long range, and faster than the crossbows used by Genoese mercenaries fighting for the French. A yard-long arrow shot from a longbow could kill a horse or a knight in chain mail at 200 yards. But innovations of this sort were few and far between. Firearms capable of being fired as quickly or accurately as the longbow were not developed until the nineteenth century.

There are several major lessons to be learned from studying the evolution of weapons. First, new weapons or dramatic improvements in old ones often—but not always—create a military advantage for the side possessing them. But that advantage in time may be nullified (sometimes only after a *long* time) by the development of an effective defense against the new weapon, and when the enemy adopts the new weapon as well, the advantage is lost. Second, the *pace* of innovation on the development of weapons was until recently—the end of the nineteenth century—astonishingly slow. It was only with the advent of the Industrial Revolution and the application of modern science to war that the pace of change in weapons and warfare quickened to make

---

* Bernard and Fawn M. Brodie, *From Crossbow to H-Bomb* (Bloomington: Indiana University Press, 1973), page 39.

rapid obsolescence of weapons and tactics commonplace. Today we experience a technological revolution every five years. That has enormous effects on weapons technology. As a result, new weapons sometimes become obsolete before they can be produced in the numbers planned. (We will explore this problem further in Chapter Six.)

In contrast, there were few major innovations in weapons from, say, the Greeks and Romans until the nineteenth century. Siege weapons that were used in Europe in A.D. 1300 were basically the same as those in use two thousand years earlier. Throughout the Middle Ages there was almost no progress in the evolution of weapons or in methods of attack against fortifications.

The crossbow, which was a key weapon of the Middle   crossbow
Ages, had already been used by the Greeks. The sword, used with great skill by the ancient Assyrians, changed little for centuries and continued to be a standard piece of British Army issue until 1937.

Firearms also developed slowly, changing hardly at all until the nineteenth century. The flintlock musket, which   muskets
came into wide use in 1650, remained in use for two hundred years. In contrast, the World War I Springfield rifles carried into battle by American troops in 1917 were already obsolete by World War II twenty-four years later, and were soon replaced by the semiautomatic M-1 Garand.

Artillery or field guns changed little from the Middle   artillery
Ages through the nineteenth century. Cannon used in the Civil War had more in common with instruments used four hundred years earlier than with the artillery that turned Flanders Field (in France) into a moonscape in World War I. Real improvements in artillery required an expanded knowledge of ballistics; chemistry (which rapidly developed in the eighteenth century); metallurgy and the manufacturing techniques of the Industrial Revolution (nineteenth century).

Similarly, the construction of warships hardly changed from the time of the Spanish Armada (1588) to Napoleon (1805); Lord Nelson's flagship at the Battle of Trafalgar, *Victory,* was then forty years old. It was the development of steam power and armor plating of ships in the midnineteenth century that set in motion the rapid changes culminating in the development of the battleship. These armored

warships, equipped with long-range guns, were so significant in their time that countries measured their military
strength in terms of numbers of battleships. And when it
came to negotiating disarmament treaties early in the twentieth century, it was battleship tonnage that was limited.

Finally, and perhaps most important, technology has
multiplied the destructive power of weapons and the distance we can hurl them by thousands of times. Just two examples will serve here. In the thirteenth century one archer
with a longbow could shoot a single arrow and kill a
mounted knight 200 yards away. Shooting quickly and accurately, he might be able to kill twenty or thirty more before
he ran out of arrows. Multiply that archer by several hundred and one can compute—even without a pocket calculator—the destructive potential. Today one man can fire a
single missile (although in the United States two or more are
usually required to activate parallel sets of switches) and kill
hundreds of thousands of people 6,000 miles away. Multiply
that missile by several thousand and one can begin to comprehend, although dimly, the extent of the change.

We need to keep these issues in mind as we take a look
at the evolution of weapons.

STICKS AND STONES

In the beginning there were two weapons: sticks and
stones. Most sticks were wood, but a good piece of bone
would do—the jawbone of an ass, for example. Sticks were
mostly used as clubs and while a stone could also be used
this way, it was even more damaging when thrown. And this
was the origin of throwing sports in ancient times: the dis-
cus, the javelin, ritualized forms of war. By throwing a stone,
the warrior could engage his opponent beyond arm's reach.
It was even better if one stood on higher ground to throw;
then gravity helped propel the stone.

Another way to increase the distance a stone could reach
was with the sling. The primitive sling was but a simple device, composed of two thongs and a pouch. A stone was put
in the pouch and the slinger then spun the sling by the
thongs. At the precise moment—no doubt learned through

long and arduous practice—one thong would be released and the stone, carrying the energy built up in the spinning, flew out much farther than the arm could throw. (And thus did little David slay the mighty Goliath.)

Sticks and stones inflict injuries by crushing, to break your bones, as the saying goes. A knife, on the other hand, cuts. The goal in knife combat is to stab some vital organ— the heart obviously is the best—or to disembowel or even to decapitate a foe. But few wounded warriors died this way. Most bled to death more slowly.

Tie a knife to the end of a stick and you have a spear for stabbing or throwing. Mount it on a long stick and you have a pike. When braced against the ground and held at an **pike** acute angle, your pike, in concert with a good many comrades-in-arms, presents an impenetrable wall of blades to attacking infantry and cavalry. Carry a pike on horseback and you have a lance. Make a wide, heavy blade on a shorter club and you have an ax. Fashion your blade of metal, make it long and thin with a small handle, and you have a sword, a cutlass, or a saber.

All of these weapons, you will notice, are powered by muscles, usually human but sometimes animal as well. (The magnificent Clydesdale horses, featured in beer commercials, are descendants of horses originally bred to carry heavily armored knights into battle.) To be able to propel an object farther than a slinger could sling or heavier than a man could lift, however, some mechanism for storing energy had to be developed.

Enter the bow. Today's best bows are manufactured of **bows and** space-age plastics, but for most of history they were crafted **arrows** from carefully selected woods. (English longbowmen used yew.) The concept is simple: A small spear (the arrow) is propelled by a string that connects opposite ends of the bow. When the bow is drawn, energy is transferred from the archer's arm and stored in the bend of the bow itself. When the string is released, the bow returns to its original, predrawn configuration, and in so doing transfers energy through the string to the arrow.

Heavy stones could be flung with catapults. Here energy **catapults** was stored in a counterweight so that gravity would do the work; or in ropes, thongs, or hair (human worked best) which would be tightened and then released. While various mechanical contraptions that could fling a few hundred pounds of rock a few hundred yards were developed in Roman and medieval times, it wasn't really possible to throw large stones very far with any regularity or accuracy until some other means of storing energy was developed.

gunpowder   Enter gunpowder. The Chinese first developed gunpowder, using it in primitive rockets as early as the thirteenth century. The idea then spread to Europe. Cannon appeared in Europe as early as the fourteenth century, but the use of chemicals to store the energy needed to fling an object evolved quite slowly. For more than a century, cannon coexisted on the battlefield with older catapults. Ironically, the cannon were heavier and often not as reliable as the older, well-tested weapon. Yet, as knowledge both of metallurgy and chemistry advanced, cannon came to dominate.

cannonballs   Early cannonballs were made of stone, but soon iron balls were substituted. Simple balls were fine for knocking down fortress walls, but relatively ineffective against infantry (foot soldiers) or cavalry. Once cannon had made castles obsolete, warfare became more mobile, moving from siege actions to field battles. So a variety of other kinds of projectiles were **grapeshot**   developed to be shot from guns. Grapeshot was for use against personnel, essentially turning the cannon into a large shotgun as dozens of small balls (the shot), held together by a frame, were fired with devastating effect on close-ranked infantry. Thus came the order "Give them a whiff of grape." Metal balls were also put in cans (canisters) and fired from cannon.

While cannonballs do their primary damage by crushing and smashing, they could also be heated red-hot to start fires when they landed on wood or straw or a ship's rigging. Early cannon were heavy and cumbersome, usually requiring dozens of men and many horses to move them. At sea their weight was less of a handicap and they were soon found on ships of war.

chain shot   Ship's rigging could be shredded by chain shot, two cannonballs linked by a few feet of sturdy chain. Fired together, the balls tumbled end over end, ripping through sails, masts, and lines. While crushing and smashing hull and rigging was the primary goal, many sailors were maimed and slashed in turn by flying splinters of violently rent wood.

The distinction between crushing stone and piercing blade was essentially erased when clever ironmongers in the sixteenth century experimented with hollow cannonballs that could be filled with gunpowder. The so-called shell had a hole where the powder was inserted. It was ignited by the charge of the gun when it was fired. A short labyrinth of powder (later a length of cord) served as a fuse, giving time between the firing of the gun and the explosion of the shell. (No doubt a good bit of bloody experimentation was involved, and it was not until the nineteenth century that the device was perfected and widely used.)

exploding shells

So now stored chemical energy could be used to blast a target as well as to launch a projectile. And soon it became apparent that great damage could be done by the pieces of the shell fractured in the explosion. Eventually, shells were designed to exploit this fact: exploding, they would spread many lethal bits of white-hot iron or steel called shrapnel (after its English inventor) over as broad a radius as possible.

shrapnel

Today there is a wide variety of explosive artillery rounds. Some are designed to penetrate deep into concrete and steel before exploding. Indeed, there are shells meant solely to penetrate armor plate: some called "shaped charges" focus their intense energy on a single point, creating a hot gas that literally hoses its way through the armor, spraying the tank crew with molten metal; another type has a "squash" effect which transmits shock waves through the armor, violently breaking off chunks inside the tank to ricochet about, turning the crew into a human puree; and others rely on simple kinetic energy just to punch through the armor.

ASIDE———————————————————

These kinetic-energy shells consist of extremely slender, pencil-pointed projectiles, much smaller in diameter than the gun tubes from which they are fired. They are usually made of extremely hard, heavy materials such as tungsten or depleted uranium, and are designed to punch their way through the heavy armor of a tank by means of their high velocity and density, and to kill the crew with resulting metal fragments or by starting fires.

kinetic energy

Still other artillery shells are designed primarily to destroy "softer" targets—people. These burst above ground so as to spread farther their extra loads of shrapnel; some even contain "bomblets" that spread still farther before exploding again. And every artilleryman's locker contains an ample supply of HE—high-explosive general-purpose shells.

The development of shoulder-fired guns was affected as much by the problem of recoil as by the technological evolution of powder and steel. The problem is that the weight of the bullet and the velocity with which it departs the gun (the muzzle velocity, as it is called) determine the severity of the recoil. Large bullet, low speed; or small bullet, high speed, and there is no problem. Small bullets have less kickback; but with a large bullet traveling at high speed, it is much harder for a man to hold on to the gun when it fires. (Recoil was a problem for cannon, too, but at least the alert and agile gunner could dodge the "loose cannon on the deck" if recoil caused the cannon to break loose from the lines and pulleys used to anchor it in place.)

Early firearms (called arquebuses) were so heavy that they required a crutch to support them while the infantryman aimed and fired. Bullets of an inch or two in diameter were not uncommon. A slug of that size was less likely to penetrate, especially at longer ranges, although it did have a lot of hitting power—a sort of small cannonball. But as weapons have evolved from arquebus to musket to rifle,* muzzle (front-loading) to breech (back-loading), from single-shot weapons to semiautomatic "repeating rifles" to full-automatic submachine guns, there has been a corresponding tendency to reduce the size of the bullet while increasing its speed.

ASIDE————————————————————————————

The size of a gun is denoted by its bore, the inside diameter of its barrel, which, of course, determines the diameter of the bullet. All new weapons are metric, but older guns, many

caliber   of which are still in production, are designated in "caliber,"

—————————————————————————

*A rifle has grooves cut in spiral fashion around the inside of the barrel which impart a spin to the bullet, making it more accurate.

each of which is equivalent to ¹⁄₁₀₀ of an inch. Thus a .50-caliber machine gun shoots bullets a half-inch in diameter, a .38's bullet is a bit more than a third of an inch, and so on.

Today an intense debate rages among professional infantrymen both in the United States and in Europe over the proper size of the bullets their soldiers' guns should fire. One faction wants to continue to use a 7.62-mm round, the NATO standard for many years and equivalent to the .30-caliber bullet used in World Wars I and II as well as in Korea. But the now dominant party wants a smaller bullet, the 5.56 mm, which is just a hair larger than the .22 caliber known to generations of rural lads who use it for "plinking" tin cans as well as stalking rats, crows, and other varmints.

bullets

There are good arguments in favor of the smaller bullet. Basically, it has a much higher velocity; the cartridge packs a lot more powder than a boy's .22. High velocity translates into incredible killing and maiming power at relatively close ranges. This is because the bullet enters the victim's body at supersonic speeds (the *crack!* of a rifle is the bullet's sonic boom, not the gunpowder's explosion), setting up shock waves that shred tissues and organs. In addition, a light bullet is relatively unstable so it often tumbles or is deflected by bone or dense organs. Even a small slug somersaulting end over end as it decelerates from supersonic speed within a human body will make a nasty gash.

Another major advantage of small bullets is that a soldier can carry a lot of them. Fully automatic (machine-gun type) fire then becomes a battlefield norm which is psychologically rewarding to the infantryman, who is, more often than not, a frightened youth far from home. Light bullets also mean light guns with less recoil so they're easier to carry and shoot. (Keep in mind that infantrymen are routinely burdened with 50 to 100 pounds of gear.)

But there's more to the interplay between explosives and steel than bullets and balls. Early on, small bombshells were made to be thrown, thus the creation of the grenadier. In medieval times, powder-filled crocks were lit and hung (with some alacrity lest you be hoist with your own petard) on the doors of besieged castles to blow them down. Another tactic

mines

was to dig a tunnel under an enemy fortification, pack it with gunpowder, and set it off. This kind of mine was last used, to little benefit other than a big bang, in World War I; but today there is an ingenious array of mines. Some are designed to get people, the most diabolical perhaps being the "bouncing Betty," first used in World War II, which would spring up to waist height before exploding. Others are made to disable tanks and vehicles. Sea mines (originally called torpedoes, thus Farragut's "Damn the torpedoes, full speed ahead!" in Mobile Bay) have evolved considerably from the simple contact type used as late as World War II. Contemporary mines are triggered by pressure or sound and can be programmed to destroy a certain type of ship. The nicest thing about mine warfare is that you can be long gone when your mine goes off.

Yet the introduction of gunpowder did not produce immediate or rapid changes in warfare. While gunpowder gave a substantial advantage to soldiers armed with muskets (long guns) because they could do damage at a greater distance, the use and safe handling of powder was not really mastered until the nineteenth century. Because of impurities it could explode violently and unpredictably, thus threatening the gunner (and his gun) quite as much as the target. In fact, artillery was so difficult and dangerous to handle that for a long time specialists, handing down their knowledge from father to son through the guild system, would craft these weapons by hand (each one a unique and often artful creation) and man them in battle under contract to whoever wanted to fight.

gun loading

Guns were extremely unwieldy and slow to load. Because of this it was necessary to have lines, or ranks, of soldiers in battle, one behind the other, in formation, each rank firing in turn and reloading while other ranks fired. The Spanish first developed the technique of using two ranks of arquebusiers in the sixteenth century. The first rank would fire, then kneel to reload, permitting the second rank to fire. In the seventeenth century Gustavus Adolphus of Sweden deployed his musketeers in six ranks. Two fired simultaneously, then marched to the rear to reload behind the protective cover of pikemen, to be replaced by the next two ranks, and so on, keeping up a steady stream of fire. As technological improvements increased the speed of reloading, the depth of infantry formations could be decreased, until the nineteenth century, when the French under Napoleon and their British adversaries used two- and three-rank firing lines.*

Loading was a problem until the invention, in the middle of the nineteenth century, of breech loading (loading a cartridge that combined shot and powder from the rear of the gun instead of ramming it all separately down the muzzle), followed by the invention of the repeating rifle (which could fire several times before needing to be reloaded). The machine gun, which could fire hundreds of bullets automatically with one pull of the trigger, was the last of these improvements. But even as late as the Civil War, thousands of American soldiers had their right arms shot off because they had to lift their arms to reload their single-shot muzzle-loading rifles while lying behind a log in a field or a farmer's stone wall.

By the middle of the Civil War the breech-loading rifle became available, and this was probably the most important weapons breakthrough prior to the invention of the machine gun twenty years later (although a primitive precursor of the machine gun, the Gatling gun, using a cluster of rifle barrels, rotated and fired with a crank, did see some combat in the Civil War). With the breech loader, shooting became more rapid and considerably more devastating. A good rifleman could reload his weapon in seconds, increasing the total volume of fire that groups of infantrymen could produce. This gave rise in the U.S. Army to a "firepower doctrine," a tactical emphasis on the amount of bullets, bombs, and shells brought to bear on the battlefield. Wars began to have enormously increased battle casualty rates from the Civil War on as tactics failed to change as rapidly as weapons.

SCIENCE, WEAPONS, AND WAR

Until the nineteenth century, then, improvements in weapons design were largely a result of trial and error. There was little systematic research in metallurgy, chemistry, ballistics, to say nothing of systems engineering. Craftsmen tinkerers and "inventors" were called upon to improve exist-

*R. Ernest Dupuy and Trevor Dupuy, *The Encyclopedia of Military History* (New York: Harper & Row, 1970), pages 456–57, 664.

ing weapons or to develop new ones. There were few professional scientists and fewer still who studied military science. Leonardo da Vinci, for example, contributed as many innovative ideas to military science as he did to art and architecture. But such people were the exception. All that changed, however, toward the end of the 1800s.

In the nineteenth century an era of intense scientific inquiry and experimentation began. Coupled with, indeed, a part of the Industrial Revolution, the resources and means of the mass production of standardized parts evolved. New inventions appeared which transformed weapons and the way they were used. Steam power for ships and railroads, steel for rails and bridges and the telegraph affected not only everyday life, but also the conduct, strategy, and logistics of
warships war. With warships, for example, there were more changes made in the last half of the nineteenth century than there had been in the previous three hundred years. Steam power, plate armor, rifled cannon in rotating turrets made warships lacking these innovations obsolete. By the end of the century it was no longer possible, as it was in Lord Nelson's era, to have forty-year-old flagships in any first-class navy.
railroads The railroad, too, changed war. It was no accident that Prussia, Russia, France, and Austria subsidized the construction of cross-country rail lines. The Prussian railroads, in fact, were designed around the need to bring soldiers to the country's many frontiers, whereas the French railroads converged for commercial (and political) reasons on Paris. Heretofore, supplies had been carried into battle exclusively by horse-drawn wagons, but the railroad allowed a military commander to bring enormous quantities of men and matériel to a battlefront in very short order. Not only was the railroad faster, but by its very size and capability, the railroad could accommodate load after load of heavy equipment.
telegraph The telegraph, operational by the middle of the nineteenth century, also changed warfare by permitting rapid communication between national leaders and field headquarters. Prior to that time, battlefield communications were no quicker than a man on horseback with a dispatch in his case. Pigeons and semaphores (signal flags) had also been used to some extent, but they were not very reliable (despite what pigeon fanciers might claim).

The American Civil War was the first modern war. Steam power, railroads, armored ships, observation balloons, and the telegraph were all put to use in the war. In terms of what was to come, however, the most significant characteristic of the Civil War was the fact that increased firepower enor- mously increased the carnage. Photographs of Richmond reduced to rubble by Union shelling are easily mistaken for London after the Blitz. But the introduction of new weapons was no guarantee that a commander's tactics would adapt to the new reality. Generals, trained in an earlier age for very different kinds of war, continued for some time to order frontal assaults with fixed bayonets against well-defended positions. But as infantry formations encountered volley after volley of accurate rifle and cannon fire, casualties were higher than they had ever been.

At Fredericksburg, to give but one example, a three-foot wall made the difference between victory and disaster for the South. The soldiers found they could hide behind it to gain protection from Union fire, while extracting a heavy toll on the attackers. At Gettysburg, Confederate infantrymen under Major General George E. Pickett showed more courage than sense in responding to their commander's order to "Charge the enemy and remember Old Virginia!" against well-defended Union positions on Cemetery Ridge. Pickett's charge (actually a walk) marked the beginning of the end for the Confederacy. Of the 15,000 men who took part in the assault, fewer than half survived. In one division only 800 men were available for muster the next morning, out of 4,800 who took part in the attack.*

Yet to adapt tactics to changing technology would never be easy, especially as new weapons came more and more quickly into use. Indeed, the focus of modern military policy, that is, since the American Civil War, is the tension between "hardware" and "software." How weapons—the hardware—affect military thinking and behavior—the software—is a central theme in today's defense debates.

Sensing the significance of the American Civil War, many military officers came from other countries to watch. What they saw was the staggering human cost of modern warfare: half a million Americans dead; the bloodiest war in our history. But they did not learn much, as it turned out. An even bloodier war in Europe followed but fifty years later.

---

* Glen Tucker, *High Tide at Gettysburg* (Indianapolis: The Bobbs-Merrill Company, Inc. 1958), page 328.

World
War I

Technologically, the First World War (1914–18) brought to fruition everything that had been foreshadowed in the Civil War. To the increased firepower already available in the 1860s was added the machine gun, invented by the French but manufactured and used with far greater emphasis and effectiveness by the Germans, and improved artillery. Both weapons raised the human cost of frontal infantry assault, and by so advantaging the defense, made forward movement in the face of these weapons enormously costly. The result was a stagnant, bloody stalemate on the western front for most of the war.

machine
gun

Three soldiers—one to carry, one to load, and one to fire—could handle a heavy machine gun with lethal efficiency. Artillery had also improved, adding to the bloodshed. To give some sense of the firepower used in one First World War battle, British artillery is reported to have fired 4,283,550 shells (more than 300 trainloads and a year's production for 55,000 war workers) at the Third Battle of Ypres (called "Wipers" by the British troops) in 1917.*

The contest between the offense (soldiers charging across no-man's-land) and the defense (machine gunners in trenches, behind sandbags supported by mass artillery) was uneven at best. The gunners needed but to come out from their underground bunkers to their firing positions along the trench while the infantry raced from shell hole to shell hole in desperate search of cover. Again, the generals' tactics were slow to adapt to the new realities. Periodic offensives by both sides were planned, organized, and carried out with high expectations but failed to break the stalemate, and produced, instead, hundreds of thousands, eventually millions of casualties. At the Battle of Ypres the British spent five months and sacrificed 370,000 men to capture 45 square miles of mud and swamp—a total of 8,222 casualties per square mile!†

Only another technological innovation could change the situation. Introduced late in the war, the tank brought back movement into battle by allowing soldiers to walk behind it as it advanced forward in the face of machine-gun fire.

---

*Brodie, *op. cit.,* page 192.
† *Ibid.*

ASIDE————————————————————————————————————

If you have sometimes wondered how the tank got its name, here is the story: At the beginning the tank was such a secret new weapon that it was kept covered by its British inventors. To avoid revealing what was under those shrouds, they said the objects were "water tanks," and the name stuck.

tank

But military leaders were slow to appreciate the value of the tank. The few tank offensives, one of which included a young American officer named George Patton, attempted in World War I did break the German lines, but these were never followed up by sufficient numbers of ground troops to make them effective. It took twenty years and another war for the tank to become the dominant battlefield weapon.

Although none so affected the outcome of the war as did the machine gun and artillery, there were other weapons innovations during World War I. Poison gas was first used in that war, but rarely since. This fact is due not so much to a moral abhorrence of chemical warfare, but to its unpredictability. Those using gas are always in danger of being gassed themselves if the wind shifts. Moreover, protective masks and clothing were extremely cumbersome and still are. And as soon as the other side began to use gas, the advantage was lost.

poison gas

Submarines used during World War I proved effective against warships and unarmed ships early in the war but were vulnerable to destroyers (antisubmarine ships) and to mines. They had limited endurance and were very slow underwater, being powered by batteries. Again, it took twenty years and another war for the potential of submarines to be more fully realized, although by World War II the invention of sonar and radar (see below) would make defense against submarines more effective.

submarines

The airplane—America's glamour weapon in World War II—fought in World War I but had little bearing on the outcome. No weapon introduced in that war could compete for effect with the machine gun and artillery. More than anything else, they accounted for the 10 million dead in battle.

WORLD WAR II AND BEYOND

World
War II

However bloody the First World War, World War II was worse. Sixteen million soldiers died in battle in World War II and perhaps as many as 60 million people (including 20 million Russians) were killed, all told.

Apart from the numbers of civilian dead, World War II marks a major turning point in the history of weaponry and warfare: the ultimate marriage of scientific and engineering talent in the service of war. With the systematic, massive application of science and industrial production, the pace of innovations in both offensive and defensive weapons accelerated to dizzying speed. Policy makers are still trying to find ways to adapt to the revolutionary developments in warfare it spawned. Nuclear weapons and missiles top the list; and we will have much to say about these later.

The tank and the airplane, as we have noted, first appeared during World War I, but it was not until the German Blitzkrieg (lightning war) of 1939–41 that the two weapons were used together and with such devastating effect. Tank battles became enormous. At Kursk, in Russia, 6,000 tanks and assault guns (artillery) on both sides battled within a few hilly square miles in 1943. (The battle is still being studied by students of military science.) Still, many World War II battles were fought without benefit of tank or airplane, in the Pacific and Southeast Asia, for example, and differed little from the infantry battles of World War I.*

In naval warfare the submarine continued to be used as an anti-ship weapon, though the submersibles of the time were small and primitive compared to today's large, nuclear-powered submarines. The Germans began the war with fewer than 50 U-boats, but their submarine "wolf packs" came close to bringing Britain to her knees in 1942 by sinking 6,250,000 tons of Allied shipping.† By the end of 1942, the Americans, and most notably the industrialist Henry J. Kaiser, were able to build ships faster than the Germans could sink them. Thus, the threat to the Allies' lifeline was overwhelmed.

---

*See John Keegan, *The Face of Battle* (New York: Viking Press, 1976), pages 284–291.
†William L. Shirer, *The Rise and Fall of the Third Reich* (New York: Simon and Schuster, 1960), page 1007.

Sonar (sound navigation and ranging), which uses sound waves and their echoes to track submarines, made them easier to locate underwater, and radar (see below) made it possible to find and attack them at night when they ran on the surface to recharge their batteries. Thus, German submarines, which had been extremely lethal against unarmed ships in World War I and early in World War II, suffered high attrition in the later years.

The really significant innovation in naval warfare in World War II was the aircraft carrier, which made it possible for opposing fleets to engage in battle with one another even though they never saw each other. This occurred first in 1942 at the Battle of the Coral Sea and a few months later at the decisive Battle of Midway. In the opening naval battle of the war, Pearl Harbor, it was Japanese carrier-based aircraft that sank or severely damaged five of the eight battleships in port. From then on, the aircraft carrier would supplant the battleship as the dominant naval weapon. Fortunately for the United States, our carriers were not in port on December 7, 1941, and were able six months later (at Midway) to sink four Japanese aircraft carriers for the loss of one of our own.

aircraft carrier

BOMBERS AND BOMBS

While there is considerable doubt over the effectiveness of Allied bombing of German cities during World War II, no weapon symbolizes that war better than the aerial bombs and the aircraft built to carry them. Bombers were, at one and the same time, the most horrible and most glamorous weapons of the war.

Bombing from the air introduced a new dimension of destruction that—in terms of the history of weaponry and warfare—makes even the destructiveness of World War I seem modest by comparison. The Germans had tried out air warfare first in the Spanish Civil War (in which they were technically not involved). When Germany's Condor Legion bombed the town of Guernica in 1937, it was a warm-up for the London Blitz of 1940. Picasso's *Guernica* captures on canvas the horror of aircraft bombing; but the citizens of Rotterdam, the people of London, and the Poles of Warsaw would all experience that horror in turn.

Goering, it is alleged, had promised Hitler that the German Heinkel, Junkers, and Dorner twin-engine bombers, each capable of carrying perhaps a dozen bombs (the Germans explicitly decided not to build heavy bombers), would destroy Britain and force the British to surrender. As it turned out, our four-engine B-17s and B-24s and the British Lancasters and Stirlings proved to be superior. Each of these Allied planes could drop seven to ten tons of bombs in a single raid, leveling cities. Air raids on Hamburg, Dresden, Tokyo, and Osaka (before the atomic bomb) killed over 100,000 people in each city.

It was the U.S. and British bombers, first in tens, then in hundreds, and eventually in thousands, that carried the war to the heart of Germany in 1943 and 1944 and 1945. And finally, it was two B-29s and two bombs that brought the war against Japan to an abrupt and devastating conclusion.

Most of the bombs dropped from airplanes during World War II consisted of heavy steel casings filled with TNT or some other chemical explosive. The bombs fell by force of their own weight, and the explosion took place on impact (or by delayed-action detonators of various kinds). Except for incendiaries, most damage resulted from their blast and fragmentation—thousands of pieces of shattered casing flying away from the explosion (hence the term "fragmentation bombs"). The shock wave was a new phenomenon, and the kinds and numbers of casualties that resulted from it were terrifying.

A shock wave behaves like a giant hammer, pounding everything within its path to bits. Structures topple and people die not just from suffocation and burning but from having legs, arms, and even heads severed from their bodies by the force of the blast. After one raid on Tokyo on January 10, 1945, the dead were so dismembered that the bodies had to be collected in pieces and trucked away.

incendiaries   Another kind of bomb was the incendiary. True, there had been phosphorous artillery shells, meant to mark the fall of shot which could also start fires on impact (phosphorus burns intensely when exposed to air), but the most devastating incendiaries were dropped from bombers. In the mass bombing raids in World War II, first on Hamburg, later on Dresden, Tokyo and other Japanese cities, high explosive bombs were mixed with incendiaries. The combination was made even more lethal and destructive when a few delayed-action, high-explosive bombs were mixed in to kill people on the ground trying to fight the fires.

The explosives used in these weapons were still, essentially, incremental improvements on gunpowder. Early in the twentieth century, however, a new chemical compound called trinitrotoluene, or TNT for short, was synthesized. It **TNT** quickly became a favorite of bomb manufacturers and of the military because it would explode only when detonated. So widely used was TNT that it also became the measuring unit for all explosive equivalents. Nuclear and thermonuclear explosions—which are of course not made of TNT—still are measured in terms of thousands or millions of "equivalent tons" of TNT.

Another kind of incendiary developed during World War II was napalm. It consists of gasoline converted to a gel to **napalm** which other flammable chemicals are added. Although napalm was sometimes dropped in mass fire raids in World War II, it was most effective against well-dug-in ground troops. If it does not directly burn the dug-in troops, it asphyxiates them by superheating the air or by consuming the oxygen in their bunkers.

Defensive innovations appeared in this period as well. The invention of the proximity fuse—a radio transmitter and receiver that could be inserted into the nose of an anti-aircraft artillery shell—made it possible for the shell to "know" when it was close to the attacking airplane, permitting it to detonate with maximum effect.

Radar (radio detection and ranging), which first became **radar** operational in 1935, permitted ground defenders to track incoming bombers hundreds of miles away. Its principle is the same as that of sonar: Instead of a sound wave, a radio wave is broadcast and reflected to a receiving antenna by the target. The length of time it takes to return to its source gives the range or distance, and the direction is known from the direction of the original transmission. Radar saved the British in the Battle of Britain. With it the Royal Air Force could concentrate their relatively few Spitfire and Hurricane fighters to intercept the formations of the attacking bombers. However, as we have seen throughout this chapter, each side soon learned how to reduce the advantage of the new weapon, in this case to jam radar by using strips of aluminum foil and other reflective materials to give false signals. Today certain aircraft (the B-1, for example) are being designed expressly to have a "smaller radar profile" than their predecessors; and if its advance billing proves accurate, the Stealth aircraft will be virtually invisible to radar. Still, the invention of radar by the Allies no doubt played a major role in all phases of World War II, especially since the Germans and the Japanese never perfected it.

ASIDE

The Japanese relied on acoustic detectors—arrays of sensitive microphones designed to "hear" the bombers' engines before they were within sight.

In one sense, atomic and later hydrogen bombs were but extensions in size of the conventional bombs we have been describing, just much more destructive. And indeed, this was an initial reaction among professional military officers all over the world (see our discussion of NSC #68 in Chapter Four). Yet, as must seem obvious today, the increase in **nuclear weapons** the magnitude of the destructive capability of nuclear weapons puts them, all of them whatever their size, into a class by themselves. This is partly because of the collateral damage they do and partly because the use of any nuclear weapon in a conflict between the superpowers could lead to nuclear world war.

Beyond the immediate blast and heat effects, which in the case of atomic and hydrogen weapons would extend tens of miles from the detonation site, there are also radiation effects. While most discussions of radiation focus on its damage to living organisms, there are unknown and incalculable meteorological consequences as well. It may be, for example, that a thermonuclear war would so disrupt the earth's atmosphere that whole areas would be uninhabitable, at least in the daytime.

In any event, both because of their effects and the fact that they have come to represent a kind of threshold no nation since World War II has dared to cross, it is safe to say that nuclear weapons are in an altogether separate category from all other weapons that have gone before.

NUCLEAR AND THERMONUCLEAR WEAPONS

At the appointed time, there was a blinding flash lighting up the whole area brighter than the brightest daylight. A mountain range three miles from the observation point stood out in bold relief. Then came a tremendous sustained roar and a heavy pressure wave which knocked down two men stationed outside the control center. Immediately thereafter, a huge multi-colored surging cloud boiled to an altitude of over 40,000 feet. Clouds in its path disappeared. Soon, the shifting stratosphere winds dispersed the now grey mass.

*   *   *

It was that beauty the great poets dream about but describe most poorly and inadequately. Thirty seconds after the explosion came first the air blast pressing hard against the people and things, to be followed almost immediately by the strong, sustained awesome roar which warned of doomsday and made us feel that we puny things were blasphemous to tamper with the forces heretofore reserved to the Almighty. Words are inadequate tools for the job of acquainting those not present with the physical, mental and psychological effects. It had to be witnessed to be realized.*

The test described was the first explosion of an atomic weapon. The place was Alamogordo, New Mexico. The occasion, the critical demonstration of whether an atomic bomb, code-named Trinity, would work. And the date, July 16, 1945. In this report, published only three months later and including an excellent history of the Manhattan Project, H. D. Smyth made history in another way by invoking the name of the Almighty in a physics journal, probably for the first time since Newton.

Indeed, the men who prepared the blast (there was one

---

* Two witnesses at Alamogordo, quoted in H. D. Smyth's "Atomic Energy for Military Purposes," in *Reviews of Modern Physics*, Volume 17, Number 4, October 1945, pages 465 and 467.

woman)—the final act in the monumental joining of physics and engineering talent that went into the Manhattan Project—were all well aware both of the powers that the release of the energy of the atomic nucleus portended and of the awfulness of the destruction that such a bomb could wreak.

Yet, with all their science, they were also naïve. They had positioned themselves—Fermi, Conant, Oppenheimer, the lot—only ten miles from the blast zone, not altogether aware as yet of the damaging effects of radioactive fallout. And, at least at that point in July 1945, none of those present could possibly know that in the 1980s there would be 50,000 thermonuclear (hydrogen) and nuclear (atomic) bombs and missile warheads, many of them hundreds of times more explosive than the bomb they had just seen go off.

Almost at once, in the aftermath of the first atomic bombings in August 1945, the terms of the nuclear or atomic age entered our language. So familiar are they to us now that we lay people sometimes feel we understand nuclear energy. Indeed, every high school physics student can recite (without necessarily understanding it) the basic principle by which nuclear energy was predicted: the equation $E = mc^2$. Yet how many of us really know what that means and how it relates to the variety of nuclear and thermonuclear weapons we have in our arsenals today?

Previously, as we have seen, the energy used to fire weapons came either from muscle power or gravity or, after the invention of gunpowder, from the exploitation of chemical reactions, that is, the rearrangement of matter at the molecular level. Now, for the first time at Alamogordo, energy would be drawn from the bonds that glue elementary particles of matter together. There is no doubt that future historians will compare the discovery of nuclear energy with that of fire. In Greek mythology, Prometheus' theft of fire brought Pandora to earth to plague him (and the rest of us) ever after. In similar fashion, the possibilities of nuclear fission and fusion give us, for the first time in human history, weapons that can destroy not just our enemies but our planet.

Although the bombs dropped on Hiroshima and Nagasaki were called atomic bombs and were popularly associated

with "atom smashing," in actual fact it was not the atoms
that were smashed but rather atomic nuclei, something   **nuclear**
smaller than the atom and contained within it. The atom, as   **fission**
late nineteenth-century scientists were beginning to discover, is not the most basic particle of matter, as had previously been thought. Rather, as subsequent discoveries
revealed, atoms themselves have numerous parts: a heavy
center, called a nucleus, made up of two kinds of particles,
positively (electrically) charged protons and noncharged
neutrons; all of which are surrounded by negatively charged
electrons.

Physicists became interested in so-called subatomic particles in the 1930s as they pursued work on radioactivity that
had begun in the laboratories of Marie and Pierre Curie earlier on. Radioactivity was the name given by the Curies to
the new set of effects exhibited by certain elements in nature (uranium, and the then newly discovered polonium and
radium). Later it was understood that these effects took
place when the nucleus of an atomic element was changing
or "decaying," as it is now called, into another. While most
common elements on earth are not radioactive, some few,
including radium, are radioactive in their natural state. So
the first step was to study radium and other naturally radioactive elements, and the next step was to induce artificial
radioactivity into stable elements.

Irène Joliot-Curie, the Curies' daughter, together with
her husband succeeded in inducing artificial radioactivity by
bombarding stable elements with subatomic (alpha) particles. And Enrico Fermi, who is an important part of our story
as a later member of the U.S. Manhattan Project to develop
the atom bomb, tried a variation on the Curies' technique by
bombarding stable elements with neutrons. In the process
Fermi *split* the uranium atoms he was bombarding, and the
rest is history.

When Fermi's free-flying neutrons hit the uranium nuclei, they produced a radioactivity measurably different from
the natural radioactivity of uranium. At first, Fermi and his
co-workers thought they might have created (or found) new
elements, such as Element 93. As it turned out, however,
there was no new element—although ironically Fermi got
the Nobel Prize in physics in 1938 for having discovered

one. Rather, the neutron "bullet" had caused the nucleus to split—a process called fission—into two previously known elements, that together were lighter in atomic weight than uranium. What had happened—as was later demonstrated and finally understood—was that fission produced two nuclear halves less in total mass (weight) than the original nucleus and that the "missing matter" had been transformed into energy.

What was particularly significant for later military and civilian applications was that, relative to the minute size of the missing matter, the amount of energy released by this fission process was *enormous*. Also, but less spectacular, some radiation in the form of gamma rays was emitted in the process.* Even more interesting was the fact that nuclear fission yielded more free-flying neutrons which would, if sufficient numbers of other fissionable atomic nuclei were nearby, continue the process of fission indefinitely. And thus the possibility of what would be called the chain reaction came into view.

ASIDE————————————————————————

Nuclear power reactors contain so-called control rods made of cadmium or similar absorbing materials that are lowered into the reactor's core at will to absorb the free-flying neutrons and sustain the fission process at a controlled rate or stop it. The heat generated by the controlled reaction is usually exploited to make steam, which in turn drives generators.

It was the creation of a chain reaction for the first time in a laboratory under the football stadium at the University of Chicago by Enrico Fermi in 1942 that gave American scientists a certain amount of confidence that they could produce a fission bomb. Still, no one was certain in 1945 that the thing would work. So, after producing the all-important chain reaction, the physicists and chemists turned themselves into nuclear engineers.

————————————————————————————

*Gamma rays are penetrating electromagnetic waves of very high frequency, very much like X rays.

The Manhattan Project (a code name given to the project to develop the atomic bomb during the war), which cost $2 billion and drew upon the work of specially built laboratories all over the country, faced a series of seemingly insurmountable problems.

First, a supply of uranium 235 (U-235), the most feasible fissionable material, had to be "manufactured." U-235 is extremely difficult to extract from uranium ore, which is made up mostly of other forms of uranium. It takes about one ton of uranium ore to supply four pounds of pure uranium. Of this amount 99.3 percent is uranium 238 (U-238), which is not as fissionable as U-235. This means that only somewhat less than half an ounce of the original ton of uranium is the fissionable U-235. Apart from the infinitely small amounts of U-235 found in uranium ore, the process of separating the U-235 and the U-238 required entirely new techniques. Since the two substances are *chemically* identical (only differing at the subatomic level), it took years for the scientists to figure out how to separate them.

The next problem was to determine the smallest amount of fissionable material which can sustain a chain reaction. This became known as the "critical mass." Even the final detonating device, the last and in some ways the most challenging piece of engineering, was so crucial a step that it remained top secret well after the Smyth report was published. Indeed, the Hiroshima and Nagasaki bombs each used a different detonating device because of uncertainties that either one would work.

Because the fissionable material was so hard to come by, only three atomic weapons were actually available in the summer of 1945. One was tested at Alamogordo and, as we all know, two were dropped on the Japanese cities of Hiroshima and Nagasaki. The bomb dropped on Hiroshima on August 6, 1945, was called *Little Boy,* and although it weighed only 8,000 pounds in total and contained only 12 pounds of uranium 235, it set off an explosion that was the equivalent of 12,500 tons of TNT. The bomb dropped at Nagasaki was called *Fat Man* because of its shape. *Fat Man* produced an explosion equal to about 22,000 tons of TNT.

ASIDE————————————————————————————————

Fabricating the fissionable material for the nuclear bombs remained problematical for some time. The bomb used at Nagasaki used plutonium 239, a new fissionable man-made element that as we now know is a waste product of uranium fission. Indeed, one of the many reasons for our current fear that nuclear weapons may proliferate beyond our control has to do with the increasing availability of plutonium 239 as a result of the ever-increasing production of nuclear power. Not many countries and certainly no terrorist group would be able to manufacture uranium 235, but an individual or group could steal plutonium 239 from a nuclear waste area and with some technical facility produce a fission bomb.

In later years, after the war, the process of separating uranium 235 from uranium was improved. (It remains secret to this day.) Because it uses so much electricity, it is, however, extremely expensive. The process is called enrichment and the objective is to increase the proportion of uranium 235 from .7 percent of the original bulk to 3 percent. Oak Ridge Laboratory in Tennessee became a major enrichment site during the Manhattan Project and remains one today largely because of the hydroelectricity produced locally by the Tennessee Valley Authority. Today two 1,000 megawatt (million-watt) nuclear reactors are used to provide the electricity required to manufacture enriched uranium for both military and civilian use.

After the war, the United States built a limited number of additional bombs and for a while enjoyed a monopoly of nuclear weapons. We will discuss in some detail the effect of this monopoly on our military thinking (see Chapter Four). But powerful as the atomic (fission) bombs turned out to be, we soon found it necessary to develop the hydrogen (H-bomb) or fusion bomb.

The H-bomb has a number of advantages over the fission or atomic bomb. Owing to the power and speed of its explosion, the atomic bomb blows itself up before the chain reaction has been fully completed, wasting, so to speak, much of its nuclear energy potential. Thus, fission weapons have a "natural" size limit of from 40,000 to 50,000 tons of TNT equivalent (kilotons). The hydrogen bomb, which fuses hydrogen nuclei (instead of splitting nuclei, as the atomic bomb does), does not depend on a chain reaction. The material simply explodes when heated up to the necessary temperature. Moreover, the materials used in producing hydrogen fusion (deuterium or "heavy hydrogen," as it is called) are less expensive and less complicated to manufacture than uranium 235 or plutonium 239. Still, some "fissionable" materials are required because the only currently feasible means of creating the necessary heat to fuse nuclei is by using a small atomic bomb as a detonator. For this reason, while our nuclear arsenals today consist mainly of hydrogen (fusion) weapons, we still manufacture atomic bombs to ignite—so to speak—the hydrogen bombs, as well as for special military applications.

ASIDE—————————————————————————————

From now on, in these chapters we will distinguish atomic bombs and atomic weapons from hydrogen bombs and hydrogen weapons as follows: we will call atomic (fission) bombs nuclear weapons, and hydrogen (fusion) bombs thermonuclear weapons. In most of the current literature both kinds of weapons are called "nuclear," but we think it important to drive home the fact that current strategic arsenals are actually made up mostly of thermonuclear weapons. Hence our terms.

———————————————————————————————————

While the United States was far ahead of the Soviet Union in the development and deployment (putting in the hands of the military) of atomic bombs after the war, we were slow to figure out how to make a workable hydrogen bomb. Our first successful detonation of a fusion weapon occurred in 1952, seven years after Alamogordo. The test, on the Pacific atoll of Eniwetok, succeeded, but the device was very large and heavy and at that point it appeared as if no transportable bomb could be devised. One year later, in 1953, our scientists detected radioactive debris coming from an atmospheric nuclear test in the Soviet Union. They were able to infer from the debris that the Soviets had not only successfully tested a fusion bomb, but that they had fused a substance called deuterium to do this. Trying deuterium,

Edward Teller and his co-workers finally perfected a transportable fusion device, and the H-bomb became available as a weapon.

Today we consider nuclear and thermonuclear weapons dangerous both for their enormous destructive power (see our discussion of blast effects on page 62) and also because of the lethal and long-lasting radioactivity they create upon detonation. Yet it was not explicitly to kill by radiation that the first bombs were developed. Einstein's famous letter to Franklin Roosevelt of August 2, 1939, pointing out the military applications of nuclear fission, does not focus on radiation poisoning or radioactive fallout from atomic weapons. Rather, Einstein understood that one nuclear chain reaction in a large mass of uranium would lead to the construction of extremely powerful bombs of a new type, and he wanted the Allies to have this weapon before the Germans perfected it.*

As we have seen, even the experts on hand to observe the explosion at Alamogordo put only ten miles between themselves and the atomic blast. Later, in the 1950s, in an effort to perfect tactical nuclear weapons for use by soldiers in the field, military volunteers were solicited to participate in the exercises with small nuclear weapons. These soldiers, it is now believed, may have been seriously contaminated by radiation at that time. Only after the effects of radiation began to be measured in Japanese victims did we begin to understand fully the long-term consequences of atomic and hydrogen bombing.

Now, as our knowledge of the fission-fusion processes increases, the military has learned how to enhance or reduce the blast from bombs in their manufacture. Very often, and the neutron bomb is a case in point, the amount of blast and the amount of blast radiation can be traded off: more radiation, less blast; more blast, less radiation. The neutron bomb—which is really just a small hydrogen bomb—has been designed to have slightly less blast and somewhat more radiation.

---

*A. Einstein, letter to Franklin Roosevelt, Roosevelt Library, Hyde Park, New York, reproduced in *Atoms in the Family,* by Laura Fermi (University of Chicago Press, 1954), page 198a.

ASIDE

The neutron bomb has periodically made headlines: first
when President Carter decided not to produce and deploy the
weapon even though we had developed it; and later when
President Reagan, without consulting our European allies,
announced (though production has still not begun) that we
would go ahead and produce it.

The neutron bomb is designed to reduce the damage it
does to property—with a marginally lowered blast effect and
a marginally increased radiation effect. Thus, it is only a little
different from any other hydrogen bomb its size. The military
calls it an "enhanced radiation, reduced blast" weapon. The
public, however, responding to the term "enhanced radiation," perceives the weapon to be somehow more deadly than
other tactical thermonuclear devices.

Hence the furor.

SIZE

When we measure the force of thermonuclear (hydrogen) weapons we talk not in terms of kilotons (thousands of
tons of TNT equivalence) but of megatons, millions of tons   **megatons**
of TNT. A one-megaton bomb, today a fairly standard size in
current arsenals, has the explosive power of one million tons
of TNT. Remember that the largest non-nuclear bomb built
in World War II had the power of 20,000 pounds (10 tons) of
TNT. Thus, a one-megaton thermonuclear bomb is 100,000
times the size of the biggest non-nuclear weapon.

To imagine a one-megaton blast, think of one million
one-ton truckloads of TNT all going off at once. In actual
fact, the TNT might do more effective damage (from a military point of view) over a larger area than the one-megaton
hydrogen bomb, partly because one million trucks would
cover a very large parking lot. On the other hand, a thermonuclear weapon can package the equivalent of a million
tons of TNT in a weapon weighing no more than about
1,500 pounds.

Not only are these megaton bombs bigger and more
forceful than anything ever known before, they are many

times more powerful (and much more compact) even than the atomic bombs dropped at Hiroshima and Nagasaki, which were measured in *thousands,* not *millions,* of tons of TNT: 12.5 kilotons in the case of Hiroshima, 22 kilotons in the case of Nagasaki. In fact, a one-megaton hydrogen bomb, if exploded, will have the blast equivalence of one-third of all the munitions used in World War II.

Atomic bombs, as we have noted, have a sort of natural size limit at about 40–50 kilotons (thousand tons) equivalence. When they get any larger than this, the bombs' explosion begins to interfere with the fission reaction. Since the hydrogen bomb has no such natural limit, the shift to hydrogen weapons reflected a desire by both sides to have larger and larger exploding devices.

Still, a certain standardization has set in. Most of our hydrogen devices average less than one megaton in size. Yet, bombs carried on aircraft are larger—5 to 10 megatons in size—and warheads mounted on missiles are usually smaller, "submegaton." Because the Soviets' missiles until now have been less accurate than ours and their guidance systems more crude (and larger), the Russians have generally produced bigger hydrogen bombs than we have. Theirs range from submegaton to 20 megatons in size, and they produced at least one 65-megaton bomb that was exploded in the Arctic in 1962. While in terms of manufacturing techniques and the physics of fusion it is now possible to build a 100-megaton weapon (100 million tons of TNT equivalence), both sides have found smaller weapons sufficiently destructive for military purposes. And the growing reliance on missiles with multiple warheads has put a premium on smaller, more compact devices.

NUCLEAR EFFECTS

BLAST

A nuclear or thermonuclear explosion is unlike any natural phenomenon on Earth, although it bears similarities to several. What makes it unique and so totally devastating is the combination of destructive effects. A nuclear explosion produces blast, searing heat (thermal radiation), direct nuclear radiation, and fallout, as well as something called electromagnetic pulse (EMP). A nuclear blast drives air away from the center of the explosion, producing violent changes in air pressure sufficient to crush even large buildings. This is called overpressure. A one-megaton weapon detonated 8,000 feet above the ground would cause sufficient overpressures to level reinforced concrete buildings within nearly a mile of ground zero (the point on the ground directly beneath the center of the explosion). Four and one-half miles away all dwellings would be leveled, all factories destroyed, and all but the strongest buildings severely damaged.

If you have ever experienced a severe hurricane (wind speed in excess of 73 miles an hour), you know how destructive such storms can be. A nuclear explosion produces winds with peak velocities of 470 *miles an hour* (more than six times hurricane force) within a mile of ground zero, and winds of at least 95 miles an hour nearly six miles from the center of the explosion. Any people caught in the open would be thrown violently against obstacles or be struck by debris and be killed. Most private residences and even the walls of steel-frame buildings would be blown away. Trees and utility poles over a wide area would be leveled. One of the most striking images showing the effects of the eruption of Mount St. Helens was the aerial photo showing thousands of acres of timber looking like so many pickup sticks scattered over the landscape. The eruption, according to the U.S. Forest Service, was equal to a nuclear explosion of between 10 and 50 megatons. The force of the eruption flattened trees and other vegetation in a fan-shaped area 8 miles long and 15 miles wide to the north of the mountain.*

The winds produced by nuclear explosion would cause similar effects.

ASIDE

The air blast creates what is technically known as overpressure—air pressure greater than that which is normal at sea level. A 2-megaton hydrogen bomb (large, but not the largest available) would create an overpressure in the immediate surrounding area of 17 pounds per square inch (abbre-

*"Mount St. Helens," U.S. Forest Service pamphlet, 1980.

Above, *view of Mount St. Helens, showing ash cloud. Over 5,000 feet of the north slope of the mountain was opened up in the May 18, 1980, blast, which had an explosive force equal to 10–50 megatons of TNT. Below, trees knocked down by blast from Mount St. Helens volcano, June 10, 1980.* (USDA Forest Service)

viated as psi). To get an idea of the effects of such an overpressure, consider the following: One extra pound of air pressure per square inch will break windows. Five extra pounds per square inch will destroy a house and rupture eardrums (this is about the level reached by a strong tornado). Twenty extra pounds per square inch does lung damage, and 35 psi destroys a building built to withstand earthquakes.

The point is that the airburst by itself—without fire or radiation effects—would kill 99 percent of the people living within a five-mile radius of the blast.

A surface burst, in contrast, is measured by its "cratering effect," the kind and size of hole it makes in the ground. Specialists in measuring blast effects at the surface describe the effects in terms of zones: The first zone, nearest to the bomb, becomes one big hole or crater. The second, at a somewhat greater distance away from the blast, is called the rupture zone because the rock in this area is churned up or ruptured. Beyond that is the plastic zone, where the rock is heaved about to the point at which it becomes unstable.

We human beings have no experience with cratering or rupture zone conditions. The strongest earthquake known to man so far compared in its effects to the conditions in the plastic zone.

To visualize the damaging effects of a surface burst, one needs to imagine a series of concentric areas around ground zero. The larger the bomb, the wider each of the zones would be: more crater, more rupture zone, more plastic zone. A 2-megaton bomb, exploding on the surface, would create a crater 1,500 feet in diameter (about the size of 30 football fields) and about 170 feet (20 stories) deep. The rupture zone would begin where the crater left off and extend another half-mile. The plastic zone, beyond that, another three-quarters of a mile.

HEAT

A substantial part of the energy released by a nuclear explosion—about 35 percent—takes the form of intense heat. heat
The temperature at the center of a thermonuclear explosion

reaches tens of millions of degrees, comparable to the heat at the core of the sun.

The heat (and the light) generated by such an explosion has tremendous effects. What happens is that all material substances in the area are not just destroyed, they are vaporized; they disappear. And the light is so great that on a clear night people looking directly at the fireball many many miles away would suffer flash blindness and second- and third-degree skin burns. The congressional Office of Technology Assessment (OTA), which has published a report entitled *The Effects of Nuclear War,* calculates that a single nuclear explosion of the size we have been talking about would result in some 10,000 severe burn cases.* The fact that the entire United States has treatment facilities for but 2,000 burn cases at one time adds to the complexities of post-nuclear recovery.

A major nuclear attack of course would involve not just the explosion of one hydrogen bomb but of hundreds. Thus we must assume that many of the wounded (burned or blinded) would not survive.

Intense heat of the magnitudes we have been describing tends to start fire storms. Fires would of course begin directly where the explosion left off, but fires would also come indirectly as a result of downed wires, exploding furnaces, broken gas lines, ignited fuel storage facilities, and the like. But these would still be fires, not fire storms. A fire storm is created when violently inrushing winds fan a fire and create **fire storms**   extremely high temperatures. Fire storms were known only very rarely in the past as a result of some natural catastrophes, but during World War II some man-made fire storms resulted from the intense aerial bombing of old cities in Europe such as Hamburg and Dresden, and in Japan when Tokyo was intensely bombed on March 9, 1945. The problem is exacerbated by what is called a "high fuel-loading factor," typical of most urban areas. Hamburg is a case in point. Because Hamburg was an old city, most of its buildings were made of wood and were built close together. Experts have calculated that Hamburg had 32 pounds of burnable material within each square foot. Eight pounds of burnable mate-

---

*The Effects of Nuclear War, Office of Technology Assessment, U.S. Congress, May 1979, page 21.

rial within a square foot is enough to ignite a fire storm. So
as the Allied bombers moved on away from the city, having
completed their attack, columns of flames rose as high as
two miles into the air, creating 300-mile-an-hour winds.

We have a novelist's description of a fire storm in Kurt
Vonnegut's paragraphs about the bombing of the German
city of Dresden in *Slaughterhouse-Five:*

> He was down in the meat locker on the night that Dres-
> den was destroyed. There were sounds like giant foot-
> steps above. These were the sticks of high-explosive
> bombs. . . . The meat locker was a very safe shelter. . . .
> A guard would go to the head of the stairs every so often
> to see what it was like outside, then he would come
> down and whisper to the other guards. There was a
> firestorm out there. Dresden was one big flame. The
> one flame ate everything organic, everything that would
> burn.
>
> It wasn't safe to come out of the shelter until noon
> the next day. When the Americans and their guards did
> come out, the sky was black with smoke. The sun was
> an angry little pinhead. Dresden was like the moon
> now, nothing but minerals. The stones were hot. Every-
> body else in the neighborhood was dead.*

Actually, most people in their shelters were dead, too. German citizens had become used to seeking shelter from
bombing raids by 1943 and many of them would sleep in
concrete bunkers overnight. But the fire storms in Hamburg, Dresden, and Tokyo turned most shelters into airless
tombs. So much oxygen was consumed by fire that people in
shelters suffocated. An estimated 120,000 people may have
died in the one raid on Dresden.†

In contrast to cities such as Hamburg, Dresden, and
Tokyo, the typical American suburb has a fuel-loading factor
of only two pounds per square foot of combustible material.
Thus such areas might be saved from fire storms. Older
American cities, however, like Baltimore and Philadelphia
would surely burn.

---

*Kurt Vonnegut, *Slaughterhouse-Five* (New York: Delta, 1969), pages 152–53.
†Precise figures are hard to come by and different sources cite both higher and
lower estimates.

RADIATION

The unique effect of nuclear explosions is, of course, radiation. Radiation is another one of those good English words that has a particular, additional meaning in physics. If you read further in this field, you will find the term radiation used by scientists both to mean the process of radioactive emission and to refer to the stuff itself that is being emitted. Radiation, as they use it, is the fast-moving nuclear particles that result when nuclei are split or fused. Since these particles can enter the human body moving at high speeds, there is of course no way to protect oneself from their bombardment, and once inside a cell they so damage the cell's structure that no normal function by that cell can ever take place again.

Two kinds of radioactive damage are distinguished by experts on the effects of nuclear explosions. The first is prompt or blast radiation, the radiation resulting from the explosion itself. The second is fallout, the downwind effect when particles of earth, rock, or other debris made radioactive as a result of exposure to the blast travel wide distances before descending to earth to do further damage. Blast radiation, not surprisingly, is very intense, but, at least with large weapons, limited to a smaller area than either the blast or the heat effects. Thus people who would be exposed to blast radiation would be "in the crater" anyway.

With smaller thermonuclear weapons the relationship between the amount of prompt, blast radiation and the amount of blast and heat is reversed: The smaller the weapon, the more casualties from prompt radiation, and the fewer casualties from blast and heat. The larger the weapon, the more casualties from blast and heat.

The effect of fallout radiation, especially of small doses over a long period of time, is a different matter. Indeed, it is one of intense controversy in the scientific community. In general, the government has been slow to admit the dangers of low-dosage radiation. And it has had to lower the "safe" dosage considerably since the issue was first studied in the 1950s.

Measuring Radiation

A radiation dose is usually measured in roentgens or milliroentgens. A roentgen is a particular unit of radiation producing certain changes (called ionization) in other atoms. There is another unit of measure, however, generally more useful in assessing health effects called the *rem,* or roentgen **rems** equivalent man. The rem is a particular dosage of radiation in man, one rem corresponding to the absorption of between one billion and 20 billion particles by one pound of human body weight.

To put radiation amounts into some perspective, consider the following: Some natural background radiation is absorbed by people all the time. Typically (depending upon the altitude at which one lives and works) it is less than $\frac{1}{10}$ rem per year. A chest X ray, for purposes of comparison, being more intense, gives the patient $\frac{1}{100}$ rem every time an X ray is taken. So 10 X rays would give the equivalent rems of one year of background radiation. In order to monitor the amount of radiation they are taking in, people who regularly work with radioactive materials, such as nuclear reactor engineers, wear a radiation-sensitive badge. When they have absorbed their safe limit (calculated at 5 rems per year), they are temporarily taken off the job.

These dosages are relatively small, but if accumulated before the body can repair itself—that is, if they are taken in rapidly with little elapsed time in between—they can be very harmful. Larger doses, the kind we are talking about, are rarely tolerable, even for a short time. The reason for this is that the body cannot—as biologists express it—stay ahead of the cell damage if the dosages are large.

Fallout

The amount of fallout resulting from a nuclear explosion depends primarily on whether the weapon is detonated on the ground or in the air (sufficiently high above the surface of the earth so that the explosion's fireball does not touch the ground). If the purpose of the weapon is to destroy a missile

Main Fallout Pattern—Uniform 15 mph Southwest Wind (1-Mt Surface Burst in Detroit). (Contours for 7-Day Accumulated Dose (Without Shielding) of 3,000, 900, 300, and 90 Rem.)

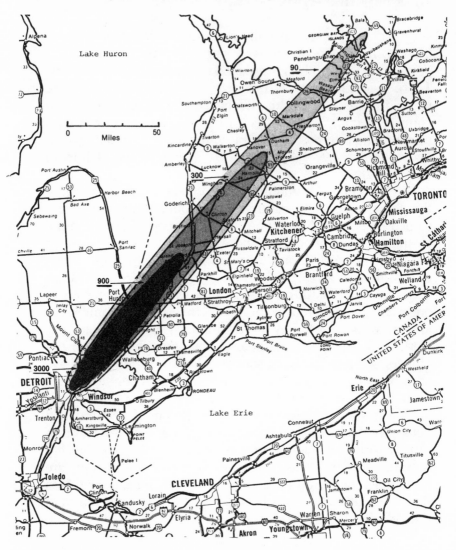

(The Effects of Nuclear War, *pages 24 and 25*)

silo, mostly underground and built of heavy reinforced concrete, a ground burst would be utilized. While a ground burst will probably cause a smaller area of destruction than an airburst (because some of the energy released is absorbed by the earth and goes into digging a large hole in the ground, the crater), it will produce considerably more fallout. When a nuclear weapon detonates at ground level, large

Main Fallout Pattern—Uniform 15 mph Northwest Wind (1-Mt Surface Burst in Detroit).
(Contours for 7-Day Accumulated Dose (Without Shielding) of 3,000, 900, 300, and 90 Rem.)

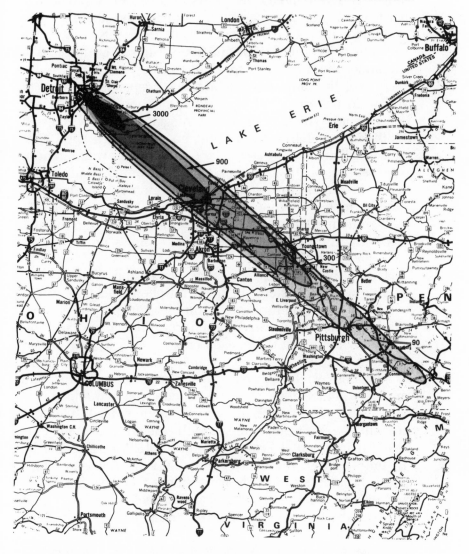

amounts of earth, rock, water, and other materials are blown up into the explosion, irradiated, then scattered downwind.

Radioactive particles in the fallout vary from the size of marbles to fine sand and even smaller fragments. The particles are the rock and dirt that have come in contact with the neutrons emitted by the nuclear or thermonuclear blast. The larger particles will return to earth relatively quickly (within a day or two), while the finer particles will remain aloft longer and will spread over a wider area. Some radioactive particles may even remain in the upper atmosphere for several years after an explosion. Fallout from U.S. and Soviet weapons tests of the 1950s and 1960s can still be detected in the atmosphere today, more than twenty years later.*

Where the radioactive debris lands depends on weather and wind patterns, and is certainly neither predictable nor controllable. When, in 1954, a 15-megaton device was tested on Bikini, an atoll in the Pacific, an unexpected wind shift caused fallout over an area 7,000 square miles wide.† These two maps show the fallout patterns that would result over a seven-day period following a one-megaton ground burst in Detroit under differing wind conditions.‡ Even just a 15-mile-an-hour wind, as you can see from the diagram, would spread harmful fallout more than 200 miles downwind of such an explosion.

Given the prevailing westerly winds and regularly appearing weather systems in our hemisphere, radiation would blanket large sections of the country for long periods of time. While people might avoid the effects of the blast radiation simply by not being there, each one-megaton weapon would create a zone of 1,500 square miles in which the amount of radiation would exceed a year's maximum in just one month. Another zone of 20,000 square miles would represent exactly one year's maximum for a year. While that amount (2 rems) won't cause death (though it exceeds current Environmental Protection Agency [EPA] standards by 10 times), given the likely poisoning of natural water supplies, the scarcity of medical treatment facilities, and other war-related dislocations, it is doubtful that people would be very healthy in these zones or that foodstuffs would grow or livestock flourish.

Since a nuclear exchange is likely to include more than one explosion, with a multitude of bombs directed to specific locations in the United States, unsafe conditions would exist everywhere.

*The Effects of Nuclear War, page 23.
†The Effects of Nuclear Weapons, U.S. Departments of Defense and Energy, 1977, page 438.
‡The Effects of Nuclear War, pages 24–25.

Besides, military strategists tend to assume that our land-based missile silos or our air bases would be first hit. But supposing the enemy were not to play by these rules? Steven A. Fetter and Kosta Tsipis, writing in *Scientific American* in April 1981, calculate the radiation damage to the country if a nuclear power plant were hit with one hydrogen bomb one megaton in size.* Because the power plant's radioactive material is especially "dirty," the lethal zone—that is, the zone where dosages would be 400 rems per day—would extend 500 square miles around the blast. An area about the size of the state of Florida (64,000 square miles) would be uninhabitable for a month, and an area about the size of the state of West Virginia (20,000 square miles) would be uninhabitable for a year. In fact, if—as the authors speculate—a one-megaton bomb hit the nuclear reactor at Racine, Wisconsin, on the western shore of Lake Michigan, Detroit as well as Chicago would be unlivable; and some fallout from this single blast would extend as far as New York.

EMP (ELECTROMAGNETIC PULSE)

A less known disturbance resulting from any nuclear or thermonuclear explosion would be the electromagnetic pulse, an electrical disturbance throughout the atmosphere similar to but far in excess of natural lightning. What happens during a nuclear or thermonuclear blast is that electrons emitted by the excited air molecules move out from the blast as an electric current. If, for one reason or another, these air molecules are blocked in any one direction (either because they are very near to the ground or because they are so high that the air is thinner above than below) an asymmetrical pattern develops. And because the earth is a big magnet, an electromagnetic wave called EMP is created. While there is no particular evidence that EMP would disturb human beings in the same way radioactive particles would, such waves or pulses could destroy microcircuitry in computers and render some of our communication systems unworkable. Fearful of this, the military has already begun to "harden" or shield communication systems and other vital

*Vol. 244, No. 4, pages 41–47.

electronic equipment that are most critical. The problem is that since we stopped testing nuclear and thermonuclear weapons in the atmosphere, we have not been able to increase our knowledge about EMP. The most we can do is to simulate the effect. Thus, there are many questions unanswered about EMP and little public discussion of it so far.*

MISSILES

Thermonuclear devices are so powerful and deadly that they tend, and understandably so, to attract the most attention in any current weapons inventory. But in terms of military strategy, the bombs or warheads are only as usable as they are able to reach their targets, and this in turn depends on their own "delivery systems." The first nuclear weapons, as we have noted, were bombs designed to be carried on aircraft and simply dropped on their targets. However, as we shall see in greater detail in Chapter Three, today the bomber has taken a second or even a third place to missiles, the most important strategic and tactical nuclear delivery systems now available.

In one sense, the missile (once called a rocket) is an old weapon. The Chinese invented rockets in the thirteenth century (along with gunpowder), and missiles not very different from those devised by the Chinese were used up to the nineteenth century, their appearance in the War of 1812 immortalized with the words "the rockets' red glare . . ." Rockets became more widely used during World War II. The bazooka was a small rocket that could, though it was hard to aim, destroy or at least disable a tank. During that war the Germans began to develop two new flying weapons, however, far more devastating than these earlier, tactical rockets: the V-1 and the V-2.

Their V-1 was, in essence, a pilotless airplane (an early form of the cruise missile, one might say) in that it was not just propelled through the air by some initial force; it actu-

---

* David W. Hafemeister, "Test VII" in *A Short Course on the Arms Race*, published by the American Association of Physics Teachers, pages 112–18. L. V. Ricketts, J. E. Bridges and J. Miletta, *EMP Radiation and Protective Techniques* (New York: Wiley-Interscience, 1976), *passim.*

ally flew after being sent off, its wings and internal engine providing sufficient aerodynamics to make it stay aloft. The V-1 came to be known, because of this, as the "flying bomb." The V-1's air-breathing pulse-jet engine made a *bzz, bzz* sound as it flew. So the British, who were the first to experience attacks by V-1s, called it the "buzz bomb."

Although the British could shoot down some V-1s, it remained a formidable weapon until its launch sites were captured. It could travel more than 400 miles per hour, an impressive speed in those years, and could cover a distance of a few hundred miles—far enough, anyway, to reach London or Antwerp from northern France or Holland. Loaded with a ton of explosives, the missile would hit the ground and explode on impact.

However powerless they were made to feel, hearing first the *bzz, bzz, bzz* followed by silence and then the weapon's explosion, the British had even more to fear from the Germans' V-2 than from their V-1. The V-2 rocket traveled 5,000 miles per hour, faster than sound; thus its noise was behind it and people on the ground heard nothing before it hit. It was, in fact, the first real ballistic missile, because it was propelled by its rocket engines and carried into the stratosphere (in an arc reaching about 70 miles high). When its fuel was shut off, it came back to earth at enormously fast reentry speeds some 250–300 miles away from where it had been launched. Looking back on the innovation, we can see now that the V-2 was more like a giant self-propelled artillery shell than like any aircraft.

As we will see in Chapter Three, with the exception of the cruise missile, most of the missiles in our current arsenals are ballistic, that is, they do not have wings or wing-like flying surfaces. Like the V-2s of yesteryear, they are launched into the air and climb beyond the stratosphere. To get to even greater heights and distances, modern missiles consist of multiple stages, each containing its own engine (or engines) and fuel supply. When the fuel of one stage is exhausted, that stage is dropped off and the next stage takes over, in relay fashion. Once the last stage has been jettisoned, the warhead-carrying "bus" coasts and ejects warheads at programmed points which then plummet back through the atmosphere to earth.

ASIDE——————————————————————————————————

Another distinction among missiles—apart from ballistic (nonwinged) and nonballistic (having winged surfaces)—is between guided and nonguided missiles. Guided missiles are directed and redirected while in flight, and may be ballistic or, like the cruise missile, nonballistic. Guidance may come from an external source such as radar signals or from an internal inertial system that uses gyroscopes or homing devices such as a small TV camera, or combinations of internal and external sources. Unguided missiles can only be aimed, like bullets; once launched, they are on their own in free flight without internal or external commands. Of our current arsenal, only small artillery rockets and some fired by aircraft are unguided. Most modern missiles are guided and, as we shall see, use a wide variety of different guidance techniques and target-seeking systems.

——————————————————————————————————————

The first time the Germans successfully launched a V-2 rocket, Wernher von Braun (the "father" both of German missile technology and of our own) is said to have quipped, "It was a great success, but it landed on the wrong planet." Perhaps he was trying to pretend that he would have preferred aiming it at the moon rather than at London. But given the primitive guidance technology available at the time, it is more remarkable that it did not land on another country.

Since the 1940s missiles have improved virtually in all respects: range, payload (or "throw-weight," as it is called, meaning the amount of weight the missile can carry), reliability, and, above all, accuracy. Guidance has developed to the point at which some missiles can perform midcourse corrections by checking their positions with a navigation satellite. The newest U.S. intercontinental ballistic missiles, for example, are now accurate to within a few hundred *feet* at the end of a 6,000-*mile* flight! Accuracy of this kind was never dreamed of by Wernher von Braun, and because of this accuracy even our hardened (reinforced) underground missile silos may be vulnerable to attack.

The point is that against missiles traveling at speeds of up to 20,000 miles per hour, there is no real defense, at least not with currently available technology. And the effects of the detonation of even one thermonuclear warhead or bomb in the megaton range are beyond anything any military expert or lay person can fully comprehend. These realities ought to be borne in mind as we inventory the strategic nuclear arsenals currently available and as we consider the evolution of our strategy of deterrence.

CONCLUSION

So from sticks and stones to subatomic particles—tiny, tiny stones indeed—and rockets, it is apparent that mankind's ability to devise ever greater sources of firepower has come a long way. Because of nuclear and thermonuclear weaponry, warfare as history has known it may no longer be meaningful. We do not know what a nuclear war would be like. No one save the Japanese has ever come close to experiencing one. It might be over quickly, with no battles in the traditional sense, no maneuvers, no fronts. . . . Or it could be a long-drawn-out affair.

The point is that even the strategic analysts whose job it is to plan for war have difficulty imagining a "nuclear exchange." With so little real experience on which to draw, they turn to computer simulations or think in terms of analogies—other wars and natural disasters. As with the machine guns and bombers of past wars, we cannot comprehend the consequences of the actual use of nuclear weapons. Some think in terms of "more" and "better" weapons, and are very much concerned when "theirs" exceed "ours." They forget the enormous destructiveness of even a few nuclear weapons.

On the other hand, it may be that our intuitive grasp of the consequences of nuclear war has prevented one.

LONG ASIDE: BREAKING THE CODE————————————————

The nomenclature and designations used by the military for identifying weapons seem rather random to the outsider. But to the military the ubiquitous letter-number designations are a meaningful code. The M-1 and M-16 are both rifles. Yet the newest Army tank is also called the M-1 (XM-1 during its experimental stages; once approved for manufacture, it became the M-1). The M-14 is another Army rifle; but the F-14 is a Navy fighter plane. The letter and the number in each case simply represent a model number within a particular category. Thus it is possible to have different items with the same letter-number designation denoting altogether different weapons. The key is understanding the category: rifle, tank, missile, warhead, bomb, bomber, ship, or whatever.

Another anomaly is the number sequencing. You might assume that the lower numbers would represent smaller systems (just as in the Mercedes 190, which is smaller than the 280 and the 450); barring that, that they came in at an earlier time. The F-111, however, was produced before the F-16; and in the case of bombers, the B-52 and B-70 came before the B-1; and the M-60 tank before the M-1.

What happens is that from time to time the numbering systems are changed. The best example of this occurred in 1962. Prior to that time the Air Force and Navy had separate aircraft designation systems. Both, for example, used the common designation F for fighters, but the Air Force numbers were serial; that is, the F-105 came after the F-84. In the Navy (recall the old joke that there are three ways to do something: the right way, the wrong way, and the Navy way) the number was serial only to the manufacturer. In other words, the F-4D was the fourth fighter design from the Douglas Aircraft Company (now part of McDonnell Douglas Corporation) but was several years newer than the F-9F, the ninth fighter from Grumman Aircraft (denoted by the second F because G was already taken by Goodyear, which had been making Navy airships [blimps and dirigibles] years before Mr. Grumman got his first Navy contract) and contemporaneous with the F-7U, the seventh fighter from the Chance Vought Aircraft Company (now part of The LTV Corporation).

But it was even more complicated than that. The A-3D3T was the third model of the third attack bomber (the *A* stands for attack) designed by Douglas Aircraft, but student radar-operator stations had been put in the bomb bay so it could be used for training, thus the *T*. All this confusion came to a head in 1961, when the Air Force decided to buy the Navy's newest fighter, the Phantom II. The Navy designated it the F-4H, the fourth fighter built by *H,* the McDonnell Company (now merged with Douglas). The Air Force, having purchased the F-106 in some quantity but having decided against buying the F-107, -108, and -109 after they had been designed, referred to its newest acquisition as the F-110. It took the Congressmen who had to authorize and appropriate the money to buy these planes some time to figure out that the F-4H and the F-110 were the same plane. They were not pleased. Neither was the Secretary of Defense, and word went out that the nomenclature would be unified.

Essentially, the Air Force system was adopted. *A* stands for attack (light) bombers, *B* for heavy bombers, *C* for cargo planes, *E* for electronic warfare aircraft, and *F* for fighters (which can also drop bombs), while *H* means helicopter and is a supplemental designation, as in *AH* for attack helicopter. In addition, *K* is for the tanker planes that refuel others in midair, *O* for small observation planes, *P* designates long-range patrol planes (which are also antisubmarine planes), *Q* denotes aircraft that have been equipped with remote controls so they can be used for target practice, *R* is for reconnaissance craft bigger than the little O's, *S* denotes antisubmarine planes (except for long-range ones, which carry a *P* designation), *T* is for trainers, *U* means general utility, and *Y* is an additional designation for prototype developmental aircraft, such as the YF-17, which evolved into the Navy's F-18 and A-18.

These letter designations can be combined as well. The KC-10 is a tanker aircraft that also carries cargo. An RF-4 is an F-4 that has had its weapons replaced by sophisticated cameras and other electronic surveillance equipment, while an EF-111 is an F-111 modified to jam enemy radar and radio communications. Even training planes get into the act; the AT-37 is a primary jet trainer adapted to light bombing missions and provided to less-developed countries such as El Salvador and, at one time, South Vietnam.

There is more. The numbers are normally followed by

another letter which denotes successive models of the aircraft. For example, the *E* in A-7E tells you that this is the fifth modification of the A-7 design. These modifications can be very extensive, including new engines and completely different electronics and weapons systems. Since the first one is always the "A" model (and sometimes not specified, as in F-16), the second one the "B" model and so on, you can usually tell which modification it is by counting alphabetically.

When the new numbering system was imposed, seriality was lost, at least for the time being. Before the change the last big Air Force bomber was the B-70; after the switch the next bomber design was the B-1. The last Air Force fighter was the F-111. Out of deference to the Navy, the F-4H became the F-4 while the F-105 remained the same. Other Navy plane numbers were integrated as best they could, but since no manufacturer had ever sold more than eleven designs of any one type to the Navy and the oldest Air Force fighter flying at the time was the F-84, there was ample room for accommodation. The first new postswitch fighter was the F-14, which has been followed by the F-15, -16, and -18. Assuming that the Pentagon does not change the system again, in twenty years only a military trivia buff will know the difference.

The often fanciful names given to aircraft originate with their manufacturers and often try to follow a theme. Lockheed, for example, pursues celestial images. Its first jet fighter was the Shooting Star, which was followed some years later by the Starfighter. Their cargo planes are named Galaxy and Starlifter and their patrol craft are Neptune and Orion. Mr. Grumman, on the other hand, must have been a cat fancier. His World War II Navy fighters began with the Wildcat, followed by the Hellcat, the twin-engined Tigercat, and the powerful Bearcat, which arrived a few months too late to fight. Grumman's first jets were the F-9F Panther and Cougar and Tiger up to today's F-14 Tomcat. Before the merger with Douglas, McDonnell Aircraft evoked the supernatural with Phantom, Goblin, Voodoo, and Demon. Their postmerger new planes are the F-15 Eagle and F-18 Hornet.

Pilots often use the numerical designations but also come up with their own names. While Douglas (before the merger) used a sky theme, as in Skyraider and Skyhawk, pilots referred to the first, a prop-driven attack bomber, as Spad in honor of its low speed and tough reliability; the second was Scooter or Tinker Toy because it was so small. Republic Aviation uses a "Thunder" on its names, but pilots named the F-105 Thunderchief the Thud or the Lead Sled. And the A-10 Thunderbolt II is affectionately known as the Warthog. Sometimes the numerical designation makes the nickname. Douglas's 1950s vintage F-4D Skyray was the Ford. North American's F-100 Super Saber was the Hun (as in *hun*dred). And just as the ubiquitous World War II Jeep came from the official designation "GP" (for general purpose), so did the UH-1 utility helicopter become Vietnam's Huey.

In Europe the system is much the same, except, of course, almost no names are the same as in the U.S. equipment. The British prefer names alone such as Vulcan, Canberra, Lightning, Buccaneer, Jaguar, Harrier, Tornado. (Interestingly enough, this antipathy toward numbers is reflected in their Army organization as well. Where we might refer to Charlie Company, First Battalion, 2d Marine Division, they will have the Queen's Own Light Horse Regiment, or some such.) The French for more than twenty years have been building the Mirage series of fighters, going through models I, II, III, IV, and V, up to the latest, the 2000 and 4000. There is a Gallic touch, though. While we name our short-ranged thermonuclear missiles Honest John or Pershing, theirs is the Pluton, soon to be replaced by Hades.

The Russians have several different aircraft design bureaus named after the aviator-engineers who started them, mostly in the 1920s and 1930s. Oleg Antonov and Sergey Ilyushin both specialized in large aircraft; Antonov's are mostly transports designated "An," as in An-22, while Ilyushin built bombers as well, such as the IL-28. The best-known Soviet bomber designer, however, was Andrei Nikolaevich Tupolev, who in the 1920s built huge planes designated ANT. Today his bureau's products are denoted with a "Tu," as in Tu-22 (a twin-jet medium-range bomber). Vladimir Myasishchev also specialized early in large aircraft, which today are lettered with an *M*, sometimes seen as "Mya."

The Russian helicopter designer Igor Sikorsky did his most notable work after seeking refuge in America. His company is now part of United Technologies. In the USSR today, both Nikolai Kamov and Mikhail Mil have design bureaus specializing in helicopters. Mil's work is today seen in the large, powerful Mi-24 helicopter gunships, operating with Soviet forces in Afghanistan, while Kamov has designed rotary-wing craft for ship-based sub hunting, most notably the Ka-25.

Fighters and attack aircraft are built by Pavel Sukhoi, whose Su-22 was the type flown by Libyan pilots when they were shot down by U.S. Navy Tomcats (F-14s) in the Gulf of Sidra in 1981. Aleksandr Yakovlov also builds fighters, his most visible product today being the Yak-36 vertical-takeoff jets that operate from Soviet aircraft carriers. But the best-known warplanes that wear the red star are a product of a two-man design team, Artyom I. Mikoyan and Mikhail I. Gurevich. MiG fighters such as the MiG-15 of Korean War fame, the MiG-21 that the North Vietnamese flew against us (and the Egyptians flew with notable lack of success against the Israelis), the MiG-23 that so concerns NATO's defense planners today, and the well-known MiG-25 (which was flown to Japan several years ago by a defector) all show the world the formidable and not-so-formidable capabilities of the Russian aviation industry.

It is interesting to reflect on the pragmatism of a supposedly Marxist state that allows technocrats of individual genius the freedom to design and develop their products within their own bureaucratic empire. We have ours as well: Boeing, Grumman, Lockheed, McDonnell, and Hughes were real people, too. But there was no General named Dynamics.

Since the Russians usually do not name their aircraft, NATO has done it for them. It is a very logical system. Fighters are denoted with words that start with the letter *f*, bombers with the letter *b*, and so on. In addition, the NATO system uses one syllable for propeller-driven fixed-wing aircraft, two syllables for jets. Thus the Bear A is a prop-powered bomber (the Tu-20), while the Backfire (the Tu-22M or Tu-26, depending on which reference work you consult) is a jet bomber. Since all fighters today are jets, we have Fishbed (MiG-21), Flogger (MiG-23), and Foxbat (MiG-25), as well as Fencer (Su-19), Fitter (Su-7), and Forger (Yak-36). And the MiG-15 of Korean War fame was known as Faggot. The same system applies to cargo planes—the Cod, Cub, or Candid; and helicopters—Hip, Hind, or Hormone.

There is lots more to this business of military equipment designations. Take Navy ships, for example. Submarines are designated "SS," nuclear submarines are SSNs, while nuclear submarines that fire ballistic missiles are SSBNs. Cruisers are CG; destroyers DD, unless they carry guided missiles, which makes them DDGs. Aircraft carriers are CVs unless they are nuclear-powered, in which case they become CVNs (the V stands for heavier-than-air, fixed-wing aircraft, but no one in the Navy knows why).

As part of a long and hallowed tradition, Navy ships have always been given proper names, in addition to their military descriptive designations, and rules of naming used to be very rigid. Battleships could be named only after states: the *Missouri* (on which the Japanese surrendered), the *New Jersey*, and others. Cruisers were named after cities, destroyers for naval heroes, aircraft carriers for battles: the *Lexington* and the *Yorktown*, the *Midway* and *Coral Sea;* and submarines for fish: *Skate, Swordfish, Shark, Pollack, Haddock*—even *Flasher*, named after a fish, not a sexual deviant. In the past, exceptions might be made but these were rare. The aircraft carrier *Enterprise*, or *Big E* as it was known in World War II, and the *Hornet*, also of that vintage, were named after sailing ships, and now the *Enterprise* has its own progeny in a nuclear-powered aircraft carrier bearing the same name.

Since battleships are no longer being built, some cruisers, notably the *California*, the *Virginia*, and the *Texas*, are named for states; but then so is the first Trident missile submarine, the U.S.S. *Ohio*. So the clear demarcations are no more.

Other cruisers carry the names of famous naval figures: *Halsey*, after the World War II admiral of that name; *Wainwright*, after the Marine general of Bataan fame; and *Josephus Daniels*, after a former Secretary of the Navy. Some aircraft carriers are meant to resonate with memories of earlier ships: the first *Ranger* was a sloop of war commanded by John Paul Jones during the American Revolution, while the newest "flattop" carries the name of a former Congressman, Carl Vinson.

Heroes are still remembered on destroyers: the *Farragut,*

the *Dewey,* the *John Paul Jones,* the *Mahan,* and the *Dahlgren,* among others. And while most attack submarines, as we have noted, are named after fish, some of the newest ones are named after cities. Others, reflecting no doubt Admiral Hyman Rickover's masterful cultivation of the Congress, call attention to the Navy's friends on the Hill: *Glenard B. Lipscomb* and *William H. Bates, L. Mendel Rivers* and *Richard B. Russell.* The names of dead heroes also decorate the missile submarines—*Lafayette, Nathan Hale, Daniel Boone, Benjamin Franklin, Will Rogers,* to name but a few—but it is noteworthy that none of our fleet has been named for a woman, living or dead.

Not to be outdone, the Army names its tanks after famous generals. Thus the M-4 was the Sherman; the M-48 the Patton; the M-551 the Sheridan; and finally, the newest tank, the M-1, is called the Abrams. Most other Army weapons just get numbers, but occasionally a gun, in this case an anti-aircraft gun, is given a proper name: the Vulcan.

Army missiles are more colorful—Sergeant, Lance, Pershing—but where the Honest John came from (an artillery rocket no longer in use) no one seems to remember.

And of course there are the acronyms. We cannot blame their invention on the military—President Roosevelt is supposed to have been the first government official to have created the "alphabet soup"—but the military carries its acronyms further than anyone else. We will soon encounter MIRV, multiple independently targetable reentry vehicles (warheads), but there is MaRV as well, a maneuverable reentry vehicle, and, to complete the trio, SAM—surface-to-air missiles.

"Alcum, Slickum and Glickum" are not a Washington law firm but air-launched cruise missiles (ALCM), sea-launched cruise missiles (SLCM), and ground-launched cruise missiles (GLCM). An ARM is not an appendage, real or metaphorical, but an anti-radiation (i.e., anti-radar) missile, and TOE is not what you dip in the water but a table of equipment. Similarly, "Knee Cap" is the National Emergency Airborne Command Post (NEACP), a Boeing 747 aircraft equipped with extensive communication gear for the President to ride in case of a nuclear attack.

The radars have colorful names, too: BMEWS (ballistic-missile early-warning system) DEW (distant early-warning system), PAVE PAWS, and Cobra Dane.

MENS is not the sign on the rest-room door, but a mission element needs statement.

And then there is the zoo: ANTS, GNATS, DOG, FROG, COD, APE, RAT, BAT, RAM, and CLAM which stand for (respectively) airborne night television system, general noise and tonal system, development objectives guide, free rocket over ground, carrier on-deck delivery, advanced production engineering, RAM air turbine, ballistic aerial target, reliability and maintainability, and chemical low-altitude missile.*

Suffice it to say that the most market-oriented automobile or home-appliance manufacturer will always have to take a back seat to the Pentagon when it comes to naming things. And if you are still confused, the Pentagon publishes a directory of acronyms and terminology to help its own people figure out what is what.

---

*Thanks to Norman Augustine for this list.

3.
The Evolution of
Strategic Weapons

WHEN ON THE SIXTH of August, 1945, an atomic bomb
called *Little Boy* fell from the bomb bay of the B-29 *Enola
Gay* and detonated 1,700 feet above Hiroshima, world attention was riveted on the bomb and what it had done to
Hiroshima, as well as to the art of war. But no particular
attention was paid to the plane. After all, its mission may
have been historic, but thousands of B-29s had been pounding Japan with high-explosive bombs for months. Yet, no
bomb is useful without some mechanism for carrying it to its
intended target. So the delivery system, though not as stun-
ning as the bomb it was carrying, had to be appreciated for
what it was, a major innovation in strategic warfare.

The distinction between tactics and strategy in military
parlance must be understood. While tactical warfare refers
to events involving forces in battle, situations where there is
direct contact with the enemy, strategic war is directed at
the enemy's basic means of support: his economy, his supplies of raw materials, his productive capacity (including his
civilian population), in short his heartland. The distinction is
as simple as the difference between blasting enemy tanks on
the battlefield and blowing up the tank factory at home.

Before the long-range bomber was invented, strategic
warfare was pretty much limited to blockade, siege, and the
burning of cropland and farm villages ("scorched earth").

Armies would starve enemy cities, lay waste to their products, and cut off their harbors from overseas supplies.

ASIDE───────────────────────────────────

It was to survive scorched earth that the Irish made their decision early in the modern period to grow the potato as their basic food instead of grain, which could be put to the torch. The potato grows underground, so the crop can be saved and the peasants can eat no matter what happens to the countryside.

──

Rarely did an aggressor aim for the total destruction of the enemy nation or its civilization. Rather, the country was seen as a valuable prize, bringing new territory and wealth to the king's coffers, loot for the army, power and prestige to the commanding general. Of course, the people under attack might burn their own bridges or even torch their own fields as a defensive measure, to deny the invader access and sustenance. But in general it was the invader who ravaged the countryside, sometimes as a punishment for natives who had fought too well, but always incidentally to the primary task of conquest.

In any case, crops (and the peasantry) would eventually grow back. Genghis Khan obliterated countless villages as Mongol armies swept across Asia, killing every inhabitant, save those few kept for slaves. In the last Punic War, Carthage was leveled, ending forever its threat to Rome's domination of the Mediterranean. And the campaigns of the Union Army in the Shenandoah Valley as well as Sherman's famous "march to the sea" during America's Civil War—destroying a 50-mile-wide swath through Georgia (and providing the setting for *Gone With the Wind*)—all were precursors of modern strategic war.

But it was the invention of the airplane and then the missile that for the first time made it relatively easy to carry the war, literally over armies and fleets, to the heartland of the enemy—the very essence of strategic war. There was little aerial bombing in the First World War, only some Zeppelin raids on England and a few British bombing runs over northern German cities. But the war ended before the British could carry out plans for bombing cities on a large scale.

At the beginning of World War II, however, the Japanese and Germans showed the world the possibilities of aerial bombing when the Japanese struck some Chinese cities and the Germans hit Warsaw and Rotterdam and brought the Blitz to London. But neither the Germans nor the Japanese came close to mastering strategic bombing. Simply put, their planes were too small: twin-engine craft that just couldn't carry enough bombs to do much damage, at least not compared to what was to come later.

ASIDE

The intellectual origins of strategic bombing lie in Italy. In the early 1920s, Giulio Douhet wrote *Command of the Air,* which fast became the bible of air-power advocates all over the world, most notably Billy Mitchell in the United States. Douhet believed that a bombing campaign would quickly demoralize the civilian population, which would lead to the collapse of the government and, with it, the war effort itself. It didn't work. Instead, bombing tended to increase civilian resistance (something we Americans experienced in Vietnam). Also, it took a while for military planners to figure out just how many tons of explosives were needed sufficiently to destroy a target (a factory, a bridge, or a railroad) so that it couldn't simply be dusted off, patched up, and put back to work the next morning.

It was America, and to a lesser extent England, which first showed the world how to build a strategic bomber. First, it had to have at least four engines. This gave it enough power to climb to high altitudes—20,000–30,000 feet in those days. Second, it had to go fast enough—maybe 200–250 miles per hour—to avoid being an easy target for fighters and anti-aircraft gunners. Third, it had to carry enough fuel to fly a couple of thousand miles while hauling enough bombs to make it all worthwhile. The first plane to do this with any reliability was the B-17, built by Boeing and dubbed the Flying Fortress.

Operating from English bases, the U.S. Army Air Corps was dedicated to the concept of precision bombing. The plan was to hit selected critical industries, which would cripple the enemy's war effort with relative efficiency. This meant they had to operate in daylight. The first target of this strategy was the German ball-bearing industry. The logic was that all machines needed bearings: no bearings, no machines, and without machines the war would soon be over.

But the German defenders were very tough. So many B-17s were lost that the mighty 8th Air Force was temporarily rendered *hors de combat*. And the ball-bearing campaign was all for naught. The Germans had previously manufactured and stored an ample supply of bearings, and whatever additional quantities they needed could be purchased from neutral Sweden. Later, long-range fighters were developed to escort our bombers and beat back most defending fighters. And other targets were picked—oil refineries, locomotive and aircraft factories, and rail yards. But the postwar *Strategic Bombing Survey* revealed that throughout it all, German industrial production continuously increased.

The British had worse luck. They built four-engine bombers, the Stirling and Lancaster, but their planes lacked speed and altitude. As a result, whenever they tried to bomb the Continent in daylight, too many of them were shot down. So they turned to night bombing. But since they couldn't see, they had to abandon all hope of precision and simply scatter their bombs about Germany's urban centers. We made a good team—they bombing at night, we in the day— and by the end of the war our combined bomber armadas were so huge that all pretense at precision could be dropped. Massive air assaults on urban centers were undertaken, culminating in the total destruction of Dresden.

The bombing of Japan was somewhat easier. Although the distances were greater and much of the flying was over water, the B-29 (which never saw action in Europe) was up to the task. Based first in China, then on Pacific islands captured after bloody Marine amphibious assaults, the 20th Air Force under Curtis E. LeMay systematically destroyed Japan's industry. Unlike the Germans, the Japanese couldn't rebuild their factories; our submarine blockade had cut them off from their raw materials.

BOMBERS: THE STRATEGIC AIR COMMAND (SAC)

When, after the war, tensions between the United States and the Soviet Union began to mount, the new Air Force (separated from the Army after the war) created a special bomber force aimed at Russia. It was called the Strategic Air Command (known popularly as SAC), and General LeMay of the Japanese bombing campaign was put in charge.

U.S. demobilization after World War II was so thorough that not one fully operational Air Wing existed in 1946. LeMay found scattered and decrepit B-29 squadrons that had little or no operational capability. But with his mandate to be the U.S. government's first line of defense against the Soviet Union, he quickly whipped aircraft and airmen into shape, imposing strict discipline and sharp professionalism on the crews. By requiring minute adherence to rules and regulations and demanding superior performance, not just in flying, but in staying on alert, LeMay gave the Strategic Air Command the status of an elite corps. Its men often had to stay so long on ready-alert that they didn't see their families for weeks at a time.

In addition, security at SAC bases was very tight. There was always the fear that some enemy would try to put the Strategic Air Command out of business by infiltrating the bases. Headquarters was put in Omaha, and most SAC bases were scattered about the Midwest; being in America's heartland put them at the greatest distance from the Soviet threat.

After the atomic bomb, of course, it was clear that we no longer needed huge formations of thousands of bombers that had carried strategic war to Germany and Japan in World War II. Instead, a smaller but still substantial number of planes, each carrying one or more bombs, would be able to do the job. By 1950 the Strategic Air Command had about 500 B-29 and B-50 (upgraded B-29) bombers, 36 giant B-36s (see below), and a stockpile of about 400 atomic bombs.

We were the world's only nuclear power. The standard war-fighting scenario went like this: Upon its outbreak, we would dispatch atomic-bomb–laden planes to destroy the Soviet Union's electrical generating capability. Such "massive retaliation" (as it was later called) would bring the war to a quick end, or so the plan went. Indeed, the Air Force demanded that plans be made for the civil administration of Russia, as well as for the management of the large number of prisoners of war that would be generated by a rapid collapse of the enemy's war effort. Thus, long before any other service had begun to rebuild, the Strategic Air Command was ready for war, a nuclear war at that. And in the

mid-1950s, SAC became a thermonuclear force when it began arming its bombers with hydrogen bombs.

The Cold War made it imperative that our airplanes have
the range to hit the Soviet Union. None of our World War II
bombers had such long range. So the aging B-29s soon gave
way to the B-50. (If you saw photographs of both planes,
however, you wouldn't be able to tell the difference. The
B-50 was no new design, just an improvement.) To achieve
still longer ranges, techniques for air-to-air refueling began
to be developed. Until special planes designed for that mission could be designed and produced, some planes in the
bomber fleet were used as airborne tankers.

From the beginning, the Strategic Air Command had a
lot of political clout. Stuart Symington, Senator from Missouri, was a great friend of SAC, and Senator Barry Gold-
water, elected in 1952 from Arizona, was an Air Force
reservist and another strong supporter of air power. But most
of all, there was Curtis LeMay himself. A World War II hero,
founder and leader of the Strategic Air Command for its first
fifteen years, and charismatic, LeMay did much by himself
to shape the course and the success of the SAC.

In 1949 there was the first of several congressional show-
downs between the Navy, wishing for a number of new large
aircraft carriers, and the Air Force, wanting to buy a fleet of
new B-36 bombers for SAC. The Air Force won. The Navy's **B-36**
carrier was canceled, although soon thereafter the Korean
War began and carrier construction got a boost. The B-36
was an immense plane with six engines (later supplemented
with four jets) mounted as "pushers" on the back of its
wings instead of on the front as is usual. Its long range made
it possible to bomb the Soviet Union from bases in the
United States. It was big enough to carry two atomic bombs.

Despite the fact that our Strategic Air Command was our
major offensive force from 1945 through 1962, the Russians
never built much of a strategic air force themselves. Near
the end of World War II, one of our B-29s made an emergency landing in Siberia after a bombing raid over Japan.
The Russians interned the plane and constructed some "re-
verse-engineered" copies, called the Tu-4. But it was Stalin's
belief, from the Russian experience in the Spanish Civil
War, that the value of air power lay in the close air support
of ground troops, not in strategic bombers.

Instead, the principal Soviet response to our long-range

bombing capability was a massive buildup in their air defenses. They even created a bureaucracy separate from their air force, called the Air Defense Force. Thousands of Soviet interceptor planes were constructed to fend off incoming bombers and tens of thousands of anti-aircraft batteries were deployed. The MiG-15—their most notable fighter of the era—caused quite a stir when it appeared for the first time in the Korean War. It was small and agile and employed a new swept-wing design which, combined with a copy of a Rolls-Royce jet engine, allowed it to approach supersonic speeds. The MiG-15 was armed with rapid-fire cannon designed to punch large holes in big bombers.

MiG-15

While the Russians have built many remarkable aircraft since, the MiG-15 was the first to show the world that they could hold their own in modern aviation technology. It saw considerable action in Korea, and though it never got to shoot at any of our B-36s, its threat to the Strategic Air Command was very real. At one point, the Air Force in response designed and built an experimental micro-fighter (called the Goblin) small enough to fit inside the bomb bay of a B-36. The idea was that the plane would be launched to fend off attacking fighters, then return to the bomber (like a baby kangaroo) and be hauled back inside. It never went into production.

In the early 1950s the Soviets did develop a few large bomber types. By this time they had detonated both nuclear and thermonuclear weapons of their own, so the threat of even a few bombers making their way to America seemed very real. One of their planes was the turboprop Tu-20 Bear A, a variant of which is now used mainly for patrol and reconnaissance (the Bear still makes news from time to time when one flies down the U.S. East Coast). The other was the all-jet (Mya-4) Bison. It caused American air defense planners to sit up and take notice when it made a surprise appearance at the Kremlin's annual May Day military parade in 1954. The Soviets had built only a few but made us believe otherwise by flying those few over Red Square many times. Our response was to ring our northern cities with Nike anti-aircraft missiles and to recruit volunteer airplane spotters—the Ground Observer Corps—as part of a major civil-defense effort.

Tu-20
"Bear"

We also bought a number of interceptor planes. The first

of these carried small unguided rockets that were to be fired in a single salvo at an attacking bomber, something the Germans had experimented with in World War II. Later models carried radar-guided missiles, some with nuclear warheads. The planes were electronically linked to a large, first-generation computer so big it occupied an entire building. It would guide flights of interceptors to the target in any weather, day or night. The last of these interceptors, F-106 Delta Darts, are still flying today. The remaining squadrons mostly are manned by National Guardsmen. The planes, now a quarter-century old, are still considered top performers at high altitudes. Ironically, we later learned that the Russians had actually built fewer than 200 bombers in the 1950s. Moreover, they lacked the air-to-air refueling capability necessary to fly to the United States, so our concern was premature.

The period from the late 1940s to the mid-1950s, however, represented a period of very rapid technological change. So even if we were ahead, we could not stand still; or at least we didn't think we could. The development of the jet engine made the B-36 a museum piece as jets came to dominate military aircraft design. Our first all-jet strategic bomber, the Boeing B-47, appeared in Air Force squadrons in 1951. Although its six early-model jet engines were so wasteful of fuel that it lacked intercontinental range, we were able to use overseas bases (and one-way missions) and thus reach the Soviet Union. Its advantage was that, powered by its new engines, it could fly more than 600 miles per hour. We eventually purchased some 2,000 B-47s in various configurations.

To gain the range it needed, the Air Force rapidly honed aerial refueling techniques. Making the refueling tanker fast enough to service jet bombers was a major problem. So a jet **jet bombers** tanker had to be built as well. The Boeing KC-135 jet tanker was the military version of the Boeing 707 airliner. Indeed, it is worth noting in passing that one of the most significant aspects of our bomber development was its impact on commercial aviation. There would be no jet airliners today without the expertise gained in designing the B-47 and the B-52. These planes led the Boeing company to a position of dominance in large, strong, efficient airplane production which it enjoys to this day.

Our next big bomber was the B-52, which has been the

B-52

mainstay of our strategic bomber force for more than three decades. Its first flight was in 1951, and operations with the Air Force began in 1955. From then until 1961, when production ceased, the Air Force bought 744 of them. Powered by eight of the latest model jet engines (mounted on four engine pods, two on each pod), it could carry four hydrogen bombs of up to 20 megatons apiece. Since its inception, the plane—called the Stratofortress by the manufacturer—has been updated many times over with more and more modern electronics (called avionics when in aircraft) and weapons systems. (One of the advantages of a big bomber, as compared with a smaller, more compact fighter plane, is that it has lots of room for modifications and additions.) Even today it is being modified one more time to carry air-launched cruise missiles.

B-52G in flight. (U.S. Air Force photo)

INTERCONTINENTAL BALLISTIC MISSILES: ICBMs

Throughout the 1950s the Strategic Air Command was the mainstay of America's national security. In recognition of that fact Congress regularly gave 50 percent of the defense budget to the Air Force. But the astounding march of post-war weapons technology rolled on, leaving the bomber behind.

In World War II the Germans had built the V-2, the world's first strategic ballistic missile. Its 5,000-mile-per-hour speed meant that, as a practical matter, once it was launched it couldn't be stopped. Both the Russians and the Americans picked up numerous German rocket scientists at the end of the war and quickly put them to work developing new missiles. But the Air Force's Strategic Air Command was slow to warm up to the rocket weapon. Wernher von Braun did his missile work for the Army, not the Air Force. Founded by bomber pilots, the Air Force was very much committed to a bomber force and anticipated nothing but problems with missiles. In the first place, they argued, it was impossible to make a hydrogen bomb small enough to be carried by a ballistic missile. (At the time they were right. Miniaturization of weapons components came almost a decade later, and it was not until 1955 that it became possible to build a thermonuclear weapon small enough to fit inside a missile.) Besides, there was no room for pilots in a missile force.

Since they had no strategic bomber fleet of any size, the Russians suffered from no such bureaucratic inertia. And since they couldn't make small hydrogen bombs either, they solved the warhead size problem simply by building giant rockets that could carry large warheads to their destinations. (Indeed, the immense size, lifting power, and throw-weight of Soviet missiles are characteristics that distinguish theirs from ours to this day.) The Soviets created the Strategic Rocket Forces, bureaucratically separate from their air force. In the fall of 1955 we observed their first ballistic missile test. In 1957 they dazzled the world when they launched the earth's first man-made satellite, *Sputnik*. The same year they conducted their first full-range intercontinental ballistic missile test.

The effect of these developments on American defense planners was electric. As we gathered data indicating that Soviet missiles were reaching intercontinental range, fears of a "missile gap" began to grow. We responded first by putting some strategic bombers on constant airborne alert. Hydrogen bombs at the ready, they would cruise about, making periodic runs to the "fail-safe" points near the Russian border. This practice became quite controversial because it seemed to increase the risk of thermonuclear war. Moreover, when a bomber crashed, radioactive debris could be spread about the site. This happened more than once. And even if the bomb casing was unbroken, recovery of the warheads was often difficult and dangerous. The last and most memorable accident of this kind occurred when two armed B-52s collided off the coast of Spain in 1964. Airborne alerts were discontinued in 1965.

In addition, we began to concentrate more on the development of intercontinental ballistic missiles (ICBMs) of our own. There were several technological difficulties to be overcome. In addition to making the warhead small, there was the problem of the guidance system. Current ICBMs operate on internal guidance. They receive no commands from the ground. To know where it's going, a missile has to know first of all exactly where it is when it starts. It needs an on-board computer to integrate its preprogrammed itinerary with the subtle changes in the earth's magnetic field as it flies over the North Pole. And at the end of its travels when it returns to earth, it must cope with atmospheric density, as well as wind and weather at the target. Finally, these data must be translated into commands to the rocket's motors, which must be able to redirect the missile's flight.

The technology of miniaturization made all this possible. And once the silicon chip was devised, miniaturization improved still more. To give some idea of the tremendous space savings in computer design, the SAGE computer, which was designed to control air-defense interceptors, was the latest product of technology in its time. It was the size of a large building. Ten years later the same computer capacity could be installed in an apparatus the size of a refrigerator. Today it takes no more space than a box of Kleenex.

Warhead reentry was another stumbling block. When an intercontinental ballistic missile flies out into space and returns to earth, its speed upon reentering the atmosphere is so great that the friction with the air will burn up any metal. Special heat shields had to be developed. Moreover, improved accuracy requires higher reentry speeds, and this imposed still greater demands on technology. Missile nose cones are designed to char on reentry, but still protect the warhead until it reaches its target. This is why our early manned space capsules were used up after just one flight. The space shuttle has special heat-resistant tiles that make it reusable, but they will still have to be replaced after a while.

The final problem involved finding a fuel. There is nothing particularly mysterious about rocket fuel; there are many types. The problems were two: the fuel's volatility and the quantity required. It takes tons of fuel to lift a few pounds of payload into space. And when the rocket passes beyond the earth's atmosphere there is, of course, no more oxygen for burning. Thus, rockets have to carry their own oxygen. Liquid oxygen is readily available, but it boils away unless kept at extremely low temperatures. This means— and it is an important detail because it limited the utility of the early missiles—that our first generation of intercontinental ballistic missiles could be fueled only immediately prior to launch, which could easily take a day. Under these conditions, quite obviously, they had no quick reaction capability.

ASIDE——————————————————————————————

You've seen on television what happens when the space shuttle launch is delayed, even for a few hours. The fuel remains loaded; but since it is boiling away, more has to be constantly added to the rocket booster. This is the same problem that faced our first-generation ICBMs. That problem was solved for the missiles in the late 1950s as storable liquid fuel was developed. But the shuttle uses the earlier fuel because it doesn't need to respond to attack, it's cheaper, and above all it's safer.

———————————————————————————————

The immense quantity of fuel necessary to launch a missile necessitated the development of engine "stages." Each stage consists of a rocket motor or motors and a self-contained fuel supply. As the fuel in one stage is used up, that part of the missile must be dropped. At the moment one engine stage is jettisoned, the next must start up perfectly. A fraction of a second's delay in ignition can throw off the missile's accuracy. Solving these engineering problems was another hurdle.

First-Generation Ballistic Missiles

Atlas   Our first ICBM was the Atlas. This liquid-fueled missile was immense and carried a single one-megaton warhead; but its accuracy was such that it could not reliably hit within five miles of its target. Although it became operational in 1960, the Air Force was never pleased with it because in addition to its inaccuracy it was difficult to maintain. Separate storage facilities were required for the fuel since the missile could not be kept with a full tank. In addition, there had to be separate housing facilities for the large maintenance crew required. The Atlas series was scrapped by 1965.

Titan I   Another early missile was the Titan I, which was almost as awkward and primitive as Atlas. Its significant feature was the fact that it was stored in a buried protective shelter—the first of our underground silos. However, it was not launched from inside the silo; rather, an elevator raised it to the surface after it had been fueled but before it was fired.

Neither the Atlas nor the Titan I had anything approaching a quick reaction capability.

There were two other liquid-fueled missiles that were members of this first generation, both of which were of intermediate rather than of intercontinental range, the Thor Thor   and the Jupiter. Sixty Thors were deployed overseas in Britain, and we devised an involved dual-key system so that the Jupiter   host nation would have some say in its launch. The same was true of the Jupiter missile, 30 of which were based in Italy, with another 30 in Turkey. But Jupiter never worked very well; in fact, those in Turkey never reached operational status, and they were scrapped by the end of 1964.

ASIDE————————————————————————————

Missile accuracy is measured in terms of "circular error CEP   probable," or CEP. This is the radius of a circle around a target within which 50 percent of the missiles fired at the target would land. Suppose, for example, that a missile has a CEP of two-tenths (.2) of a mile, about 1,200 feet—average by current standards, but by no means outstanding. If 100 missiles were fired at a given target, we could expect 50 to land within two-tenths of a mile (or closer) and the other 50 to land farther away.

Accuracy is one of the most important characteristics of a missile. The destruction of "soft" targets, such as cities, factories, and airfields, does not require much precision. But to destroy missile silos requires considerable accuracy. While a larger warhead can compensate to some degree for inaccuracy, accuracy is the most important variable. The mathematical formula for computing the ability of a missile to destroy a hardened target is $K = Y^{2/3}/CEP^2$. It looks complicated but it's not. Y represents the explosive power of the warhead in megatons. We have already explained CEP. K stands for the ability of the missile to destroy a hard target. Basically, the relationships are such that increases in accuracy (CEP) cause K to increase more rapidly than increases in explosive yield (Y).

Of course, accuracy ratings are derived from tests. There is no way to be certain the missiles would work as well in a war. For example, neither we nor the Soviets have ever fired more than a few missiles at a time, that is, in salvo. Moreover, both we and the Soviets test our ICBMs in east-to-west or west-to-east paths. But in a war they would be fired over the North Pole, that is, south to north to south. Planners devise elaborate computer simulations that attempt to account for all the variables that might possibly affect missile accuracy: weather at the target, variations in the earth's gravity and magnetic field, and so on. But short of full-scale over-the-Pole tests of each side's missiles, there is no way to be certain that our (or their) ICBMs would be as accurate as we think they are.

It is easy in hindsight to fault the U.S. military for relying so long on the long-range bomber as our major strategic weapon. We forget how primitive this first generation of missiles were. Because we could not store their fuel in the missiles, they could only have been used—if at all in this period—in a premeditated way, or with some days' warning, so that they could be prepared for launch. They were ideal for scientific purposes, but not serious retaliatory weapons.

The Russians had these problems, too. Indeed, according to Roger Hilsman, a high State Department official in the Kennedy administration, Soviet Premier Nikita Khrushchev decided—against his science advisors' warnings—to use his *Sputnik* rockets as ballistic missiles. The Russian scientific

Soviet ICBMs

community knew these wouldn't work because they were too delicate and complex to function as weapons. To be useful, weapons have to be at the ready at all times and be maintainable by ordinary technicians. Khrushchev's scientific advisors were right. The first Russian missiles were so heavy that they cracked their launch pads. We received reports that at least one high Soviet defense official was killed during this period when one missile exploded during a test launch.*

It was common Soviet practice, we later learned, to store the missile warheads in secure bunkers miles from the missile launch site. Whether this was because of inexperience with missiles or because of a need to maintain absolute control over thermonuclear weaponry, we don't know. But now it is clear that by the end of the 1950s their missile capability, though astonishingly better than we had thought it could be, hardly constituted the "missile gap" for us that John F. Kennedy made an issue of when he ran for President in 1960. The Soviets had but four operational ICBMs in 1960, the United States 18.†

In any event, during the Cuban missile crisis of October 1962, when our reconnaissance reported that some Soviet missiles were being assembled in Cuba, the Russians had no more than 85 intercontinental ballistic missiles deployed, and probably because of inadequate means of communication with their missile launch crews (called "command and control"), they didn't even put them on alert. In contrast, the United States had nearly 300.‡

Hilsman believes that the reason Khrushchev put missiles in Cuba was to make up for the failure of his ICBM program. Medium-range ballistic missiles based in Cuba would have the same striking power as long-range missiles in the Soviet Union. We were using medium-range missiles based in Turkey at the same time for the same reason. Khrushchev's plan, as we all know, backfired and brought us to a nuclear confrontation. In his memoirs Khrushchev says the whole affair was a trick to get the United States to

*Roger Hilsman, *To Move a Nation* (New York: Doubleday, 1967), page 163.
†"Missile Gap: 1957–1960," Center for Defense Information, unpublished paper, 1981, page 3.
‡*Ibid.*

promise not to invade Cuba (this was 1962 and the United States had sponsored an invasion at the Bay of Pigs just one year earlier). The Cuba-based missiles, he wrote, were meant to be just pawns in a diplomatic gambit.

THE TITANS

It is hard to say whether the Titan II was the last of the first generation of U.S. long-range missiles or the first of the second generation. Like the earlier missiles, the Titan uses liquid fuel, but unlike the earlier missiles, the Titan could be prefueled and stored underground for immediate launch in

Launch of a U.S. Air Force Titan II missile from Cape Canaveral, Florida. (U.S. Air Force photo)

response to attack. Nonetheless, its fuel continued to give trouble. It is highly toxic when exposed to the atmosphere, and as a result dangerous to handle. It is so corrosive that over time it can destroy the missile's fittings, sealants, and valves, making it difficult to keep ready.

It was a Titan II that exploded in 1979 in Damascus, Arkansas, when an airman dropped a socket wrench into the silo. The wrench bounced and tore a hole in the side of the missile, releasing the fuel. The crew fought the resulting fire for several hours, but the missile blew up, killing one crewman and injuring others. The silo's blast cover (designed to resist nuclear explosions from above and not explosions from below) was blown off and the warhead was thrown some distance from the silo. The 9-megaton warhead broke into several pieces but did not explode.

hard silos The most significant innovation with this weapon was that it was placed in a "hard" silo. The system was designed so that our missile launchers would be hard enough to endure a Soviet attack and still be able to fire back. Soviet warheads at this time were not very accurate, with CEPs of no better than a half-mile and usually much greater. So despite the large warheads they carried, it was relatively easy to design a silo that could survive an attack. Given the low probability of a direct hit, Titan silos were built to withstand 300 psi of overpressure generated by the detonation of a thermonuclear warhead.* (Remember that 5 psi will level a house, 35 will destroy a concrete and steel building.)

These underground housings are called silos because they are vertical concrete structures similar to grain storage silos, except that they are buried in the ground. (Indeed, the extensive excavation and construction required for the Titans were such that the missiles deployed around Tucson, Arizona, remain the largest public works project in the history of that part of the Southwest.) There are nine levels of retractable workstands so that the work crews have access to all parts of the missile.

Each Titan silo is accompanied by a command bunker, the two being linked by a tunnel. It has living quarters,

---

*House Military Appropriations Subcommittee, Military Construction Appropriations Hearings for FY 1982, Part 6, page 275.

ample supplies of survival rations and water, plus escape hatches for the crew. Equipment and structures are mounted on heavy springs to absorb the shock of a nuclear explosion. At all times the control center is crewed by four Air Force men (and now some women, too): two officers and two enlisted men. The enlisted men are technicians who perpetually maintain the missile. The liquid fuel is so corrosive that tiny leaks constantly occur in the complex plumbing of the rocket's motor; hardly an hour goes by that some repair isn't needed.

When these systems were being designed, there was considerable concern within the military (and the public) that without fail-safe mechanisms, some "nut" could fire a missile and start World War III. To prevent this, an elaborate command-and-control system is in place. The crew has no knowledge of the intended target and the missile cannot be launched without an electronic authorization from central headquarters, which would get authorization from the President (known officially as "National Command Authority").

Titan II launch complex.

But even then, it is necessary for both officers to turn their launch control keys simultaneously. They wear the keys around their necks, and the locks that launch the missile in the command module are placed far enough apart so that one person cannot turn both.

In addition, each officer wears a snub-nosed .38-caliber revolver. It is obvious that such a weapon is meant to be used only if someone in the bunker needs restraint. In such an event it would be difficult to get help from outside because the command bunker is sealed off by two heavy blast doors. It is possible for the crew to launch the missile in the absence of a National Command message. But this could occur only if several days elapsed without any communication from headquarters.

If you have occasion to pass by a missile silo, you could miss it. From the road—and most, though not all, are not near heavily traveled highways—you would see nothing more than an area the size of a suburban lot with chain-link fence topped with barbed wire around it, some low concrete bulges, and a small forest of antennas. As in other facilities of the Strategic Air Command, security is quite tight. In addition to the armed officers deep in the bunker, security forces armed with rifles patrol the surface in trucks and the air in helicopters. There is a central headquarters for the missile wing where launch commands and other orders are relayed to the individual silos. Also, the wing has a maintenance facility. Periodically, warheads or missiles must be pulled out and sent back to the shop for work.

Originally, there were 54 Titan IIs (now 52) deployed in three states: Missouri, Arkansas, and around Tucson, Arizona. The southerly locations were chosen to give the weapon a few more minutes of warning time before the arrival of Russian missiles. The Titan is not very accurate by today's standards but is armed with the largest thermonuclear warhead in our arsenal: 9 megatons.

MINUTEMAN

Relatively few Titans were deployed, because by the time their development was completed something better was available: solid rocket fuel.

ASIDE————————————————————————————

The fueling problem was solved in two steps. First we found a way to make the liquid fuel storable, but storage was expensive to maintain and the fuel remained dangerous. Modern solid fuel was developed somewhat serendipitously by the Thiokol Chemical Company while its researchers were trying to find new ways of synthesizing rubber. The solid rocket fuel they came up with solved the problem of liquid fuel, but it had problems of its own. It is not immediately obvious how you "turn off" a solid that is burning. You can stop a liquid fuel burn simply by turning off the valve that feeds the fuel to the engine. But to stop a solid fuel burn required a new engineering innovation, a way of dispersing the thrust of the engine through "blowout ports" so that the forward thrust of the missile would be stopped.

solid fuel

————————————————————————————————————

Because of its solid fuel, the Minuteman was a much simpler weapon to take care of. Like a rifle cartridge, its motor can be left relatively unattended for long periods of time. For this reason each Minuteman command bunker is responsible for *10* (not one, as in the Titan installations) of the missiles.

Moreover, Minuteman silos are somewhat harder than the Titan silos, built to withstand about 2,000–2,500 psi overpressure.* So a Russian missile could land closer without destroying it. The silos were designed to give the missiles plenty of "rattle room" as well.

The most salient characteristic of the Minuteman missile is its relatively small size. Whereas the Titan was 104 feet long and 10 feet in diameter, weighing 300,000 pounds, the first Minuteman was less than 60 feet long and 5 feet 10 inches in diameter, weighing but 72,810 pounds. In addition, its warhead was considerably smaller. Minuteman I carried no more than a one-megaton warhead, compared to the Titan's 9. Note that this was a choice made by the Pentagon. At the time we were perfectly capable of manufacturing much larger missiles. But by the mid-1960s the military

————————————————

*Aviation Week & Space Technology, January 11, 1982, page 21; also House Military Appropriations Subcommittee, *op. cit.,* page 275.

Above, *Minuteman III missile in an underground silo.* Below, *launching of a Minuteman III missile from Cape Kennedy.* (U.S. Air Force photos)

believed that given the relatively high accuracy of the weapon, a smaller warhead could easily do the job. Keep in mind that you need 16 megatons in a single warhead to destroy the same area as four evenly spaced one-megaton explosions.

Minutemen were deployed along the northern Great Plains, again in the center of the Continent but this time about 1,000 miles closer to the Soviet Union than the Titans. While this meant, of course, that there would be a few minutes' less warning time of a Soviet assault, it also meant that the missiles would be that much closer to their Russian targets. In all, 1,000 Minutemen were deployed in North Dakota, South Dakota, and Montana. And in 1966, Minuteman I was replaced by Minuteman II, a somewhat more accurate version equipped with decoys (called "penetration aids") to confuse Soviet defenses. Later, some Minuteman IIs were equipped with ERCs, the emergency rocket communication system. Instead of warheads, these missiles carry radio transmitters that broadcast the nuclear weapon release codes to the remainder of our nuclear forces as well as to European and Pacific Commands.

The points to keep in mind here are first, that while the Russians were building very large ballistic missiles, we deliberately built small ones; and second, that although we had originally planned to deploy 1,200 or more Minutemen, we decided on our own volition that 1,000 would be enough.

SUBMARINE-LAUNCHED BALLISTIC MISSILES: SLBMs

The idea of launching strategic missiles from submarines had bounced around for a decade following World War II. At first, planners thought the submarine would have to surface before it could fire (indeed, one early concept had ballistic missiles being launched from converted cargo ships). Although the first discussions of undersea launching involved the adaptation of the Jupiter to submarines, it was obvious to submarine officers that a liquid-fueled missile would be far too dangerous to have on board. So it was the development of solid fuel that made it possible to put ballistic missiles in submarines.

In addition to solid fuel technology, a means had to be developed for launching from underwater. After some experimentation, a method was devised using compressed air to eject the missile from the submarine while it is cruising about 20 feet under the surface. The missile "pops up," and the instant it clears the water's surface its engines ignite, sending it on its way. (Now this technique can be used to "cold-launch" ICBMs, but more about that later.)

nuclear-powered submarines

The application of nuclear power made the submarine an infinitely more significant member of our "strategic weapons family"; with nuclear power, it never has to surface to recharge its batteries or replenish air supplies. On-board systems continually regenerate oxygen for the crew, and since the propulsion system requires none, the submarine becomes an entirely self-sufficient, mobile, underwater launch pad.

Polaris and Poseidon

The Navy's first ballistic-missile submarine (several had been equipped with early cruise missiles some years before), the *George Washington,* joined the fleet in 1960 and that same year tested the first submarine-launched ballistic mis-

The first nuclear-powered fleet ballistic-missile submarine, U.S.S. George Washington, *under way.* (U.S. Navy photo)

sile (SLBM) from underwater. The *George Washington* had begun its life as an attack submarine, but prior to its completion it was cut in half and a section containing 16 missile launch tubes was spliced in. In all, 41 submarines of this type were built in the early 1960s and each was equipped with 16 Polaris missiles, the first of our SLBMs. The first Polaris missiles had a range of 1,200 miles; these were later replaced with improved models with 2,500-mile range. The longer the range of the missiles, the more square miles of ocean a submarine can hide in and still hit Soviet targets.

A Poseidon missile is launched from the nuclear-powered fleet ballistic-missile submarine U.S.S. James Madison. *(U.S. Navy photo)*

ASIDE———————————————————————————————————

So much was invested in the development of nuclear propulsion for submarines that our electricity-generating utilities
were encouraged to use similar reactor systems for their
power plants. The fact is, if you were going to build a nuclear
power plant from scratch (as have the Germans and French)
instead of adapting a nuclear reactor made for the Navy, you
wouldn't use a water-cooled type. Rather, you'd want a so-
dium-cooled reactor because the kind of accident that occurred at Three Mile Island (where the reactor core was
exposed) would take more than a day to take place in a so-
dium-cooled reactor (it only took a few minutes on that day in
Pennsylvania). But the nation had invested such large sums
in the Navy's design, and there was so much public relations
capital to be made by using "atoms for peace," that it was the
water-cooled reactor that was marketed in the United States.

———

Since the tolerance of the crews for long undersea voy-
ages remains the only constraint on nuclear-powered submarines, each is manned by two complete crews, one called
"blue" and the other "gold." This permits the Navy to maintain an average of more than 50 percent of the nuclear-
powered ballistic-missile submarine fleet at sea at all times
(a much better record, as we shall see, than the Russians).
In addition to utilizing nuclear power, submarine design
improved so as to make the craft much quieter while under
way. This was done through a variety of new technologies,
the most important of which was the ability precisely to balance the massive complex of gears, shafts, and turbines that
transmit the power of the steam generated in the nuclear
reactor to the propeller. (One thing that makes a submarine
detectable is the noise of its machinery.) Also, soundproofing
insulation was widely used and hull design was perfected to
enable water to flow smoothly over the hull without causing
turbulence, also a cause of undersea noise. (Interestingly, a
major source of data on this technology came from the study
of porpoises.) Finally, propeller design was perfected to reduce the turbulence (called cavitation) generated when the
propeller turns. However, one source of noise—the pumps

needed constantly to circulate cooling water through the reactor—could not be completely eliminated.

Nuclear power provides not only total self-sufficiency for the submarine, but much greater speeds as well. In World War II the maximum speed of a submerged submarine was rarely more than 12 miles an hour, and that for only short sprints. The exact top speed of nuclear-powered submarines is secret, but it is believed that they can go faster than 30 miles per hour. At full speed, however, submarines are noisy (propeller cavitation is impossible to avoid, for example), so to avoid detection submarines routinely patrol at low speeds, rarely more than 10 miles per hour.

ASIDE

You may find it confusing, but our missile-bearing submarines and the missiles they carry often, but not always, bear the same name. So, for example, our first missile submarines were called Polaris and carried Polaris missiles; our second generation was Poseidon, again after the missiles they carried; and the same is now true for our latest, the Trident. But as with most of the nomenclature you will meet in this book, there are exceptions. We find the Navy now putting Trident missiles in some of our older Poseidon submarines, and there is even some talk of using a variation of the Trident missiles—yet to be perfected—in place of the MX.

Since the submarine is constantly moving, it is almost impossible to attain the targeting accuracies with an SLBM that are inherent in an ICBM. When Polaris was first developed, underwater navigation technology was relatively inaccurate, commonly more than five miles off. If the missile's guidance computer did not know exactly where it was when it started, it would be impossible to program an accurate trajectory. So our first submarine-launched missile was designed to get a navigational fix on the North Star—Polaris—to reorient itself in space before reentry. Still, the first submarine-launched ballistic missiles had no more than a one-mile accuracy, only about half as good as that of their land-based contemporaries.

But in time sophisticated on-board inertial navigation systems—a complex array of state-of-the-art gyroscopes linked to computers—could ascertain the submarine's position within a few yards. Even so, a submarine is always subject to the subtle movements of the sea, which impart minute but significant momentum to the missile, making it a few yards less accurate than if it were land-based. The next gen- **Trident** eration of submarine-launched missiles (the D-5 Trident IIs) will use several navigational fixes from NAVSTAR satellites to fix accurately both their position and velocity. This is sup- posed to allow SLBMs accuracy close to that of land-based missiles.

ASIDE————————————————————

Interestingly enough, some years later we learned that many of our first-generation Polaris SLBM warheads were duds. It seems that a change in one of the safety devices on the warheads' trigger was made but never tested. Radiation within the warhead reacted with chemicals in the trigger's explosive charge and, over a period of time, caused critical parts to corrode and fuse together. The flaw was detected in 1965 and extensive testing in 1966 revealed that "three were bad to one good." The A-1 warheads were modified using parts from a newer model Polaris. By 1968 the modifications were complete.

See Walter Pincus, *The Washington Post,* December 2, 1978, page A4; December 3, 1978, page B6.

————————————————————

command Command and control of submarines is far more difficult **and control** than with land-based missiles. After all, if worse comes to worst, you could always send a messenger to a missile silo. But communication with a submerged submarine is full of risks. If the submarine radios to home base it may give away its location if the communication is intercepted. Commands to the submarine from home base are impossible unless the submarine commander knows when and about where to ex- pect to receive a message and makes himself somehow avail- able. Otherwise he cannot be found, by either friend or foe.

The single basic goal of submarine-launched missile strategy is make the ship invisible, hence invulnerable. To accomplish this, the Navy issues very general orders to its commanders: to cruise, for example, in certain sectors of ocean during certain time periods. How and where the cap-tain enters the appointed sector and where within it he cruises are known only to him, and these sectors are a few thousand miles square. So his location is kept secret from the Russians by keeping it secret from us. Included in the commander's orders are stipulated times when he is to come close to the surface—within 50 feet—and trail a long antenna from the back of the ship. Navy planes known as TACAMO (Lockheed C-130s), which trail their own antenna wire nearly a mile long behind, are used to relay information to the submarines. Because of the low frequency of the radio, it is difficult to get more than a few words sent. But by using codes, a variety of commands are possible within these restrictions.

However, this system is too limited to have immediate emergency communications with the submarine fleet. The Navy has tried for years to build a land-based, very low-frequency radio transmission grid in the United States, but they have been thwarted by objections from the people (and their Congressmen) who live in the chosen areas. It can't be put just anywhere because it needs certain subterranean geological formations to work. The Navy wanted to put it in Texas at first. Failing that, the Navy opted for Wisconsin; rebuffed there, it favored the Upper Peninsula of Michigan. The neighbors object because they don't want the disruption that would come from burying mile upon mile of underground cable. So now the Navy is willing to string the antenna cables above ground, but people still fear environmental problems caused by the radio waves and have a natural concern arising from the certainty that they would immediately become a primary target of the Soviet Strategic Rocket Forces.

The idea is to use this very low-frequency radio not to transmit long, complex messages but rather as a bell ringer to alert the submarines' commanders to come close to the surface for a longer message. Maybe space satellites able to communicate directly with submarines will rescue the Navy from this dilemma (blue-green laser technology shows promise of being able to penetrate seawater to some depth). Although even here, disclosure of the submarine's location is again a risk.

All this means that, unlike the land-based missile, which

cannot be launched without an electronic command from Washington, the submarine is very much on its own. It is not immediately obvious how the submarine commander is to know that there is a war on, much less that he is expected to fire his missiles. Should a message to launch be received, whatever communication mode is used, the control procedures require that the commander of the submarine, his executive officer, and his weapons officer all agree to it.

So while communication is an obvious weakness with submarine-launched ballistic missiles and reduced accuracy is an additional but minor disadvantage, the fact is that they are invulnerable because they are invisible; they are invisible because they operate underwater; and because no one except their commander and his navigation officer ever knows for certain where they are. As a result of these strengths, the nuclear-powered missile-bearing submarine has been described by some weapons experts as the most nearly perfect deterrent ever conceived. Navy men refer to them as "Big Boomers."

THE TRIAD

By the time of the Cuban missile crisis in 1962, all three components of what has come to be known as the Triad were in place. We had missiles housed in underground silos able to reach the Soviet Union from locations along the northern Great Plains or the Southwest. We had Polaris submarines cruising the oceans' waters, invisible and virtually untrackable, equipped with missiles and armed with nuclear warheads aimed at Soviet cities. And we still had our Strategic Air Command bombers ready to fly on 15 minutes' notice.

bombers   Each leg of this three-legged stool has its strengths and weaknesses. The bomber force is, of course, slow (it takes about eight hours to fly to the Soviet Union from the United States) and is vulnerable on the ground as well. It is impractical to build hard shelters for a fleet of big B-52s. Add to that the fact that they need very long runways to take off; even if the airplanes survived, it seems likely that the runway would be severely damaged after any nuclear attack.

But bombers have one great advantage: they can be launched at the first inkling of an attack. And if 30 minutes or even three hours later it turns out that the whole thing was a mistake, they can come home. Of course, if tensions mount, they can be dispersed to various airfields around the continent, which further complicates the enemy's attack plan.

A certain segment of the bomber force is always kept on continual 15-minute ground alert. Since we can expect a minimum of 15–20 minutes' warning of a massive Soviet ballistic missile launch, there is time for the bombers to get away. Also keep in mind that each bomber needs a tanker or two for midair refueling if it is to reach its target. The tankers would have to get aloft, too; but many of them are already part of the National Guard and are relatively well dispersed around the country.

One other advantage of bombers is their flexibility. Their orders and designated targets can be changed in flight, even after penetrating Soviet airspace. Their crews can observe the destruction of a target and make an immediate decision as to whether to hit it again or to choose another target.

With land-based missiles, the only real disadvantage (but a significant one, as we shall see) is that their position is fixed. Everyone knows exactly where they are at all times. That is also their advantage, of course. Because they are fired from known positions, ICBMs are our most accurate **ICBMs** missiles. Meanwhile, the primary advantage of the third leg of the Triad, the SLBMs, is that the submarines that carry **SLBMs** them are essentially undetectable, even with the latest methods of antisubmarine warfare. Hence they give our strategic force "survivability." Their disadvantage is that they are less accurate, relative to land-based missiles, and more difficult to command and control.

The point is that the three systems complement each other. Our strength is in the mix. Bombers can quickly respond to any warning and still be recalled; land-based missiles can deliver precise retaliation within 30 minutes; and submarines contribute survivability to the Triad. Whatever happens, the Big Boomers will survive and be ready to shoot. And every enemy knows this.

In 1962 the bombers were still the most powerful leg of

the stool, both in terms of warheads as well as megatonnage. The strategic objective for the following dozen or so years was to build up all three legs of the Triad in terms of increased accuracy, improved range, survivability, and numbers. There was never a formal policy decision to have a three-legged strategic force. The term Triad (sometimes called the trinity of weapons earlier on) simply evolved as three distinct thermonuclear systems developed.

SOVIET SECOND-GENERATION MISSILES

The Russians were far behind us (further than we thought at the time) and their second-generation ICBMs did not begin to be deployed until the mid-1960s. The Russians **SS-9** indulged their penchant for large missiles in the SS-9 (SS stands for surface-to-surface), 308 of which were deployed in hard silos in the center of the Soviet landmass. This monster missile was comparable to our Titans, only bigger: 120 feet high, 10 feet in diameter. It was relatively inaccurate, with a CEP of seven-tenths of a mile. But the Russians tried to compensate for its inaccuracy by installing a 20-megaton warhead on it. Popularly thought of as a "city buster" (because of the size of its warhead), it had the practical effect of leading American military planners to believe that—among other things—our carefully constructed "invulnerable" command centers (in Cheyenne Mountain, outside of Colorado Springs, and Mount Weather, near Washington, D.C.) were no longer safe.

The SS-9 was liquid-fueled, as was the next Soviet mis- **SS-11** sile of the era, the SS-11. The Russians deployed, in all its "mods" (modifications), nearly 1,000 SS-11s during the next several years. These missiles had one-megaton single warheads, but with accuracy never better than half a mile. It seems clear that the Russians had not mastered solid-fuel technology at the time. Their first solid-fueled ballistic mis- **SS-13** sile was the SS-13, of which they only deployed 60.

The Russians also began building ballistic-missile submarines, after we did. Again, their technology was far behind ours, their SLBMs were much less accurate (with CEPs of about two miles), and they even mounted some early-model missiles on diesel-powered submarines. Since their submarine-launchable missiles were (and still are) liquid-fueled, this made them particularly dangerous to operate. More importantly, however, the Soviets have yet to master the technology necessary to make their submarines run silently. Thus theirs are more easily detected than ours, especially given superior Western antisubmarine warfare technology. Also, the propulsion technology in their nuclear-powered submarines appears inferior to ours. They've had more than a few accidents at sea; our patrol planes have observed surfaced Russian submarines transferring casualties to other vessels. The Secretary of the Navy noted in March of 1982 that Soviet sailors had been killed at sea in accidents related to the nuclear propulsion plants of their subs.*

So although the Russians have built more ballistic-missile submarines than we, they normally cannot keep more than 10–15 percent of them at sea at any one time (compared to more than half of ours, on average).

STRATEGIC DEFENSE

As strategic weapons were developed, the effort to find some defense against them continued. There are two ways to defend against nuclear weapons: active and passive. Active defense seeks to neutralize or destroy the attacking weapon before it hits. Passive defense, on the other hand, tries to limit the damage resulting from the attack. Anti-aircraft and antimissile defenses are active; the building of shelters, evacuation of cities, and the construction of hardened missile silos are passive. Early-warning devices can contribute to either active or passive defenses.

As Soviet strategic striking power began to grow, the United States turned some attention to both active and passive defenses. The Soviets did the same.

To provide warning against Soviet bombers we built arrays of radars across Canada, first the Pinetree Line, later the DEW (distant early-warning) line. As Soviet ballistic-

active defense

The Washington Post, March 17, 1982, page A3.

missile capability grew, we built the BMEWS (ballistic-missile early-warning system) radar in Greenland, Alaska, and Britain. (The first time the BMEWS radar was put into operation, its waves bounced off the moon, reflecting in the radar scopes as a massive Soviet attack. Several anxious minutes passed before the operators realized what was going on.) Later, we added satellites capable of detecting within minutes the launch of Soviet missiles. The purpose of all early warning is to provide the quickest possible indication of a strategic attack on the United States, to give the President the maximum time to assess the situation and decide on an American response.

But what was that response to be? Would it ever be technically feasible to knock enemy missiles out of the sky? As early as 1945 the Army began to experiment with surface-to-air missiles for attacking incoming aircraft. Soon thereafter began a decades-long attempt to meet the challenge of building an antimissile missile to defend against the Soviet threat. **ABM** The effort to build an anti-ballistic missile (ABM) began in earnest in 1958. We needed radars to find and track enemy warheads, high-speed computers to process radar information on the trajectories of many incoming objects; we had to find a method to discriminate real warheads from decoys; above all, we needed ways to guide interceptors to the enemy warheads. If we used nuclear-armed interceptor missiles, we had to decide whether they would explode the enemy warhead or scramble its delicate electronics by means of radiation (neutron warheads were first developed for this purpose).*

By 1967 the decision to go ahead and develop a "thin" ballistic-missile defense system designed mainly to defend against the Chinese was announced by Defense Secretary Robert S. McNamara. The decision was immersed in controversy, both because of its cost and because some people feared that it would make some areas even bigger targets once it was built. So it is useful to go back and see what was actually proposed, particularly because it bears on some current weapons controversies.

---

*For a detailed discussion of defense against missiles see Ernest Yanarella's *The Missile Defense Controversy* (Louisville: University of Kentucky Press, 1977).

An ABM can have one of two functions, or both: to defend large areas, mainly cities; and/or to protect land-based missiles, lest the increasing accuracy of enemy missiles make them vulnerable to attack.

It was generally recognized in 1967 that the available technology was not good enough to provide what Robert McNamara called an "impenetrable shield over the U.S.," i.e., a "thick" ABM to protect cities. But intelligence reports suggested that the Soviets were building an ABM system around Moscow, and possibly at Leningrad, too. The Johnson administration believed the Republicans would "make a campaign issue out of an alleged ABM gap" in the 1968 campaign.*

Also, it was felt that the Chinese might have a modest ICBM force by the mid-1970s, but intelligence estimates of the state of Chinese ICBM development turned out to be very wide of the mark. Even today the Chinese have a very limited ICBM capability. But in 1967 the threat seemed plausible. At the time hostility toward China was high, and the Chinese were thought to be so wildly irrational that they might not be deterred by our overwhelming superiority. After all, didn't Mao brag that the Chinese would emerge from a nuclear war as the dominant nation? †

Thus the decision was made to begin building a thin ABM system that would provide some protection against a Chinese attack. It seemed to some a good idea; after all, it would defend against the Chinese and the Republicans at the same time.

Following his narrow victory in the tumultuous 1968 election, President Richard M. Nixon chose to continue the ABM program. McNamara's anti-Chinese system, now called Safeguard, was slightly modified to protect some of our Minuteman sites. And this decision fueled one of the most intense public debates on a weapons system seen in the United States since World War II.

---

* Morton Halperin, "The Decision to Deploy the ABM: Bureaucratic and Domestic Politics in the Johnson Administration," reprinted in Richard Head and Ervin Rokke, eds., *American Defense Policy* (Baltimore: Johns Hopkins University Press, 3rd ed., 1973), page 478.
† Stuart Schram, *The Political Thought of Mao Tse Tung* (New York: Praeger, 1969), page 409.

From one point of view—that sketched out in testimony before Congress by Army general James Gavin—following a policy of "no-first-strike" attack on any enemy, "We are obliged to develop an air defense capability. . . . Otherwise we will invite attack and expose our people . . . to destruction and to fruitless loss."* The opposite point of view held that the deployment of an ABM system would fuel the arms race, because with every effective antimissile defense measure, the other side would need to build more missiles or add more warheads to circumvent it. Besides, or so aroused ABM opponents argued, to send up nuclear warheads to burst over our own territory (the proposed system employed nuclear warheads, although non-nuclear ABMs are under discussion today)—given the radiation and other effects—was not worth it. So even after the technology to locate, track, and destroy incoming missiles had been developed, a large-scale ABM system was dropped in the early 1970s.

ASIDE———————————————————————————————

For a number of years in the early to mid-1970s the Army and the Air Force played an interesting game. The Air Force test-launched ICBMs from Vandenberg Air Force Base in California, aiming them at Kwajalein, an atoll in the Pacific. On Kwajalein, Army ballistic-missile defense specialists, as part of the U.S. ABM research and development program, attempted to track and simulate the destruction of these incoming warheads. Thus the Air Force was able to test the effectiveness of its "penetration aids" and the Army had "live targets" against which to test ABM capabilities.

———————————————————————————————————————

passive
defense

In the mid-1960s the United States toyed briefly with passive defense measures—civil defense. An effort to persuade the American people to build fallout shelters was mounted by the Kennedy administration. Some home owners built shelters; and shelters in public buildings were marked, stocked with crackers, medical supplies, and water. But civil defense was never popular with the American people and interest quickly faded. We still spend money on

*Yanarella, *op. cit.*, page 32.

pamphlets and personnel who explain how to build base-
ment shelters and devote considerable bureaucratic energy
to devising various schemes for maintaining the continuity
of government in a post-thermonuclear war environment.
The current emphasis is on plans to evacuate U.S. cities in
the event of a crisis. Yet while the federal government has
asked officials of all major cities to devise evacuation plans,
many cities have refused.

The Soviets, always more defense-minded than we, built
an extensive system to defend against bombers and began
an ABM system around Moscow as an extention of their
anti-aircraft system. Research continued there as here, but
the 1972 SALT I agreement stopped construction of ABM
systems in both countries (see Chapter Seven). In comparison with American measures, Soviet civil defense efforts are
thought to be more extensive; but the extent and value of
their civil defense activities have become controversial here
in the last few years. They certainly have a larger bureaucracy devoted to the task than we, with a senior military officer in charge.

Skeptics, however, argue that if the bureaucracy that
manages civil defense is anything like the one that manages
their agriculture, Soviet civil defense is likely to be somewhat less than effective. We know they have built shelters
for key segments of their population, although most people
would still be expected to evacuate. Despite their efforts they
remain in many ways more vulnerable than the United
States to nuclear attack. Their population and industry are
heavily concentrated in the European part of the Soviet
Union, and much of their new industrial construction is still
in these dense urban areas.

ASIDE————————————————————————————————

The Russians, who are famous for black humor, have a
joke about civil defense. One Russian asks another, "What
should you do when the nuclear attack warning sounds?"

"I don't know," the second answers.

"Wrap yourself in a shroud and walk slowly to the cemetery," says the first.

"Why walk slowly?" asks the second.

"So as not to cause panic."

It is clear that offensive forces still hold the upper hand technologically. Any ABM system can be "saturated" by massive ballistic-missile assault and confused by the decoys called penetration aids carried by all U.S. missiles. In effect, defensive weaponry becomes a "warhead sponge" for the offense. The Strategic Air Command responded to Soviet air defense measures by further modifying the B-52 fleet with sophisticated electronic countermeasures and equipment designed to blind or mislead their radars. In addition, our bombers have been equipped with short-range attack missiles (SRAM), which, armed with nuclear warheads, are designed to be fired at the Soviet air defense radars and surface-to-air missile (SAM) sites as the B-52s penetrate enemy air space.

As new technologies become available and existing ones are perfected, ballistic-missile defense may appear to become feasible once more. Indeed, there is concern in the Pentagon that the Soviets may decide to scrap the 1972 ABM treaty and rapidly deploy an ABM system of its own. There are also some in the United States who believe we should do the same. However, for the present, most experts agree that our own security is well served by preserving the ABM treaty.

MIRVing

One way to increase the strength of your missile force in order to overwhelm an enemy ABM system is to manufacture and deploy more missiles. But another means is to put more warheads on the missiles you already have. Because of the immense size of their ICBMs, the Russians could and did put multiple warheads on some of their SS-9s and SS-11s (called multiple reentry vehicles, or MRVs) and we did the same with later models of the Polaris. But multiple warheads still land on the same target, doing more damage, to be sure, but not increasing the number of targets the missile can hit.

It's more "cost-effective" to develop the means, called MIRV (for multiple, independently targetable reentry vehicles), to hit several different targets with the same missile. In any case, the 1972 SALT I agreement banned the construction of additional ICBM launchers (silos) by either side. So the option of building more missiles was precluded, but multiple warheads were not. MIRV may be simple in concept, but the technology is extremely complex and difficult to master.

A missile's flight consists of a boost phase, a coast through space, and reentry through the earth's atmosphere. After its motors burn out they are separated from the front section of the missile. The warheads are carried on this section, called the "bus." As the bus coasts through space, it is oriented toward a particular target and a warhead is dropped off. As it coasts farther, it is reoriented and another lethal passenger gets off; and so on, until all warheads have been sent on their way. In this manner many targets over a substantial area can be hit by a single missile.

Mock-up of the upper portion of an MX missile, showing the bus, warheads (black cone-shaped objects), and nose shroud. (photo courtesy of the Avco Corporation)

The full consequences of MIRVing were not anticipated by defense planners. The technique evolved out of attempts to add decoys to existing missiles in order to throw off the enemy's antimissile defense systems. If several dummy warheads were to separate from the main missile during reentry, the enemy's antimissile capability would be strained in locating, tracking, and hitting them all. But it soon became obvious that once the technical problems of multiple targeting had been solved, we might as well put thermonuclear warheads on all reentry vehicles to increase the breadth and density of our attack rather than fooling around with decoys.

We first began testing MIRVs as early as 1968 and began to deploy them in 1970. Missile guidance was also greatly improved in this period. With more knowledge about the earth's atmosphere and its magnetic field, combined with much better mapping of the earth from satellites, more data than before could be put into computer guidance systems. By the mid-1970s we began to know not just how many miles away Moscow was, but how many yards, and all this contributed to more precise aiming of our Minutemen.

Another improvement came from further miniaturization **Minuteman** of computers. This permitted us to make the Minuteman **III** even more capable while retaining its small size. The next generation, known as Minuteman III, contained three MIRVs. These were more accurate than anything we had built before, having CEPs of two-tenths of a mile (about 1,200 feet). This was subsequently improved still further by more guidance modifications. Five hundred and fifty Minuteman IIs were replaced with Minuteman IIIs in the mid-1970s, leaving 450 Minuteman IIs still deployed. In the next few years the Air Force plans to replace an additional 50 IIs with IIIs.

In the late 1970s Minuteman III was further upgraded and its capability to hit hard targets improved substantially. The command-data buffer system permits ground control quickly to update the missile's computer with the latest satellite weather data at its intended target. The system also makes it possible to retarget the missile's warheads in less than half an hour. Previously, this task took almost a day.

Still another modification, the NS-20 guidance system, also installed in the late 1970s, has improved the missile's accuracy to the point at which its current CEP is believed to be 900–1,000 feet.* In addition, 300 Minuteman IIIs have been equipped with the new Mark 12A warhead. The explosive yield of the Mark 12A is about .335 megaton, or twice as powerful as the .170-megaton warheads originally installed on Minuteman III. The more powerful warheads have replaced older warheads one for one. The combination of increased yield and accuracy makes the Minuteman III a formidable counterforce weapon in its own right. Also significant is the fact that all Minuteman missiles have been hardened to withstand electromagnetic pulse, which means they are more likely to be effective in a large-scale thermonuclear war. The point is, these improvements give us the accuracy to permit us to target not just Russian cities, industry, and military bases, but some missile silos and command bunkers as well.

We should also keep in mind that our SLBM force has undergone improvements too. Today we have 31 of a newer type of submarine that carries Poseidon or Trident missiles. And now we're building the much larger Trident submarines. These Big Boomers still carry 16 MIRVed missiles each, except for the new Trident, which has 24. All of the original Polaris submarines have been retired or converted into attack submarines. So today the United States has a total of 32 ballistic-missile submarines. Poseidon and Trident missiles, like the Minuteman, are solid-fueled, and each is equipped with as few as 8 or as many as 14 MIRV warheads. Poseidon warheads are approximately 40 kilotons each, or about twice the size of the bomb that destroyed Nagasaki.

CATCHING UP

Throughout the period from the late 1940s to mid-1970s the United States remained ahead of the Soviet Union both in incremental technical advances and in major breakthroughs. We moved from liquid to solid fuel earlier than they. We had greater accuracy in our missile guidance for

*Aviation Week & Space Technology, March 22, 1982, page 18.

most of the time. We had more and better bombers and our submarine-launched ballistic-missile capability was by far superior to theirs.

During this period the Russians relied almost exclusively on their land-based ballistic missiles as their primary strategic weapon and to some extent held our European allies hostage with their medium-range missiles directed west. Their goal was to deploy more and bigger missiles to compensate for their greater inaccuracy. Today Soviet missiles boast one principal advantage over U.S. missiles—greater throw-weight or payload-carrying capacity.

Beginning in the early 1960s (notice how the Cuban missile crisis becomes a seminal event in the evolution of strategic weaponry), the Russians decided to build up their missile forces to match (some would say surpass) us. We hadn't really expected them to. We thought they would accept second-rate status. McNamara even went so far to conclude in 1965 from his intelligence sources that "The Soviets have decided they have lost the quantitative race and are no longer seeking to engage us in that contest." There was no indication, he went on to say, that the Soviets were seeking to develop a strategic nuclear force as large as ours.*

He was wrong.

Of greatest concern to American policy makers today is the latest generation of Soviet ICBMs: the SS-17, SS-18, and SS-19. While all are liquid-fueled, they are much more accurate than earlier Soviet systems and all carry MIRVs. Both **cold launch** the SS-17 and SS-18 are "cold-launched." Recall that we developed this technique for submarine-based missiles. Its advantage in a land-based system is that the rocket exhaust does not incinerate the interior of the launch silo. Supposedly, this means the silo can be reloaded with another missile with relative ease. In the case of the normal "hot" launch it would take weeks, if not months, to rebuild the silo's innards before another missile could be emplaced. With cold launch a silo can be reloaded in a few days.† This, as we shall see in Chapter Seven, has consequences for arms control agreements. We have been counting missile

---

* William Van Cleave, "The US Strategic Triad," in *The US War Machine,* page 63.
† See U.S. Department of Defense, *Soviet Military Power* (Washington, D.C.: U.S. Government Printing Office, 1981), page 56.

launchers (not missiles) because we have been able to assume that one launcher could be used for only one missile.
The SS-17 is 80 feet long and 8½ feet in diameter and has   SS-17
been tested with both a single warhead and with four
MIRVs. So far, 150 of them have been put into SS-11 silos.

More awesome is the SS-18, which is 11 feet in diameter   SS-18
and 120 feet high. SS-18s have been retrofitted to 308 silos
originally built to hold the SS-9. Because of their immense
size, it has been estimated they could carry as many as 30
MIRVs, but they have been tested with but 10. Imagine the
cold launch of such a behemoth: a missile ten stories high
being blown by hot gases from its silo, then igniting and
roaring off into the stratosphere.

The SS-19, in contrast, is hot-launched. It is about the   SS-19
size of our proposed MX, and has been tested with as many
as six MIRVs. The Russians have deployed about 300 of
these, also in converted SS-11 silos. So, all told, the Soviets
have nearly 1,400 ICBMs (including 580 remaining SS-11s)
in place, which can carry some 4,800 thermonuclear warheads. These latest-model missiles have accuracies close to
ours, that is, CEPs of two- or three-tenths of a mile—maybe
less.

In addition, the Russians have built a new Typhoon-class
missile submarine that, like our Trident, is bigger than the
Washington Monument and carries 20 long-range ballistic
missiles. Also, they are working on a new strategic bomber
designated by the Pentagon as the Ram-P (NATO code
name Blackjack), which appears similar to the B-1, only a bit
larger. Of course, they also have more than 200 Backfire
bombers which could attack the United States flying high
and slowly, although most agree they are medium-range airplanes (with two engines each) for attacking European targets and ships at sea (see Chapter Four).

In the United States the race is carried on through new
improvements to each leg of the Triad. For the bomber force,
a new bomber called B-1 is already in prototype and scheduled to join the Air Force in 1986. Cruise missiles (see below) are now being bought to mount on modified B-52s; a
new ballistic-missile submarine, the Trident, has been designed, and the first of many, the U.S.S. *Ohio*, has been accepted by the Navy; and a new land-based ballistic missile,
known as MX, is under development.

CRUISE MISSILES

The evolution of the cruise missile into a major strategic weapon in our time is an interesting case study. Interesting because it is a qualitative as well as a quantitative leap. In some ways the cruise missile is but an improvement on the Germans' V-1, the "flying bomb" we discussed in Chapter Two. In the 1950s the Navy and Air Force explored the possibilities of cruise missiles, developing the Regulus and Snark and Navaho [*sic*] before dropping them in favor of ballistic missiles.

Boeing AGM-86B air-launched cruise missiles are shown on the wing pylon of a B-52G. (official Department of Defense photo)

Boeing air-launched cruise missile (ALCM) shown in flight. (U.S. Air Force photo)

What brought the cruise missile back into prominence as an exciting new weapon of the 1980s is the technology for miniaturization we talked of earlier. We can now make a jet engine and computerized guidance system so small that we can mount these on a cruise missile no more than 20 feet long and less than 2 feet in diameter. It first made headlines when, in 1977, President Jimmy Carter canceled the B-1 bomber program and said he wanted to upgrade the old B-52s instead with air-launched cruise missiles.

B-1 BOMBER

The B-1 had been recommended by the Air Force because as Soviet radar improved, our old B-52s were becoming too "visible" to the enemy to be expected to fly into Soviet airspace and survive. To solve this problem a long-range combat aircraft with a lower "radar profile" than the B-52 was designed. The B-1 is a smaller plane than the B-52 (although it weighs nearly as much) and is shaped to deflect more than reflect radar waves. (Radar works best when it can bounce off flat surfaces.) The B-52, with its large flat sides and tall vertical stabilizer, is a good reflector of radar energy.

Prototype B-1 undergoing flight test. (photo courtesy of U.S. Department of Defense)

But another way to solve the survivability problem is to have the bomber remain beyond the reach of Soviet defenses and launch cruise missiles. These weapons can penetrate enemy airspace and hit the target because of their smaller size and greater numbers. Cruise missiles, programmed to fly close to Russian terrain, can successfully evade radar defenses while the mother ship, flying far from these defenses, remains safe.

Another advantage of the cruise missile is that it is cheap, compared to the cost of an all-new bomber fleet. We are currently producing about 3,000 air-launched cruise missiles at an estimated price of $1.5 million each (excluding the cost of the thermonuclear warhead). B-1s will cost at least $300 million apiece.

ASIDE———————————————————————————

The current plan for the so-called air-breathing leg of Triad (air-breathing because it consists of airplanes and cruise missiles powered by jet engines, which require air to run, as opposed to rockets, which carry their own oxidizer), is to build 100 B-1 bombers. But until the first squadron of B-1s joins the Air Force in 1986, B-52s will continue to serve both as penetrating bombers and standoff cruise missile carriers.

When the B-1 becomes available, it is to assume the more demanding penetrating bomber role, while the remaining B-52s will be just cruise missile carriers. When the new Stealth bomber (designed to be virtually invisible to radar) becomes available, about 1990, the B-1 will be shifted to the role of cruise missile carrier, after serving only five years or so in the role of penetrating bomber, for which it was expressly designed.

TRIDENT SUBMARINE

The new Trident missile submarine is 560 feet long. Stood on end, it's as high as the Washington Monument. Yet it is so quiet that if you were swimming and it cruised within 100 feet you'd never hear it. Trident carries 24 missile tubes, each bearing a Trident missile having a range of 4,000 miles. Since each missile will carry approximately eight MIRV warheads of about 100 kilotons each, the submarine at any one time will be carrying 192 thermonuclear warheads, each one about eight times the size of the atomic bomb we dropped on Hiroshima. And these warheads can be delivered almost anywhere in the world from underwater.

Trident's great size is one reason for its high cost, which, including missiles, will probably end up between $2.5 and $3 billion each. Yet these figures are but estimates. We shall not know the full cost of the Trident system for a number of years. Initial cost projections were on the order of $1.5 billion, so we have already had to revise our estimates considerably. The Navy plans to buy at least 15 Tridents but so far only 10 have been funded.

As noted earlier, the first Trident, the U.S.S. *Ohio,* joined the fleet in 1981, giving us a total now of 32 nuclear-powered missile submarines in our arsenal.

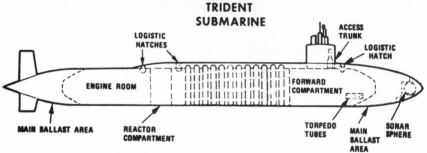

The illustrations show a Trident submarine, U.S.S. Ohio, operating on the surface, and a schematic drawing of the ship. (official U.S. Navy photo)

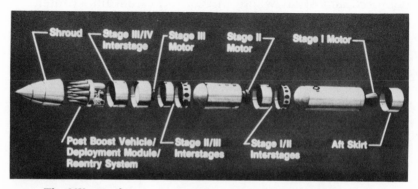

The MX missile.

MX

The MX is our newest intercontinental ballistic missile,
and is still under development. The first test flight is expected in the middle of 1983. What's confusing is that "MX"
has come to stand in the public's mind both for the new
missile itself and for the mobile-basing scheme that was
originally planned for it. Even though the basing plan was
scuttled by President Ronald Reagan, many people think
that the *M* in MX stands for "mobile." It does not. MX means
"missile experimental."

The MX is larger than the Minuteman, being 70 feet long
and nearly 8 feet in diameter, and weighing 190,000 pounds.
It is designed to carry at least 10 MIRV warheads, compared
to the Minuteman's three. In one configuration the MX
would carry the same warhead as is being put on several
hundred Minuteman IIIs, the Mark 12A, or it could be
equipped with a larger number of smaller warheads. The Air
Force is considering still a third warhead possibility so it's
not at all clear what size warheads the MX will finally have.
With the Mark 12A, the MX would be a ten-shot Minuteman
III with slightly better accuracy.* Another difference is that
it is designed for a cold launch, which gives it (in theory, at
least) the added advantage of being reloadable into the same
silo in a long, drawn-out nuclear war.

The most interesting aspect of the missile has been its
proposed basing schemes. In 1974 the Air Force asked Congress to fund a follow-on missile to Minuteman. Their
grounds were that the Minutemen were becoming vulnerable in their hardened silos, owing to increasingly accurate
and far more numerous Soviet warheads. Congress went
along on the condition that they find some basing mode
other than a fixed silo.

In response the Air Force came up with a number of
mobile-basing ideas, ranging from the carrying of the missile **basing**
on the C-5 cargo plane (or on some specially built aircraft), **planes**
to a very controversial system of "multiple protective shel-

---

*See *Aviation Week & Space Technology*, March 22, 1982, pages 18–19.

ters" covering several thousand miles of desert in Utah and Nevada. The idea was to shuttle the missile from one hardened shelter to another in a "shell game" meant to confuse the Soviets. But President Reagan vetoed the multiple-shelter idea in 1981, and the Air Force planned to put 40 to 50 of them in rebuilt Minuteman silos until they could figure out what to do with the rest. However, the Senate Armed Services Committee rejected this plan in March 1982, and froze funds for MX until a better basing scheme could be devised. The Pentagon plans to deploy 200 MXs some day. The whole thing will cost somewhere between $30 billion and $40 billion for the entire project, depending on what basing mode is finally agreed upon.*

Since many of these systems are still in development, their future is by no means assured. They are discussed in more detail in Chapter Eight.

WAR IN SPACE

There is growing concern today about the strategic implications of weapons designed to attack space satellites. We rely on satellite reconnaissance for intelligence about Soviet developments and weapons deployment; even more importantly, we have satellites designed immediately to detect the launch of any Soviet missile. By using more than one satellite of this type, it is possible to track Soviet missile launches. Indeed, this system would give us our first warning of any Soviet missile barrage, a minute or so before we could detect them on radar.

But the Russians have demonstrated the capability to attack satellites in low earth orbit. Basically, their system is a kind of primitive space "hand grenade." It is a satellite with a maneuvering capability that is launched into an orbit parallel to the target, maneuvered close in, and exploded.

We, too, are working on a new antisatellite system (we

---

*For a good comprehensive and readable review of the MX controversy see Herbert Scoville's *MX: Prescription for Disaster* (Cambridge: MIT Press, 1981).

built one in the mid-1960s) although ours works differently. Our system includes a two-stage rocket launched by an F-15 fighter which will send a "miniature homing vehicle" toward the satellite so that they will collide and be destroyed by impact.

OTHER COUNTRIES HEARD FROM

In any assessment of strategic arms inventories it is easy to forget that the United States and the USSR do not exist in a vacuum. Great Britain, France, and China now have nuclear weapons. India has detonated a "peaceful nuclear device" but has not built weapons. Israel and South Africa may have nuclear weapons or could build them quickly. And most experts believe that Pakistan and Argentina are not far from having their own as well.

The British have four ballistic-missile submarines and have decided to buy Trident missiles, while the French have five and are building a sixth. The Royal Air Force boasts a small fleet of Vulcan bombers, which, although they are of B-52 vintage and are gradually being retired, can deliver nuclear weapons.

The French have 18 silo-based MRBMs (medium-range ballistic missiles) as well as mobile tactical nuclear missiles. The Chinese are hard at work developing MRBMs and ICBMs, too, and it would not be surprising to discover that Israel had the capability to hit targets a thousand miles or more away.

CONCLUSION

It is obvious that there is no paucity of strategic nuclear armaments in the world today. In fact, the total global stockpile consists of about 15,000–20,000 strategic nuclear bombs or missile warheads (and this does not include nonstrategic or tactical nuclear weapons stationed in Europe and elsewhere). In the U.S. arsenal there are 1,052 ICBMs carrying some 2,000 separately targetable warheads. These are located on 52 Titan missiles and 1,000 Minutemen. Each of our 32 missile-bearing submarines carries 16 or 24 missile tubes with a total of about 5,000 warheads, more than half the U.S. total. Finally, we have about 300 long-range bombers, carrying about 2,000 bombs and missiles.

For the Russians, the arsenal includes 1,398 intercontinental ballistic missiles carrying a total of about 4,800 separately targetable warheads, many of them larger than American warheads, 80 missile-bearing submarines with 950 missiles and 2,000 warheads, and about 100 Bear and Bison long-range bombers all carrying hydrogen bombs of several megatons each. All told, they have about 7,500 strategic warheads and bombs; we have perhaps 9,000. How these weapons affect our thinking about war is quite remarkable, as we shall see in our next chapter.

4.
Deadly Logic: The Deterrence of War

I have spent my life in the study of military strength as a deterrent to war, and in the character of military armaments necessary to win that war. The study of the first of these questions is still profitable. But we are rapidly coming to the point where no war can be won. War implies a contest. When you get to the point where . . . both sides know that in any outbreak of general hostilities . . . destruction will be reciprocal and complete, possibly we will have sense enough to meet at the conference table with the understanding that the era of armaments is ended. . . . Already we have come to the point where safety cannot be assured by arms alone, their usefulness becomes concentrated more and more in their characteristics as deterrents than as instruments by which to obtain victory over their opponents. . . . In this regard today we are as clearly separated from the end of World War II, as the beginning of this century was separated from the beginning of the 16th century.

—DWIGHT D. EISENHOWER

TWO TECHNOLOGICAL OFFSPRING of World War II have irreversibly changed our view of the world. We developed the one, nuclear weapons; and the Germans developed the other, long-range ballistic missiles. And although these weapons have never accounted for more than 15 percent of our total military budget, they have come to dominate the way everyone, military and civilian alike, thinks about our national security.

From the beginning, our nuclear weapons were never expected to shield Americans from an enemy attack the way anti-aircraft guns, battleships, tanks, or infantry could have done in the past. Nuclear weapons could be used only to threaten or to retaliate. They can attack the enemy before he attacks us, preemptively, or after he attacks, in a punitive way. So the only way to begin to come to grips with the complexities of nuclear strategic doctrine is to recognize that these weapons exist to not be used. With nuclear arsenals, we and the Soviets have been holding one another hostage for decades. And this is precisely the meaning of deterrence.

The most important military consequence of the discovery of atomic and later hydrogen weaponry, then, was to change our military focus from *offense,* attack, and *defense,* protection from attack—the two historical strategies of war— to *deterrence,* prevention of attack.

To the individual missile commander whose job it is to be ready to fire his weapon at any time, but whose hope it is never to have to do so, the reality is harsh and confining. It is like training surgeons who will never operate, writers who will never publish. And it is particularly hard on military professionals whose ultimate test comes in combat.

It is a harsh and difficult reality for us all. As early as the 1940s, shortly after the first atomic bombs were dropped on Japan, perceptive observers began to anticipate some of these dilemmas. Winston Churchill, for one, described the United States and the Soviet Union as two scorpions imprisoned in a bottle: one scorpion cannot kill the other without being killed itself. A group of scientists, knowledgeable about nuclear energy and therefore perhaps more nervous about our prospects for survival, put a "doomsday clock" on the cover of the first edition of their magazine, *Bulletin of the Atomic Scientists.* And as military developments followed one upon the other with the deepening Cold War in the years immediately after World War II, they would move the hands on their clock closer or farther from doomsday (midnight).

In October 1949, for example, when the Russians exploded their first atomic bomb, the doomsday clock went to three minutes before the hour; and in September 1953, when it was clear that the Russians had tested a hydrogen bomb, the hands of the clock moved closer still. Later, in 1963, when we signed the nuclear test-ban treaty with the Soviet Union, banning tests in the atmosphere, the clock moved back to seven minutes to midnight; and in July 1968, with the signing of the nuclear nonproliferation treaty (in which many nations agreed not to acquire nuclear weapons), to 12 minutes before. (Today the clock is at four minutes to midnight.) War, the scientists were trying to demonstrate with this symbol of the clock, would never be just war again. It would be planetary suicide.

Public opinion on this issue was greatly influenced by John Hersey's book *Hiroshima*. First published in *The New Yorker* in 1948, the book described in detail what had happened in Hiroshima after we dropped the first atomic bomb. Fewer people may have been killed there than died in conventional fire-bombing raids on Dresden and Tokyo during World War II; but nuclear weapons, though not fully understood by many, were universally perceived to be infinitely more horrifying.

But while many people, including scientists, immediately recognized "the Bomb" as ushering in the atomic age, military thinking did not change quickly. In the spring of 1950 the National Security Council issued a policy paper (NSC #68), the first to set out the basic idea of deterrence. The NSC attempted to respond strategically to the breakup of the World War II alliance and the growing gap between American and Soviet interests in Europe. Also there was a good possibility that the Soviets might soon have a number of nuclear weapons, as well as the means to deliver them. Yet, while NSC #68 called for a military program that would have us create a stock of atomic weapons and as quickly as possible develop hydrogen bombs as well, it also called for an increase in conventional weaponry.* All of this was necessary, so the logic went, to prevent the Soviets from exploiting their military power around the world.

NSC #68

---

*NSC #68 is reprinted in *Naval War College Review*, May–June 1975, pages 51–108.

CAPABILITY ANALYSIS

We begin our analysis of postwar military strategic doctrine with NSC #68 because it reflected in pristine form what in military parlance is called "threat" or "worst-case" or
capability
analysis
(usually) "capability analysis." The idea here is to calculate the enemy's total projected military power, based on industrial output as well as current weapons inventory. Then, assuming that what the enemy can do it will do, it proposes a counter-policy to meet any and all of the projected eventualities. By definition, then, capability analysis tends to drive military preparedness; for if the enemy has the ability to build so many tanks or so many bombers or so many submarines, it requires us to have an antitank, an antibomber, and an antisubmarine capability large enough to deal with these worst-case projections. But in fact the enemy might easily build fewer tanks or submarines or aircraft. For military planners, however, the prudent response is to assume that the enemy will do everything he can.

In the real world, military judgments are qualified by political and budgetary considerations which take into account other factors. The state of political relations between the two countries, budget priorities, values, and competing demands for national resources all play a role. But in the initial evaluation, professional soldiers have to ask for more and better weapons than we currently have. They feel they must assume the worst.

A good example of how capability analysis can exaggerate an enemy's potential concerns the Soviets' Backfire bomber. This is a twin-engine aircraft with variable geometry (swing wings). It has the "capability" to bomb the United States from Russia only if the following assumptions are made: first, that it would fly high and slowly (perhaps 300–400 miles per hour to conserve fuel); and second, that it would be able to fly undetected, zoom in fast, drop its bombs, and land unscathed in Cuba. All these assumptions seem improbable. Yet according to capability analysis, since the bomber can technically fly this far, some kind of military response must be designed to meet the threat.

(Actually the Pentagon and independent analysts agree that the aircraft is most suitable for peripheral missions—

against our aircraft carriers, perhaps, and against European and Chinese land targets. It is not designed to attack the United States.)*

In any event, soon after NSC #68 appeared, the North Koreans attacked South Korea and President Harry Truman felt compelled to respond. The United States found itself fighting in a non-nuclear—conventional—war, which became a stalemate after the Chinese intervened. The unpopularity of the Korean War was a key factor in the election of Dwight Eisenhower in 1952, who had promised to "go to Korea" to end it. The important point here is that the Korean War, unpopular though it was, resulted in a fourfold increase in defense spending. Our military budget went from about $16 billion in 1950 to more than $44 billion in 1952 (and this was not a period of high inflation). Moreover, military spending did not return to pre-war levels after it was over.

Despite or perhaps because of his past military experience, Eisenhower was not comfortable with capability analysis. Once the Korean War was settled, he believed—and said so publicly—that it was too expensive to meet every possible enemy capability. He was not the only one who thought so. At the time some American defense experts advanced the notion that the Russians were deliberately trying literally to bankrupt the West by making us keep up with impossible capabilities. (Similarly, some U.S. weapons—long-range bombers, for instance—have been justified over the years partly on the ground that they force the Soviets into spending a great deal more on air defenses.) Moreover, the Korean War instilled in some U.S. military planners a determination to avoid future land wars in Asia.

MASSIVE RETALIATION

As a result of this concern, Eisenhower and his Treasury Secretary, George M. Humphrey, decided to rely on the fact that we alone had a supply of atomic bombs and strategic aircraft (airplanes able to penetrate Soviet airspace from

*Soviet Military Power, page 63; and Robert Berman, Soviet Airpower in Transition (Washington, D.C.: The Brookings Institution, 1978), page 26.

bases in Europe) and not to compete in terms of mass with the Soviet Union's army. This was an important new direction for American policy. It was dubbed "Bigger bang for the buck," or "More rubble for the ruble." But the term that stuck was coined by Secretary of State John Foster Dulles: "massive retaliation."

If the Russians threatened any of our vital interests anywhere, we would threaten to "level them" using our atomic advantage rather than fight another Korea-type war. Dulles never said we must go to war. He said we must display a willingness to go to war, or in his words, "We must be prepared to go to the brink of war." (Hence the term "brinkmanship.") Indeed, his thinking was consistent. For if we didn't flaunt our atomic power, the new strategic doctrine would not work. The weapons had to be waved like big sticks. We had to be good bluffers.

brinkman-
ship

Under this doctrine—and the period is full of ironies since President Eisenhower had been General of the Army before entering politics—conventional forces, that is, the Army's ground troops and the Air Force's fighter planes, reached their lowest ebb in the postwar period. The Army was actually reduced in size and shipbuilding slowed (although the United States could still rely on the massive Navy built during World War II). Only the Air Force, and particularly the Strategic Air Command, got increased support. By 1955, as we have noted, SAC's big bombers, first the B-36s, then the all-jet B-47s and B-52s—in all, about 1,300 aircraft capable of carrying nuclear bombs—became the keys to American military preparedness.

Zero Sum and Nonzero-Sum Gaming

At about the same time, from an entirely different corner of America, that of the mathematicians, a new kind of thinking developed that would substantially contribute to the language, if not the thrust, of the doctrine of deterrence. The theory of gaming, or "game theory," presents the notion that there are two kinds of games that people and nations can play: the zero-sum game and the nonzero-sum game.* In a

---

*John von Neumann and Oskar Morgenstern, *The Theory of Games and Economic Behavior* (Princeton, N.J.: Princeton University Press, 1946), *passim*.

zero-sum game, anyone who wins does so at someone else's expense; or, to say it differently, anyone who loses causes someone else to win. (If the value of what one side wins is $+1$, the value of the other side's loss must be -1. Thus, $+1-1 = 0$.) So the game is pure competition and conflict. Playing it, you assume your opponent is doing his best to do you in. (After all, you are doing the same to him.) This means you have no need to communicate with him and your basic strategy is to maximize your winnings, which always come at his expense, while minimizing your losses. This is known as the "minimax" strategy.

In nonzero-sum gaming, outcomes in which both sides win or lose are possible. The goal in nonzero-sum gaming is not to "win" in the ordinary, competitive sense of the term but to find mutually advantageous solutions. For this to work you must communicate in some way with the other players, and compromise rather than maximize your own gain, to co-operate instead of competing.

Of course, such games do not exist in pure form in real life and no theoretician would be foolish enough to claim they do. Rather, we think of tendencies toward zero-sum and nonzero-sum play. An illustration of how games are actually mixed in the real world can be taken from the playing field. Sports and competitive games can be said to be zero-sum in their play, given their scoring systems. You either win or lose. Everybody knows that. But they are non-zero-sum in their organization. For if there is no mutual agreement to play at all and to play by certain accepted rules, there is no game. So before anyone can play a zero-sum game, they have to play a nonzero-sum game to get started.

But the most significant lesson to be gained from game theory is from a game called "the prisoners' dilemma." Imagine you and an acquaintance are arrested for auto theft. The district attorney holds you incommunicado from each other and tells you that he has enough evidence in hand to convict both of you of auto tampering, a misdemeanor. That will get you six months in the county jail. But he doesn't have enough evidence to get you for auto theft, a felony, which would cost you five years in the state prison. He offers a deal. If you confess and the other prisoner doesn't, he will let you go free and convict your accomplice of the felony on the basis of your testimony. But he also says that he has offered your acquaintance the same deal. So if both of you talk, you'll both get five years in prison. If just one talks, then he goes free and the other gets the five years. And if neither talks, both of you get only six months in the can.

Thus the dilemma: do you talk or not?

If you were to substitute "arming" or "engaging in arms control" for "talking" or "not talking," you get a clear picture of the strategic dilemma that we face with our nuclear rival. If one side arms and the other does not, then the side that arms had an advantage over the one that does not. But if both sides arm, then both lose. The only way that both can win is to agree together to control weaponry.

At least so the theory goes.

Nonzero-sum games require bargaining. A secret weapon in a nonzero-sum game makes no "sense." The players must show what they have and communicate in some way. Some time ago a Congressman who had seen a model of a Polaris submarine in a toy shop complained that we were showing the Russians "what we have" for the price of a toy. He entirely misunderstood the game of deterrence. Certainly, the location at any given time of any one Polaris submarine is and has to be unknown. But the fact that these vessels exist and have certain capabilities must be known to the other side as part of our "play." How otherwise can the other side be deterred if it does not know what we have?

To be sure, the Russians have behaved more secretively than this principle of mutual deterrence would suggest, even to the point of concealing information on military matters from their own high officials. At one stage of the SALT I negotiations, a Soviet general complained to his American opposite that by openly discussing the capabilities of Soviet weapons in the talks, we were revealing to Soviet civilian officials information that they had no business knowing, a complete turnaround from the normal expectations of what should be kept secret from whom.*

---

*Interestingly, the United States provided all the numbers—on both U.S. and Soviet weapons—that provided the basis for the negotiations. Later, in SALT II, the Soviets agreed to provide information on the size of their strategic forces.

By the end of the 1950s the policy of massive retaliation had apparently lost its credibility. Widespread criticism had appeared in print. In his campaign for the Presidency in 1960, John Kennedy charged his opponent Richard Nixon (Eisenhower's Vice President) with responsibility for a "mis- **missile gap** sile gap" between the United States and the Soviet Union, and for neglecting U.S. non-nuclear forces. The fact is, influential military analysts had begun to worry that if massive retaliation did not deter an enemy from attacking our interests somewhere on the globe, we would not have the conventional forces ready to fight it. Army Chief of Staff General Maxwell Taylor was among the first to recognize this and in 1956 urged that flexible response be substituted for massive retaliation.

But perhaps the most significant factor undermining our reliance on massive retaliation was the launching of the world's first space satellite, *Sputnik*. Americans had been **Sputnik** certain that, despite their rapid development of atomic weapons, the Russians were still backward in their scientific and technical capabilities. (After all, we thought, they couldn't even make a ball-point pen. How could they catch up with us in space?) We assumed that our space satellite, the *Vanguard*, would be the first up. We were wrong. This demonstration of Soviet rocketry contributed as much as anything to an American (and, more significantly, a European) loss of faith in massive retaliation as an effective policy. If the Russians could put a satellite into orbit, what else could they do? They might build ICBMs and destroy our bombers before they could take off. This was especially worrisome to us since we had been slow to shift from aircraft to missiles in our strategic nuclear arsenal.

ASIDE————————————————————————————

One immediate result of *Sputnik* was an impetus to science education in this country. Identification of potentially able scientists and engineers through high school physics courses was an early goal. Another effect was accelerated work on our own missile system, including the Jupiter (Army), Atlas, Titan, and Minuteman (Air Force), Polaris (Navy), and others. (See Chapter Three.)

In effect, our nuclear monopoly had given us the luxury of playing what seemed to be a zero-sum game with the Russians. It was implicit under massive retaliation that it was they who would lose, and lose big, in any ultimate confrontation. But the beginnings of a Soviet intercontinental thermonuclear striking capability revealed that it was really a nonzero-sum game we were in; one which we could lose, too. Or so it appeared at the time.

In hindsight our fears were not fully justified. These first-generation Soviet missiles were crude, unreliable, and not very accurate. Moreover, the Russians built fewer missiles than our capability analysis had led us to expect, although they carried larger warheads than ours. But what ultimately destroyed massive retaliation as doctrine even more than *Sputnik* and John Kennedy was the flaw inherent in its logic. That we would use nuclear weapons to respond to an attack on America was never in doubt. But what seemed less and less likely was that we would use nuclear weapons to respond to something distant and less directly threatening, like, say, a Soviet invasion of Afghanistan or, for that matter, West Berlin. Who could believe we would risk the destruction of the American people for such relatively minor provocation? It may well be that Dulles never intended massive retaliation to apply to such contingencies, but with the comparative neglect of conventional forces that coincided with the policy, the United States found itself with few options.

And so the first strategic doctrine to deal with a situation in which our rivals as well as ourselves had nuclear weapons was abandoned. By 1960, the Americans no longer had any kind of monopoly on nuclear weapons, and our threats to use atomic bombs in response to even minor provocation lacked believability.

We had to find something else.

FLEXIBLE RESPONSE

In place of massive retaliation, the Kennedy administration—made up mostly of men who had fought as junior officers in World War II—offered the concept of "flexible response." Through it we sought to remedy the flaws in massive retaliation, in particular the disproportion between means and ends. Anticipating Communist subversion around the world, the plan was to build up conventional land forces to be able to strike back wherever and whenever the Communists moved in. Still, the game was mostly competitive and the objective was "winning," that is, zero-sum.

At the time, you may remember, Communist subversion rather than nuclear attack seemed a more serious threat. All this was occurring long before the split between the Soviet Union and China. And in this period China appeared to be self-aggrandizing in Korea and in its support of the Vietnamese insurgency against the French. Also, Americans were still chafing over Castro's takeover of Cuba in the late 1950s. So when Castro sent his co-revolutionist, Che Guevara, to South America to spread the doctrine of the Cuban revolution, the threat seemed even more real. Thus, even before the term "third world" was coined, the Kennedy administration wanted to be able to battle Communist takeovers in much of the underdeveloped world.* It feared, and rightly so, that, our atomic weapons notwithstanding, we would be impotent to contain (as the phrase went) Communism without land forces and weapons.† Indeed, as Chairman Mao was fond of saying, the United States might turn out to be "nothing but a paper tiger."

Another new notion that helped make flexible response an attractive alternative to massive retaliation was the "domino theory." If we lost Laos, it was argued, we would lose South Vietnam. If we lost South Vietnam, we would lose Cambodia. If we lost Cambodia, we would lose Thailand.‡ And if we lost Thailand, we would lose the Malay Peninsula. And so on, until—in its most primitive version—we lost California. With such scenarios confronting him, it was almost inevitable that Kennedy would promise, as he did in his inaugural address in 1961, that we would "pay any price, bear any burden" to assure peace around the world.

domino
theory

*Barbara Ward, *Spaceship Earth* (New York: Columbia University Press, 1966), page 79.
†George Kennan invented the term "containment."
‡Events have shown that those four states that comprised former Indochina (Laos, North Vietnam, South Vietnam, and Cambodia) have indeed "fallen," in spite of American efforts. But Thailand has maintained its independence for more than a century even through the Japanese occupation of its neighbors. The question is, Did their "fall" damage U.S. security?

Conventional forces were substantially increased. John Kennedy revived the Green Berets, the Army's Special Forces which had been created in the early 1950s for an entirely different purpose. Ironically, the Green Berets—who were to make their reputation for good or ill in Vietnam— had been founded in the expectation of World War III in Europe. American soldiers, specially trained or recruited to speak the languages of eastern Europe, would infiltrate behind the Iron Curtain and train insurgents who would harass the Red Army from the rear. These Special Forces, however few in number, were never popular with the top brass; and so the Army was in the process of disbanding them when Kennedy took office. But Kennedy turned this policy around. He ordered that they be redirected away from eastern Europe and toward worldwide counter-insurgency. Thus the Green Berets became a prime instrument of flexible response.

The reasoning behind flexible response is as follows: If a landlord wants to evict a tenant or get him or her to pay the rent, the landlord might turn off the heat. And if that didn't work, turn off the water, instead of beginning formal eviction right away. In the same sense, our new strategy of flexible response involved "decomposition of the threat," or, as it was sometimes called, "incrementalizing of the threat."

The lessons of the Vietnam War are still undigested. But one thing we learned from that war was that "incrementalism" can lead to mutual escalation. As everyone now knows, we sent in a few advisors, and they sent in a few, too. We sent in some troops. They sent in some more. After a while both sides had so much invested that we were stuck. Not being a specialist in foreign relations or military strategy, Lyndon Johnson kept on Kennedy's people—the "best and the brightest," author David Halberstam would later call them. Nonetheless, the President soon found himself with 500,000 troops in Vietnam and an incensed public at home, chanting, "Hey, hey, LBJ, how many kids did you kill today?" When, after the Tet offensive, General William Westmoreland asked for just another increment, 50,000 more troops, what was Johnson to do?

Johnson was like the youth who has purchased an old car for $100, sunk some repairs into it, to the tune of, say, $400, and then finds himself confronted with a major repair estimated at $600. What do you do with a car that's worth $100, has $500 invested in it, and now needs $600 more? The President finally realized he had a lemon in Vietnam, but it took several more years and another President to get us out.

One other painful lesson for the military was that air power has its limits. Remember that the airplane, especially the bomber, was the glamour weapon of World War II. We started bombing in Vietnam, hoping destruction from the skies would cause the North Vietnamese to stop sending troops into the south. When that didn't work, we bombed some more. Some analysts argue that if we had bombed North Vietnam as intensively in 1968 (under Lyndon Johnson) as we bombed the country in 1972 (under Richard Nixon) we would have beaten them. Indeed, they argue that we had it won until Watergate effectively ended any further bombing. But most strategists today believe that the Vietnam War could simply not have been won only with airplanes.

A third aspect of the war that has influenced political and military thinking since was that it was covered daily and in detail on American television.* No viewer, however uninformed about weapons and strategy, could miss the point that the United States had given the South Vietnamese the very best weapons available, but that they hadn't made any perceptible difference. In fact, our most sophisticated weaponry fell into enemy hands as our allies panicked and ran.

In fact, several senior generals and high Pentagon officials have admitted that the Vietnam War did more to cause the deterioriation of U.S. military forces than almost anything else. As a result of the high cost of running the war, the services neglected investment in new weapons and equipment. Moreover, the tempo of fighting took its toll in terms of greater-than-normal wear and tear on existing weapons. Ships, aircraft, tanks, and vehicles of all kinds wore out; maintenance was neglected; replacements delayed. The Pentagon is still trying to catch up.†

---

* Peter Braestrup and Burns Roper, *Big Story: How the American Press and Television Reported the Crisis of Tet 1968 in Vietnam and Washington* (Boulder, Colo. Westview Press, 1977).

† Michael Maclear, *The Ten Thousand Day War* (New York, St. Martin's Press, 1981), Chapter 17, *passim*.

THINKING ABOUT THE UNTHINKABLE

Perhaps, in terms of thermonuclear strategy, the most important new writer to appear in the late 1960s was Herman Kahn. Located today at his Hudson Institute, Kahn first achieved prominence while working for the Rand Corporation with two books, *On Thermonuclear War* and *Thinking about the Unthinkable*. Kahn proposed that America should actually prepare for thermonuclear war as a way to gain maximum credibility vis-à-vis the enemy. If deterrence were to be effective, Kahn argued, this country had to have the capability of surviving at least a nuclear first strike.

ASIDE———————————————————————————

The term "first strike" refers to an initial attack with nuclear weapons. A disarming first strike is one in which the attacker attempts to destroy all or a large part of its adversary's strategic nuclear forces before they can be launched. A preemptive first strike is one in which a nation launches its attack first on the presumption that the adversary is about to attack. (This definition is taken from Herbert Scoville's, *MX*, cited earlier.)

———————————————————————————————

Kahn's book went into great detail as to how it would be possible to survive such an attack. His point of view was essentially zero-sum in that he felt a thermonuclear war might not only be survivable but winnable, if we were prepared for it. In Chapter Two there was a long discussion about the immediate and long-term effects of thermonuclear explosions. But Kahn minimized the impact of these physical effects. He went so far as to estimate how many "megadeaths"—introducing a new word into our vocabulary—the country could sustain and still survive. In fact, he predicted, public hysteria, not death and dislocation, would be our greatest problem.

megadeaths

Another influential strategist, Albert L. Wohlstetter, criticized our manner of deploying our strategic nuclear weapons. When deterrence was the threat of massive retaliation, we kept most of our bombs loaded on Air Force bombers parked on open airfields, vulnerable, as Wohlstetter noted, to an enemy first strike. Indeed, they invited attack because with one massive strike the enemy could knock out virtually everything we had. To prevent this, Wohlstetter said, we needed to have a more decentralized nuclear deployment scheme. Some of our planes had to be in the air at all times, while other nuclear weapons needed to be put on other kinds of delivery systems—submarines, for example—or buried in underground missile silos.

Indeed, just before and during the Vietnam War, the United States expanded its ICBM force, and the first Polaris submarines joined the fleet. Recall that in 1960 our thermonuclear arsenal consisted largely of B-52s, carrying gravity bombs. Also in place were the Thor and Jupiter IRBMs, based in Europe, and a few Atlas and Titan ICBMs—all part of the Strategic Air Command. The expansion of our missile force accomplished during Kennedy's term in office gave us some short-term advantages. Yet the Soviets' continuing ability to match these improvements led to many of the nuclear dilemmas that we face today.

Kahn saw quite clearly that there was no way to defend against a first strike. All we could do was to be able to absorb it and retaliate, that is, to have a "second-strike" capability. Hence his desire to see us confront the real possibility of a thermonuclear exchange.

Robert McNamara played an important part in dealing with the shifting strategies that emerged from these debates. Coming to office in 1961, under Kennedy, with the criticism of massive retaliation in the background, he saw the problem of credibility very clearly. What was happening was that the logic of nonzero-sum gaming as it relates to the prisoners' dilemma was in the process of making a slow transition from academic speculation to actual public policy. In essence, prisoners' dilemma is a nonzero-sum game that appears zero-sum to the players. The symbolism of the prosecutor's threat becomes in the real world the awesome destructive capabilities of nuclear weapons. The root of the dilemma facing you as prisoner lies in trying to divine the intentions of the other, and to communicate yours to him. In the game the question is simple: Will he talk or won't he? In national security policy the questions are more complex but reflect the same uncertainty about intentions: To what extent will he arm? Will he attack and under what conditions? And, can we trust him? And you, of course, present the same mystery to him.

The problem of credibility lies not so much in the weaponry as in the will to use it. But even more important is the fact that such will must be communicated—i.e., the others must believe you. So, in effect, the essence of credibility, which is the essence of deterrence, lies completely in the perceptions of others. In the case of the prisoners, the task is simply put. If he talks, you will, too. But if he remains silent, you will do the same despite the fact that you would profit from confessing in the face of his silence. With thermonuclear strategy, the zero-sum component is stated with equal simplicity. If he attacks, you will retaliate. But the cooperative aspect of the equation goes beyond the simple understanding that your weapons will remain unused as long as do his. It is implicit in the game that one player's restraint in the acquisition of weapons must be acknowledged and reciprocated in some comparable way by the others if the system is to work. It would be some time before this latter aspect of the prisoners' dilemma would have a meaningful impact on strategic thinking.

Unlike some theoreticians and military experts, McNamara focused on the problem of cost. How much, he asked, are we going to have to pay for a credible deterrent? Until his tenure as Secretary of Defense (and he stayed on in the position until 1968) there had not been a system in the Pentagon for doing what became known as "cost-benefit analysis." No one could tell the Secretary when he first arrived how much security we were buying with what weapons and at what price. On the one hand, of course, true national security, like human life itself, cannot be "costed" and "benefited." But what McNamara was after with his Planning Programming Budgeting System (PPBS) was some specific measure or measures of the effectiveness of our military preparedness, as well as of our deterrent capability. Slowly McNamara came to understand, and tried to communicate to others in the Pentagon, that more weapons did not necessarily buy more security. His approach and his intention were meant to make more rational the strategic policy that he had inherited.

When he first came to office, the United States had three times as many nuclear warheads and strategic delivery systems as the Soviet Union. So, not surprisingly, his first impulse—essentially zero-sum in nature—was to maintain this overwhelming advantage. In a commencement address given at Ann Arbor, Michigan, in June 1962, McNamara made his position clear. We needed, he said, a strategic force capable of hitting different kinds of targets. The principal U.S. military objective in the event of nuclear war should be the destruction of Soviet weapons and military forces, so as to give the Soviets the maximum incentive to avoid attacking U.S. cities. At the same time, he noted, the United States would have sufficient striking power, even after a surprise nuclear attack, to destroy Soviet cities and industrial centers if necessary (a second strike). But he was clearly saying that both sides should of course avoid such a disaster.

targeting strategies

The technical terms for these "targeting strategies" are "counterforce" and "countervalue." Counterforce refers to the ability to hit an enemy's military forces, which consist of both "hard" targets (mainly missile silos and command centers built of reinforced concrete and buried underground) and "soft" targets (such as airfields and shipyards). Hitting hard targets demands a high degree of confidence in your weapons' accuracy.

hard and soft targets

Historically, the Air Force was best able to provide this precision because bombers actually see their targets, at least on radar, before they let their weapons go. (In World War II, bombardiers bragged that they could put their bombs into a pickel barrel from 25,000 feet.) In addition, as we have learned, land-based missiles are more accurate than those aboard submarines.

counterforce

Countervalue strategy refers to the annihilation of enemy cities and industrial capability. Since these targets are large and soft, much less accuracy is needed to do the job. Obviously, accuracy sufficient for missile silos can be used on cities, but missiles that are only accurate enough to hit cities cannot reliably "kill" hard military targets.

counter-value

These distinctions have sometimes been considered mutually exclusive. In fact, American nuclear forces have never been targeted on cities per se. Our war plans have always included large numbers of military and industrial targets.

But in the Soviet Union, as in the United States, many industrial and military facilities are located in or near cities. Thus, if we were to start using nuclear weapons (which, of course, deterrence seeks to avoid), the distinction between counterforce and countervalue would largely disappear because of the realities of nuclear weapons and how they would be used to fight a war. Still, the distinction appears and reappears in the strategic debate. The reasons for this bring us back to the heart of deterrence logic.

As we try to make some sense of the debate between counterforce and countervalue targeting scenarios, we must concede that at first glance the advantages of a counterforce capability seem overwhelming. After all, these enemy missiles are aimed at us. If we could knock them out, we'd be spared thermonuclear destruction, or so it appears. But, on second glance, we have to ask ourselves, what happens next? If we (or they) were to proclaim that the enemy's strategic weapons were our first target, then we would deny him his deterrent. If they did the same (and how could we expect them not to?) they would deny us ours.

Moreover, the distinction fosters the dangerous illusion that it might be possible to fight a nuclear war in some limited way, in which only nuclear weapons and military facilities are targets while cities are spared. Given the thousands of nuclear weapons that would be involved, their size, and the proximity of military targets to cities and population centers in both countries, a limited counterforce nuclear war is simply not possible. When World War II began, there was a sort of gentleman's agreement among the belligerents that cities would not be bombed. It did not take long for this to break down. And it is hard to imagine that nuclear weapons would be any different.

As McNamara got deeper into the strategic debate, he began to realize that our attempt to maintain absolute strategic superiority would always be subject to Soviet force improvements. Every time the Russians built something new, we would be obliged to double and redouble our efforts. By 1964 a perceptible shift had occurred in the Defense Secretary's thinking. He began to articulate a new idea, that of the "damage-limiting strategy." This concept recognized the impossibility of achieving overwhelming superiority and acknowledged the fact that America would inevitably suffer considerable damage—Herman Kahn's analysis notwithstanding—in a thermonuclear exchange. Thus, from an emphasis on offensive weapons, designed to retaliate, McNamara moved to a concern with defensive weapons and policies that would limit the damage occurring to the United States and its people if deterrence failed.

DAMAGE LIMITATION AND ASSURED DESTRUCTION

Two components of this new policy were the ABM system (the first military proposal, incidentally, to stimulate public protest since efforts to ban atmospheric testing in the 1950s) and a comprehensive civil defense program of shelters stocked with survival food and gear. The ABM system was politically unpopular because Americans felt that protective defenses around cities would make them targets instead. And the shelter program went the way of the Edsel. Although considerable funds were spent, the American people for reasons of their own yawned through it all. A few built backyard shelters and schoolchildren of the era will remember being taught what to do when the sirens blew, but indifference was the norm.

ABM

civil defense

The following year another new concept surfaced in McNamara's thinking. He called it "assured destruction." He was still trying to define "enough" so he could cap the development and deployment of strategic weapons. McNamara's systems analysts concluded that beyond a certain level, more nuclear weapons produced only limited returns. They calculated that the equivalent of 400 one-megaton bombs would destroy about 60 percent of the Soviet Union's industrial capacity and kill 50 million to 100 million Russians. Additional weapons above that number would result in only marginal increases in destruction. In short, they would not be cost-effective.

assured destruction

While it is probably true that more Americans than Russians would die promptly in a thermonuclear exchange (because of the greater megatonnage of Soviet nuclear weapons), our plan was to destroy with our weapons virtually all their petrochemical, fuel, and fertilizer plants, their steel and smelting, electrical generating and transportation capability, chemical industry, and motor vehicle production. Then, it was predicted, the Russian winter would take care of the rest. In less than a year, so the scenario went, the Union of Soviet Socialist Republics would be reduced to bands of starving peasants roaming the barren steppes.

McNamara did not let go of the damage-limiting strategy right away. At first he thought it was compatible with assured destruction. We would give the enemy a paralyzing hit while doing everything possible to minimize our own losses. But by 1967 it dawned on him that if the Soviets chose the same combination of strategies, we might be entangled in impossible opposites. Any Soviet damage-limiting effort (ABMs on their territory and civil defense, for example) would threaten our assured-destruction plans, and we would be forced to take steps to nullify their efforts. The Soviets, for their part, could easily nullify our efforts to limit damage to the United States by various military measures.

In essence, like any prisoner of the dilemma, the Defense Secretary now seems to have understood the futility of a zero-sum strategy which dictated the unending purchase of more and better thermonuclear weaponry. So he came to realize that more weapons simply did not buy more security, especially if we were to assume—and we had to—that anything we would build, the Russians would also build later on. He never used the term, but it was obvious that once both sides had an assured-destruction capability over the other, strategic reality would have reached a kind of stability

MAD   with "mutual assured destruction." And with this came the most unfortunate, if most apt, acronym of the whole strategic debate, mutual assured destruction—MAD.

Another irony in the story illustrates the role played by the perceptions of the adversary (in this case, us) in deterrence, because at the time mutual assured destruction was being embraced by our side (the early 1960s), the Russians had but a limited capability for attacking the United States. To be sure, their ability to develop both atomic and hydrogen weapons had come quickly and had caught us by surprise, but they did not yet have many intercontinental ballistic missiles, and the ones they had didn't function very well. At the time, their intercontinental bomber force, which consisted of about 135 aircraft, posed only a token threat to the United States. It did, however, cause us to spend a lot of money for air defense. Since it is zero-sum thinking, worst-case analysis had again imputed to the enemy's then-current capability, something that could and only would be actualized in the future.

By 1966 the basic elements of our present nuclear deterrence force were in place. As we have seen, it comprised a Triad involving three delivery systems: Air Force bombers, mostly B-52s; land-based missiles in hard silos, Titan and Minuteman; and submarine-launched missiles, the Polaris. Even though McNamara had tried to limit warhead expansion, the 3-to-1 nuclear superiority America had had at the beginning of his term had grown to 4 to 1 at the end. This was largely because the United States deployed its second-generation ICBMs at a faster pace than the Soviets. The deployment of MIRVs (multiple independently targetable re-entry vehicles) in the early 1970s would further increase the U.S. advantage.

ASIDE

It is perhaps appropriate to tell here the story of the ultimate deterrent, the doomsday machine, not that it was ever seriously considered as a policy option. But in its essence it does represent a perfectly rational extension of the logic of deterrence. This ultimate deterrent was to be a hydrogen bomb or a series of hydrogen bombs so huge and/or so strategically placed that they could destroy the planet, either by splitting the globe in two or by driving the earth out of its orbit.

doomsday machine

Its critical aspect would be its trigger. It would be set to activate automatically if any thermonuclear weapon landed on American soil. And once the machine was set, it could not be disarmed by any person, American or adversary. Thus, with a doomsday machine in place, the United States would possess the ultimate threat. We would announce to the world that if any thermonuclear weapon fell on the United States, the whole earth would be immediately destroyed.

ARMS LIMITATION

Spurred by the Cuban missile crisis, during which many people (including Nikita Khrushchev and John Kennedy) thought we had come closer to thermonuclear war than ever before (or since), both the Soviet Union and the United States began to realize the need for some kind of negotiation and cooperation (i.e. nonzero-sum behavior) to limit or at least to channel the competition in certain ways. As a result we began to negotiate what would become a series of seventeen treaties dealing with arms limitation, nuclear testing, and prohibiting weapons of mass destruction in areas such as outer space and the ocean floor. One of the first ideas that
hot line surfaced is popularly known as the "hot line," a direct communication link between the command-and-control structures of the White House and Kremlin. Later on, other countries would be given "extensions" on the line (actually a teletype, not a telephone wire), but at the outset it was meant to permit direct communication only between the top American decision-makers and their Soviet counterparts. This mutually recognized need for rapid communications was an acknowledgment of the nonzero-sum nature of the situation we both found ourselves in. And as a link between national military command structures, it represents the first time in human history that the decision-making institutions of two major powers were continually connected.

The second idea was an atmospheric test ban, and the treaty outlawing nuclear tests above ground was signed by the Soviet Union and the United States in August 1963. In January 1967 the two countries concluded an outer-space treaty that banned weapons of mass destruction from being deployed on satellites. In July 1968 both sides and other countries, too, concluded a nonproliferation treaty designed to keep still more countries from "going nuclear."

Nonproliferation is an important strategic issue. In the beginning, of course, the United States had a monopoly on nuclear weapons, one soon broken by the Soviet Union. By the late 1960s, however, France, Great Britain, and China had nuclear weapons, although none had the same number and kinds as we. People began to worry about the "nth coun-

"*n*th country
problem"

try problem" (*n*th meaning any number). Assuming there is a given possibility of nuclear war if there are only two nuclear powers, when a third power is added, the probability of war increases; if a fourth is added, it increases still more; and as more and more (*n*) countries join the nuclear club, a point is reached—mathematically—at which war becomes inevitable. This is the *n*th country problem.

The logic has some flaws. It can be argued that as a nation gains the capability to manufacture hydrogen bombs and to create technically sophisticated delivery systems, it will find itself in much the same position as the United States and the USSR, namely with too much to lose from war. On the other hand, a terrorist organization, having much less at stake than an advanced country, may think differently on these issues; or one insane leader, temporarily in charge, might well not think at all. Or, for that matter, an Israeli or South African leader, facing certain annihilation for his country, might take the nuclear step.

Another factor contributing to the superpowers' readiness to sign a nonproliferation treaty was that the Russians were being pressed by their ally, the People's Republic of China, into giving them nuclear weapons, or at least assistance in developing them, and we were (then, not now) being pressured by some of our allies to do the same. By signing a nonproliferation treaty with one another, both countries had an excuse, if they needed one, for not handing over nuclear weapons to anyone else. At the same time, the United States and the Soviet Union were extracting commitments from non-nuclear nations to eschew nuclear weapons. As one way of inducing the non-nuclear powers to refrain from acquiring nuclear weapons, the two countries agreed to negotiate reductions in their own nuclear arsenals.

In February 1971 détente was in full bloom. The Soviet Union and the United States concluded a seabed treaty whereby each promised not to put nuclear weapons on the ocean floor. In September 1971 an "accidental measures" agreement was signed, providing that both sides would inform one another of their missile test launchings. This was meant to prevent any misreading by either side of any missile activity. But it wasn't until May 1972 that the first significant step in strategic arms limitation was undertaken with the signing of the SALT I agreement.

SALT I dealt exclusively with strategic arms. These, as defined in the treaty, are intercontinental weapons, capable of traveling from one continent to the other. This means that only bombers, ICBMs, and SLBMs could be dealt with in the treaty (although bombers were excluded). Indeed, SALT I was meant to initiate a whole series of agreements that were to put some limits on the production and deployment of nuclear delivery systems. And SALT II (and later SALT III) would have continued these arms limitations even further.

We will treat SALT I and SALT II in some detail in Chapter Seven. What is interesting to us here in tracing the evolution of nuclear strategic doctrine is the complex thinking about antiballistic missile systems in terms of deterrence; and the difficulty in measuring "missile equivalency." From this point on, although the arms limitation process turned out to be even more protracted and difficult than was anticipated—Salt II was never formally ratified, and the SALT III talks, now called START, only got under way in June 1982—the possibility that we would be negotiating arms control had to be part of the deterrence considerations.*

SALT I actually comprised two agreements: 1) a treaty to limit antiballistic missile systems (ABMs); and 2) an agreement to freeze the total number of intercontinental land-based missile launchers and submarine-based missile launchers at the then current inventory levels.

The ABM discussions were particularly interesting in terms of deterrence thinking. Superficially, a missile system able to shoot down enemy missiles is attractive because it seems to bring the more appealing idea of protection (as opposed to a balance of terror) back into the nuclear equation. But in fact it can undermine deterrence insofar as it presents the possibility that a country can be protected from retaliation. So the mutual vulnerability, on which deterrence is based, evaporates when we build antiballistic missile systems. So long as an enemy can block our counterstrike, the enemy might be willing, in fact tempted, to start a nuclear

*Eugene Rostow, President Reagan's director of the Arms Control Agency, called the continuing strategic arms limitation discussions "strategic arms reduction talks." So SALT became START in 1981.

war. (The same argument can be advanced about civil defense. If the Russians were to evacuate their cities tomorrow—especially if this were a period of rising tensions—would we not think that a provocative act?)

Another objection to the ABMs was that given the primitive antiballistic missile technology of the time, any ABM system could easily be overwhelmed by an attacker willing to launch more weapons than could be absorbed by the defensive system. So that if each country built an ABM system and then went ahead and built enough additional missiles to overwhelm the other's, vast amounts of money (a minimum of $50 billion in the United States alone) would have been spent for no net gain in security to either side. (In game theory terms, if both sides go this route, nobody wins and everyone is poorer.)

ASIDE———————————————————————————————

ABM critics reasoned: In World War II, a good air defense was one that could shoot down 20 percent of the enemy's attacking aircraft, because eventually, at that rate, the cost to the enemy in downed planes and lost pilots would become prohibitive. This is essentially what happened to the German Luftwaffe in the Battle of Britain in 1940. When the Royal Air Force became capable of regularly shooting down 20 percent of the incoming German bombers, the Germans had to cancel their campaign. Within a few months they did not have enough bombers left to continue the fight.

But in a nuclear exchange a 20 percent success rate has no meaning at all, at least in view of offensive weapons now available to both sides. Nuclear bombs can inflict such heavy damage that it matters little whether 20 percent are destroyed en route. If an ABM system is going to work at all, it has to be pretty close to perfect to protect us; that is, the anti-weapon weapon must destroy virtually all the incoming missiles.

———————————————————————————————

For all these reasons, both sides agreed to limit their antiballistic missile systems to two sites, later reduced to one each. And the treaty has remained in force to this day. (Our ABM site was built at Grand Forks, North Dakota, and for reasons of economy was decommissioned after completion at the insistence of Congress. The system was called Safe-guard.)

The second treaty—to freeze long-range intercontinental missile launchers from land- and sea-based locations—was far more political and controversial. In terms of "who got what," the Russians appear at first glance to have "won" SALT I. After all, they were allowed more missiles than we (1,618 for them as against 1,054 for us) with a much greater cumulative megatonnage. But this kind of "bean counting" can be misleading. In fact, SALT I left us with more war-heads despite the greater number of missiles the Soviets were permitted to keep. More importantly, our warheads were much more accurate than theirs, a fact which balanced their higher megatonnage. And even more importantly, the Soviets were then several years away from MIRVing their sea-based missiles, and the United States had already begun to do this.

In fact, some people within the U.S. government had wanted to include a MIRV ban in SALT I because MIRVing would multiply the numbers of warheads whatever the lim-itation on numbers of missiles. But they were unsuccessful. In fact, despite SALT I, a new arms escalation ensued, not so much in numbers of missiles (which were limited) but in numbers of warheads on missiles. Minuteman III missiles, which replaced Minuteman II in the period after SALT I, carry three MIRVed warheads. Minuteman II carried only one. And the Poseidon submarine-launched missile (though not armed to this strength) can carry up to 14 separate nu-clear warheads. With MIRVing in view, then, the limitation on missile launchers was not nearly as effective in limiting nuclear arms as one might have hoped.

Still, it was a start. We were talking about arms limitation with our nuclear rival and we were beginning to agree on certain limitations.

What is interesting about SALT II, which began in 1972 and was put on hold when the U.S. Senate refused to ratify the treaty in 1979, is that while this treaty was never ratified either by the Senate or by the Supreme Soviet, both nations have done nothing, and say they will do nothing, to "under-mine" it.

The second thing to note about SALT II is how the game

of deterrence is played once two superpowers start to bargain. Most lay people do not appreciate the degree of detail that goes into such treaty negotiations. In order to place numerical limitations on nuclear weapons, Russians and Americans together must define what weapons are. We have already seen that weapons in SALT I were defined quite narrowly as missile launchers, and numbers of actual warheads were not covered by that treaty. If there are 10 nuclear warheads on one missile, is this counted as one weapon or 10? Or, if we have agreed to limit cruise-missile-carrying airplanes, how do we make it possible to distinguish from satellite photographs the airplanes equipped with such missiles from those that are not? Or, to take a third example, if the Russians build two models of the same missile, one carrying one warhead each, the other carrying MIRVs, how can we count one separately from the other?

Solutions to these dilemmas take an enormous amount of patient negotiation, and the process has introduced entirely new terms and new requirements into strategic planning. To solve the third dilemma, for example, the Russians agreed to count all missiles tested with MIRV warheads *as if* they were equipped with MIRVs (even the ones that were not). And to meet the Russians' need to know which of our B-52s could carry cruise missiles, we in turn agreed to make visible changes in these airplanes so that they could be counted separately.

The point is that today deterrence requires a new and special kind of relationship with the Soviet Union. It is a fragile relationship, too, as post-Afghanistan problems have shown. Essentially, it requires assurances as well as threats, since we have to be assured that they do not have weapons that they agreed not to have, and when challenged, as provided for in SALT, each side has to provide the other with such assurances. To do this, we have to exchange an enormous amount of detailed information about our weapons systems and also make it possible for each side to verify—that is, count and confirm—what the other has.

It is in this context that the concept of a "secret weapon" takes on a very different meaning. It is still vital to prevent the other side from obtaining detailed information on the performance, specific capabilities, and designs of U.S. weapons. But on the other hand we have to tell in general what weapons we have and at the same time not interfere with efforts to verify that we are in compliance with the agreement. And the Russians have to do the same.

Secrecy and security are always politically sensitive, particularly in times of crisis. As a result, judgments as to how much verification is enough have always been as much political issues as technical ones. To say something is "political" means that reasonable people can and do disagree over what is "adequate." This is one of the key issues in the debate over SALT II.

Typically, the problem is asymmetrical; that is, different for each side. While the United States publishes large amounts of data on its weapons and military forces, the Soviets are compulsively secretive about everything their government does and even more so about defense matters. In short, it is harder for us to verify their weapons than it is for them to verify ours. Moreover, many Americans believe the Soviets will lie and cheat if it suits their purposes. Indeed, at one time or another most governments find reasons to lie to their own citizens, to say nothing of foreign governments, so there is good reason for caution. Nevertheless, the Soviets' record of compliance with international agreements in general and arms control accords in particular has been pretty good. When the agreements have been precisely and carefully drafted, there have been few problems. When there have been ambiguities, either deliberate or inadvertent, problems have arisen.

The MX missile basing system, proposed by the Carter Administration and rejected by President Reagan, illustrates some of these problems. The basing plan as originally proposed called for the construction of 4,600 shelters to conceal 200 missiles. Each missile was to move at random among 23 shelters (hence 4,600 shelters for 200 missiles), 22 of which would house dummy weapons to complete the deception.

The purpose of the scheme was to make it impossible for the Soviets to know with certainty where the real missile was housed. So they'd have to attack all 4,600 shelters to hit but 200 missiles. This they could not do, since SALT II would have limited the number of missiles and warheads they could deploy. But since under SALT II it was essential for the Soviets to be able to verify that 4,600 shelters held but 200 missiles, the shelters were designed with removable roof ports, allowing reconnaissance satellites to see inside.

Since the basing scheme has been dropped, the point is not how expensive or land-wasteful it would have been. Rather, it demonstrates how very difficult it is to meet each new arms escalation and at the same time keep our rival informed about our total strength.

From the Russian point of view, arms limitation was attractive for political as well as economic reasons. Their leaders, among the oldest in the world, vividly remember World War II and continue to be influenced by that experience, which cost them 20 million lives. Moreover, the Soviets have no real allies, with the possible exception of Cuba. Countries such as Poland, Hungary, Czechoslovakia, Rumania, and the other Eastern-Bloc "allies" cannot be counted on in time of war, a fact reemphasized by recent events in Poland. Even China, once an ally and partner in Marxism, is a potential enemy today.

While the United States has to worry only about the Soviet Union and its Cuban ally, the Russians have to consider us, western Europe, the Chinese. Even the Israelis have demonstrated the will and the military capability for a whole range of offensive moves. For now, as far as the Soviet Union is concerned, Israel is simply a potential base for U.S. forces. One day, however, it might be a real enemy.

The French nuclear force is not large by our standards, but the French have five Polaris-type submarines, each loaded with 16 hydrogen-warhead–equipped missiles. In addition, the French have land-based missiles and a small bomber force. The British, too, have four Polaris submarines (and will soon buy the Trident missile) and a bomber force of their own; and the Chinese have intermediate-range ballistic missiles and bombers all within range of at least some Soviet targets.

The Soviets have still another reason for pursuing arms control agreements and détente in general. They were (and still are) anxious to acquire Western technology and trade credits as a way of injecting some growth into the otherwise sluggish nonmilitary sector of their economy. Détente provides them with the opportunity to do so.

ASIDE————————————————————————————————

Critics of détente, many of whom occupy responsible positions in the Reagan administration, argue that not only did U.S. trade with the Soviets not moderate their international behavior, but that it actually helped strengthen Soviet military capabilities. It is alleged, for example, that recent Soviet improvements in missile accuracy were the direct result of the 1972 sale by the Bryant Grinder Corporation (approved by the Nixon administration) of 168 precision ball-bearing grinders. Precision ball bearings are a vital component in the gyroscopes used in missile inertial-guidance systems. The Soviets might have gotten comparable grinders elsewhere if we had not sold them, but probably not as quickly, and there is good reason to think the sale helped them.

————————————————————————————————

THE PERIOD AFTER DÉTENTE

While SALT I (and SALT II, to the extent it is adhered to) imposed real restraints on the United States' and Soviet Union's military machinery, in the period immediately following, both nations pressed ahead, building weapons that were not limited under the agreement. We developed a new generation of small, accurate, low-flying (to get under enemy radar) cruise missiles. These pilotless aircraft can be land-based, but will usually be carried by bombers or submarines. At the same time, the Russians, following the U.S. lead, equipped many of their long-range missiles with MIRVs.

For reasons even the experts cannot agree on, the Russians began speeding up the arms race, or at least their share of it. New tank companies appeared in eastern Europe; new ships joined their fleet; and a new generation of missiles from each of their four "design bureaus" emerged. Some observers claim that although the Russians were willing to talk arms limitation, at the same time they were spending half again as much of their national budget on weaponry as we.

ASIDE————————————————————————————————

Figuring out how much the Soviets spend on arms is not easy. Their budget is secret and their pricing structure—as they have a socialist economy, in which products are not bought and sold on the basis of supply and demand—is hard to make sense of. Also, ruble-dollar exchange rates are difficult to gauge. The CIA computes Soviet defense spending by estimating how much it would cost the United States to buy the same military forces the Soviets buy. It is acknowledged that this inflates Soviet spending figures by applying military pay scales that are current here to the very large Soviet manpower totals. (In fact, we know the Soviets pay their recruits far less than the United States does.) Nevertheless, it does provide a rough standard by which to evaluate the size of the Soviet military effort.

It has been suggested that for comparison purposes a reverse methodology be used to compute how much it would cost the Soviets to buy American forces. The trouble with this approach is that the Soviets would find it impossible to match some Western technology at any price.

————————————————————————————————————

Another destabilizing factor was the increased missile accuracy on both sides. You will recall that Titans and Minutemen were placed in underground hard silos, which protected them from all but a direct hit from a nuclear warhead. The then available missiles weren't accurate enough to get such a direct hit so our ICBM fleet was invulnerable. Thus we had a real stability with MAD (mutual assured destruction), since, whatever happened, both sides had a sure second-strike capability that no nuclear first strike could eliminate.

This situation was substantially changed when far greater missile accuracy became available to both sides toward the end of the 1970s. Once technology advanced to the point at which it was possible to "put the silo in the crater," silo-based missile invulnerability was no more.

Using intelligence estimates of the number, accuracy, and destructive power of Soviet warheads, contrasted with the estimated hardness of our Minuteman silos, we can calculate mathematically how a Soviet attack could in theory destroy all but a few random surviving Minutemen. (Of course, no one can be sure either theirs or ours would be that accurate in a real war, and no one wants to find out.)

Still, some Americans think that the Russians are really playing a zero-sum game and are seeking strategic superiority. If the Soviets could remove our land-based missiles in a single disarming first strike, then, these analysts believe, the United States could be deterred from retaliating, out of fear that the Soviets would then—in a second strike—destroy our cities, something we could not prevent. At least they could blackmail us with such a threat. If this were true, then we might indeed have a "window of vulnerability," as President Reagan has claimed.

The scenario—to play it back slowly—would go something like this: Accompanied by a propaganda barrage aimed mainly at western Europe, calling for "peace and disarmament," the Russians fire a missile salvo that eliminates most of our 1,052 ICBMs. Then they announce to the world that they have disarmed us in the name of world peace, and urge immediate top-level negotiations. If, using its submarine-launched missiles, the United States retaliates against Soviet cities instead of coming to the peace table, then they—the Russians—will have no choice but to reply in kind, destroying American civilization. What is the President to do? Does he order retaliation in the face of a threatened second barrage? Or does he knuckle under?

Note the change here. We have always assumed that the scenario would be a threat followed by a strike. Now, with enhanced missile accuracy, the strategists are beginning to worry about a strike followed by a threat to strike again. And this is why the military wants a "secure" MX (which would be protected by new ABMs) and a "hard-target kill capability" for the submarine-launched ballistic missiles.

In fact, many analysts doubt that any sane leader would choose the "strike first, threaten later" scenario. They note that the Russians are nothing if not cautious. ICBM accuracy is, in the final analysis, a highly speculative prediction. And the Soviets have no assurances that we might not just launch our ICBMs before theirs arrive.

ASIDE————————————————————————————————————

The idea of firing our ICBMs before they could be destroyed by incoming Soviet warheads is officially known as "launch under attack" (LUA) or "launch on warning" (LOW). In common debate, it is normally assumed that such policy is destabilizing—puts a "hair-trigger" on the balance of terror. After all, what if it was a mistake? What if your radar picked up a flock of geese or had some internal malfunction giving you false warning of an attack? Nonetheless, it is the simplest and most inexpensive way to close the window of vulnerability: simply to let the Russians know that *any* attempt at a disarming first strike will fail because our missile commanders will launch their weapons before they can be destroyed. (The option is of course always there whether we make it *policy* or not).

Keep in mind that our solid-fueled Minutemen have a particularly rapid acceleration rate which permits them to be fired at literally the last minute.

Spurgeon Keeny, Jr., and Wolfgang Panofsky describe the problems very well in an article in *Foreign Affairs*. A successful attack on U.S. Minuteman missiles would require at least 2,000 weapons of one-megaton size (if 2,000 weapons can be called a "limited" attack, then words have lost all meaning). It has been estimated that such an attack could kill up to 20 million Americans, and a minimum of 8 million to 10 million under all but the most optimistic assumptions. Death and destruction on such a scale have no equal in the American experience. It seems incredible that any Soviet leader could count on an American President suing for peace in circumstances in which some 10 million American citizens were dying. After all, the United States would still retain 75 percent of the strategic forces on submarines and surviving bombers and ICBMs as well as its entire economic base.*

Still, the new fears were real, and the principal actors since 1976—the Pentagon, the Congress, and the President,

---

*Spurgeon Keeny, Jr., and Wolfgang Panofsky, "MAD vs. NUTS," *Foreign Affairs*, Winter 1981–82, page 295.

in this case Carter and Reagan—responded with a new two-fold program: 1) a plan for expanding (modernizing) U.S. strategic nuclear weapons and delivery systems—cruise missiles, B-1s, and MX; and 2) a reemphasis on the concept of "flexible response." One of President Carter's last major defense policy decisions as President, in the summer of 1980, was to issue P.D. (Presidential Directive) #59. As U.S. strategic doctrine, P.D. #59 was designed to take advantage of a new nuclear warhead, the Mark 12A, which is carried on the Minuteman and is proposed for the MX. The Mark 12A is the most accurate warhead we have ever had. With it we can now reasonably expect to hit a Soviet command bunker or missile silo 6,000 miles away, matching what we assume to be a Soviet capability. The idea here is not new. It is intended to enhance deterrence by giving the Commander-in-Chief options between all-out thermonuclear war or nothing. What if, for example, the Russians were to use nuclear weapons somewhere in the world? Would the President launch a total retaliatory strike? Without "flexible response" capability, that is his only choice. With "flexible response," it becomes possible to retaliate in a tit-for-tat mode. This is called the "countervailing strategy." The objective is to convince the Russians that they will be successfully opposed at any level of aggression they choose.*

counter-
vailing
strategy

We have met this doctrine before. Gerald Ford's Secretary of Defense, James Schlesinger, argued during Ford's administration that we should have the capability to "exchange warheads" with the Soviet Union on a limited, controlled basis. And Robert McNamara, as we have seen, toyed with similar notions. The United States has had the capacity to strike Soviet military targets for almost as long as we have had nuclear weapons. These new doctrinal excursions represent more than anything else attempts to give nuclear weapons some diplomatic clout; to make nuclear weapons appear usable and therefore make threats believable again, as they had been in the late 1940s and early 1950s, when our nuclear monopoly was unchallenged.

"surgical
nuclear
strike"

The problem is that no one has yet devised a believ-

---

*Harold Brown, 1982 DOD *Annual Report,* page 40.

able scenario for a limited thermonuclear war between the United States and the Soviet Union. As Khrushchev said during the Cuban missile crisis, "The knot is drawn too tight." Once hydrogen bombs—even one—start landing on native soil, the enormity of the damage and the old human tradition of an eye for an eye add up to certain escalating retaliation.

Perhaps more important than these intellectual gyrations are our new programs for modernizing and expanding U.S. nuclear forces. Along with P.D. #59, President Carter decided to build an elaborate system of shelters, the MX multiple protective shelter basing mode, to protect U.S. land-based missiles from Soviet attack, and at the same time to provide the United States with additional highly accurate missiles of its own. President Reagan, however, has scrapped the multiple protective shelter scheme and replaced it with several military programs, some new, some not so new. The Reagan plan would put a small number of MX missiles in existing Minuteman silos while continuing the search for other basing schemes (perhaps an air-mobile system, in which they would be kept in the air at all times on specially built airplanes). In addition he has revived, for the moment, the B-1 bomber and plans to build 100 of these very costly aircraft ($200–$300 million each). And the development of a new type of bomber, the Stealth, designed to elude Soviet defenses, has been accelerated. Finally, the Navy will develop a more accurate submarine-launched missile—the Trident II (or D-5, as it is officially known).

Though this program for modernizing U.S. strategic forces is meant to close the "window of vulnerability," it is still something of an enigma. During the 1980 election campaign, the President made much of the threat to our deterrent posed by new Soviet weapons. Yet the strategic programs he has decided upon do little to remedy the vulnerability problem, at least in the short run. The Reagan scheme depends on a number of as-yet-untested technologies on the one hand—the MX missile and the Stealth bomber—and another bomber, the B-1, which was rejected in 1977 by President Carter as already obsolete, on the other. The MX missile, with its ability to knock out Soviet missile silos, remains, but not the proposed protective basing scheme designed to protect it from a Soviet attack. We are left with enormous "capability" but much mutual vulnerability nonetheless.

The Reagan program illustrates nicely the dilemma inherent in nuclear weaponry. New technology produces new and ever more "capable" weapons. But despite much effort there are few ideas put forward, and fewer still that make much sense, and our attempts to devise new concepts come up time and time again against the same irreducible truths. However hard we try to extract some political or diplomatic mileage out of our nuclear arsenal, the result is the same. In war and politics, means and ends must balance; they must be suited to one another. But after each new round of weapons developments and each round of elaborate scenarios and revised doctrine, we return to the simple fact that nuclear weapons are a means without any appropriate ends. We always return to deterrence—weapons that exist only to ensure that the other's will not be used.

ASIDE

Some people feel that once a nation possesses an assured destruction capability, more weapons add nothing to security. Even Henry Kissinger when queried on the subject responded once, "What in the name of God is strategic superiority?" Admiral Rickover, upon his retirement, pointed out that one missile-carrying submarine carries enough thermonuclear warheads to devastate every Russian city of more than 100,000 population. One Poseidon-equipped submarine can fire 160 MIRVs that could kill perhaps 30 million Soviet citizens. From this point of view, the reality of thermonuclear weapons remains fixed: when you have enough, you have enough.

CONCLUSION

The problem is essentially the extent of one's grasp on reality. Reality is the weapons. Reality is that no nation can reasonably expect to fight a thermonuclear war against a comparably armed enemy, and win. To be sure, there will be survivors, and they, in inimitable human fashion, will somehow muddle on; but their world will be so radically different from ours as to make it literally unimaginable.

To make matters worse, there is no way to tell if deterrence is working. It's like the old joke about the clown who keeps snapping his fingers to keep the wild elephants away. Must work, he figures. No wild elephants around here. We'll never know for certain. But we will know all too well if deterrence fails.

5.

Weapons for Fighting "Conventional" Wars

THROUGHOUT HISTORY warriors have been guided by one fundamental goal: seek out, close with, and destroy the enemy. The achievement of this goal has always been simple in concept, requiring but two things: mobility or "maneuver" and firepower—mobility to close with the enemy, and firepower to destroy him. Even today virtually all weapons, no matter how complex or sophisticated, and most tactics for their use are nothing more than efforts to apply these two basic principles. Of course, some armies emphasize one more than the other. For many years the Israeli army has emphasized maneuver. Rather than slug it out with more numerous Arab armies, it has developed tactics designed to take advantage of what it does best—maneuver rapidly, surrounding and checkmating its opponents. The United States and the Russians, on the other hand, have emphasized firepower. (Some military reformers argue that we should emulate Israeli tactics of rapid maneuver and mobile warfare.)

The major technologies of the twentieth century have tremendously enhanced both maneuverability and firepower. The airplane, the internal combustion engine (and the many vehicles that grow out of that invention), and the missile have increased both the speed with which fighting men and military equipment can be moved, as well as the distances they can cover. We saw the beginnings of this when the railroad was introduced for military transport, increasing the speed of a foot soldier from 4 to 25 miles per hour or more, in addition to being able to bring enormous quantities of heavy equipment to the front. Today we have increased the soldiers' speed to 600 miles per hour, the fighter pilots' to 1,400 miles per hour (more on short sprints), and the speed of an unmanned weapon (such as a short-range ballistic missile) to as much as eight times the speed of sound. Helicopters further increase infantry maneuverability, making it possible to hop over obstacles and enemy strongpoints, to "vertically envelop"—to use the military's term—the enemy on the battlefield with even greater speed and effectiveness than paratroopers did in World War II.

The volume, accuracy, and increased destructiveness of modern firepower are literally incredible. Recall our story of the machine gun and how it created a "firepower doctrine" among the generals. Today every GI carries his own automatic rifle—the equivalent of a machine gun—and he can call also upon a wide variety of heavy machine guns, artillery (cannon), short-range precision-guided missiles, and even bombs dropped by aircraft circling over the battlefield. And airplanes and missiles can carry more firepower farther and faster and deliver it with greater precision than ever before.

Ships have always embodied both mobility and firepower. And while the speed of surface ships has not changed very much from World War II, firepower has very much increased with the development of ship-to-ship cruise missiles, which give small ships the capability to sink large ones. Once upon a time the size of a ship determined the volume of firepower it could deliver. The bigger the ship, the heavier the guns—and the more of them—it could mount. Large ships usually were also more heavily armored and able to absorb a lot of damage. That's why the battleship in the pre-World War II period was considered such a potent weapon. But today, with precision-guided cruise missiles, the relationship between size and firepower is disappearing (although bigger ships can still absorb greater damage without sinking).

Range has also increased in the new Navy. As we noted, aircraft flying from aircraft carriers extended the range at which ships could deliver firepower several hundred miles. Today even small ships can deliver firepower farther than World War II battleships could. The largest World War II naval guns could hurl a 16- or 18-inch (in diameter) shell, weighing perhaps a ton, some 20 miles. The anti-ship cruise missiles of today have ranges of from 50 to 300 miles and the ability to follow their target even as it tries to evade. Because of the tremendous capabilities of these weapons, the challenge for the Navy today is to find ways to defend against them. These means include radar-directed, computer-assisted, rapid-fire guns, air-defense missiles, as well as electronic and other countermeasures to confuse the attacking cruise missiles' guidance systems.

The term "conventional" is used in today's military to mean non-nuclear. But many of the nominally non-nuclear systems that we describe can also deliver nuclear warheads with minimum changes to the basic delivery system. A soldier needs five minutes to substitute a nuclear "shell" for a high-explosive one in the two most common types of conventional artillery. (Getting permission from Washington—which would, of course, be required—takes a good deal longer than making the adaptation.) The nuclear shells are stored, to be sure, in central facilities and are closely guarded and under the control of high-ranking military officers. Moreover, they incorporate electronic devices called "permissive action links" (PALS) which require special codes and/or keys to be activated. Warships carry nuclear depth charges and rocket-assisted torpedoes for attacking submarines, as well as high-explosive versions of the same weapons.

The point is that nuclear warheads, weapons, and bombs are fully integrated into what are nominally conventional arms. Of course, we can fight a purely conventional war, as we did in Vietnam; but the nuclear capability is always there, available to be used, and our enemies know that. (Soviet conventional forces are the same, quickly adaptable to nuclear shells, bombs, and missiles.) This is especially true of our forces in Europe. In the event of a Soviet attack they would attempt to stop that attack using non-nuclear weapons, but could turn to nuclear warheads of many different kinds as a "last resort," if they were unable to stop the onslaught by conventional means. U.S. war planners' objectives—even if such nuclear weapons were used—would be to contain the war and bring it to an end at the lowest level of violence. That is, to prevent escalation to all-out nuclear war. The danger, of course, is that once the nuclear threshold is crossed, no one knows if escalation could be contained (see Chapter Seven for more on this).

FIREPOWER

For the individual soldier the first and most readily available sources of firepower are the weapons he is able to carry: his rifle (the most important one), ammunition, hand grenades (which are small bombs), and grenade launchers (similar to what the police use to fire tear-gas shells).

THE M-16 RIFLE

For American soldiers today the M-16 rifle (the *M* stands simply for model) is the basic infantry weapon.

ASIDE

The M-16 is a comparatively small-bore weapon (at 5.56 mm) compared to the .30 caliber (approximately 7.62 mm) of the M-1 Garand rifle, which was standard during World War II and the Korean War. The M-16 is gas-operated, meaning that the hot gases produced by the explosion of the powder in the cartridge are used to operate a mechanism which extracts the spent cartridge from the chamber and puts a new one in its place. This means the rifle can be fired semi-automatically (as fast as you can pull the trigger, with one shot for each pull), or automatically, like a machine gun, firing as long as the trigger is depressed or until it runs out of ammunition or burns out its barrel. When fired automatically, the M-16 can fire at a rate of 650–850 rounds per minute (the latest model is limited to three-shot bursts, in the interest of conserving ammunition). Yet it weighs little more than eight pounds, is 39 inches long, and can use either a 20- or 30-shot magazine (ammunition container).

The M-16 rifle was a controversial item even before it entered service, although it is difficult to imagine that something as simple as a rifle could give rise to so complex a

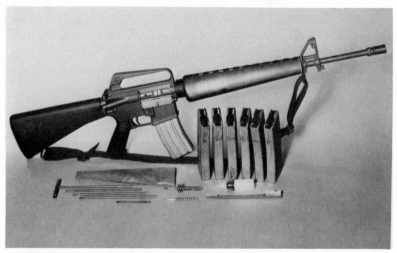

M-16 rifle. (U.S. Army photo)

debate. Designed and developed privately by weapons designer Eugene Stoner (who called it the Armalite, or AR-15, after the company that first produced it), it was resisted by the Army for many years because it failed to meet certain Army specifications. (James Fallows in *National Defense* devotes half of a chapter to this debate.) Nevertheless, it was found to be effective and reliable in repeated tests. More importantly, troops in Vietnam found it so superior—the Air Force had previously adopted it for its own security forces— that individual soldiers were willing to spend their own money to get one to replace their Army-issue M-14.

Eventually, an Army version of Stoner's design, the M-16, was made available in Vietnam, thanks to the personal intervention of General William Westmoreland and Robert
AR-15 McNamara, Secretary of Defense. But while the AR-15 was found to be extremely reliable (that is, it didn't jam while in use), the M-16 frequently malfunctioned. Numerous complaints by troops led to a Congressional investigation of the rifle. The Army insisted (and still does) that the M-16's problems were due to poor training and maintenance. James Fallows blames the Army's weapons designers, who, largely for bureaucratic reasons, insisted on modifying the weapon and on using a different ammunition from that for which Stoner had designed the gun.*

* James Fallows, *National Defense* (New York: Random House, 1981), pages 88–89.

Today these problems have been largely corrected, and the M-16 continues to be the standard U.S. infantry weapon. It has also been sold extensively abroad and is being produced under license in other countries as well.

MODERN ARTILLERY

The infantryman's opponents are other soldiers (or groups of soldiers) similarly equipped, as well as enemy artillery, tanks, and aircraft. To extend his firepower beyond the range of his individual weapon and those of his comrades, a soldier can call upon a variety of different kinds of artillery (cannon). These vary from portable types, called mortars, that can be carried in two pieces to a location by a couple of men and which fire a small projectile a few miles, to long-range artillery which have to be towed by big trucks or are self-propelled on tank-like vehicles and can fire projectiles as much as 20 miles or more.

Cannon used to be very hard to aim properly, as we saw in our history of earlier periods. Today aiming is done in some instances in the same manner as guided missiles are aimed, namely by compact guidance systems. The Army's new Copperhead is a laser-guided shell fired from a 155-mm (about 6 inches) cannon, a pretty standard size. A forward observer on the ground or in a helicopter or spotter plane shines a laser beam on the target as one shines a flashlight in a darkened room. The Copperhead's guidance system detects the laser light reflected off the target and guides the shell to it at ranges from 2 to 17 miles away. Operated this way, the shell is accurate enough to hit a moving tank.

Copperhead

The accuracy of modern artillery is also being greatly enhanced by modern electronic technology. Targets such as enemy artillery can be located by radar and computers, which together can track a shell fired by the other side, calculate its point of origin, and provide the artillery crew with a target location. Artillerymen call this fire directed against other artillery "counterbattery fire."

Artillery accounted for more than half of all casualties in World War II, and today, against soldiers, artillery is four

Towed howitzer, 155 mm, M-198. (U.S. Army photo)

Self-propelled 8-inch howitzer. (U.S. Army photo)

times more lethal than it was then. It is without doubt the weapon infantrymen fear most.*

SURFACE-TO-SURFACE MISSILES

To deliver firepower at still longer ranges, say 45–75 miles away, missiles such as the Lance are available. These **Lance** are surface-to-surface missiles (similar to the long-range strategic missiles housed on submarines or in underground silos, but having much shorter ranges). Like the strategic variety, these are ballistic, meaning that they are preprogrammed to travel in a high-arching trajectory, as much as 140,000 feet high, and then come flying back only 75 miles away at three times the speed of sound. Even though the missile has not traveled out of the earth's atmosphere, from the foot soldier's point of view, psychologically and militarily, it has the same effect. The Lance can be equipped with either a nuclear or high-explosive warhead.

Lance missile and self-propelled launcher. (U.S. Army photo)

* Donald Vought and J.R. Angolia, "The U.S. Army," in *The U.S. War Machine,* ed. Ray Bonds (New York: Crown, 1978), page 80; also James Dunnigan, *How to Make War* (New York: William Morrow, 1982), page 70.

ASIDE———————————————————————————————

The Lance is about 20 feet long and weighs 2,800 pounds. It uses a storable liquid fuel. While production of the Lance ended in 1980, the Army plans to purchase 340 new nuclear warheads for these missiles between 1981 and 1983. These won't be "neutron" bombs, as the Army had intended, but they could be quickly convertible to that warhead. The reason for this change is the popular opposition to neutron bombs in Europe.

———————————————————————————————

For attacking targets still farther away, ground forces can call upon longer-range missiles such as the Pershing **Pershing II** (500-mile range), and eventually the newer Pershing IIs (1,000-mile range) and the ground-launched cruise missiles (1,500-mile range). Since they are part of a very intense current controversy, we treat both new weapons in some detail in Chapters Seven and Eight.

In the major wars that have been fought since World War II—in Korea, Vietnam, and the Middle East—artillery has been a key instrument of destruction. Vietnamese targets were hard to find in the jungles, so artillery was sometimes used for what is called "harassing and interdiction" fire. This involved shelling areas designated as "free-fire zones" and it sought to contain enemy forces on a somewhat random or scattershot basis. In the Middle East, Syrian artillery, for example, firing from the Golan Heights, damaged or destroyed Israeli settlements so effectively that one of the main military objectives of the Israeli offensive in the 1967 war was to seize the Golan Heights. And it is also one reason the Israelis are so unwilling to give it up. In the case of the Golan Heights shelling, long-range missiles were not needed. The targets were but 20 miles away. Some short-range missiles, however, of Soviet design were fired at Israeli cities from Egypt during the 1973 Middle East war, also for harassing purposes. But in that war the Egyptians used a massive artillery barrage in support of their Suez Canal crossing operation against fixed Israeli fortifications (called the Bar-Lev line) on the Sinai side of the Suez Canal. And Israeli artillery took a heavy toll of Egyptian attackers. But even though the Israeli emplacements were heavily protected by sandbags and protective earthworks, the shelling caused considerable destruction and sufficient disorganization to make reinforcement of their positions costly and difficult for the Israeli army. Many of the soldiers manning these positions were eventually captured by the Egyptians.

The Soviets have always looked to massed artillery to provide a large part of the firepower that would be needed by their ground troops, and they have built large numbers of comparable weapons. Soviet and Warsaw Pact forces in Europe are equipped with more than 9,900 pieces of artillery (NATO has about 9,500) and more than 26,000 tanks.*

TANKS

In the event of war the Soviets would use their tanks quickly to slash through NATO defenses and advance deep into Europe. Some analysts fear that given their number of tanks, they could reach the English Channel before NATO could get its act together. Others, noting the unreliability of Soviet tank engines, doubt that they could move so far so quickly.

Tanks represent not only enormous firepower but a way of greatly increasing maneuverability in war. As we noted earlier, the tank was developed as a way of countering the machine gun, and insofar as it embodies both mobility and firepower in one vehicle, it is a potent weapon on the battlefield. Armored warfare was an important part of World War II. But since then it has taken on a new look in the hands of the Israelis, who have perfected the tactics of rapid maneuver using tanks. The Israelis rely on the maneuverability of their armored forces and on the initiative of their tank commanders. In the 1973 war, for example, in a daring operation they used a tank force to cut through a gap between two Egyptian armies. They were able to move behind the Egyptians' positions, cutting off their sources of supply and destroying their air defense missiles. The maneuver surrounded the Egyptian 6th Army and essentially left them naked to air attack. The Sinai desert is particularly well

---

*International Institute for Strategic Studies, *The Military Balance* (London) 1981–82, page 124.

suited to this kind of warfare, owing to its open spaces, but northern Europe with open plains is good tank country, too.

The tank, as this maneuver shows, has taken over the military role that cavalry (mounted) units performed in the past. In fact, tank units are sometimes called armored cavalry in today's armies, and the insignia worn today by American tankers have taken the old cavalry insignia of two crossed sabers (the curved swords used by cavalry) and superimposed a tank profile on them. General George Patton, one of the greatest American tank commanders, believed that a tank's greatest asset is its tracks, i.e., the means by which it moves.

In the American Army, the M-60 main battle tank is the mainstay, having been in service, with various modifications and improvements, since 1960. Each M-60 (the A-1 model) **M-60** weighs 53 tons, carries a crew of four—commander, driver, gunner, and loader—and is equipped with a 105-mm cannon and two auxiliary machine guns. It is powered by a conventional diesel engine. While tank guns are cannon, they are different from the cannon we have been describing in that they fire shells at higher velocity and with a flatter trajectory than artillery, and are particularly designed to destroy other tanks.

M-60A1 tank. (U.S. Army photo)

To increase the accuracy of their guns, the newer M-60s have been equipped with laser range finders, computer fire-control systems, and thermal night sights.

ASIDE————————————————————————————————————

More than 10,000 M-60s have been built by the Chrysler Corporation over the years, 7,000 of which are in current service. The 1982 price of each M-60 is about $1.2 million.

———————————————————————————————————————

While the M-60 was a major contributor to the Israeli victory in the 1973 Yom Kippur War against the Soviet-built T-62 tank, which formed the bulk of the Syrian and Egyptian tank forces, since that war the Syrians have acquired a newer and more powerful Soviet-built tank, the T-72.* In response the Israelis have built a new tank of their own design called Merkava, or "Chariot." The U.S. Army has also ordered a new tank, called the M-1 Abrams, named for the M-1

M-1 tank. (U.S. Army photo)

————————————————————————————————————

*The M-60 proved superior by far in gun range, accuracy, and shell penetration; and in the hands of the talented Israeli tank commanders permitted the Israelis to destroy more than half the Syrian tanks. (Lawrence Whetten and Michael Johnson, "Military Lessons of the Yom Kippur War," in *The World Today*, March 1974, page 108.)

late General Creighton W. Abrams, who was a protégé of General George Patton, the great tank commander of World War II. It has been under development for ten years, but only recently (1981) entered limited production. Also built by Chrysler, the Abrams weighs 61 tons (compared to the M-60's 53 tons) and incorporates a number of innovations designed to enable it to defeat any existing Soviet tank.

One improvement is in its armor. It has a superior layered armor, developed by the British to withstand the shaped charges we talked about in Chapter Two.* Shaped charges, you will recall, are designed particularly to destroy tanks by focusing the heat of the explosion on a very small point, creating a jet of molten metal that can melt its way through the heaviest armor. While the exact details of this armor are classified, we know that it employs layers of different materials, including ceramics, to defeat the purpose and effectiveness of the shaped charges, giving us another example of how a weapon creates a counterweapon which in turn creates a counter-counterweapon in the drive for military equipment superiority. While providing protection against shaped charges, the M-1's armor may be vulnerable to kinetic-energy shells, which use a slender and very heavy projectile to punch through tank armor.

In addition to having this new armor, the M-1 Abrams is equipped with sensitive night sight, which by translating heat emitted by an enemy tank into a visible image permits the gunner to aim its 105-mm main gun and hit another tank in complete darkness as far away as 2,000 yards (more than a mile). It also features a sophisticated, computerized fire-control system that allows the tank to fire accurately while on the move.

ASIDE————————————————————————————

The Army is planning to purchase 720 M-1s in 1982, and a total of 7,000 over the next few years, at a cost of about $2.6 million per tank, or more than twice the cost of the M-60 (*The Washington Post,* January 6, 1982, page A-21).

———————————————————————————————————————

*Christopher Foss, "U.S. Ground Forces Weapons," in Bonds, *op. cit.*, page 88.

Its high cost and sophistication have led to considerable criticism; also, the fact that it has an airplane-type turbine engine (instead of a diesel engine) has been a point of contention. While permitting faster speeds (more than 40 miles per hour on roads and more than 30 miles per hour on rough terrain, in comparison to a 30-mile-per-hour maximum for the M-60), the engine is subject to frequent breakdowns. According to a General Accounting Office (GAO) report, the tank can average only about 48 miles before the engine needs essential maintenance and 43 miles before the transmission has to be gone over.* Moreover, its very hot exhaust makes the M-1 vulnerable to heat-seeking missiles (see below). It appears that unless these problems can be fixed, the prospects for the tank in battle may not be as glowing as its appearance and other features might lead one to believe.

Another problem is the amount of fuel required by tanks. Weapons procurement choices entail all sorts of consequences, some unanticipated. The decision to produce the M-1 has meant that the Army will have to buy additional fuel trucks to supply the M-1's thirsty new engines (it uses almost 4 gallons of fuel for every mile it travels), and these could cost more than $60 million. Also costly and unanticipated is the need to purchase still another support vehicle (called derisively in the press the "M-1's butler") to dig holes for the M-1. When tanks fight from fixed defensive positions, they usually dig in behind piles of earth. These are not quite foxholes, but the idea is the same. In the past, tanks could be equipped with bulldozer blades to do the digging, but the M-1's engine and transmission are not up to the strains of the job; they are too delicate. So the Army now wants to buy an armored combat earthmover (ACE) to dig ACE holes for the M-1. And these fancy bulldozers will cost more than $1 million each for the 600 that the Army claims it will need.†

Soviet tanks, like so many of their other weapons, are Soviet tanks rugged, in some ways even crude, and robust. They have a lower silhouette, which means they are somewhat harder to hit. This also makes them more cramped and uncomfortable

*GAO Report, MASAD, 82–87, December 15, 1981; quoted in *The Washington Post,* January 6, 1982, page A21.
†*The Washington Post,* February 9, 1982, page A1.

inside. Because of this, it was said that the ideal Soviet tank crewman is a left-handed midget (he must be left-handed because in at least one model the loader must use his left hand to load the gun). Indeed, they do recruit especially small men for their tank crews. The latest-model Soviet tanks, the T-72 and T-80, have substituted a balky and unreliable automatic loader for the fourth crewman, and they may also be subject to even more frequent breakdowns than the M-1. It was also found in the 1973 Yom Kippur War that their tank guns could not be depressed enough to allow them to fire over hills and sand dunes. The Israelis, using American and British tanks, found they could park on the back side of a hill, in defilade, and depress their guns to fire at targets on the other side. With Soviet equipment the Arabs had to get on top of the hill to shoot, exposing themselves to Israeli fire in the process.

Another significant difference between Soviet and American tank design is that where we have four-man crews— driver, loader, gunner, and tank commander—they have but three, with the result that fewer men have more work, especially vital maintenance.* Smaller crews mean that the So-

Soviet T-72 tank. (Department of Defense photo)

*Dunnigan, *op. cit.*, pages 56, 63.

viet tanks can be smaller, but if their automatic loaders break down they are in serious trouble. Battles are often won or lost on the basis of such differences.

ANTITANK WEAPONS

Just as the tank was designed to counter the machine gun, antitank weapons are another major category of conventional arms designed to counter the tank. Of course, the tank is still thought to be the best available means for defeating another tank. (The Israelis destroyed 10 Syrian tanks for every one of theirs lost in 1973.*) But new weapons have been created which enable infantrymen to attack them with greater effectiveness than in the past. The TOW antitank   **TOW** missile (the letters stand for tube-launched, optically tracked [meaning a human eye tracks the missile], wire-guided) is a little too heavy for one soldier to carry, but several soldiers can move it to a location and mount and fire it from a tripod. It can be mounted on a Jeep or other vehicle, or even on a helicopter for increased mobility, but the point is that one soldier standing on the ground while optically tracking the missile can destroy a tank.

ASIDE——————————————————————————————————

Here's how it works: After the missile leaves the launcher, guidance fins unfold and the optical tracker on the launcher picks up an infrared (heat) source on the missile's tail. The strength of the TOW is its accuracy. The guidance unit on the launcher can pick up any deviation in the missile's flight path and automatically issue correction commands via hair-thin wires to the missile while it is in flight. So long as the gunner keeps the cross hairs of the optical sight on the target, he can score a hit (*Army Green Book*, 1980–81, Association of the United States Army, page 42).

———————————————————————————————————————

To follow a TOW missile to its target, which is necessary with optical tracking, a soldier firing the missile will have to expose himself for as much as 20 seconds to enemy fire. In open country this would be a serious problem.† However, in

* *Ibid.*, page 48.
† Fallows, *op. cit.*, page 23.

The U.S. Marine Corps test firing the TOW missile. (U.S. Marine Corps photo)

Europe, TOWs are expected to be fired from prepared defensive positions or from inside armored vehicles.

In the first two days of the 1973 Yom Kippur War, the Egyptians destroyed or disabled many Israeli tanks with a Soviet wire-guided antitank missile called the Sagger, similar to but not as good as the TOW. (Parts of the battlefield looked as if they had been attacked by giant spiders because they were covered with webs of guidance wires left behind by these missiles.) Later in the war, however, the Israelis developed tactics (mainly the use of machine-gun fire from tanks) that rendered the Saggers relatively ineffective. Nevertheless, the initial successes of these missiles sparked an intense debate everywhere over the future of the tank. Since the German Blitzkrieg of World War II, the tank has been the dominant offensive weapon on land. But after 1973 it appeared to some as if cheap, precision-guided missiles might make the tank obsolete and return the advantage to the defense. To counter the new antitank missiles, designers began an intensive search for new and improved tank armor (just as gunpowder caused mounted knights to increase the weight of their armor in the thirteenth and fourteenth cen-

Sagger

turies)—hence the new composite-layered types of armor—while considering the development of smaller, more maneuverable tanks and armored vehicles. In addition, the Army set about devising new tactics to try to neutralize antitank missiles of this type.

One effective means of countering wire-guided antitank missiles is to use smoke screens, because if the gunner can't see a target, he can't hit it with an optically guided weapon. Another important method for countering such missiles is to operate tanks in association with both infantry and artillery—what is called by the military the "combined arms team." Infantry can locate and destroy other infantrymen equipped with antitank missiles more effectively than can tanks. Artillery can also help protect tanks by firing on areas occupied by infantrymen with antitank missiles, making things "too hot" for infantrymen effectively to fire their missiles. And finally tanks can use their machine guns to kill infantry armed with antitank missiles.

As tank design improves and new tactics are adopted to counter wire-guided missiles, the missiles themselves are improved and tactics are adopted to improve their effectiveness. The TOW has been improved with a new warhead and night sight and mounted on armored vehicles so that gunners need not expose themselves to enemy fire. The advantage today may still lie with the tank, but its dominance has been shaken. NATO would use tens of thousands of antitank missiles, fired from aircraft and helicopters as well as from ground positions, to try to stop a Soviet attack on western Europe. The Soviet advantage in numbers of tanks is not so great that they could be certain of penetrating the wall of missiles and other antitank weapons they would surely encounter. One thing the 1973 Middle East war (and the 1982 war over the Falklands) made quite clear is that in any future war immense quantities of very costly equipment on both sides will be lost.

A-10

Another way to counter tanks, of course, and possibly the best way, is from the air. Firing from the air is traditionally, and by agreement among the services an Air Force function. Indeed, one of the several "missions" of the Air Force is to provide "close air support" for troops battling on the ground. The fact is that for many years the Air Force gave this mission rather short shrift. What ground troops need is air support just ahead of their positions, and until the Air Force developed the A-10 airplane, front-line air support was being provided by airplanes that had not been specifically designed for that purpose. Beginning in the mid-1960s, the Air Force began to study the problem and eventually designed a new plane for the express purpose of providing close support to ground troops.

The A-10 came out of the ground troops' need for close support in the Vietnam War, but the first prototype did not fly until 1972, and it played no role in that war. However, it is now available for any conventional war that might be fought in the future. The plane is designed to drop bombs and fire missiles while flying slowly and not very high over the battlefield. Specifically, the A-10 is now envisioned as engaging Warsaw Pact tanks in a war in Europe in what is called Battle-of-the-Bulge type weather, meaning low clouds, little visibility. The aircraft is specialized for destroying Russian tanks and for this purpose has a powerful 30-mm automatic cannon mounted in the front of the plane. To get the gun into the very center of the plane (for more accurate fire), the plane's nose and landing gear has had to be built off to one side. It is so funny-looking as a result of all these Warthog   design peculiarities that pilots have dubbed it the Warthog.

The plane can carry two dozen 500-pound bombs in addition to its gun and can fly comfortably at the slow speed of 300–500 miles per hour. Since it flies so slowly, it has to be able to survive a lot of ground fire; and to protect the pilot, a kind of "bathtub" made of very strong titanium armor has been built in which the pilot sits. The fuel tanks are filled with a fire-suppressing foam, and its twin engines are mounted on the tail sufficiently separated so that a hit on one will not necessarily knock out the other. In essence, it is a flying tank.

The Air Force plans to buy 733 of these planes (manufactured by Fairchild–Republic Company). The Air Force asked for $357 million in fiscal 1983 to buy 20 A-10s (about $18 million each).

smart   Among the weapons that the A-10 can fire are so-called
bombs   smart bombs and the Maverick missile. During the Vietnam

Two A-10s in flight.

2,000-pound laser-guided smart bomb. (U.S. Air Force photo)

War the Air Force was frustrated by its inability to destroy difficult targets, such as bridges, unless many flights of many aircraft were sent out. The fact is that it is not easy to drop a bomb exactly on a target, especially a small one, when a plane is flying at 500–600 miles per hour and dodging anti-aircraft fire from guns and missiles at the same time. Therefore, Texas Instruments, Incorporated, developed an inexpensive laser guidance system that could be strapped onto a standard gravity bomb, making it a very effective guided missile.

What happens is this: A laser designator, either on the ground or in the aircraft, shines on the target. The "seeker" within the bomb homes in on the laser light reflected from the target. Unpowered, the bomb simply glides toward its target, guided by its fins, which in turn are activated by the guidance unit.

Maverick   Another weapon that such aircraft can carry nowadays is the Maverick, a precision-guided air-to-ground missile designed to destroy tanks, bunkers, and other small protected targets. Early versions of the Maverick carried a television camera in the missile's nose and were limited to daylight use. These were used extensively in Vietnam, and during the 1973 Yom Kippur War the Israelis used them, too. Later versions employ a laser guidance system (like the smart bomb), which makes them effective at night or in smoky and hazy conditions. The Maverick has a range of about 14 miles and carries a 140-pound high-explosive, non-nuclear warhead. A still more sophisticated version, the infrared-imaging Maverick, has so far been an expensive failure.

More than 28,000 Mavericks have been manufactured.

During the Vietnam War, before the A-10 was available, the helicopter was found to be effective in performing some of the functions that the A-10 was later designed to do. But the helicopter has advanced our Army's maneuverability as much as, or more than, it has contributed to firepower, so we will talk about it a little later on.

Armament specialist checks AGM-65A Maverick missile before loading it on an F-4 aircraft for a mission. (U.S. Air Force photo)

BOMBS

Bombs that are not smart are still pretty lethal. These are referred to as "iron bombs," or "dumb bombs," and are in essence modifications and improvements on the high-explosive bombs we had before Hiroshima. So drastically did the introduction of nuclear bombs change thinking about war that all non-nuclear weapons immediately became "conventional." The catchall phrase "conventional weapons," however, blurs the many distinctions and variety in types of conventional munitions.

Unlike strategic weapons, conventional bombs and warheads do not share a common explosive. Moreover, they may be designed to do a specialized task, or to perform more generalized functions. Some pierce tank armor; some (called fuel-air explosives) produce a powerful blast that is used to flatten trees and other vegetation to create landing zones for helicopters (as in Vietnam) or to kill troops in deep bunkers by concussion, and, incidentally, to kill or incapacitate any troops who happen to be near the blast. Other kinds of bombs contain lots of smaller "bomblets" that are dispersed over a wide area and spread shrapnel even farther. White phosphorous bombs are used to illuminate targets; napalm bombs to start fires and suffocate dug-in soldiers; and if and when nerve gas is ever used, it could be delivered by still another variety of bomb.

Still, the most numerous bombs in our arsenal are called general-purpose bombs; they consist of high explosives that detonate on impact.

MOBILITY AND MANEUVER

"Mobility" in the military refers to a number of different kinds of missions: carrying troops from the United States to potential war zones, and in battle ferrying them from place to place within a war zone, and allowing them to move rapidly, in association with tanks, for example.

The "miracle" of World War II, in addition to our rapidly mobilized industrial capability, was our country's ability to get millions of soldiers and millions of tons of equipment overseas. To do this we used ships almost exclusively. And in a conventional war in Europe, the Middle East, Africa, or the Far East, we would still have to rely on ships to move heavy equipment long distances. However, we now have very large air transports, notably the C-5A, and others which can move war matériel far more quickly than ships.

CARGO PLANES

C-141 Starlifter

One of the most successful long-range transport designs has been the C-141 Starlifter, made by Lockheed. This plane carried many American troops to Vietnam and home again. It can fly 154 troops or 70,000 pounds of cargo up to 6,000 miles without refueling. The Air Force began purchasing C-141s in 1965 and eventually bought 284 planes. (A program to stretch their length, therewith increasing the cargo capacity of the planes currently in service, was completed in mid-1982.)

As the Army's equipment got bigger and bigger, another cargo plane, the C-5A, was needed to carry outsized equipment such as tanks, and even more soldiers and tonnage.

USAF C-5A in flight. (U.S. Air Force photo)

However large the C-141, it just wasn't big enough for some purposes.

The C-5A transport was one of the most controversial—some say scandalous—weapons procured in the past decade. Called the Galaxy by its manufacturer, the Lockheed Corporation, the plane is similar to a C-141 in appearance and function but much larger, in fact, one of the largest airplanes ever built. To see one parked at an airport next to the largest civilian or commercial plane is to feel its enormous girth. *Newsweek,* at the time of its purchase, dubbed it "Moby Jet."

C-5A
(Galaxy)

"The Galaxy," writes author Berkeley Rice, "is not merely huge, only 18 yards shorter than a football field, it has a 223-foot wing span and a tail six stories high. Its four 16-foot, 70,000-pound turbofan jet engines are twice as powerful as any in existence and could furnish electricity for a city of 50,000 people. Its cavernous fuselage can swallow 14 jet fighters, 50 Cadillacs, or any 250,000-pound assortment of tanks, helicopters, cannons, trucks or other equipment."*

The C-5A's size was matched by its cost. The price of the entire plane rose from the 1965 contract estimate of $20 million apiece to nearly $60 million, and brought the cost of the total program from an original price estimate of $3 billion for 115 planes to somewhere about $5 billion for only 81. Moreover, a provision in the original contract committed the Air Force to pay higher prices on subsequent deliveries because of the cost overrun on the first batch of planes. Indeed, because of the complexity of the contract, no one really knows, despite numerous cost studies, what the C-5A finally did cost.

ASIDE——————————————————————————————

Despite its massive size, the plane climbs quickly and is capable of reaching speeds of over 600 miles per hour. It can land, unload its cargo, and take off again on a 4,000-foot dirt runway (a Boeing 707 needs 10,000 feet); this, in weather conditions that would shut down civilian airports. Supposedly the C-5A can operate at temperatures ranging from an arctic

*Berkeley Rice, *The C-5A Scandal* (Boston: Houghton Mifflin Company, 1971), pages 1 and 2.

65 degrees below zero to the steaming 120-degree heat of Southeast Asia. A built-in "malfunction detector" is supposed to monitor electronically 600 test points, locate any troubles, and print out repair instructions.

What makes the C-5A particularly useful in far-off places is that the pilot can land it on unpaved runways and in an emergency bring the plane to a halt in only 500 yards, much less than normal stopping distance. It can "kneel"—that is, lower itself nearly three feet for loading and unloading so vehicles can drive up or down its built-in ramps.

The nose of the plane swings up on hinges so that cargo can be removed at both ends at the same time, cutting normal load/unload time in half.

ASIDE————————————————————————————

Load/unload time is extremely critical in forward battle zones such as Vietnam. If a plane stays on an airstrip—however well defended—for too long it becomes vulnerable to enemy ground fire.

The C-5A was conceived in 1962 as a means of permitting the United States to deploy fully equipped forces around the world on a day's notice. It was felt at that time that if we could send troops from the continental United States that quickly, we would not have to station so many troops and so much equipment in foreign countries, giving us, on balance, a cost-saving. In addition, it would have given us the "flexible response" capability the Kennedy-McNamara team wanted us to have at that time. (See Chapter Four for a discussion of flexible response.)

Just 12 such airplanes could have handled the entire Berlin airlift, which required 224 planes in 1948. A fleet of 100 C-5As could transport 15,000 combat troops and their equipment from the United States to Europe in twenty-four hours. As one Defense Department official noted, "This will mean that an Army division in Kansas is just as much on the front line as one in Germany."* It came to be thought of not just as the world's largest airplane, but as a kind of total defense system—a mobile military base.

*Rice, *op. cit.*, pages 3–5.

Indeed, the C-5As (and the C-141s) played a major role carrying supplies to Israel during and shortly after the 1973 Israeli Yom Kippur War. More than 22,000 tons of matériel, including 29 tanks, were shipped in just the two months of October and November 1973.

In early 1982 the C-5A was again at the center of controversy. Analyzing its long-range transport options, the Air Force decided that it now wants a new transport plane, the C-17, to be built by McDonnell Douglas in St. Louis. Yet the Administration has ordered a new Lockheed contract for about 45 modernized C-5As (called the C-5B).   **C-5B**

Once soldiers are delivered to the place where they are supposed to fight, they are still dependent on ground transport to move them around. During World War II most of the infantryman's mobility came from his feet. Soldiers marched across Europe much as the Roman legions had two thousand years before. Who can forget Bill Mauldin's immortalization of Willie and Joe, two GIs, ragged, unshaven, and always complaining about their sore feet. They epitomized the foot soldier of that era. Jeeps and trucks provided some mobility then and now, but most GIs did more walking than they cared to.

Korea didn't change this pattern all that much. In Korea we were basically still using World War II technology. In Vietnam infantrymen still had to walk, but significantly less so than in the past, helicopters providing much mobility. Today's foot soldier is more likely to ride into battle and in armored carriers designed to protect him from enemy fire, likely to be far more dense and lethal than during World War II.

ARMORED VEHICLES

World War II made the Jeep a part of the modern Army. It was ubiquitous, reliable, cheap to build, but it wasn't armored. The M-113 armored personnel carrier is about as common today as the Jeep was then. Essentially a metal box, the M-113 is designed to carry eleven fully equipped soldiers   **M-113** and a two-man crew into battle, providing protection from small-arms fire. Its simplicity of design and its versatility have made it one of the most popular vehicles of its type in

M-113 armored personnel carrier. (U.S. Army photo)

The M-2 Bradley infantry fighting vehicle (IFV). (Department of Defense photo)

the world. Its principal flaw is that its aluminum armor is vulnerable to shaped charges.

The Israeli army, which uses the M-113 in large numbers, has affectionately dubbed it Zelda. Some 70,000 M-113s have been produced by the FMC Corporation and under license by the Italian firm of OTO Melara, since the M-113 was first introduced in the early 1960s and it is still being produced. The U.S. Army, our National Guard, and the Marine Corps have 35,000 of these vehicles in service, while more than 20,000 have been sold abroad. The M-113 can be found transporting military forces in more than forty countries at this time.

ASIDE

The M-113 comes in many variations: mobile command posts, cargo carriers, ambulances, missile-launcher carriers, mortar carriers, light tanks, armored recovery vehicles (tow trucks, to us), bulldozers, and bridge layers. More recently, M-113s have been equipped with launchers for TOW anti-tank missiles, thus giving them the ability to destroy main battle tanks as well.

Despite the M-113's long record of service with our own forces and those of other countries, the Army is ready for a new armored vehicle, and has spent twenty years designing one called the infantry fighting vehicle, which will weigh twice as much as the M-113, be eight times as expensive (nearly $2 million apiece), and still retain the vulnerable aluminum armor of the M-113. In place of machine guns, the new vehicle will be equipped with a turreted 25-mm automatic cannon, making it look like and be like a tank.

As in many other instances of high technology, for the price of one new vehicle the Army could buy eight improved models of the older M-113s.

There is an interesting pattern in the development of troop-carrying vehicles in recent times. What started out as a relatively simple and inexpensive armored personnel carrier has become in time something that looks like a light tank. In the same way the helicopter, which began in Vietnam primarily as a mode of getting troops over inhospitable terrain and in and out of the remote areas favored by the Viet Cong, became in time a gunship. The story of the helicopter's metamorphosis is worth telling, both because of the interplay between battle needs and weapons design and because with the attack helicopter the Army has got itself a fighting Air Force all its own.

HELICOPTERS

"The introduction of the combat helicopter," believes Army Chief of Staff General E. C. Meyer, "revolutionized warfare."* The helicopter was not originally designed to be a combat aircraft. It has neither long range nor high speed; it is not a bomber or a fighter. In the past, helicopters found their greatest military use (as anybody who has watched *M*A*S*H* knows) in evacuating wounded from battle zones and in rescuing downed pilots. (Recall Bill Holden and Mickey Rooney in *The Bridges of Toko-Ri.*) Indeed, its potential as a source of firepower was not anticipated at all, until almost by accident the Army came to rely on the helicopter for close air support in Vietnam.

The problem was that according to Pentagon regulations "close air support" is an Air Force function. As we noted in the discussion of the A-10, this mission was specifically assigned to the Air Force when it separated from the Army after World War II. But over the years the Air Force neglected its close-air-support obligations, and by the time of Vietnam there was no Air Force plane flying that could fully and effectively meet the needs of ground troops; that is, by dropping bombs on enemy strongpoints a few hundred yards ahead. The Air Force kept buying planes designed for what is called "interdiction": bombing bridges, railways, and truck convoys deep in the enemy's territory. But such planes fly too fast to be as effective as the Army would have liked.

During the Vietnam War the Army discovered that if it placed a few guns on the small transport planes used to supply isolated outposts, it could suppress enemy ground fire as the planes flew in. But when the Air Force found out about these guns, it made the Army remove them. It was an Air Force, not an Army, function, said the Air Force, to shoot from the air. In fact, Air Force people would routinely in-

* American Enterprise Institute, "Conversation with E. C. Meyer," January 27, 1981, page 7.

Top: *UH-1 Huey helicopter.* Bottom: *AH-1G Cobra attack helicopter.* (U.S. Army photos)

spect Army spotter planes to be sure that they carried only smoke rockets—for marking targets—and not weapons.

By the 1960s helicopter technology had advanced to the point at which the helicopter could become an effective weapons platform. The vehicle for this new application was the UH-1 helicopter, or the Huey, as it came to be called. **UH-1** Built by the Bell Helicopter Company, its turbine engines gave it power and speed not possessed by earlier helicopters. Although the Huey was originally procured for liaison and general utility flying (transport)—the *U* in "UH" stands for utility—the troops soon found other uses for it. At first, just a couple of machine guns were mounted in the doors, but as the Vietnam War intensified, rockets, grenade launchers, and more powerful machine guns were added. And so the helicopter gunship was born. Bell modified the basic Huey airframe from a ten-person transport to one that would accommodate just a pilot and a gunner, and more weapons. The helicopter was renamed the Cobra. With the Huey and **Cobra** the Cobra, Vietnam became the first helicopter war (see Francis Ford Coppola's *Apocalypse Now*) and the Army had gained its very own air force.

Still another use for the helicopter was to come. During the so-called Easter offensive in 1973, the North Vietnamese tried a surprise blitzkrieg type of assault across the demilitarized zone. The Army quickly gathered up some TOW missiles (see above)—still in the experimental stage—and hurriedly hung them on some helicopters. They fired about 85 missiles in this fashion and with them destroyed more than 60 North Vietnamese tanks and other vehicles. As a result the Easter offensive was stopped, and suddenly everyone realized that properly armed helicopters could crack a tank assault. (The new YAH-64 has been specifically designed to do just that. However, as have so many new weapons, it has been plagued by severe cost overruns.)

Despite the new importance of helicopters as fighting vehicles, their principal use still remains providing transport in general, and all the services (including the Air Force) now have them. The bigger ones—the kind used for the aborted Iranian rescue mission—can now carry 50–60 people or a substantial amount of heavy equipment. Another large helicopter on one occasion carried 147 refugees and their belongings in Vietnam, and was regularly used to pick up damaged aircraft.

FIGHTER AIRCRAFT

We have already seen that many weapons combine both firepower and mobility: the tank, the new armored personnel carrier, the helicopter—but none do so better than modern fighter aircraft.

American fighter planes today are the best in the world, but it was not always so. In World War I, Eddie Rickenbacker and the men of the Lafayette Escadrille flew French planes. At the beginning of World War II, our fighters were distinctly inferior to those of the British, Germans, and Japanese. They were too slow and unmaneuverable. True, P-40 Claire Chennault's Flying Tigers (P-40 Warhawks) were Warhawk able to hold their own against the Japanese over China in 1940, but they employed hit-and-run tactics against Japanese bomber formations. They didn't stick around to fight. A less successful design was the P-39 Aircobra, which was so bad that we gave them all to the Russians (who at that moment in their history were grateful for anything they

could get). And the P-38 Lightning, an expensive twin-engine fighter, proved ineffective in Europe. Fact is, the best
fighter we made in that era, the P-51 Mustang, was an inexpensive, company-funded development that was rejected by
the Army Air Corps and first bought by the British. The British found the design promising but its performance anemic,
so they substituted a more powerful engine for its original
American engine. The Rolls-Royce Merlin, the British engine, was later manufactured in America, and the P-51 made
history. Escorting our bombers, the P-51 cleared the skies of
German fighters and made possible the extensive bombing
of Germany in 1944 and 1945.

P-38
Lightning

P-51
Mustang

The original conception of the fighter plane was the pursuit ship—hence the *P* in P-40 and P-51. The objects of the
pursuit were enemy bombers, a relatively simple quarry because bombers were not particularly fast or maneuverable.
But experience quickly showed that the real problem was to
successfully engage the enemy fighter planes escorting the
bombers. And to penetrate the fighter screen, the attacking
planes and their pilots had to be better than their defenders.
Fighter planes, being maneuverable, are harder to hit. Indeed, those fighter planes that were most agile turned out to
be the ones that got through; our fighters, up to the beginning of World War II, were simply not maneuverable
enough.

What we did to compensate—apart from outproducing
our enemies during World War II—was to develop heavily
armed and armored fighter planes which, despite their lack
of agility, could outlast if not outperform the Germans and
Japanese. After the war in recognition of the change of role,
the Air Force, now an independent bureaucracy, changed
the "P" designation to "F" for fighter. The P-80 became the
F-80; the P-51, the F-51; and so on.

By the end of World War II, once we had swept most
enemy fighters from the sky, fighter planes began to earn
their keep by carrying bombs. Bomb racks were added under
the wings; gun sights were adjusted for dropping bombs or
shooting rockets; and pilot training syllabi were modified for
the additional bombing mission. The P-47 Thunderbolt (for
which the A-10 Thunderbolt II was named, in the tradition
of giving a new plane the name of an older, very successful
model that is no longer in the force) was perhaps the best
example of the new genre. It was such a large airplane that

P-47
Thunderbolt

RAF pilots would razz their American counterparts, saying if they got into a dogfight in the air, the Americans could undo their shoulder straps and run around in the cockpit to avoid incoming bullets. Yet it had such a powerful engine that several good-sized bombs could be mounted under the wings, and its lack of agility meant that it provided a good, stable platform for bombing; thus the birth of the fighter-bomber.

In Korea the all-around superiority of American planes and pilots was again demonstrated in a way that set a very high standard indeed for the subsequent performance of American planes and pilots. Our F-86 Sabre jets, which were as close to pure fighters as any American aircraft of the post-World War II era, succeeded in shooting down 14 Soviet-built North Korean MiG-15s for every one of our planes the Koreans were able to shoot down. Overall, U.S. planes shot down seven of theirs for every one of ours that was lost. This enviable success rate was the result of both the superior skill of U.S. pilots and the superiority of U.S. planes, especially their engines, fire-control systems—that is, gun aiming—and overall maneuverability.

F-86 Sabre jet

In the years after Korea, American fighters became heavier, somewhat less maneuverable, and less purely fighters. The fighter was evolving into the multipurpose fighter-bomber. The most successful and famous plane of this type was the F-4 Phantom II. The F-4 was originally designed as a high-altitude fleet air defense interceptor for the Navy, but it was so versatile that it was subsequently purchased by the Air Force. It was one of the planes that engaged Soviet-built

F-4 Phantom II

Right side view of an F-4G. (U.S. Air Force photo)

MiG-21s in Vietnam. The plane can be used as an interceptor to attack enemy bombers, as a fighter in air-to-air combat, and as a fighter-bomber to attack ground targets with bombs and missiles. Not only was it the workhorse in Vietnam, it has been in extensive combat in the Middle East with both the Iranian and Israeli air forces. It is now (since the mid to late 1970s) being gradually replaced in the Air Force by F-15s and F-16s and in the Navy by F-14s and F-18s (see below).

More than 5,000 F-4s in nearly twenty variations have been built by the McDonnell Douglas Corporation since the aircraft first flew in 1958. More than 1,600 of these have been sold abroad to about a dozen different nations, where the plane will doubtless remain in service for many years to come.

The plane is a two-seat (pilot and radar/weapons officer) twin-engine jet fighter-bomber capable of speeds in excess of 1,450 miles per hour, twice the speed of sound, or Mach 2.2.

ASIDE————————————————————————

The Mach number, named after Ernest Mach, a German scientist who studied aerodynamics, is the ratio of a certain speed to the speed of sound. Mach 1 is the speed of sound, about 715 miles per hour at sea level on a standard day (the speed of sound itself varies according to altitude and temperature; sound travels slower in less dense air). Mach 2, then, refers to twice the speed of sound; Mach 2.5 to two and one-half times the speed of sound; and so on. Airplanes designated as capable of flying at Mach 2.5, like the F-4, do not fly at those speeds very often or for very long, owing to the high rate of fuel consumed at these speeds (this is also why the Concorde supersonic airliner is not profitable). Another disadvantage of high speed capability is that the stress on the airframe is so great at those speeds that the airplane has to be especially designed to withstand it. This increases cost of production for what might be, given the infrequency of flying at top speeds, very little payoff in the end.

———————————————————————————————————

The Phantom can carry up to 16,000 pounds of bombs, almost as much as a World War II four-engine bomber could carry. It has a combat radius—the distance it can fly in a single mission and still return to base without refueling—of up to 1,000 miles, depending on the size of its weapons load, how fast it flies, and the altitude at which it flies.

The characteristics that made the F-4 so versatile and effective as a fighter-bomber made it less effective in dogfights against enemy aircraft. In Vietnam, when it came to aerial combat, the F-4 didn't perform quite as well against Soviet planes as had our Sabre jets in Korea. When we totted up the score during and after that war, it seemed as though American planes and pilots had lost much of the edge that they had demonstrated so convincingly in Korea. In Vietnam we managed only about a 2-to-1 superiority over the North Vietnamese, who for the most part flew Soviet-built MiG-21s, direct decendants of the MiG-15s we had faced in Korea. Now it may seem as though 2-to-1 superiority is a pretty good record; but when we remembered Korea, this ratio seemed tantamount to defeat, and sent U.S. military analysts scurrying around to find some explanations.

One reason we didn't do quite so well, our analysts concluded, was that we had neglected pilot training. Not that our pilots were untrained. Quite the contrary—their overall flying skills were still as good as ever. But what was needed was a different kind of training—more realistic, more like real aerial combat of the kind that might be encountered in a real war. In an effort to provide this kind of training, a series of special aerial-combat training programs called Top Gun and Red Flag have been instituted, in which U.S. pilots flying our best planes are pitted against other U.S. pilots flying planes meant to resemble Soviet aircraft and using Soviet-style tactics. Indeed, the so-called aggressor squadrons go to great lengths to simulate the Soviets. They study Soviet tactics, wear Soviet-style uniforms, and even have pictures of Lenin on the wall, and in all respects try to behave in the air as would the Soviets.

At the very end of the Vietnam War we were finding out that pilots who had been through this training were performing much better in aerial combat than those who had not. It is now a standard part of fighter-pilot training.

The improved training was one response to the less-than-outstanding combat record in Vietnam. Still more sophisticated fighter aircraft were the other. What we were seeking in the next generation of fighter planes was increased maneuverability and all-around dogfighting capability. Another consideration was what the Soviets had up their sleeves. We knew that the new MiG-23 was already flying, and we knew it was an improvement over older Soviet aircraft. It has the variable geometry (swing wings) and other features not found in the MiG-21. Still, we did not know how good it was going to be. As it turned out, the MiG-23—which first appeared in 1967, along with the MiG-25—is probably no better in capability than the Phantom. It smokes heavily, accelerates and turns no better than the old F-105 (which, you will recall, was called the Lead Sled), and carries a copy of our early-version Sidewinder missile.* But the Air Force wanted to maintain our edge, and the Soviets are now testing still newer planes. So we went ahead and built two extremely sophisticated planes, the F-15 and the F-16.

The resulting aircraft are probably the best of their kind in the world. Both have been designed to win dogfights with enemy fighters so as to gain and maintain air superiority over the battlefield. This is their primary mission. With some accessories, however, they can also carry conventional (and, in the case of the F-16, nuclear) bombs and missiles for attacking ground targets. This is their bomber mission. Thus, despite the initial intention to produce "pure" fighters, both planes have again evolved into multipurpose airplanes.

It was the proposal to sell these bomber accessories—bomb racks and extra fuel tanks—to Saudi Arabia in 1981 that made the Saudi arms deal so contentious in the U.S. Congress. We agreed to sell the Saudis 60 F-15s in 1978 with the express promise to the Congress (and indirectly to the Israelis) that we would not sell bomb racks and external fuel tanks to go with them. These accessories would of course have permitted the Saudis to use their F-15s as fighter-bombers as well as fighters, and the added fuel tanks would give the planes the additional range needed to carry those bombs as far as Israel. Hence the Israeli protest. The AWACS, which got more publicity during the congressional debate on the arms sale, is a flying radar station which was meant primarily to help the Saudis detect hostile aircraft approaching their territory. It has an offensive function as well, in terms of guiding fighter planes to their targets, and was therefore another source of Israeli concern. Despite the Israeli protest, the U.S. government sold the Saudis both the AWACS and the complementary equipment.

*Pierre Sprey, "What Quality vs. Quantity Issue?" Briefing memorandum, mimeographed, 1982.

F-15 Eagles. (U.S. Air Force photo)

Powered by two Pratt & Whitney F-100 engines, the F-15 has a top speed of Mach 2.5 and can fly as high as 100,000 feet (its "ceiling"), more than twice as high as commercial airliners. The ratio of power to weight—high power, relatively low weight—is what makes it so maneuverable as well as fast. As a result it is the most maneuverable plane in the world, and is capable of accelerating while flying straight up. Equipped with powerful radar, it is claimed, the F-15 can detect aircraft from as far as 100 miles away (although it must be remembered that at these distances the pilot cannot easily tell whether the aircraft are friendly or hostile). Armed with two kinds of air-to-air missiles and a 20-mm cannon, it is a formidable opponent. Besides, its large fuel capacity gives it a combat radius of up to 600 miles, and even farther with supplementary fuel tanks.

As well as to Saudi Arabia, we have sold the F-15 to Israel and Japan. The Israelis used the F-15's radar to great effect over Lebanon in 1982, and it helped them shoot down more than 80 Syrian planes. It is very popular with nations that can afford it.

Such high performance has its price. The U.S. government proposed to buy only 42 F-15s in 1983, each costing a little more than $38 million. Plans call for the eventual purchase of more than 700 of these aircraft, but even that—

because of price—may change. During the 1970s the Air Force began to recognize that the cost of the F-15 would make it difficult to purchase very many, and so it requested that a second fighter—simpler, less capable, and less expensive—be procured. That was the origin of the F-16. A combination of both aircraft is supposed to give the Air Force what is known as a "high-low mix," that is, a mixture of high performance, high-cost weaponry, and weapons of somewhat lesser capability. Indeed, the Air Force anticipates purchasing about 1,400 F-16s. In the 1983 budget request, 120 F-16s will cost more than $16 million each, as against some 700 F-15s at a bulk rate cost of $30 million each (or almost twice as much).

The main difference between the F-15 and the F-16 is   F-16
that the F-16 is lighter, smaller, does not have long-range radar, and has only one engine. The Air Force is planning to use the two together, flying a pair of F-15s together with a pair of F-16s; the F-15s will function as the "long eyes," identifying targets and directing the F-16s to them, while the F-15 continues its mission of "search and destroy."

Many more countries are willing to purchase the cheaper F-16, built by the General Dynamics Corporation, than the

F-16 at Nellis Air Force Base, Nevada, December 1979. (U.S. Air Force photo)

more expensive F-15, built by McDonnell Douglas: Norway, Denmark, Belgium, and the Netherlands have already ordered the F-16 and are helping to build the aircraft under special joint-production agreements. Greece, Israel, Egypt, Pakistan, and Venezuela have also agreed to purchase it.

F-111 (TFX) The most controversial airplane built in the 1960s meant for both the Air Force and the Navy was the F-111, called in its design stages the TFX. The reason for its notoriety is that—as we shall tell in some detail in our chapter on defense decision making (Chapter Six)—in this instance the Department of Defense tried to get the Navy and the Air Force to share a single airplane design. The experiment, in terms of the bureaucracy, was not a success. While the Air Force version was purchased in some quantity, the Navy version was never produced because it had become too heavy. Instead, the Navy went ahead and built a different plane. But in terms of technology the Air Force version remains one of the most advanced fighter-bombers in the world.

The plane was built to accomplish a particular mission for the Air Force: bombing ground targets from low altitudes. The reason we began to become interested in low-altitude bombing was that Soviet radar had improved by the mid-1960s so much that high-altitude flying through Soviet air space was no longer feasible. After Gary Powers' U-2 was shot down in 1960, the Air Force changed the direction of bomber design. From ever higher and faster capability, they went to low-level for radar evasion.

Additionally, the F-111 was designed to fly off short runways—the kind we might encounter in remote areas. To do this it was given a swing-wing design. For high-speed flight the plane's wings are swept back, and for fuel-conserving slower speeds they are extended straight out. Several airplanes now have this feature (such as the Soviet Backfire bomber, which we described in Chapter Four, and the MiG-23). What made the F-111 unique is that when it was first built it was the only aircraft in our arsenal that had the capability of flying at supersonic speeds at ground level. (Today the F-15 and F-16 can both do that.) Another innovation is the escape capsule for the crew. If it is necessary to bail out, the entire cockpit is jettisoned and the crew floats to earth still comfortably seated within. (We discovered in the 1950s that even when pilots successfully bailed out of planes flying at supersonic speeds, they were severely injured by hitting an "air wall" as they left the plane. Hence the escape capsule idea.)

ASIDE

To appreciate the capability of the F-111 (called the Aardvark by its crews), some specs are perhaps necessary here: At high altitudes the aircraft can exceed Mach 2.5. Its range is 3,800 miles; or 4,700 miles in a variation, the FB model. It carries one 20-mm cannon and 3,300 pounds of bombs. It is manufactured by the General Dynamics Corporation in Texas and about 375 of the 506 F-111s originally purchased are still flying with the Tactical Air Command, and 66 with the Strategic Air Command. The Australians bought 24 at $22 million each in 1976. It is harder to figure out what we have paid for the plane, because in 1975 the price was $17 million each for 12 and in 1972 $9.7 million each for 96.

Today the F-111 is being converted for electronic warfare (under the new designation EF-111) at $57.5 million each. EF-111 Electronic warfare involves the following scenario: One plane in a flight of bombers (called the "Wild Weasel") will be equipped with radar-jamming equipment and anti-radar missiles instead of bombs. If the enemy uses their radar, they are hit by anti-radar missiles, which home in on their radar signals. If they don't use their radar, they are no threat to the bombers coming in behind. It is the use of the two different kinds of aircraft in combination that allows the bombers to reach their targets, much as escorts enabled bombers to reach their targets in World War II.

An exception to the recent trend toward ever more sophisticated and expensive fighter-bombers is the F-5. It is a F-5 comparatively inexpensive (at about $5 million for the "E" model) lightweight fighter, simple in design, reliable to operate, and easy to maintain, but still able to fly at supersonic speeds. It is also the first U.S. jet fighter aircraft expressly designed and built for export.

The evolution of the F-5 (and its sister, the T-38 training T-38 plane) is unusual in that in this instance the contractor (the Northrop Corporation) kept pushing a design it believed in, even though the original contract with the Navy had been canceled. In the mid-1950s Northrop designed a small fighter that could take off and land on the Navy's so-called jeep carriers. These small aircraft carriers, produced in large numbers during World War II, were retired, however, before the Northrop plane was ever purchased. Later, Northrop used the basic design to build the Air Force's first supersonic trainer aircraft, the T-38. More than 40,000 pilots have trained in the T-38 and it is still in active service. It was also used by the Air Force's aerobatic demonstration team, the Thunderbirds.

Because of their belief in the design, Northrop went ahead and at the company's own expense built a fighter version which came to be called the F-5 Freedom Fighter. Beginning in the early 1960s, the Air Force purchased large numbers of the F-5 for export to friendly countries, first under the Military Assistance Program (MAP) and later through the Foreign Military Sales (FMS) program.

ASIDE————————————————————————

Under MAP the United States provided some friendly countries with free military equipment. In the mid-1970s, at the insistence of Congress, this program was all but phased out and cash-and-credit sales were substituted.

———————————————————————————————

The F-5 became popular abroad because it is an inexpensive and reliable "air defense" weapon, which is designed to defend a given area against other airplanes and is especially favored because it is more than a match for the widely sold Soviet MiG-21. By the end of 1976 twenty-four countries, including the United States, were flying F-5s.

Northrop F-5E fighter. (Photo courtesy of Northrop Corporation)

Despite its virtues and popularity abroad, the F-5 has never been very popular with the U.S. Air Force. Rather, it is used primarily for simulating enemy fighters in the combat training of pilots because of its similarity in size and performance to the MiG-21. In a series of mock battles over the Nevada desert in 1978 called ACEVAL/AIMVAL (air combat evaluation, air intercept missile evaluation) pilots flying the smaller, less sophisticated F-5E found that by using a combination of unorthodox tactics and superior numbers, it was possible for them to defeat the Air Force's and the Navy's top fighters, the F-15 and F-14, something they could never expect to do in one-on-one dogfights.

ACEVAL/ AIMVAL

ACEVAL/AIMVAL got into the popular press when, in June 1981, CBS-TV featured the mock battles in its five-part series "The Defense of the United States." Drawing on comments by critics, CBS concluded that the tests demonstrated the need to buy cheaper, less sophisticated aircraft in larger numbers, rather than fewer, more sophisticated, more expensive ones. Unlike Top Gun and Red Flag, which were and are training exercises, ACEVAL/AIMVAL was an attempt to test air combat tactics, as well as the capabilities of all the fighter aircraft and air-to-air missiles in use by all the services. Thus it was a chance for the military to have a look at a variety of U.S. fighters pitted against one another. Because these were war games, there were rules, and those who disagree with CBS's conclusions argue that it was the artificiality of the rules that kept the more sophisticated planes from winning the battles.

The F-14s (Navy fighters) and the F-15s (Air Force fighters), for example, were required *visually* to identify their targets before firing their missiles—although with their radar they were of course able to detect the targets long before they could see them. The reason for the requirement was that radar cannot tell whether an incoming fighter plane is friend or foe. Radar cannot "read" insignia, or "see" shapes of planes. All the pilot gets is a blip on a screen, indicating that another plane is in the neighborhood, coming from a certain direction, at a certain speed and altitude. So it is quite probable that fighter pilots would be required—even in a real war situation—to follow "rules of engagement," among which might be the rule that the pilot visually identify the incoming aircraft before firing.

ASIDE

There are some clues that might give pilots a sense of whether an incoming plane is friendly or not (such as the direction it is coming from), but in the confusion of air combat these might not always be reliable. Therefore the Air Force is trying to perfect some electronic devices that would enable the distinction to be made. Current NATO doctrine establishes "corridors of flight" for our aircraft in a war. Any plane outside the corridor would be fair game.

Another condition of the tests was that they were done in clear weather over the Nevada desert, conditions not likely to be found in Europe. Also, communications and electronic jamming were not allowed.

What makes ACEVAL/AIMVAL so fascinating is that these tests pitted American planes against one another in different numerical combinations: one on one, one on two, one on four, and so on. The tests produced at least one clear conclusion: Superior numbers are important, and so is pilot skill. But in one-on-one encounters between planes equipped with heat-seeking missiles such as the Sidewinder (see below), planes tended to destroy each other (so lethal are these weapons). In two-against-one encounters, no matter how sophisticated the single plane, the two always defeated the one. These results have shaken some of the previously held assumptions about the advantages of very expensive, very sophisticated high-performance aircraft. Writing in *The New York Times Magazine* of February 14, 1982, Senator Gary Hart (D.-Colo.) reflects some of this new thinking when he says:

> . . . the real debate is between two different definitions of quality. The Pentagon defines quality in technical terms: high technology equals quality. The military reform movement defines quality tactically, in terms of the characteristics that are most important in terms of actual combat.

It's interesting that in all the years that fighter planes were acquiring more and more sophistication and higher and higher price tags and undergoing revolutionary changes in design, most of the publicity attendant on their evolution

was restricted to magazines and books read by specialists in
the field. Only now is the public getting an opportunity to
hear about these debates. One of the reasons is that this debate reflects a larger issue, not so much the question of how
much we should spend on defense, but rather what we
should spend our money for.

The Navy, of course, has its own air force, and the F-14   F-14
is the Navy's current first-line fighter aircraft (comparable in
many ways to the F-15). It is the latest in a long line of Navy
planes built by the Grumman Corporation (Grumman has
been building Navy planes, in fact, since the 1930s). Designed and built to fly from the decks of aircraft carriers, the
swing-wing F-14 is a two-seat, twin-engine "air superiority"
fighter and interceptor. Its primary mission is to protect its
carrier and other ships from attacks by enemy aircraft and
cruise missiles.

To locate and destroy the enemy planes, the F-14 is
equipped with sophisticated radar and electronics capable of
tracking 24 targets—200–300 miles away—simultaneously,
and/or guiding six long-range Phoenix missiles to separate
targets as far as 100 miles away. It also carries the Sidewinder air-to-air missile (see below), a 20-mm gun, as well
as other types of missiles and bombs.

The F-14 can reach a top speed of over 1,500 miles per
hour (Mach 2.34) and has a combat radius of about 1,000
miles. A large part of the airplane is constructed of titanium
(stronger and lighter than steel but also much, much more
expensive) and this, plus its high performance, its radar, and
its other electronic systems, has made the airplane—at almost $47 million per plane in the 1983 budget—one of the
most expensive fighters ever built, so far.

The Navy originally intended to purchase a total of 722
F-14s, but the escalating cost has forced a change and it
now plans to acquire only 497 F-14s.

Seventy-seven F-14s were sold to the Shah of Iran during
the mid-1970s in a very controversial arms sale.

ASIDE

It has been alleged that the Grumman Aircraft Company
paid "commissions" to Iranian agents to improve chances for
the sale and then added these commissions to the cost of the
plane. Later, when the Long Island firm got into financial
difficulty, as a result of F-14 cost overruns, Iran loaned the

company a total of $200 million to insure delivery of its planes. The loan saved Grumman from serious financial difficulties, possibly bankruptcy, and the company is now making a profit on the F-14.

As is the case with the Air Force's F-15 (see above) the Navy has also decided to go for a high-low mix, supplementing the costly F-14 with a simpler, less expensive aircraft,

F-18   the F-18. Like the F-14, the F-18 has been plagued with technical problems.

The F-18 evolved in an interesting way. In 1975 the Air Force staged a competitive "fly-off" between General Dynamics Corporation and Northrop. The winner of what was then billed as the defense contract of the century (because such a large order was at stake) was to produce the Air Force's new lightweight fighter plane. General Dynamics won the contest and its plane became the F-16 (see above). Northrop's losing design became the basis for the F-18. (The Navy insists that its fighter planes must have two engines, an important safety feature for aircraft designed to fly over open ocean, far from land.)

The F-18 is a single-seat, twin-engine, carrier-based fighter plane designed to defend the fleet against attacking aircraft. (Its "attack version," the A-18, will go after ground targets with bombs and missiles.) While originally intended to be a less costly supplement to the Navy's F-14, its cost has also escalated to the point where it costs about the same as

F-14A Tomcat fighter aircraft with an AIM-9L Sidewinder missile under a wing. (U.S. Navy photo)

An F/A-18 Hornet. (U.S. Navy photo)

the F-14, and many critics now believe that the Navy would be better off buying more F-14s and existing A-7s and not purchasing the F-18 at all.

TACTICAL MISSILES

When many of the aircraft we have been describing go into battle, they carry air-to-air missiles in addition to their internal guns. The missiles are mounted, as the picture of the Sidewinder below shows, on the outside of the airplane.   **Sidewinder**

The Sidewinder shown below is mounted on the wing of a Navy F-14 fighter plane. The F-14 can carry as many as eight Sidewinders as well as four long-range Sparrow   **Sparrow**

Sidewinder air-to-air missile. (U.S. Navy photo)

Phoenix missiles, or six very long-range Phoenix missiles and two Sidewinders.

Originally a Navy design, the Sidewinder is now the standard U.S. dogfight missile. It is designed to shoot down enemy aircraft at short range (less than 10 miles), and it combines sophistication with reliability. It has an infrared guidance system which detects and homes in on the heat produced by an aircraft's jet engine. With fewer than two dozen moving parts and fewer electronic components than an average radio, it has proved to be one of the most reliable weapons of its type in the world, and has been copied both by the Soviets and by the Israelis.

Early versions of the 7-foot-long missile first entered service in 1956. The latest version, the "L" model, weighs 180 pounds and is very highly regarded by fighter pilots—and with good reason. With earlier versions the pilot had to "get on the tail" of an enemy fighter plane—get behind the enemy plane—in order for the missile to work. Newer versions are effective when fired at enemy aircraft from almost any direction. Sidewinders were used to shoot down two Libyan fighters over the Mediterranean in 1981, and by the British to shoot down numerous Argentinian aircraft in the Falkland Islands war.

More than 110,000 Sidewinder missiles have been produced by the Raytheon Company and Ford Aerospace. The Sidewinder has also been licensed for production in West Germany.

To defend ground troops and installations against fighter-bombers, the United States and the Soviet Union have developed many different kinds of anti-aircraft or surface-to-air missiles (SAMs). These weapons have played a vital role in **SAM** recent wars, especially in the Middle East and Vietnam, and the vast majority of aircraft losses in those wars were to SAMs and anti-aircraft guns.

The picture below shows Hawk missiles on a tracked **Hawk** launching vehicle. The Hawk is a radar-guided air-defense missile designed to shoot down (using a high-explosive warhead) enemy aircraft within 22 miles and at a maximum speed of more than 1,600 miles per hour. The Hawk can

Hawk surface-to-air missiles (SAMs) on tracked launcher. (U.S. Army photo)

engage virtually any kind of aircraft at almost any combat altitude and any speed. Thus, in service since 1960, the Hawk is still one of the most reliable and effective missiles of its type in the world, although it is cumbersome. It has already been used in combat both by our forces in Southeast Asia and by the Israelis in the Middle East.

Stinger   Another type of air-defense missile, the Stinger, can be fired by one man from a portable launcher. A Soviet version was used by terrorists on at least one occasion to shoot down a civilian airliner. The Army has been trying to develop a replacement for the Hawk, called Patriot, for many years but the system has been plagued by cost and performance problems.

ASIDE

Some 22,000 Hawks and more than 5,000 improved Hawks are currently in service with U.S. forces. In addition, more than 5,000 of these missiles have been sold to more than twenty foreign countries. In the United States the Hawk is produced by the Raytheon Company. Abroad, it is being produced under license by a consortium of NATO countries and by Mitsubishi of Japan. A single missile costs less than $200,000, but a "battery of Hawks" (three missiles, a launcher, and associated radar and support equipment) cost about $6 million in 1978.

Soviet ground forces are equipped with large numbers of air-defense missiles more or less similar to the Hawk, as well as other types with greater and lesser range and considerable mobility, and guns to supplement the missiles. These provide the Russians with dense and overlapping protection for their ground troops and armor. It is assumed that in any future war many airplanes would be lost to such ground defenses. Indeed, using Soviet air-defense missiles in the 1973 Yom Kippur War, the Egyptians took a high toll of Israeli aircraft, although they fired about 50 missiles for every aircraft shot down. Airplanes can avoid SAMs via electronic countermeasures, meant to confound the missiles' guidance, or by flying evasively and low. But in flying low, aircraft become vulnerable to anti-aircraft guns, the most sophisticated of which employ radar to track targets and aim. In Vietnam 80 percent of U.S. aircraft losses were to guns.*

*Dunnigan, *op. cit.*, page 121.

To enable aircraft to counter missiles designed to counter them, the United States has developed missiles that home in on the radar signals used to guide some air-defense missiles. Over Lebanon in 1982 the Israelis completely foiled the Syrians' Soviet-built SAMs and destroyed them with such missiles fired from aircraft and from the ground.

Thus the game of cat and mouse between offense and defense continues.

AWACS

For fighter aircraft to bring their firepower to bear against other fighter aircraft, they have to find them first. This can be done in a number of ways. The simplest is to rely on the pilot's eyes, which of course are somewhat limited. To enable fighter aircraft to see "beyond visual range," aircraft are equipped with powerful radars. The Soviet air force, in contrast, relies heavily on ground-based radar to find the enemy and direct its pilots there. The U.S. Air Force, while relying heavily on the radar carried by individual aircraft, has also built a special plane called AWACS (advanced warning and control system) to help our pilots find the enemy, direct them toward the enemy, and in general orchestrate an air war.

E-3A AWACS aircraft. The large round dome visible on top of the aircraft houses the radar antenna. (U.S. Air Force photo)

AWACS   AWACS became a household word in mid-1981, during
the Reagan administration's hotly contested sale of five of
these aircraft to Saudi Arabia. Israel's supporters in and outside of Congress tried to block it. The ensuing argument produced all kinds of debates about the aircraft, basically a
Boeing 707 equipped with sophisticated radar, computers,
and other electronic equipment.

Opponents of the sale played up the aircraft's effectiveness and the threat it would pose to Israeli security. Proponents of the sale (including the Pentagon), in an effort to
soft-pedal the threat to Israel, emphasized its limitations.
Proponents did such a good job that one Senator was moved
to say they made the plane sound like a "piece of junk."

A piece of junk it's not. Its radar is good enough to detect
high- and low-altitude aircraft as well as naval vessels—this
is what is called its "look-down capability"—250 to 350 miles
away. Its radar can track 600 targets simultaneously while
its computers can identify and interpret data from over 240.
In addition to intelligence gathering and observation of military activities, AWACS can direct combat aircraft—fighter
planes and attack aircraft—against other airplanes and
ground targets.

In Chapter Two we referred to the important role played
by radar in the Battle of Britain in 1940. It allowed the Royal
Air Force to concentrate its limited fighter aircraft where
they were most needed. AWACS aircraft would allow NATO
to do very much the same thing in any air war in Europe
and would be what the military call a "force multiplier."
Moreover, look-down capability gives it the ability to detect
enemy aircraft trying to fly under the cover of ground-based
radars.

The first AWACS joined the U.S. Air Force in the mid-
1970s. By the end of 1981 the United States had 23 in its
inventory and had plans to purchase 2 more in 1982. Because these aircraft are so expensive—about $100 million
apiece—they have been purchased in only limited numbers.
Four E-3As have been stationed in Saudi Arabia, where they
have been keeping an eye (so to speak) on the Iran-Iraq war
since September 1980. They'll remain there until the five
AWACS we are selling to the Saudis are delivered in 1986.
Even then, 30 U.S. Air Force crewmen and more than 400
civilian technicians will be needed to help operate and maintain these aircraft and to teach the Saudis how to use the

sophisticated gear they carry. Other U.S. AWACS aircraft are stationed in Europe, where they monitor both NATO and Warsaw Pact air activities. In addition, NATO nations have bought 18 AWACS of their own.

The Soviets have recently begun to produce a similar system. However, they have lagged behind the United States in developing the look-down radar capability.

NAVAL WEAPONS

Although it might appear at the outset that the Navy is a very different kind of fighting force from the others, if for no other reason than the medium—water—with which it is traditionally associated, today's Navy can also be understood in terms of firepower and mobility. Ships, as we noted earlier, are thought of today as mobile platforms that carry all sorts of weapons—guns, missiles, torpedoes, aircraft, all equipped with both nuclear and non-nuclear explosives. The Navy has moved from the sea to the air, and, if we include the Marines as part of the Navy (which they are), to land as well. In some senses, then, it is no longer just seafaring, but a self-contained fighting force of its own.

This has led, as we shall see, to some serious interservice rivalry between the Navy and the Air Force over fighter plane design and over missions. Who is to say, really, whether it is an Air Force or a Navy mission to lay mines from the air in enemy harbors? Or whether it is an Air Force or a Navy mission to launch ballistic missiles from submarines? In Brazil, the aircraft carrier is considered a joint operation between the Navy and the Air Force. The Navy runs the ship, and the Air Force flies the planes. In Canada there is now a single force which combines Army, Navy, and Air Force missions.

From the end of the nineteenth century through 1941, the battleship was the queen of the seas. So central was the battleship to any nation that considered itself a sea power that in the 1930s, in an effort to prevent war among the naval powers (the United States, Great Britain, Japan, Italy, and France at the time), a treaty setting ceilings on battleship construction was signed in the expectation that if the nations could avoid a battleship-building competition, they could avoid war.

Battleships, as we have noted earlier, played a relatively minor role in World War II, but the treaty points up the high value that nations put on their battleships before the war. In fact, the reason the Japanese attacked us when they did and where they did, at Pearl Harbor, was to devastate our battleship fleet. Ironically, the Japanese planes that attacked Pearl Harbor flew off Japanese aircraft carriers, disproving at that very moment their theory. And six months later, at the battles of the Coral Sea and Midway in 1942, we turned the tide of the war in the Pacific with our aircraft carriers. Thus the battleship ceased to be the centerpiece of the modern Navy. There are those who accuse some of today's admirals of being as wedded to the aircraft carrier as yesterday's admirals were to the battleship. Be that as it may, the aircraft carrier remains both a golden memory and the heart of U.S. naval striking power.

The Navy today has 13 large aircraft carriers, as well as 12 helicopter carriers for amphibious operations. (The Soviets have only five helicopter carriers, three of which carry a few vertical take-off aircraft.) The largest aircraft carrier, the *Nimitz,* weighs 90,000 tons, while others, such as the *For-*

U.S.S. Nimitz. (U.S. Navy photo)

restal, are a third smaller. Some of the larger ones are nuclear-powered.

The Reagan administration has requested funds in its FY
1983 budget for two more nuclear-powered aircraft carriers,
costing (exclusive of aircraft) $3.5 billion each.

Despite the Administration's vote of confidence in the
carrier, its future is by no means certain. Extensive deployment of anti-ship cruise missiles—not only in the Soviet
navy but in the navies of other, lesser countries—has caused
many analysts to wonder whether our naval resources
should be invested so heavily in a few very large and expensive ships. Big carriers, after all, make big targets, and
the *Nimitz* (more than 1,000 feet in length, or three football fields laid end to end) is one mighty big target in an
open sea.

While the aircraft carrier was essentially an anti-ship
weapon in World War II, in the 1950s carrier-based aircraft
were given an additional, strategic mission (along with the
Air Force's long-range bombers) to deliver nuclear weapons
against targets deep inside the Soviet Union. This mission
required large, long-range aircraft and even larger carriers to
accommodate them. As a result, carriers grew to about twice
the size of their World War II predecessors. Other classes of
U.S. Navy ships have also grown in size, although for different reasons (see below).

As nuclear-powered ballistic-missile submarines joined
the fleet in the early 1960s, carriers began to assume other
missions. In Vietnam carrier aircraft bombed the north and
provided close air support for U.S. and South Vietnamese
troops. There is general agreement today that carriers are
especially valuable as mobile air bases in what are called
low-threat environments (meaning low threat to the carriers). Because bases maintained in other countries can
always be attacked (either militarily or politically), carrier-
based aircraft might be used to protect access to Persian
Gulf oil supplies, for example, if the routes to the Middle
East were blocked.

Where the aircraft carrier is likely to be less useful is in
the context of a major European war. Not many analysts
believe aircraft carriers could operate effectively close to Europe, given the threat posed by Soviet ships, submarines,
and land-based aircraft. Navy leaders, on the other hand, argue that the carrier could be an effective weapon on the

flanks of Europe, in the eastern Mediterranean or in the waters off northern Norway, and note with some justification that aircraft carriers can absorb a great deal of punishment.

Even though carriers are equipped to defend themselves, they do not and cannot operate alone even in so-called low-threat regions. They must have escorting destroyers (like the Spruance class; see below), cruisers, and submarines for their defense.

ASIDE

Their normal complement of 75–90 aircraft usually includes high-performance fighter-interceptors such as the F-14 (see above), as well as the mini-AWACS, the E-2C Hawkeye. They also carry Sea Sparrow anti-aircraft missiles and Phalanx rapid-firing guns (more than 3,000 rounds per minute). Their antisubmarine arsenal includes S-3 antisubmarine planes, and antisubmarine helicopters equipped with sensors and weapons.

Carriers depend as well on escorting tankers to replenish their own fuel (for those that are not nuclear-powered) and the aircraft fuel they carry for their airplanes.

One important peacetime use of the carrier is to provide a naval presence or, as the military puts it, to "show the flag" in a part of the world that might need reminding of our nation's power. Toward this end the Navy operates carrier task forces (the carrier plus supporting ships) in the Mediterranean, Pacific, and Indian oceans. While at any one time three or four of these task forces will be "forward-deployed" in these regions, others are completing maintenance, overhaul, and training cycles at various bases in the continental United States.

Since World War II there haven't been many opportunities for the major powers to test some of their most advanced weapons themselves. Therefore the several Middle East wars, in particular the 1967 and 1973 wars between Israel and the Arabs, have been important incubators and testing grounds for new military ideas and hardware.

While the public remembers these wars primarily as land wars, with the tank as the most visible weapon, in fact, naval forces played significant roles in both the 1967 and the 1973 Arab-Israeli wars, which as a result have been studied with considerable interest by naval planners in other countries.

When in 1967 the Egyptians sank the Israeli destroyer *Eilat*, with a Soviet Styx cruise missile, it sent a shock wave through the U.S. Navy. (The sinking of H.M.S. *Sheffield* by a French-made Exocet missile in the spring of 1982 made a comparable impression on the American public fifteen years later.) The U.S. Navy had relied exclusively on carrier-based aircraft for attacking other ships, as we noted above, and some within the Navy high command had been skeptical of anti-ship missiles altogether. Meanwhile, the Soviets, who had no aircraft carriers, went ahead and developed cruise missiles instead. And the United States found itself in 1967 having to come to terms with a new reality.

These missiles give any small vessel the ability to sink ships many times its size. Therefore new defenses capable of protecting the fleet from the fate of the *Eilat* needed to be found, and a U.S. anti-ship attack missile had to be developed as well. The Harpoon is one product of that search.

Most U.S. Navy warships are now equipped with the Harpoon. It can be launched from ships and submerged submarines, and it can be carried and launched by a variety of naval aircraft as well. The Harpoon has already been sold to NATO and to Israel, Saudi Arabia, Iran, and South Korea. Another, larger anti-ship cruise missile, the Tomahawk, can fly more than three times as far as the Harpoon.

Harpoon missile

The loss of the *Eilat* stimulated drastic changes in the composition of the Israeli navy and its tactics. Cruise missiles can give small ships great firepower. At the same time, defense against cruise missiles requires maneuverability, speed, and countermeasures. With these principles in mind, the Israelis got rid of their old, large destroyers, similar to the *Eilat*, and instead built a fleet of small, fast, and agile patrol boats. These they equipped with anti-ship missiles of their own design and construction, called Gabriel. They also devised tactics and countermeasures to confuse the guidance of Egyptian and Syrian anti-ship missiles, and their careful preparation paid off.

During the 1973 Yom Kippur War, Israeli missile boats roamed the western Mediterranean at will, boldly raided Syrian ports, and sank several Arab ships and missile boats without losing one of Israel's. The Arabs fired more than 50 cruise missiles at Israeli ships without scoring a single hit.*

*Dunnigan, *op. cit.*, page 177.

Harpoon anti-ship missile is launched by U.S.S. Badger. It has a range of about 90 miles and carries a 500-pound (non-nuclear) high-explosive warhead. (U.S. Navy photo)

Harpoon missile in wing of P-3 aircraft. (U.S. Navy photo)

The 1971–72 India-Pakistan War drove home the same lesson. Indian navy missile boats sank a large Pakistani destroyer, the *Khyber,* off Karachi.

The U.S. Navy has not gone out to purchase small missile boats, but is trying to do the next best thing: namely, put anti-ship missiles onto new and existing surface ships of all kinds, including most of its destroyers and frigates. (Destroyers tend to escort aircraft carriers; frigates, generally smaller in size, escort less important ships.)

The newest destroyer-class Navy ship, outfitted now with anti-ship missiles, is the Spruance, named after the World War II admiral Raymond Spruance. The Navy has built 31 of these.

Spr class
destroyers

Their main task is to protect aircraft carriers not only from submarines, but from other threats as well. To do this, in the face of the enormously increased sophistication in the kinds of weapons that can threaten the aircraft carrier, they have to be equipped as follows: two 5-inch multipurpose guns for use against ships, aircraft, and shore targets; a launcher that can carry eight missiles for use against ships or submarines; ship's masts carrying antennas for three different radars, one for tracking ships, one for tracking aircraft and missiles, and one for general surveillance; just behind the rear exhaust stack, a helicopter hangar and landing platform; below the waterline, the ship's sonar and its six torpedo tubes, three on each side of the stern.

The Spruance is also being equipped with the Phalanx rapid-firing 20-mm gun for defense against cruise missiles and possibly even with the Sea Sparrow anti-aircraft missile. The total cost of each of these ships was about $350 million.

Phalanx

That's the bigger ship.

Now the smaller, frigate class is the first of a class of 25 simple, relatively inexpensive, general-purpose escort ships. To be protected against all possible threats, this ship will have to carry: a general-purpose missile launcher for both anti-aircraft, anti-ship, and antisubmarine missiles; one 3-inch general-purpose gun, a Phalanx rapid-firing anti-cruise missile gun, six torpedo tubes, and a pair of antisubmarine helicopters. And it is one of the simpler, less expensive warships being built by the Navy today.

Some people argue that given the vulnerability of our larger ships to Soviet cruise missiles, we would be smart to purchase a much larger quantity of these smaller ships.

A Spruance class destroyer. (U.S. Navy photo)

Guided-missile frigate, Oliver Hazard Perry class, FFG-7, under way. (U.S. Navy photo)

After all, for the price of one aircraft carrier, we could buy a dozen or more fast frigates. In effect, the debate here parallels the controversy over fighter aircraft procurement—the high-low mix issue discussed above. (We shall refer to this again in Chapter Eight.)

The Soviets have one of the largest fleets of attack submarines in the world, 220 torpedo attack (both nuclear-powered and diesel-electric) and about 70 equipped with cruise missiles (also both nuclear and diesel-electric). Although they are noisy and subject to breakdowns, they are still a source of great concern to the United States. (The Germans started World War II with 57 U-boats.)

The principal antisubmarine weapon is, of course, other submarines; and U.S. "attack submarines" are all nuclear-powered and among the best in the world. They are equipped with sophisticated sonars capable of detecting enemy ships and submarines more than 60 miles away.* But apart from submarines themselves, Navy patrol aircraft are among the most effective antisubmarine weapons available. The U.S. Navy has for years used the P-3 Orion for this purpose. The plane is a long-range, land-based, antisubmarine aircraft (a military version of the old Electra airliner, built by Lockheed in the late 1950s). It is equipped with a variety of

P-3 Orion

P-3B Orion patrol aircraft in flight. (U.S. Navy photo)

*Dunnigan, *op. cit.*, page 165.

sensors designed to locate and to track enemy ships and submarines. It also carries a variety of weapons: mines, homing torpedoes, and the Harpoon anti-ship missiles. Sensors include radar, so-called sonobuoys (small floating devices which detect sounds produced by submarines), and a magnetic anomaly detector (the long, slender object protruding from the aircraft's tail), which detects magnetic disturbances in the ocean caused by the presence of the submarine's steel hull.

The P-3 also carries computers which analyze the signals received from its various sensors in order to pinpoint a submarine's location. The computers are programmed to compare signals received with signals produced by all known targets within its memory.

Additionally, the newer models of the P-3 will have infrared sensors which are sensitive to the heat left underwater by the engines of a passing submarine.

CONCLUSION

Crystal-ball gazing is uncertain at best and even less useful when we try to anticipate wars of a kind that have not yet been fought. Given the amount of information we have about some recent wars, however, we can venture a number of observations. First, in future wars the losses on both sides in terms of military equipment will be extremely high. In the 1973 Middle East war, for example, nearly 3,000 tanks were lost by both sides in less than three weeks. That number represents one-half of the total pre-war tank inventory of all the combatants. More than 500 aircraft, one-third of the total pre-war inventory, were also destroyed.*

Second, given the density of weapons now in Europe—the tanks, ground-to-ground missiles, air-to-ground missiles, and ground-to-air missiles, as well as artillery—conventional warfare is likely to be "devastatingly lethal."† There are now in Europe alone 26,000 Soviet tanks, 17,000 NATO tanks, perhaps as many as 100,000 antitank missiles (NATO),

* *SIPRI Yearbook, 1974* (Stockholm International Peace Research Institute) (Cambridge: MIT Press, 1974), page 151.
† Vought and Angolia, *op. cit.*, *U.S. War Machine*, page 80.

thousands of mobile air-defense weapons on both sides, and thousands of attack helicopters.

That is, even without the nuclear option, any war in Europe using these kinds of weapons will be so devastating as to approach—over a wider area—the amount of devastation created in no-man's-land between German and Allied lines during World War I.

Apart from the loss of equipment, the number of casualties cannot even be estimated, but they will certainly be very high. Units, moreover, are likely to be cut off from their main forces and may find themselves fighting isolated engagements with little or no direction from higher command. The mobility available to both sides—tanks, armored personnel carriers, and helicopters—may make for very fluid battles, with soldiers moving back and forth and even engaging one another behind their own lines. Indeed, the concept of front lines may cease to have any meaning in such a war. Command and control, of course, will become extremely difficult. High casualties among officers will cause command responsibility to devolve on lower-ranking officers. Confusion and chaos, what Karl von Clausewitz called "the fog of war," will be widespread.

Even the air environment will be dense, not only with fighter planes fighting one another but with SAMs of many kinds as well as gunfire. Whatever the maneuverability and speed of fighter planes (on both sides), it is unlikely they will survive long in such a weapons-packed environment. Indeed, because of the vast quantities of matériel that will be consumed in such a conventional war, the belligerents will quickly use up even large stocks of weapons and supplies. Thus, it is hard to imagine such a war lasting very long. But then, that's what everyone thought in 1914.

For many years, for all these reasons, some Europeans have taken the position that in terms of likely devastation there is little to choose between a conventional war and a nuclear war on their territory.

They may be right.

6.

Why We Buy the Weapons We Buy

THE ARRAY OF WEAPONRY that appears in Chapters Three and Five are but survivors of a long and complex process from "weapons concept" to deployment. Along the way many ideas are discarded, while others get so far as to generate immense stacks of paper, yet never get to the "bending metal" stage. Still others are designed, transformed into a few prototypes, and tested but not bought in any quantity. Some of these also-rans can be found lined up in the "boneyard" at Davis-Monthan Air Force Base in Tucson; a few are in museums; while the most unfortunate wind up as scrap.

The process by which some weapons are purchased while others are scratched is not easy to follow. From the weapon's point of view, the process is one long series of hurdles—some higher than others. From the perspective of those people in the Pentagon responsible for weapons development and procurement, the task is (for some of them) to bring the new system to fruition and (for others) continually to assess and reassess one weapon against another, while trying at the same time to fold in budgetary considerations and the overall mission or purpose for which the weapon is intended.

From the vantage point of Congress—as one House Armed Services Committee staffer put it—the weapons procurement process looks rather like a freight train: once a project gets rolling it is very hard to stop. One reason for this is that in the beginning Congress may allocate funds for re-

search and development (R & D) without attending much to
details. Since initial R & D is not normally as costly as production and because a weapon's early specifications are
often at the frontiers of science, it is very difficult for non-
scientists (or congressional staffers) to figure out just what
is going on. Yet, having sunk money in a project, Congress
and the Pentagon are often reluctant to cancel it. In fact,
there is but a 4-percent chance that a weapons program will
be canceled each year after it has passed its first year.* And
even cancellation may not be final. President Carter killed
the B-1 bomber in 1977 only to see it revived by President
Reagan in 1981.

No one is really satisfied with the weapons procurement
process. Every few years it gets "reformed," usually with
each change of Administration, and new ways are established to monitor, evaluate, and decide which weapons to
buy. Yet the system remains under constant attack. Some
critics see the weapons we buy as the inevitable outcome of
close and incestuous ties within the military-industrial complex. For others they are the product of the biases of powerful Congressmen who sit for decades on the Armed Services
committees of the House and Senate. For still others, weapons are the output of self-serving bureaucrats intent on
perpetuating themselves and increasing their empires, bureaucrats who are often uninterested in identifying or admitting to failures in the weapons systems with which they are
associated. For example, early in 1982 a serious vulnerability
in the Army's new M-1 tank (its lack of protection against a
very common type of antitank ammunition) came to light. It
turned out that the Army had known about this weakness
for many years. But the program managers were reluctant to
report it "upstairs," lest the entire project be canceled (as
had happened before with two other tanks).

ASIDE

The Council on Economic Priorities, a group generally
critical of Pentagon policies, attributes the system's failures
quite specifically to the military-industrial complex. Pierre
Sprey and Jack Merritt, both former Pentagon officials, in

*Norman Augustine, "Augustine's Laws and Major Systems Development Pro-
grams," 1980, page 20.

contrast blame bureaucracies that reward those who expand the organizations' budgets and power. Norman Augustine, a vice-president of Martin Marietta Corporation and formerly of the Defense Department, feels "bad management" is the cause: too much centralization, too rapid rotation of managers, too little competition, and unrealistic inflation estimates. The Project on Military Procurement puts the blame on inadequate operational testing. Even the Reagan administration acknowledges there is a problem and has called for more realistic cost estimates; the buying of weapons in larger, more economical quantities; and multiyear procurement.

See Gordon Adams, *The Iron Triangle* (New York: The Council on Economic Priorities, 1981), passim; also Merritt and Sprey, "Negative Marginal Returns in Weapons' Acquisition," in Head and Rokke, *op. cit.*, pages 494–495; also Norman Augustine, "Just How Good/Bad Is the Defense Acquisition Process?," *Government Executive*, February 1982, pages 27–34; also Dina Rasor, "Fighting With Failures," *Reason*, Vol. 13, No. 12 (March–April 1982), pages 19–28; also Deputy Secretary of Defense Frank Carlucci, Testimony before Senate Armed Services Committee, February 8, 1982, pages 6–8.

"not invented here" One favorite expression in the Pentagon is "not invented here." Ideas that originate outside the Pentagon, or even in other departments of the Pentagon, are not likely to be taken seriously. The Army evaluated a German tank and thought about building it in the United States before deciding to purchase the M-1. But hardly anybody, inside or outside the Defense Department, had any doubts as to how the evaluation would turn out. It was going to be rejected because it was "not invented here." The same was true of the M-16 rifle. It took the Army years before it replaced the Army-designed M-14 with the cheaper, more effective, but privately designed M-16. Meanwhile, our GIs in Vietnam had to spend their own money to buy AR-15s (the civilian version of the M-16) before the Army agreed to adopt the weapon.

NORAD In another recent case, the Air Force's North American Air Defense Command (NORAD) fell six years behind schedule and came in $150 million over budget while "modernizing" the computer system that helps guard the United

States against enemy attack. The new system, according to a congressional committee, is no better than the one it replaces. In criticizing NORAD, Congress said the Pentagon had refused to accept valid criticism and was inclined to blame problems on "unwarranted intrusions by oversight agencies." Meanwhile the computer in question produced three false alerts of imminent Soviet attack between 1979 and 1980.*

Since most citizens are exposed to nothing more than local newspapers and national news magazines, they usually do not find out about weapons in the design or prototype stages. Yet other people do. These matters are covered regularly and in depth by magazines such as *Scientific American*, *Aviation Week & Space Technology*, *Military Enthusiast*, *Armed Forces Journal*, and *Aerospace Daily*, among others. Without such exposure, the general public hears about weapons systems only when there is some foul-up or a major cost overrun. The B-1 bomber, the M-1 tank, and the Trident submarine were under development for years before their ballooning costs became part of the daily news. Indeed, the infrared-imaging Maverick missile, which proved troublesome in numerous tests over several years, found its way into *The Washington Post* only a few months before the decision to produce it in large numbers was scheduled to be made.

Short of studying thousands of pages of transcripts of congressional hearings (including some reading between the lines) and following the trade literature, there is no way for the public to track a proposed weapon from its emergence as an engineering possibility to its deployment with U.S. forces. Yet when, in the context of the military budget, citizens finally do hear about a weapon, they want to know how come it costs so much. And who decided that we needed that weapon anyway?

Who decides indeed? is the key question. And no one— neither the critics nor reformers nor Congress nor journalists—can answer this question easily. That's because such decisions are not made the way we make personal decisions.

---

*House Committee on Government Operations, "NORAD Computer Systems are Dangerously Obsolete," Report No. 97-449, U.S. House of Representatives, March 8, 1982.

We tend to think of decisions both big and small as events, moments, after which things change: a new appliance is purchased and carted home; a job or project is begun or finished; a contract is entered into or terminated. But procurement decisions—the ones that determine which weapons, at what price, in what number, and when—are not single events, but many and multilayered, instead. The process, in short, is diffuse.

There are many moments along the way when the projected weapon nominally comes up before a decision-making board or committee, the Secretary of Defense, or Congress. But often as not, the decision is effectively foreclosed in advance, either because of sunk costs or proprietary interest on the part of the service or the manufacturing company, or because—at least since arms control talks have been going on—we need the weapon as a bargaining chip in the next round of negotiations. (The last argument has been applied in turn to the B-1, Trident, cruise missiles, and MIRV.)

Even when there is a history of substantial cost overruns, we are unlikely to cancel programs in midstream or penalize the producer. To wit: the Lockheed C-5A, which cost, in the end, about nine times what was originally anticipated. Again, the point is that it is hard to stop the process once it has been set in motion. This accounts for part of the growth of the defense budget (unable to choose, we try to do it all) and the difficulty of apportioning ultimate responsibility for the weapons that are finally procured.

Yet some ideas are abandoned even before the testing stage, while they are but engineering designs and "weapons concepts." Why is this? What makes one weapon attractive to the military and another not? While it is difficult to generalize for all weapons in every service, the two almost irresistible criteria are new technology in the form of "innovative design" and the promise of "high performance." A fighter plane that is more maneuverable, faster, with a powerful long-range radar (like the F-15), will often be appealing to the Air Force because it seems to offer a winning edge. A bomber with a smaller radar profile, like the B-1, promises the same. So, too, a tank like the M-1, using a new kind of engine (gas-turbine) and achieving higher speeds than before (40 miles per hour) and built with exotic new armor. Or smart missiles like the Maverick. All seem worth developing. These are the kinds of weapons that start off with a great deal of support because they seem to make it possible to fight and win a war more effectively than before. And in some instances they even perform up to their advance billing.

There are, of course, some other not entirely "rational" considerations that seem to operate in the choosing of weapons: there is an inclination to think that if a weapon (or any other product) costs more than another and can do more, it is necessarily better. To balance this tendency, former Secretary of Defense Robert McNamara tried to introduce the idea of "systematic cost-benefit analysis" into the decision-making process. As we shall see, the results were mixed. But it is interesting to note that an independent study commissioned by McNamara in 1961 showed that while costs often exceeded expectations and weapons were generally late in coming on line, in terms of the military's "performance goals," weapons were almost always satisfactory or better. And that remains true even today. Weapons achieve 75 percent of their performance goals most of the time.*

But whether the performance goals are the right ones is another issue. Critics would argue that the Pentagon's performance criteria are often wrong and that the evaluation process is not nearly as objective as it is made to seem. But more about that later.

No one denies that politics plays an important role in weapons procurement, not so much in the concept stage but in choosing one manufacturer's product over another. When Robert McNamara selected the General Dynamics TFX design over Boeing's in 1966, in the face of Air Force and Navy preference for Boeing, there were accusations of political influence and charges that the Texas-based corporation was selected because Lyndon Johnson was then President. It wasn't true, but the fact that Lockheed has a major plant in Georgia (and Senator Sam Nunn is on the Armed Services Committee) is cited as one reason that it gets so many cargo plane contracts, even in the face of past enormous cost overruns.

*Norman Augustine, "Just How Good/Bad Is the Defense Acquisition Process?," *Government Executive*, February 1982, pages 27–34.

WAR VS. PEACE: THE BOTTOM LINE

So why do we buy the weapons we buy?

Military forces—armies, navies, air forces alike—are assembled, trained, and armed for but one purpose: to make war (although deterrence is another benefit). War is the ultimate test of weapons (as well, of course, as of tactics, training, and leadership). It provides a clear and unambiguous bottom line: success or failure, victory or defeat.

Weapons that are ineffective or unreliable on the battlefield are identified, discarded, and replaced or improved. Soldiers will not fight with equipment in which they have little confidence. And there is no reason why they should. Examples of expensive weapons that failed the test of battle are numerous. We've already mentioned the episode of the M-14 vs. M-16 rifle. Also in Vietnam, the Sparrow missile, designed to shoot down enemy aircraft, worked only about 8 percent of the time. The Sheridan tank gained a reputation as a deathtrap because of problems with an innovative, but faulty, type of ammunition. Back in World War II, the P-38, an expensive twin-engine fighter plane, was chased from the skies over Europe because of its poor maneuverability. And the Soviets have had similar problems. Their Sagger antitank missile was the major failure of the 1973 Middle East war.

The point is that the only real test of a weapon's effectiveness is its combat performance. Obviously, in peacetime the trial of combat is not available. The same is always true of nuclear weapons. So the Pentagon has to find other standards by which to evaluate them, none of which is perfect. Sometimes we can watch someone else's war and observe our weapons—and theirs—in battle. This is the significance of the several Arab-Israeli wars, which come up again and again in our description of conventional weaponry. The 1967 and 1973 wars, indeed, have been among the very few since World War II fought with truly modern arms. We learned from the Israelis, for example, that the hydraulic fluid used in M-60 tanks was highly flammable, but not until several hundred Israeli tankers burned to death. Vietnam also provided us many opportunities to observe weapons in battle, and some of our most important conventional weapons decisions—the shift to the M-16 rifle and the use of helicopters to knock out tanks—were made as a result of that experience.

Weapons in prototype are tested, but in the absence of war, testing is done by computer simulation and in laboratory and field tests. Mock-combat exercises (such as ACEVAL/AIMVAL) are also important. But as military theorists from Clausewitz on have pointed out, in actual combat there is "friction," or "the fog of war," which can cause laboratory-tested weapons to perform poorly. So the problem for testers is (or should be) how to best simulate real-life battle conditions.

The point is that politics affects defense procurement in several ways. Bureaucratic politics, in the form of interservice rivalry, is one. The Army, Navy, and Air Force compete with one another for resources and tend to view any weapon that serves their own particular missions as "successful." There has been a great deal of competition over "roles and missions," and one reason for this is that with any enlargement of a military responsibility (that is, a new mission) comes the opportunity to purchase new weapons to carry out that task. The Air Force, for example, has never been fond of the close-air-support mission for which it has had responsibility since 1948. But at the same time it has been reluctant to give up this mission altogether because it might permit the Army to acquire combat airplanes of its own. As it is, Pentagon regulations restrict the Army to combat helicopters and light observation planes.

Most weapons begin (or should begin) within the context of a service's mission. Sometimes ideas are generated by the "users"; but just as often an aggressive and talented manufacturing company will come up with a proposal just because it wants to do the work. Sometimes the weapons concept originates with scientists and engineers in a national weapons laboratory. But in most cases, a new weapon is but an improvement on or a replacement for an older one. Because of this, many contractors tend to specialize in certain kinds of equipment, and if they produce one system they can often count on producing its successor. Lockheed, for example, has been our principal cargo-plane producer; McDonnell Douglas, our main manufacturer of Air Force fighter planes; Grumman, the favored fighter-plane builder for the Navy. Raytheon specializes in missiles, while FMC produced the M-113 armored personnel carrier and will also produce its follow-on, the Bradley infantry fighting vehicle. Chrysler made the M-60 tank and developed its successor, the M-1. As we will see below, specialization is reinforced by the fact that in many cases only a single manufacturer is capable of producing a given type of weapon.

Part of the reason for the extensive cooperation between the military and the defense contractors, then, is no more complicated than the fact that the services want to have their weapons built and the builders want very much to build them.

The United States has been producing and purchasing weapons for a long time, but we haven't always done it the way we do today. In 1795, Congress established the first government-owned arms factory in Springfield, Massachusetts. At the Springfield Arsenal, Eli Whitney (who later **arsenal** invented the cotton gin) introduced innovative mass-produc- **system** tion techniques to produce muskets. In time, arsenals in other parts of the country were built to produce virtually all the Army's weapons. The Watervliet Arsenal near Troy, New York, made cannon, and still does. The arsenals at Watertown, Massachusetts, and at Rock Island, Illinois, produced other artillery components as well as tanks. The Frankford Arsenal (near Philadelphia) and the Picatinny Arsenal (near Dover, New Jersey) turned out bullets, shells, and explosives. But the Springfield Arsenal had a near-monopoly on all the muskets and rifles used by U.S. troops in all wars until the beginning of World War I. The standard infantry weapon used by Union troops in the Civil War and by our doughboys in World War I carried the name Springfield rifle.

The Navy was less self-sufficient than the Army and relied a lot on private shipyards between the two world wars. Still, it operated large shipyards of its own on both coasts. The Navy yards at Portsmouth (New Hampshire), Boston, New York, Philadelphia, Norfolk, Mare Island (California), Puget Sound, and others produced all kinds of vessels, from battleships to submarines.

contract The arsenal system, to be sure, was bureaucratic, slow, **system** and inefficient. For example, it took the Springfield Arsenal thirty years to design and field the Army's first semi-automatic infantry rifle, the M-1 Garand, used in World War II

and Korea. In contrast, most of the $50 billion spent by the
Pentagon to purchase weapons and equipment in 1981 went
to privately owned companies. (See Appendix II, page 388.)
Only about 80 government-owned plants remain today and
many of these are operated by private contractors. On the
other hand, there are some 25,000–30,000 private firms classified as "prime contractors" for the Defense Department
and an additional 50,000 subcontractors who supply parts,
components, materials, and services to the primes. There are
some 3,500 companies engaged in aerospace production
alone, and together these firms employ about 5.8 million
people.

World War II greatly expanded the size of the defense
industry. The vast quantities of weapons and equipment
needed could be produced only by mobilizing all U.S. industry. "Rosie the Riveter" and her co-workers produced staggering amounts of weapons and munitions: 310,000 aircraft,
88,000 tanks, 900,000 trucks, 411,000 artillery pieces, 10
battleships, 27 aircraft carriers, 211 submarines, 358 destroyers, and more than 12 million rifles. In 1944 the United
States was completing Liberty cargo ships in fifty days, turning them out literally faster than the Germans could sink
them. And in one furious month—March 1944—U.S. industry made more than 9,000 military aircraft. In contrast, during the entire decade of the 1970s we built, on average,
about 300 military aircraft a year. Of course, the comparison
is not completely fair since in 1944 we produced little else
but weapons, while the United States was not mobilized for
war in the 1970s. Still, there are many who doubt we could
match the feats of 1944 even if we tried.*

THE CAST OF CHARACTERS:
THE DEFENSE COMMUNITY

Directly and indirectly the weapons acquisition process
today involves billions of dollars, thousands of organizations,
and millions of people. Some are in uniform, but most are
civilians. They work in the Pentagon or in private companies

*The Ailing Defense Industrial Base: Unready for Crisis. Report of the Defense
Industrial Base Panel of the Committee on Armed Services, December 31, 1980,
pages 8, 12.

while some engage in applied research in weapons laboratories and others toil on Capitol Hill. Collectively, they are
known as the "defense community."

The Pentagon players are so profuse and varied that they
fill dozens of pages in the Pentagon telephone directory. All
the services are represented, as are the Office of the Secre-
OSD tary of Defense (OSD) and the Joint Chiefs and their staffs.
Other parts of the executive branch of government are also
involved. These include the Central Intelligence Agency
(CIA) and the Office of Management and Budget (OMB),
among others.

ASIDE───────────────────────────────

The Pentagon phone book is about 400 pages long—about
as big as the directory for a small city, which in many ways it
is. It even has white and yellow pages. The white pages contain the usual alphabetical listing in the usual fine print (Secretary Caspar Weinberger is listed there under the W's, like
anyone else). You can let your fingers do the walking
through the Pentagon's yellow pages but you won't find any
ads, just an organizational directory with several major divisions: the Office of the Secretary of Defense and DOD-wide
agencies (17 pages); the Department of the Army (25 pages);
the Navy Department (52 pages); the Air Force (13 pages);
and a miscellaneous section (9 pages). It also contains two
pages of office abbreviations, beginning with AAFBD and
running through WSEG. The first stands for the Army and
Air Force Exchange Service Board of Directors and the last
for Weapons Systems Evaluation Group.

───────────────────────────────

Industry players consist of thousands of large and small
firms that produce everything from ablative materials (heat
shields for missile nose cones), abrasives, or aircraft to yokes
for cables and wires. Also involved are an assortment of trade
associations and public relations and advertising firms as
well as independent lobbyists. Although it is not easy to draw
the lines, about 10 percent of our labor force is tied in one
way or another to military procurement. Workers in plants
producing missiles or ammunition are clearly dependent on
the military, but so are merchants and saloonkeepers near
military bases who depend on money spent by GIs; and scientists at universities and research centers whose buildings,

laboratories, graduate assistants, and staffs are paid from military contracts.

Then there is the Congress, including the 535 elected members as well as their office staffs, plus a half-dozen major committees on both sides of the Hill with their own staffs. In addition, there is the Congressional Budget Office, Congressional Research Service, General Accounting Office, and the Office of Technology Assessment, all of which have substantial crews of defense specialists who are involved one way or another in weapons acquisition and defense budget decisions.

The giants of U.S. defense production—that is, the largest prime contractors—are familiar names to us all. They are among the major corporations of U.S. industry: Boeing, General Dynamics, Grumman, McDonnell Douglas, Northrop, Rockwell, and United Technologies. These have been among the top ten recipients of defense contracts for nearly a decade. Between 1970 and 1980 they received a total of more than $100 billion: 25 percent of all business done by the Pentagon. They also got another $11 billion in contracts from the National Aeronautics and Space Administration (NASA). Government is their largest customer, accounting for half of the gross. Indeed, in the case of Grumman, the government accounts for 80 percent of its business (they would have to sell a lot more buses and canoes to match their defense sales). For Boeing, on the other hand, with its large sales of civilian airplanes, sales to government account for only 31 percent of its total sales.* **the primes**

In contrast to the primes, most subcontractors are not well known, yet they are dotted about the nation and provide significant employment as well as essential products. Parts for Northrop's F-5 fighter are made by York Industries of Emigsville, Pennsylvania; Superior Manufacturing of Long Island City, New York; the Ceco Corporation of Portland, Oregon; Breeze-Illinois of Wyoming, Illinois; and many other firms. These are only a few of the thousands of firms supplying essential parts, components, and materials without which none of the primes could operate. **the subs**

Any successful, well-managed business does its best to stay in close touch with its customers, and good customers

*Gordon Adams, *op. cit.*, page 41.

get special treatment. What is true of business in general is especially true of the defense industry, but there's one major difference: their best customer is the U.S. government. Needless to say, they work very hard at cultivating those ties that bind them together.

To do this, all top defense firms maintain Washington offices (more than 500 other corporations do the same). Many employ former (and future) Defense Department officials and retired military officers. They track legislation and policy decisions as well as provide information to Congress and executive-branch bureaucrats. These Washington representatives report to the top management of their companies, explore new business opportunities, and keep tabs on old ones. Because it decides on defense spending levels and new weapons systems, Congress is a major focus of lobbying activities. But Defense Department officials who manage existing weapons programs and develop new ones are another major focus, too. So is the State Department's Office of Munitions Control, which reviews and licenses all foreign sales of weapons and military equipment.

In addition, all major defense firms maintain political action committees, mechanisms by which individual employees (and more importantly the corporation itself) make campaign contributions to favored elected officials. Trade and professional associations hold conferences and conventions, publish magazines, testify before congressional committees, and perform many of the same activities that the largest firms' Washington offices undertake. A sample of these associations are the Aerospace Industries Association, the Air Force Association (made up of retired Air Force people as well as civilian friends of the Air Force), the Association of the U.S. Army and the Navy League, with a similar membership, the American Defense Preparedness Association, the National Security Industrial Association, the Electronics Industry Association, and others.

PROFITS

While there is a widespread belief that companies doing business with the government—especially military business—do very well, the profit picture in fact is mixed. Large increases in defense spending by the Reagan administration may turn out to be as much a source of problems as opportunities. Much of the defense industry's production equipment is old (more than twenty years, in many instances) and inefficient. Investment in new equipment has lagged behind U.S. industry as a whole. While larger firms have generally made as much as comparable civilian manufacturers, subcontractors (usually small and medium-sized firms) have not. As a result, the number of such suppliers has declined.*

Still, there is money to be made, because a standard contractual procedure is to charge the government "cost plus," meaning that all the costs attendant on the development and/or manufacture of the item will be reimbursed, "plus" an agreed-upon percentage of profit. The system is open to abuse, not so much on the usually fixed rate of profit, but because of the almost limitless amount of costs that can be charged to the contract. So, as a result, cost overruns have become an often scandalous part of the weapons procurement story. Today there is a 91 percent chance that a weapon will experience an overrun which will average 52 percent of the cost—and that's not counting inflation.†

So despite a mixed profit picture defense contracts are   "buying in"
worth a lot of money. Contractors assume, with good reason, that the government will not force them to operate at a loss (they are, after all, necessary for the nation's security) and will reimburse their costs while ensuring them a profit. Besides, once the contract is signed, the firm doesn't have to market the product. Sales, as a rule, are guaranteed. Thus these companies will go to great lengths to obtain defense work. Sometimes they contract for a development project at an unrealistically low price, even if it means losing money. After all, if their people have done all the development work on a new weapon, they're really the only ones who know how to manufacture it. So the company management can be reasonably confident that it will be able to come in with the lowest bid on the production contract, and its losses on the development project will be recouped. This is called "buying in." Indeed, the military will often knowingly accept a bid it knows to be unrealistically low because it and the contractor have a stake in a weapons program and want to get "a foot in the door," so to speak.

*The Ailing Defense Industrial Base, page 17.
†Norman Augustine, "Just How Good/Bad Is the Defense Acquisition Process?," page 27.

Indeed, once a contract is signed, there are lots of ways to ensure profitability. Contracts can be and often are renegotiated; higher costs are usually covered and follow-up contracts offer numerous ways to recoup initial losses. Certainly, as regards the larger weapons, once the contract is in hand, the government has no place else to go. To get the weapons they've paid for, the military sometimes has to offer the company a financial "bailout" to keep it in business.

Of course, as noted above, whenever large contracts are at stake, politics enters in as well. Companies based in Texas or California don't have to lobby their Congressmen and -women; they are quite naturally favored by their delegation. Before World War II the Goodyear Aircraft Company (now Goodyear Aerospace) had large cotton farms in Arizona, the cord being used to reinforce tires and aircraft fabric. The president of the company told Arizona's Senator Carl Hayden that he would be doing them both a favor if he would persuade the War Department (there was no Pentagon or Defense Department in those days) to place military installations in the state. But not just any kind of facility; what they wanted was something new—air bases. He did and they did. Today Arizona has three major Air Force bases, as well as a couple of Army installations and a Marine Corps air station. And Goodyear has a large, prosperous plant southwest of Phoenix right where the cotton farms used to be.

There are legendary sagas about Congressmen and -women lobbying to get military goodies for their home districts. L. Mendel Rivers of South Carolina was chairman of the House Armed Services Committee for many years. The story went that if one more military installation were placed in his congressional district (around Charleston, South Carolina) it would sink. In fact, today the area contains no less than eleven major Navy installations, an Air Force base, and an Army post. Thirty-five percent of the payrolls in the district come either from military installations or defense industries.* At least Rivers was evenhanded. He gave all the services a chance to build bases and spend money in his district.

---

* Michael Barone, Grant Ujifusa, and Douglas Matthews, *Almanac of American Politics* (New York: E. P. Dutton, 1978), page 772.

ASIDE————————————————————————————————

When the Air Force decided not to produce the C-17 transport, which would have been built by the McDonnell Douglas Corporation, headquartered in St. Louis, the Missouri Senators issued a joint statement challenging the decision. "The Air Force," they said, "had specifically concluded that the C-5A [the Lockheed bid] could not meet those military needs . . . we can only wonder what happened to the needs of our military forces." Senator Nunn of Georgia, in contrast, in whose state Lockheed resides, saw the decision as a "tremendously positive enhancement of our military airlift capability as well as a major economic boost for the Lockheed-Georgia Corporation, our state and region." (*Aviation Week & Space Technology,* February 1, 1982, page 24.)

But before the 1983 Defense Authorization Bill left the Senate, Henry Jackson of Washington managed to delete the money for new C-5s and insert a provision calling for the Air Force to buy ten used civilian Boeing 747s built in his state. This was strongly opposed by Senator Nunn but was supported by both Senators from Kansas, since the work necessary to convert the airliners from civilian to military use would be done there. And Senators Eagleton and Danforth of Missouri backed the move as well. The House supported the C-5.

————————————————————————————————

From time to time the Department of Defense has proposed closing or reducing in size more than 600 military bases as a cost-cutting measure. But most stay open owing to congressional resistance. Edmund S. Muskie (when in Congress) and Edward M. Kennedy, however critical they may be of defense spending, are always ready to defend Maine's Loring Air Force Base or the Boston Navy Yard.

Another problem is that defense spending is not evenly distributed over the entire country. Naval installations are usually in states that have ocean boundaries. Some Army bases were built during earlier conflicts with Mexico, or when the primary mission was killing Indians. The Sun Belt allows for more flying days and there is abundant open land in the West for government use. As a result of this situation, 204 Congressmen and -women from 16 northeastern and midwestern states have organized an "Economic Advancement Coalition" to press for more defense spending in their areas. They argue that while together they comprise 45 percent of the total American population and pay, together, 50 percent of all income taxes, they house only 20 percent of the military bases and only 14 percent of all military personnel, and they can expect to receive only 9 percent of those new military installations now being planned.

Of course, Congress's role in the weapons procurement process involves a good deal more than just bringing home the bacon for the home district. Each year the Armed Services committees of the House and Senate must review and authorize Pentagon programs before money can be voted by the Appropriations committees. Thus, congressional decision-making on weapons programs is somewhat separated from spending. The Armed Services committees review Pentagon weapons and activities in some detail every year, and they authorize procurement and R & D plans as well. Each service gets its turn to testify. Every year the parade of brass trooping through the halls of Congress to explain what they're doing and why takes months to complete. Committee staffs, as well as members, acquire considerable expertise on weapons programs and the committee veterans, men like Senator John Stennis (D.-Miss.) or Congressman Melvin Price (D.-Ill.), have long memories. The record of these annual authorization hearings runs to thousands of pages and is a gold mine of information on Pentagon weapons programs for anyone who cares to peruse it. (The Soviets collect and study these hearings with great care, as do many researchers and journalists.)

While Congress has the power to shape the defense budget, it has not always used it. For twelve years after World War II it never vetoed a major weapons request or force-level recommendation made by the executive branch.* The Vietnam War changed all that. In the early 1970s, Congress began to reassert its prerogatives in defense and foreign policy. In the years since, it has created some new tools and refurbished some old ones, to influence defense and foreign policy decisions.

For example, in 1981 it enacted the Nunn Amendment, which is designed to allow better monitoring of increases in the costs of weapons systems. The amendment was described by Common Cause as a "breakthrough for Congressional control of the military budget" and is designed to

*Samuel Huntington, *The Common Defense* (New York: Columbia University Press, 1961), page 133.

provide early warning of excessive cost overruns.* But early warning is useful only if Congress has the will to act on the information. Despite post-Vietnam congressional activism and an apparent interest in doing a better job of monitoring Pentagon spending, there are still many in Congress who believe their only task is to give the Pentagon what it wants. As Charles Bennett (D.-Fla.), chairman of the Seapower Subcommittee of the House Armed Services Committee, put it, "The main function of Congress is to get whatever national defense is needed. Oversight is not a major function."†

Yet far more significant than the politics of military procurement is that unlike the rifles and wagons of earlier times, the overwhelming majority of military purchases are for products that have no civilian use. True, missile guidance technology may have accelerated the production of the microcomputers used in calculators, word processors, etc., but what civilian use is there for a B-52? (After World War II various entrepreneurs tried to start airlines using surplus converted B-24s, and failed because the old bombers were simply not economical to fly.) Of all the vehicles produced for the military, only Jeeps and cargo planes (such as the venerable C-47s, the military version of the DC-3) have been salable on the surplus market for anything other than salvage or scrap. Surplus military rifles are sometimes adapted for hunting; but with these few exceptions, military procurement is a one-customer market. This means that there is no free market, no competition with other buyers.

ASIDE———————————————————————————————

Sales of weapons to foreign countries are perhaps a partial exception. Most weapons sales are through the Foreign Military Sales, or FMS, program. Under FMS, the Defense Department buys the equipment in question and resells it to the foreign buyer, adding a small administrative charge to the price. A smaller portion of foreign sales of weapons is direct commercial transactions between American firms and foreign governments. In both cases, however, the government must approve and license all sales.

———————————————————————————————————

*The Christian Science Monitor, March 25, 1981, page 3.
†The Washington Post, October 4, 1981, page A29.

sole-source contracts   Not only is there but one customer for most military hardware, there is usually only one supplier, or at best a few. Military products usually have "specs," or specifications, so peculiar to the individual weapons system that the product needs to be tailor-made and can rarely be bought "off the shelf." (Although some off-the-shelf products might work as well and be much cheaper.) There is only one company that makes Trident submarines (General Dynamics Corporation), and just one shipyard can build aircraft carriers (in Newport News, Virginia). There is one that produces tanks (formerly the Chrysler Corporation, but they recently sold the facility to General Dynamics because Chrysler needed the money), and one that makes armored personnel carriers (the FMC Corporation). For the so-called big-ticket items, meaning high-cost weapons, there's usually no competition. So a vast preponderance (70 percent) of all military procurement is through "sole-source" contracts or is otherwise let without competitive bidding.* Competition does exist at the front end, i.e., the development stage, but this has the effect of encouraging buy-ins, since low bids, even if unrealistic, often win.

ASIDE———————————————————————————————

Defense industry analyst Jacques Gansler esimates that the Pentagon could save as much as 30 percent on the cost of many weapons if it were willing to find a second company to produce those items now made by one. So the Air Force is planning to use dual-source procurement for fighter plane engines. Both the F-100 engine, built by Pratt & Whitney for the F-15 and F-16, and the F-101, made originally for the B-1 by General Electric, will be purchased. Lieutenant General Kelly H. Burke, Deputy Chief of Staff for Research, Development, and Acquisition, said that the object is to sustain competition among producers over a period of years and that the Air Force would give "70 percent of the buy to the superior bid and 30 percent to the inferior bid with the idea of providing competition next year." (Paul Mann, "Air Force Intending Dual Engine Purchase," *Aviation Week & Space*

———————————

*D. Horan, GAO statement before Subcommittee on Procurement and Military Nuclear Systems, House Armed Services Committee, June 16, 1981.

Technology, May 31, 1982, page 14.) Yet while dual-source procurement may be effective for a variety of products, many weapons have no alternative manufacturer.

It's the system, always the system. Pentagon cost estimates are supposed to take inflation into account. Sensible enough. But the Pentagon is part of the executive branch and the Secretary of Defense works for the President. When Presidents spend a lot of time fighting inflation, they want the public to believe they are being effective. Hence they require the Defense Department to use inflation estimates that are politically palatable. So when inflation continues to climb, as it did in the past several years, the price of weapons rises faster than was projected.* In its fiscal 1983 budget DOD encountered the opposite problem—inflation lower than expected as a result of using "historical experience" to calculate inflation rates. Thus the budget contained funds to offset inflation that did not materialize.

Sometimes the military is in a hurry to get a weapon into production. Then it will begin to let contracts before design specifications are complete so as to "lock in" programs. The Navy, for example, began construction of the Trident submarine even though a mere 15 percent of the engineering drawings were ready. Not surprisingly, they had to make many changes along the way. And changes in specifications drive up costs. Just ask anyone who's built a house what happens when you change the plan partway through construction.

Yet the fact is, technology is always changing. A project takes years to complete (the average for major weapons is eight years; 10 years or more is not unusual). Commonly, it's not finished before some previously unthought-of possibility occurs to the buyer—a new target acquisition capability, different radar, a more powerful engine, or some other "nice to have" feature. When this happens, design changes are made, sometimes costing billions of dollars, and the taxpayer

---

* Representative Dave McCurdy, chairman, Special Panel on Defense Procurement Proceedings statement, October 28, 1981.

picks up the tab. And when the Soviets have, or are purported to have, a new capability, this, too, forces more design changes that result in cost overruns.

The people who manage Pentagon weapons programs understand quite well how the system works. They know that if costs rise, Congress usually comes up with the money. If it doesn't, they can always reduce the size of the "buy," that is, build fewer items, which raises unit costs and reduces production efficiency. They also understand that bureaucrats' power and prestige are based on the size of the programs they manage. Furthermore, as members of the military, they believe that what is really needed is weapons that outperform any others, which leads to what Deputy Secretary of Defense Frank Carlucci has called "the last five percent syndrome." The last 5 percent of performance—that extra edge military men lust after—can increase costs by as much as 50 percent.* As the costs of weapons go up, the number of weapons purchased goes down, and we get less defense for our money. One defense analyst, with some bitterness, has described this process as the "curve of unilateral disarmament." That is, without intending to disarm, we end up having fewer weapons than before.

COST OVERRUNS

The absence of a free-market system is one key to understanding the particular problems of weapons acquisition. The genius of the free-market system, as no American needs to be reminded, is the feedback—the "bottom line"—that it gives the entrepreneur. If you're selling automobiles, you know well how your car measures up to the competition; and, more importantly, you know to the penny just how good a job you're doing selling them. In other areas, the distribution of so-called nonmarket goods (such as education, law enforcement, and the like), it's hard to measure performance. The bottom line, then, has to be something ar-

---

*House Committee on Armed Services, "Weapons Acquisition Policy and Procedures: Curbing Cost Growth." U.S. House of Representatives, 1982, page 27.

tificially created for that purpose, like "publish or perish" in the university or traffic ticket quotas for policeman; in short, some kind of bureaucratic measure of success.

Since there is no peacetime bottom line for military hardware, evaluation standards must be invented. For plywood, sheet steel, or peanut butter, there is a market which creates, presumably, a fair market price and provides a comparative test of quality. But if the Navy wants to buy a Trident ballistic-missile submarine, something that has never before been designed or built, it should not surprise us that the bid for the first one turns out to be $20 billion, $30 billion, or even more short. No one knows how much the Trident weapons system actually costs, and we won't know until it is all done and we can add it up. And of course there is no competitor.

So a system which demands "cost optimism" in the bidding phase results in cost overruns once the contract is landed. But in the absence of market discipline, defense company management often gets quite sloppy, if not larcenous. A Rand study of military contractors, commissioned by Defense Secretary McNamara in the early 1960s, found that five times as many engineers were put on military projects as were assigned to comparable civilian ones in the same company. Yet there was no correlation between the size of the development team on a project and the success of the venture as a whole.*

So once the contract is in hand and the military is dependent upon the company to finish the job, "costs" escalate. Part of the cost is "overhead," which tends to escalate with little oversight from auditing agencies. Slick P.R. materials, called educational by the contractor and therefore allowable as "costs," tend to promote the weapon. Advertisements, not allowable as costs, but part of the contractor's anticipated profit, do the same.

A market relationship is absent in other ways as well. When a company begins dealing with the government, the government takes over many of the functions ordinarily reserved to the private sector. The government chooses the product and is very specific in describing what it wants. The

*Adam Yarmolinsky, *The Military Establishment* (New York: Harper and Row, 1971), page 262.

Eyes on the olive branch, but arrows at the ready.

The American Eagle's stance on the Great Seal of the United States symbolizes what our country's great leaders have taught for two centuries: Seek peace from a position of strength.

President George Washington captured its meaning in his first message to Congress in 1789. "To be prepared for war is one of the most effectual means of preserving peace."

Today, the United States Air Force F-15 Eagle is a manifestation of the Great Seal's symbology. Strong enough to win, awesome enough to deter. By its very presence it is an expression of national will.

F-15 Eagle
MCDONNELL
DOUGLAS

Sample of a defense contractor's advertisement, technically not a part of project costs, but paid from company profit. (Photo courtesy of McDonnell Douglas)

government states its price. It can pick the subcontractors and suppliers. It also can dictate employment practices, such as "equal opportunity" requirements and the like. Companies working for the military often are operating so far out of the normal market system that Pentagon bureaucrats sometimes end up substantially managing the whole company or, at least, significant parts of it.

Another complicating factor is that the military commonly insists on what is called state-of-the-art design. This makes it difficult, if not impossible, to anticipate costs. Design requirements that are on the frontier of the known engineering world create so many ambiguities and unknowns that engineers assigned to these projects find it useful (indeed necessary) to categorize them as "known unknowns" and "unknown unknowns." The known unknowns are the details you know you're going to have trouble with. Unknown unknowns are the ones that won't show up until you are well into the project.

state-of-the-art

ASIDE————————————————————————————

For example, in the late 1950s newly developed combat aircraft were approaching the physical limits of winged flight. They couldn't go much higher without rocket engines. Speeds were as great as 2,000 miles per hour, albeit in a shallow dive. The problem was how to control the airflow into the engine. Regardless of the plane's speed, the air inside the engine cannot exceed the speed of sound; if it does, the supersonic shock wave will stall the engine, perhaps even wreck it. The task, then, was to find a way to regulate the flow into the air intake (technically called the inlet ramp.) Devising a variable inlet ramp was a tricky technical problem. But the point is, this was a known unknown; the engineers didn't have the solution when they began, but they knew what the problem was.

An unknown unknown, on the other hand, is completely unanticipated. While it was expected that fast planes would require variable inlet ramps, high speeds also presented some surprises. Paint, for example, tended to peel off. More significant was the fact that the heat, and other stresses generated, caused the airframe to expand a bit. And when the plane slowed, it cooled and contracted. This constant flexing loosened the aircraft's myriad hydraulic connections. So the fluid leaked out, which was quite critical since hydraulic pressure operated the plane's controls, flaps, and brakes. Eventually, new connectors were devised and retrofitted that held tight despite the flexing. The thing to keep in mind is that it would have been much easier and a lot cheaper if our engineers had known about the problem beforehand.

The airlines, in contrast, do not demand state-of-the-art designs for precisely these reasons. And when it is necessary to modify a contract—as in the shift from a three-man to a two-man cockpit in the new Boeing 767—the airlines have to pick up the tab. In the case of the cockpit redesign, Boeing anticipates that the additional work will cost each customer from $2 million to $3 million per plane.* But it is worth it to the airlines, since they'll save half a million each year in operating costs. It is noteworthy to recall that no U.S. carrier was willing to commit to Boeing's supersonic transport design in the early 1970s. The airlines felt they couldn't make money with it. Indeed, the British/French supersonic transport, the Concorde, has not been able to make it commercially. And the same is true of the Soviet design, the TU-144.

Military demands for the state of the art are understandable. The Navy or Air Force doesn't want to be surprised. They don't want to buy a new fighter only to discover that the Russians are about to build something better. Its goal is to maximize performance, often with little regard for cost. Since few of the weapons being built today will actually see combat, weapons performance tends to get defined in technical terms rather than in terms of usable combat capability. And, as noted above, some expensive, complex state-of-the-art systems turn out to be losers in battle.

DOD: THE DEPARTMENT OF DEFENSE

At the heart of the defense community is the Department of Defense, the DOD. But organizational charts notwithstanding, the Department is not really one unified organi-

---

Aviation Week & Space Technology, December 7, 1981, page 28.

zation but rather a bureaucratic layer cake, consisting of several agencies and bureaus with many layers of authority.

As cabinet offices go, the DOD is comparatively new. Prior to World War II the Army was represented at the cabinet level by the War Department, the Navy by the Navy Department. Both services operated as independent fiefdoms. Each had its own separate bureaucracy, its own budget, its own institutions for training officers (West Point and Annapolis), and its own traditions and ways of doing things (the "Army way" and the "Navy way"). Cooperation was extremely rare, requiring the equivalent of an international treaty or a presidential directive. World War II provided an impetus for increased cooperation. It demonstrated the importance of combined air-sea-land operations, and it proved that a joint command structure could work reasonably well. But the end of the war brought a return to the rivalry of the pre-war period.

ASIDE———————————————————————————————

In 1946 one Air Corps general had the temerity to ask whether we needed a Navy at all. Not long after, an Air Force general suggested that we abolish the Marine Corps as a separate service. The Marines, he said, were nothing more than a "small bitched-up Army talking Navy lingo." (Huntington, *op. cit.*, page 309.)

———————————————————————————————————————

President Truman had no desire to see a return to the kind of parochialism that had existed before the war, and he believed that a unified Department of Defense was the only answer. The National Security Act of 1947 was an attempt to do this. At least it was a start. It gave legal status to the wartime Joint Chiefs of Staff and created a new Department of Defense to replace the old cabinet posts of Secretary of War and Secretary of the Navy. The DOD was given its own cabinet-level Secretary. (The act also created the CIA, the National Security Council, and the U.S. Air Force as a separate service.)

National Security Act of 1947

The Joint Chiefs of Staff—the three military commanders (as distinct from the civilians appointed to the positions of Secretary, Under-Secretary, and Assistant Secretary in the three services)—were now required to report to their respective civilian bosses; and the three Secretaries, in turn, were under the Secretary of Defense.

Old habits, however, die hard; and the old bureaucracies, especially the Navy, resisted change. The 1947 legislation did not produce a unified department but rather a loose confederation of three military bureaucracies presided over by a weak Secretary of Defense. The services and their allies in Congress, by carefully limiting the powers of the new Secretary, saw to it that the military services would continue to enjoy substantial autonomy. Not surprisingly, each service responded differently to the challenge. The Navy, which had long benefited politically from its own separate access to the President through the Secretary of the Navy, resisted the measure. The new Air Force was delighted with equal and, as we shall see, sometimes more-than-equal status with the two older forces.

ASIDE ──

Most people forget that the Air Force was part of the Army (bureaucratically speaking) throughout World War II. The issue of an independent Air Force had been controversial in the 1920s and 1930s, surfacing most dramatically in the Billy Mitchell affair. General Mitchell was an Army aviator with an abiding faith in his weapon. The conventional military wisdom of the day saw aircraft as scouts at best. Mitchell demonstrated, against orders, that aircraft could sink battleships with bombs. But World War II seemed a vindication of air power. Vast fleets of B-17s, B-24s, and B-29s routinely bombarded Germany and Japan and, in appearance at least, pounded the Axis into submission. Whatever the case (and the effectiveness of World War II bombing missions is still being debated), the aviators and their "birds" captured public and congressional imagination. This fact, in conjunction with the simple bureaucratic reality that air squadrons required hundreds of thousands of ground support personnel, led the Army high command to fear that the tail might come to wag the dog. Thus, by 1947 the Army brass were happy to be rid of the fly-boys and their toys.

──

The initial arrangement didn't work very well, and it took a series of amendments to the original act to strengthen the responsibilities and to augment the power of the Secretary of

Defense. In 1953, after years of difficulties in trying to get the new organization to function (difficulties which included, among other things, the suicide of the first Defense Secretary, James Forrestal), additional powers and staff were added to the office of the Secretary of Defense.*

One problem was and remains interservice rivalry. Even after the Department was created, disputes among military branches tended to play themselves out in Congress. For years the Air Force got two dollars for every one dollar the Navy and the Army each received, owing in part to its better congressional connections and in part to the dominance of the Strategic Air Command. (Today the Navy gets the lion's share of the budget.) Instead of accepting the Defense Secretary's judgments on new weapons, the Army, Navy, and especially the Air Force would fight out their battles in Congress, particularly within the Armed Services and Appropriations committees. This led, as we shall see, to years of poor planning, nonstandardization of weapons and parts, and some redundancy in weapons systems.

Since it found itself unable to deal with the competition, Congress finally in 1958 amended the National Security Act one more time and handed over ultimate authority for the determination of "roles and missions" of the various services to the Secretary of Defense. Congress retained control over military spending as a whole.

Conflicts between the services and the Secretary of Defense are still common today, and a great deal of what goes on inside the Pentagon—weapons procurement in particular—can be understood only if one understands these tensions and conflicts. It is the individual services—the Army, Navy (and Marines), and Air Force—that largely manage the development and procurement of weapons. The Secretary of Defense and his staff play their part, but the services have a way of getting what they want most of the time. The problem is that while no Army, Navy, or Air Force officer *outranks* his civilian Secretary or the Secretary of Defense, most will surely *outlast* their civilian superiors. Therein lies the nub of the problem.

---

* Forrestal "destroyed his health while trying to make this loose confederation of three military departments work." Charles J. Hitch, "Evolution of the Department of Defense," in Head and Rokke, *op. cit.,* page 347.

Well into the 1960s, despite efforts at reorganization for efficient management, the services resisted the kind of centralization that the creation of the DOD had been intended to provide. The Army, for example, had a Jupiter missile with about the same capability as the Air Force's Thor. But while the two missiles had identical missions, they had no interchangeable parts.

Typically, the government would discover that while the Air Force was selling surplus oxygen regulators on the East Coast for 50 cents apiece, the Navy was putting through a rush order for the same equipment at $250 each. Not only was there no central purchasing or coordination of weapons systems, there weren't even efforts to integrate targeting strategies or war scenarios among the services. Indeed, it seemed as though no Secretary of Defense could make the system work.

CENTRALIZING DOD: THE McNAMARA ERA

At the start of his tenure as Secretary of Defense in 1961—a post he would hold for eight years, longer than any other Secretary before or since—Robert McNamara was given a Navy briefing about the new Polaris submarine-launched ballistic missile program. During the briefing he is reported to have interrupted the slide show to ask how the Air Force's targeting priorities fit in with the Navy's. There was an embarrassed silence, or so it was reported. The Navy, it appeared, did not know or care what the Air Force was planning to hit, and the reverse was true as well. It was one thing to buy different belt buckles, crash helmets, radios, and oxygen regulators; but to have no joint targeting strategy was too much for the new Secretary to tolerate. And so SIOP was born.

SIOP   SIOP, the Single Integrated Operating Plan, combines Air Force and Navy strategic target planning. It is continually being updated and adjusted as missile batteries and bombers are modified and as submarine deployments shift. Today it forms the centerpiece of our thermonuclear war planning.

Defense Supply Agency   In the same vein, McNamara also combined the various military supply organizations into one Defense Supply

Agency, so that we would avoid the embarrassing scandals of the right hand selling surplus at pennies on the dollar while the left hand was paying a premium to rush-order the same thing. Henceforth, all the services would issue the same socks and underwear, shoes and belts. Odd though this may seem, this order generated a great deal of resentment among uniformed personnel. (The Marines in particular were upset because their standard-issue belt buckle was of a distinctly different design and could be used to open beer bottles.)

But McNamara had a much larger agenda. For better or worse, he revolutionized the Defense Department. Drawing deeply on his background, first as a systems analyst in World War II (he held the rank of major) and then a professor of management at MIT, he had made his reputation as the savior of the Ford Motor Company, which in the late 1940s was approaching bankruptcy under the iron hand of its founder, Henry Ford. McNamara helped turn Ford around and make it profitable again. In the Defense Department, McNamara's goal was simple: to bring systematic cost-benefit analysis to the DOD.

His effort to impose cost-benefit analysis was, to say the least, controversial. Not all decisions, many argued, could be reduced to such calculations. How does one calculate the "cost" and "benefits" of morale and leadership, for example? And how about the contribution to U.S. prestige and deterrence of having a reputation for producing the best equipment in the world? McNamara evoked a gut-level reaction in the military. After all, didn't big bombers exist for bold men to fly? Great warships for intrepid men to sail? Powerful tanks for brave men to ride into combat? What did he offer instead? Young "number crunchers" fresh out of grad school, slide rules (the pocket calculator hadn't yet been invented) dangling from their belts.

McNamara took one of the more obscure bureaucracies within the office of the Secretary of Defense and made it central to his purpose: the Office of Systems Analysis, or OSA. In 1961 there were only six professionals in OSA. By 1968 there were 200. The job of these "whiz kids," as they were derisively called by old-line military personnel (one kid was Harold Brown, from the California Institute of Technology, who returned in 1977 to be Carter's Secretary of Defense), was to ferret out from the line-item budgets answers to tough questions: Precisely what kinds of capability are we buying? How much do weapons systems really cost? How can we better standardize weapons development and purchasing?

McNamara's objective was to eliminate program overlap and to ensure that the overall directions of the military were being clearly thought out and stated. Otherwise, he felt (correctly), these goals and programs could not be objectively evaluated; and he, the Secretary, could not make rational decisions as to which ones to fund and which to cancel.

This was revolutionary thinking, and not all of it took hold during McNamara's tenure. In the past, technology and "the threat" had tended to drive the system. If something could be done (or built) it would be, especially if the Soviets might beat us to it. If it was possible to make an airplane fly five times the speed of sound (around 3,500 miles per hour) at 80,000 feet, then we should build one. The Soviets might do it if we didn't, and in any case, faster and higher flying had to be better. Today there is a substantial debate in the Congress and in the nation over the military's traditional preference for complex "high-performance" weapons over cheaper, simpler, and often more reliable equipment. But at the time, no one outside of McNamara and his crew was challenging that view.

From the systems analysts' point of view, the traditional procurement process started at the wrong end of the problem. Rather than "buy solutions," they said, we should first clarify goals—what the military call "missions." If a mission was defined as being able to destroy a certain kind of target in a certain kind of weather in the face of certain kinds of hostile countermeasures, the most "cost-effective" solution might not necessarily be the weapons system under review, but perhaps an altogether different idea. "Define the mission," the whiz kids were demanding. Only then could they come up with a rational solution.

To accomplish all this, the Secretary first had to reorganize the way the Pentagon thinks about its assets. The military is hardware-oriented. The Army has tanks and guns, the Air Force planes, and the Navy ships. It was traditional for them to see their roles as extensions of their weapons.

McNamara, in contrast, viewed defense as a whole and, more importantly, as a process. For example, rather than treat bombers, ICBMs, and SLBMs only as separate entities, he also viewed them collectively as "strategic retaliatory forces." Similarly, he saw air and sea lift as part of the same mission and insisted on viewing separate and distinct programs for cargo ships and cargo planes as components of that mission. Obviously, this approach tended to ride roughshod over the traditional, time-honored service demarcations. Nevertheless, he established seven functional categories and insisted that the military budget be organized around them.

One of Robert McNamara's most important contributions to management of DOD was the establishment of the Planning Programming Budgeting System, PPBS for short. PPBS **PPBS** is a comprehensive system employed by the Defense Department to manage defense programs and plan budgets. It has been modified some since McNamara installed it in the early 1960s, but not so much that he wouldn't recognize it today. The process begins with the assessment by the intelligence community of threats, and to counter these envisaged threats the military services plan military requirements— weapons, force levels, and so on—over a ten- to fifteen-year period. Programming is the next step and probably the most important one, involving as it does the setting of priorities among weapons programs and of spending limits. Programs and their costs are then assembled to produce the annual defense budget and the five-year projections of defense spending, which are revised annually. We'll get a closer look at how the system works in practice in the pages that follow.

The TFX

There is probably no better example of the strengths and pitfalls of McNamara's desire for systematic weapons procurement than the saga of the TFX (later known as the F-111). The idea for a "tactical fighter, experimental" (hence the letters TFX) came into being, it is alleged, after an excursion on an aircraft carrier that McNamara, this time accompanied by President John F. Kennedy, took in 1961. The

Navy was proud of its large and varied fleet of planes. It had day fighters and all-weather fighters, heavy bombers and light bombers, big anti-submarine patrol planes and small anti-submarine patrol planes, and as many different kinds of helicopters. In the midst of the grand display, McNamara and Kennedy wondered, "Why do we have so many different kinds of planes? Why can't we build some common aircraft?"

On the drawing board at that time were two new planes, one planned for the Navy and one for the Air Force. McNamara wanted to combine the two into a single aircraft design that would serve the needs of both services. He never intended for the two services to use identical planes, but rather for the two versions to have sufficient commonality of parts (about 85 percent) to reduce development costs and to achieve some economies of scale in their manufacture (common practice in the automobile industry).

The plane the Navy had on the drawing board was called the Missileer. It was designed to "loiter"—a technical term meaning to fly slowly at high altitudes over the fleet—and to carry long-range air-to-air missiles to shoot down enemy planes hundreds of miles away. To do this the plane was to house a powerful radar antenna in its nose. The Air Force, meanwhile, was planning a fighter-bomber (to replace their F-105, known to those who flew it in Vietnam as the Lead Sled because of its poor maneuverability), a new plane capable of supersonic speed at low altitudes and able to use short, unimproved airfields. Its mission was to destroy ground defenses and other targets with tactical nuclear weapons or conventional bombs.

You don't have to be an aviation expert to perceive that the two services had very different missions in mind: the one aircraft was to fly close to the ground, using complex new terrain-following radar to guide it automatically; the other (the Navy plane) to have maximum performance at high altitudes and to operate from aircraft carriers. The services both doubted that one plane could be built to meet both sets of requirements. Yet McNamara wanted to use the same basic design for both. He believed that more than $1 billion could be saved not only on the initial purchase but also over the life of the aircraft, owing to reduced maintenance costs.

"It was," Henry Trewhite notes in *McNamara,* "a shotgun marriage with McNamara holding the gun."*

McNamara won the first round. He held a design competition that winnowed the field down to two competitive bids, one proposed by General Dynamics (in association with Grumman Aircraft), the other a Boeing design. The intention was to choose one and have the Navy buy a few hundred for fleet air defense while the Air Force would buy as many as 1,500 to serve as fighter-bombers. The military found both designs acceptable but chose Boeing's because it seemed to offer better performance at lower cost, in other words, "more airplane for the money."

McNamara worried both that the Boeing design would be too costly and that it would take too long to build something so innovative. He was concerned about production difficulties associated with its variable-geometry wings, as well as with its terrain-following radar system for flying at treetop level in bad weather. (The pilot sets the controls on automatic, and the plane virtually skips over the ground sometimes no more than 50 feet high, missing poles, mountains, and buildings, a major technological achievement, but a complex system to create.)

One way to make such a decision is to have a "fly-off": **fly-off** build prototypes of both planes and test them against each other. But to save money McNamara chose to make the decision based on the design proposals alone. He was willing to compromise on performance in order to get a better handle on costs. Some feel he may have been under some political pressure, too, to choose the Texas-based General Dynamics design because the Vice President was from Texas, and Texas had been in the Kennedy column in the 1960 election (while Washington State, where Boeing was located, had not). Yet months of congressional scrutiny found no conclusive evidence of political favoritism. Nevertheless, the military wanted the Boeing plane, whatever the politics. One general was quoted as saying, "A second-best airplane is like a second-best poker hand. It's no damn good."

McNamara's view, that we didn't always have to buy the

---

*Henry Trewhite, *McNamara* (New York: Harper & Row, 1971), page 34.

"best," ran counter to deeply held Pentagon values. As a result he won the battle over the TFX but lost the war. McNamara believed the General Dynamics design was closer to the common Air Force–Navy plane he was looking for, and selected it. But the Navy version became too heavy for carrier operations, and because of this the Navy never bought the plane, now renamed the F-111. Its two test models ended up in the boneyard. Instead, the Navy designed and eventually bought the F-14, a Grumman plane which incorporated the wing-sweep mechanism, the engines, and the radar and missile systems of the TFX. And the Air Force bought a few squadrons of F-111s, some of which now serve as strategic bombers (the FB-111) while others are being modified for electronic warfare. After McNamara was gone, the Air Force got what it really wanted, its own brand-new fighter, the F-15 Eagle.

THE PERIOD AFTER MCNAMARA

McNamara tried, one might say, to "maximize management," but many of his reforms were seen as interfering with military prerogatives and were fiercely resented by the services. The reasons are not hard to discern. The Secretary centralized power in the Department of Defense, usually at the expense of the services. And after McNamara left office, his Office of Systems Analysis was substantially downgraded. Nevertheless, systems analysis has not disappeared and, in fact, has been upgraded again under subsequent Secretaries. Today the Army, Navy, and Air Force all have their own systems analysts to enable them to compete better with those who work for the Secretary of Defense. If you want to play the game, they have concluded, you have to adapt to changes in the rules.

But some reforms remain. Joint weapons programs are more common though not yet the rule. The Navy is buying an Army helicopter to be based on frigates and destroyers. The Air Force and the Navy together are developing a new air-to-air missile to be carried by their fighters. In addition, the Army and Air Force are working on joint tactical radio systems. Similarly, cruise missile development has been a combined Navy–Air Force effort, although the services also maintain separate offices.

Still, there is some foot-dragging. A 1975 DOD directive giving responsibility for production and control of all ammunition to the Army has not fared so well. The Army has so far been able to wrest control over only 60 percent of the $16-billion store of non-nuclear ammunition. The other services control the rest, hide some of it from the Army, and continue to purchase more independently.* Still, despite its uneven implementation, common ammunition procurement has already saved about $200 million over the past six years.

Mission budgeting is now standard, although the old line-item system still coexists. Cost analysis has been broadened to include not only the cost of buying a new weapon but its cost over its life (including maintenance and operation). Today even Congressmen and -women understand the concept of "life-cycle costs," thanks to Robert McNamara.

THE WEAPONS PROCUREMENT PROCESS TODAY

THE THREAT

How does the process work today? It begins with an analysis of "the threat."

The CIA (known around Washington as "the Agency") and the DIA (the Defense Intelligence Agency) are constantly reviewing and updating information on foreign military forces—friendly, hostile, and potentially hostile. They provide information on what is called the "order of battle," numbers and kinds of weapons, size of armies, navies, and air forces, quality of training, organization, deployment, and so on. From these data, classified guidebooks used by government officials are compiled. The CIA and DIA are not the only ones working on this. The State Department also has a Bureau of Intelligence and Research, and each of the military services conducts intelligence work on its own.

Special attention of course is paid by all the intelligence operations to the Soviet Union, other Warsaw Pact countries, North Korea, Cuba, and Libya, because we want to know more than numbers. We need to know where troop

*The Washington Post, January 18, 1982, page A9.

concentrations are and where they are moving, how large and what the scope of defense production is, what foreign scientists are contributing, and how stable the political leadership is.

Some of these data come from espionage, but a lot more come from remote electronic sources: photographs from aircraft and from satellites. We analyze their communications, called COMINT, and their electronics (the characteristics and effectiveness of their radars for example), called ELINT. Once in a while the public gets a glimpse of the degree of detail that is collected in this fashion. In the March 1982 briefing on Nicaragua, for example, photographs were displayed not just of military bases and airfields, but of tanks and even trucks on the ground, and our specialists were even able to identify these vehicles by type. Presumably, we have similarly detailed photographs of Soviet bases, factories, training facilities, military exercises, operations, and movements of troop units, too. We shall see in the discussion on arms control how critical these technical sources are for verification of compliance with arms control agreements. The point here is that these data provide a picture of the military capabilities of potential adversaries (and friends) and give us some insight into their military plans.

Assessing intentions, of course, is a good deal more difficult than analyzing capabilities. Because of this, the intelligence community tends to focus more on military capability, and from this "capability analysis" to make estimates of "the threat."

The way that weapons perform, particularly Soviet weapons, is of special interest to the Pentagon. We want to know how good the opposition is and to identify weaknesses that in case of war might be exploited (somewhat in the tradition of scouting an opposing team in sports). In 1974, for example, when a Soviet missile submarine sank in the Pacific, our CIA and Navy undertook a complex and costly operation to raise it in order to get information on its design and construction (also to find out more about the weapons it carried). The Soviet MiG-25 flown by a defector to Japan several years ago was examined piece by piece before it was returned to the Russians (in crates; neither we nor the Japanese were willing to reassemble it for them). We did the same with captured Soviet weapons taken by the Israelis in the 1967 and 1973 Arab wars. In fact, we have standing agreements with Israel and a number of other countries to share such information whenever and however it should come our way. (As a result of this cooperation we have a small arsenal of Soviet weaponry, including MiG fighters, tanks, surface-to-air missiles, rifles, and other items.)

Some of the information we get from these "borrowed" weapons is reassuring. The MiG-25 was made up of much less titanium and aluminum and more steel than our intelligence sources had anticipated, and, in general, the aircraft was crude by American standards, capable for example of only very short sprints at high speeds. The automatic loader on the Soviets' T-72 tank frequently breaks down and its diesel engine (based on a 1928 design) has a life of only about 250 hours.* Former DOD official Norman Augustine notes that despite their huge inventory of about 50,000 tanks, the Soviets are stuck—at any given moment—with more broken-down tanks than all of ours put together.†

The Soviets devote even greater effort to obtaining information about our weapons and intentions. They obtained considerable information from U.S. weapons captured in Vietnam. They can also get a great deal from published sources, ours being a much more open society than theirs. But they are willing to use illegal means as well. Several years ago they stole a Sidewinder missile from West Germany and studied it. To prevent the Soviets from getting one of our F-14 fighters, the U.S. Navy went to considerable trouble in 1976 to recover an F-14 that had crashed off Scotland. It was carrying Phoenix missiles and complex new radar.

With so many different intelligence agencies plowing the same fields, inevitably some of their analyses do not coincide. While the public is rarely privy to these debates, they go on all the time. And from time to time, to bolster its position, one agency or another will leak information. One such leak, publicized in March 1982, was the report from the Pentagon's Director of Research and Engineering to the effect that the Soviets would soon have a space-based laser

---

*Pierre Sprey, personal communication, March 21, 1981.
†"Augustine's Laws and Major System Development Programs," self-published, page 39.

weapon—a prediction quickly disputed by American scientists as well as by the Air Force. The point is that this information, correct or not correct, was supposed to have been classified.

If intelligence estimates are used to plan defense budgets and weapons procurement, as well as to justify them, the question of their accuracy is very critical. While our information about current military strength may be reliable, the further into the future we try to predict, the harder the task has to be. The alleged bomber and missile gaps of the mid- and late 1950s substantially overestimated Soviet potential at that time; but then we were also wrong when we assumed about ten years later that the Soviets would accept numerical inferiority with respect to strategic nuclear weapons.

An analysis of "the threat" goes beyond mere observation of other countries' current military capability. The threat is also perceived as a future potential. Thus, what might exist sometime in the future becomes a factor in considering our military response. How do we know what an enemy's future capabilities might be? The only way is to be on that frontier ourselves.

DEFENSE SCIENCE

Not formally a part of the Pentagon, but intimately associated with it, are the so-called national weapons laboratories such as Lawrence-Livermore (near Berkeley, California), Los Alamos (near Santa Fe, New Mexico), and Oak Ridge (near Knoxville, Tennessee). Beyond these labs is the wider defense science community, made up of hundreds, possibly thousands, of scientists and engineers working in think tanks and universities, supported by research funds from the Department of Defense.

Several of the weapons laboratories evolved out of the atomic bomb project in the 1940s. Some were given specific assignments associated with the design of the bomb. The Radiation Laboratory of the University of California at Berkeley and the Oak Ridge laboratory, for example, had the job of separating the isotope uranium 235 from uranium 238. As we said in Chapter Two, the task of producing the fissile fuel was one of the great stumbling blocks to making a usable bomb, and it took hundreds of thousands of man-hours to do the job. Los Alamos, of course, was the headquarters of the Manhattan Project, where the engineering and manufacture of the bombs took place. After the war the government decided not to disband these centers, but rather to make them into permanent national laboratories, lest the skilled personnel which had been trained and assembled there be too widely dispersed and "lost."

By that time the hydrogen bomb was already under development, and since then scientists in these labs have been pressing the frontiers of weapons science and technology further all the time.

ASIDE————————————————————————————————

The management of these laboratories varies. Oak Ridge, Lawrence-Livermore, and Los Alamos are owned and managed by the U.S. government. The Sandia Laboratory, also in New Mexico, is managed by Western Electric, although directed and run, of course, by scientists. Oak Ridge for part of its history was closely connected with Du Pont but is now managed by Union Carbide. The Rand Corporation, a well-known think tank, was begun as an Air Force enterprise, but for many years it has been an independent, nonprofit organization, although it performs work under contract to DOD and other state and federal government agencies.

————————————————————————————————

The reason defense science is so important is that, as we have seen again and again, technology plays a significant role in driving weapons development toward new and sometimes unanticipated frontiers; and it is the scientists—not the military—who are on those frontiers. By themselves scientists do not make defense decisions in the way the President, the Secretary of Defense, and the Congress do. But insofar as they provide the military with new weapons possibilities, they determine what are called the parameters within which many defense decisions are made.

The relationship between the defense scientists and their sponsors (the Air Force, the Navy, and the Army, or the Defense Department acting by itself) is extremely intimate. While it would be unusual for a military person to be formally employed by a university or a government-owned laboratory, it is not at all unusual for the military liaison person to be a virtual commuter between the Pentagon and the applied physics laboratory, the engineering institute, or the lab in which a particular new weapon idea is being developed. The funding is, of course, entirely military in origin, making the liaison person the ultimate project manager, if not the immediate boss.

Scientists at national laboratories working in close communication with one another have periodic meetings with their military liaison. Once a breakthrough occurs, a meeting is called of all the national specialists—both civilian and military—within days. Normally scientists have to await publication of other peoples' findings or an annual convention to be apprised of new results. But in the case of defense science there is no time to wait. If the quickly called meeting concludes that the idea is promising, the next step is to "weaponize the concept." That assignment will be given to one of the national labs, where scientists approach the problem through modeling the possibility and analyzing some of the questions inherent in it, using powerful computers. The purpose here is to try to anticipate, before production, the consequences of such a system's development.

If it turns out that the idea indeed can be weaponized, the concept will be passed on through the military liaison to higher-ups. The Secretary of Defense and the Defense Science Board make a judgment on whether to continue the investigation.

The Defense Science Board is just that: a group of distinguished scientists who have made their reputations in areas related to weapons research (Edward Teller, "father of the hydrogen bomb," was chairman of the board for some time), who meet regularly and who are on call to advise the Secretary on technology and weapons science. In addition to this, they are also the people the Defense Department will call on to testify before congressional committees on weapons budgets, the impact of arms limitations agreements on our technological posture, and other significant issues at the point where science and defense overlap.

Whether working for the weapons laboratories or in their own labs, scientists remain scientists, independent-thinking and determined to find truth. The issue here is not whether or not they have been co-opted by the government, but how their work affects policy.

PARING THE "WISH LISTS"

The threat, as perceived through the national intelligence estimates compiled by the intelligence community, in combination with the weapons possibilities unearthed by defense scientists together set the "defense requirements" for the immediate and long-term future. These requirements are nothing more than the military's views of the kinds and numbers of forces and weapons needed to defend the United States and to carry out "national policy." Commonly referred to as "wish lists," they typically contain everything the services would like to have, irrespective of cost.

This done, the next and really most important stage is called programming, and it is at this point where the hard realities imposed by limited dollars are introduced into the process. Here the services' wish lists are pared down to realistic levels. Here important choices are made among different programs, rating them in relative importance and setting weapons priorities. Obviously, high-priority programs will command the most resources—people and money— while those of low priority may be dropped entirely or strung along on limited budgets. The basic reality is that the nation simply can't afford everything the services would like to have. The kinds of questions asked at this point are: How large should the Navy be? How many ships of what types should be built in a given year? How many Army divisions should be maintained? How many aircraft and missiles should be supported? What weapons research programs should be funded and at what levels?

Early in this phase of the cycle, the services produce what are called Program Objective Memoranda, POMs for **POMs** short. These describe the hardware for each service, as approved by the Secretary of Defense, usually for the first year of a five-year plan. These, in turn, are used to develop the annual defense budget, while the five-year projections are altered every year to reflect new developments. All of this is submitted to Congress for review and approval each year.

Taken together, the POMs are supposed to combine the perspectives of the uniformed services on what military forces are needed (given the threat) with the Secretary of

Defense's understanding of how best to allocate the available money among the various services and missions.

EVALUATING WEAPONRY

Once a weapons system has been selected—either because it counters some threat, reflects an important new scientific breakthrough, or simply is part of some existing weapon's modernization—a program office for that weapon is established within the particular service to which it is assigned and a program manager named. If the weapon is important (and expensive) like the MX, B-1, M-1 tank, or Trident missile submarine, the program manager may acquire a staff of from 250 to 500 people (uniformed and civilian) to oversee the work. This bureaucracy parallels the contractor's team, and they work closely together during the life of the project (thus the "close and incestuous ties").

In short, the "layering" of the Pentagon cake is further divided according to weapons programs. (Perhaps marble cake is the better metaphor.) We have a bureaucracy (the weapons program office) within a bureaucracy (the military branch) within a bureaucracy (the Department of Defense). And all these people—those within the Pentagon quite as much as those outside—have vested interests in the particular weapons programs; their livelihoods and careers depend upon their success.

To assure that these weapons programs are moving along on schedule and retaining their cost-effectiveness, the Secretary of Defense has established a review agency, the Defense Systems Acquisition Review Council (DSARC), which is made up of top Defense Department officials who review the program at various established milestones in its evolution.

Milestones I, II, and III   The first stage, called Milestone I, involves the "validation of the requirement." Here the DSARC explores alternative systems, settles on a weapons hardware concept, and sets a dollar threshold for the project. Succeeding there, the next decision point—Milestone II—involves a commitment to the engineering, testing, and evaluation of a limited number of prototypes. If the program still survives, it comes to

Milestone III, where a decision is made as to whether to go into production. Under the Reagan administration many of these Milestone III decisions are being made by the services themselves.

In the case of big-ticket items, of course, the commitment to a prototype (Milestone II) can mean the spending of billions of dollars. Because of this, few large weapons systems will be canceled after this stage is reached. At Milestone III the Secretary of Defense may decide neither to produce nor to cancel, but to produce a limited number of weapons and continue testing until performance goals are met.

What kinds of data does the DSARC consider? Test results certainly are among the most important. But as we noted earlier, the only true test of how good a weapon is is the test of battle. Without this, the system is full of ironies: the less popular weapon will be subjected to more rigorous analysis than the favored system; and the more expensive the weapon, the less it will be assessed.*

When highly tested and expensive weapons fail to perform adequately in what limited combat experience we have (in Vietnam and in the Middle East), people begin to question the testing methods used. As early as 1970 an outside panel of experts recognized the need for more realistic operational testing of weapons and urged the creation of a new evaluation agency. Despite the creation of such an agency, however, favored weapons are still being coaxed through tests so that they will pass muster, and serious deficiencies are still being ignored. Operational test results of the Army's M-1 tank, for example, were routinely adjusted by "scoring conferences," in which officers decided which equipment failures to count (in the official statistics) and which to throw out. Of course, it makes good sense to discount trivial failures that would not reduce combat effectiveness, but 1980 congressional hearings found that the Army was discounting major engine and transmission failures as well.†

Even more significant is the lack of coordination between these two distinct and separate sets of activities, weapons

---

* "Augustine's Laws," page 20.
† Dina Rasor, *op. cit.*, pages 22–23.

evaluation and budget planning. While quite obviously DSARC (weapons-evaluation) decisions have important consequences for defense spending, there are few opportunities within the Pentagon's decision-making process for the two sets of activities—weapons evaluation and weapons budgeting—to be related.* Indeed, the weapons cost figures used by the services to develop their budgets are often nine months old by the time they get to the Congress for review, and eighteen months old by the time the budget goes into effect.

WHERE IT ALL COMES TOGETHER: THE DEFENSE BUDGET

Today weapons procurement represents about 25 percent of the annual defense budget, but since the development and deployment of these complex systems sometimes take as long as ten years, decisions made in one year have budgetary consequences for many years to come. Indeed, two total-dollar figures that made their way into the news during 1982—the annual Pentagon budget and the five-year weapons modernization budget—were particularly confusing.

The point is that defense incorporates a good deal more than just weapons. But how much more and what more is hard to determine. The federal budget, for example, always includes a large amount (about $24 billion in the 1983 proposed budget) for the cost of caring for veterans. This money, allocated to the Veterans Administration, could be considered the residual cost of wars past, but it is not part of the defense budget.

Another disputed item is the cost of the space program. Some of the National Aeronautics and Space Administration's activities are military in nature, but it is hard to tease out the military activities from the purely scientific ones. The space shuttle, for example, is intended to contribute to future space exploration and even the harnessing of solar energy. But it has been given a much greater carrying capacity to meet the Defense Department's needs, such as put-

* House Armed Services Committee Report, 1982, page 6.

ting reconnaissance satellites in orbit or at a future date to service laser weapons in space. So how do you calculate the cost of that extra capability? It's just not possible.

Even with the budget for nuclear armaments there is an accounting difficulty. Nuclear warhead production, which today costs about $5.5 billion annually, is technically a part of defense expenditures but not included in the Defense Department's budget. Since warheads are produced by the Department of Energy, they fall under that budget instead. (This is a holdover from the days when the former Atomic Energy Commission dealt with all nuclear production.)

Another more general source of confusion about the budget stems from its terminology. When Congress approves the Defense Department's "annual appropriations," it gives DOD "budget authority," which is the right to incur new debts, hire personnel, and sign contracts for the purchase of goods and services. But normally the Pentagon is not able to use all its budget authority for a given year *during that year,* for the simple reason that it takes time to negotiate contracts, hire staff, and pay for all their activities. So the amount actually spent (that is, the checks drawn on the U.S. Treasury) in a given year, called "outlays," is usually *less* than budget authority. In fact, only about three-quarters of the actual expenditures in any year results from budget authority approved *in that year.* The rest comes from money left over from previous years.

budget authority

outlays

But, in any case, not all the money spent by the Pentagon comes from its budget authority. Some funds come from the sale of weapons, surplus goods, or other items; some of it from balances available from previous years. So we have still a third category called "total obligational authority," which represents the Defense Department's total spending program for each fiscal year, irrespective of how that spending is financed.

For the 1983 fiscal year, which began October 1, 1982, the Pentagon actually expected to spend (its "outlays") $221 billion. But if the United States became involved in hostilities during that year, the outlays would be much higher.

There are other ways to think about the cost of defense. One is to see it in terms of the proportion of the federal budget—29 cents out of every dollar—or of the gross national product—almost 6 percent in 1983. But perhaps the most important figure is its proportion of the money Congress actually can control in any given budgetary year. Because three-quarters of the total federal budget is previously obligated (for Social Security, interest on the national debt, etc.), the federal government has only so much "disposable funds"; and of this amount 78 *percent* will be spent meeting the military's needs.

The specific purposes for which defense dollars are spent are also confusing because different systems of categories are used to describe them. The Pentagon uses functional categories called "Major Force Programs" (a McNamara innovation).

ASIDE————————————————————————

Major Force Programs are as follows: strategic forces, general-purpose forces (the largest chunk), intelligence and communications, air lift and sea lift, National Guard and reserve forces, research and development, central supply and maintenance, training, medical and other personnel (second-largest chunk), administration, and support for other nations (foreign military sales).

————————————————————————————————

But the Pentagon's budget is also split among the services: the Navy (and Marines) get the most these days, followed by the Air Force; while the Army gets the least.

To confuse matters further, Congress uses its own set of categories to distinguish Pentagon spending within DOD. These are their budget titles: military personnel, retired pay, operations and maintenance, procurement (the weapons chunk), research and development, and "revolving" management funds.

The calendar is a good part of the problem. Congress meets every year and passes, or tries to pass, an annual budget. But the gestation cycles for weapons systems, as we have seen, do not necessarily correspond with the earth's around the sun. So things get out of phase. The weapons procurement cycle has essentially four phases: 1) concept, 2) development and testing, 3) production, and finally 4) modification and improvement of the weapons once they have been manufactured and sent out to active military units. There is also considerable overlap among the phases, especially development, production, and modification.

So the program's own bureaucracy lives on beyond a production decision. Production and deployment are usually spread over several years, and modifications and improvements are often made along the way. The same program office that saw the system through development performs the modification function as well. It keeps the users in the field aware of the latest maintenance routines and "fixes" for problems that inevitably occur. In effect, we see a bell-shaped curve wherein a program starts very small (in terms of dollars and people assigned to it), grows into the prototype and development phase, peaks at the production phase, and then gradually recedes in the operations and maintenance stage. It is terminated only when the system is scrapped.

The unit cost, then, of any one weapons system—that is, the cost of any one airplane or any one tank or any one rifle—must reflect all the foregoing: hundreds of peoples' salaries and benefits, office costs, physical plant, travel, etc. For example, in the Defense Department's fiscal 1983 budget request, $3.9 billion was asked to build but seven B-1 bombers. That's $523 million per plane. But this is not to say that each subsequent B-1 will cost that much. If more are produced, the unit cost will decline. And if more than our planned 100 B-1s are eventually bought, according to the contractor's chairman of the board, their unit price will be but $60 million–$70 million each.*

Contractors are not unaware of public and congressional concerns over military procurement. They feel as trapped as anyone by the dilemmas of overlapping bureaucracies and conflicting spending cycles. Their greatest desire is for "multiyear procurement"—that is, a firm commitment from the government to purchase a quantity of weapons over a number of years. The way it is now, they don't know if a program will survive from year to year, and even if it does, they never know how many weapons will be bought each year. This makes it difficult to plan ahead; to buy new material and to contract for subsystems in quantities large enough to get volume discounts on their price. Also, the system discour-

*Air Force, March 1982, page 22.

ages them from investing in expensive computer-controlled machines and advanced tools that could reduce the price of production. (As it is today, some of our most advanced weapons are essentially built by hand, like Ferraris).

The Reagan administration has turned a sympathetic ear to the contractors' complaints. Yet it is approaching multiyear procurement with some caution since there are some obvious pitfalls. Who, after all, wants to be locked into a long-term commitment to a weapon that proves to be a dog? So the idea is first to award multiyear contracts for systems that are bought in relatively large quantities and have proven their worth. Cruise missile engines and laser-guided artillery shells are thought to be likely candidates for the future, and early in 1982 a multiyear contract was awarded to General Dynamics for F-16 fighter production. In the 1983 fiscal year 15 programs were selected for multiyear contracts.

CONCLUSION

At about $50 billion a year, weapons procurement is the fastest-expanding portion of our defense budget. And with nearly six million people involved in weapons development and production, it is clearly one of America's major industrial efforts and a growth industry. Some weapons now being planned may not see "action," i.e., deployment, until the year 2000. By that time space-age equipment—laser and particle beam weapons—may render them obsolete. Indeed, ideas now in the minds of scientists and engineers might completely alter our weapons thinking. International developments not now anticipated (who could have foreseen an Argentine invasion of the Falklands?) could dramatically change our strategic doctrine and tactical war-fighting scenarios. We may even agree to limit armaments in ways that could fundamentally alter procurement plans.

In the face of so many uncertainties, how can responsible spending for national security take place? And how do we get control over the weapons freight train so that we can stop or redirect it when realities change?

Every time some antimilitary group gathers on the Pentagon steps to protest defense spending, somebody working there inquires out loud: "Why don't you picket the Congress? That's where decisions are made." But he could just as well have said, "Picket the White House." Or "Picket the weapons laboratories." Or "Picket General Dynamics." Or "Picket *Aviation Week & Space Technology*." The point is, as we have seen, no one group or institution by itself determines weapons policy.

Clearly, defense procurement is the single most complex process by which policy is made in our society. No one fully controls it, and indeed, while this is an inherent characteristic of all democratic processes, more and more people are beginning to wonder whether we can afford it.

7.

Controlling the
Arms Race

ONE OF THE FIRST things that strikes the uninitiated looking at arms control today is that the people negotiating on both sides are not out to rid the world of nuclear weapons. Rather, most arms controllers simply want to stabilize the existing relationship of mutual deterrence, and to reduce the chances of a nuclear war. Indeed, recent bilateral arms control agreements between the United States and the Soviet Union have grown out of a recognition by both countries that despite deep political and ideological differences, they share a self-interest in avoiding the use of nuclear arms. They recognize that the United Nations notwithstanding, there are no lawmen to preserve peace and to provide security on the international scene; and while arms are one path to security, limitations on armaments can provide another. Thus, as currently practiced, arms control rests on the same fundamental motive that propels nations to produce and buy weapons in the first place: a self-interested search for security.

ASIDE———————————————————————————————

Since the early 1960s a sharp distinction has been drawn between the terms "arms control" and "disarmament," with arms control by far the more commonly used term. In *Arms and Influence*, Thomas Schelling notes that arms control aims at stabilizing mutual deterrence by reshaping military forces to reduce or eliminate any incentive that might exist to attack. If the military forces of two potential enemies are such that an attack will yield no advantage to the attacker, peace will be assured. Disarmament, on the other hand, aims at eliminating military forces, whatever their character, in the belief that weapons themselves are a cause of war.

A LITTLE HISTORY

Historically, one way to control arms has been to disarm an adversary through victory in war. (Though that has its limitations, too, as the world discovered in the 1930s when Germany unilaterally threw off the restrictions the Treaty of Versailles imposed on its military.) But compared to military victory, the peaceful limitation of armaments is a much more difficult and far less dramatic process which requires lengthy negotiations among nations that are sovereign equals. Arms control agreements, then, are no more (or less) than limits nations impose on their own armaments in exchange for comparable self-imposed restraints by others. And if they are to be effective and lasting, such agreements must serve the interests of all parties.

Examples of arms limitation agreements are not hard to find in history. Early in the nineteenth century the United States and Britain successfully negotiated the Rush-Bagot agreement after two wars in North America between the two countries. We must remember that at the time the Redcoats were hated and distrusted quite as much as the "Reds" are today. Nonetheless, both sides agreed to limit naval forces on the Great Lakes (and Lake Champlain) to a few ships on each side. It worked, sparing both the cost of maintaining navies on the Great Lakes, and the security of all parties was enhanced. (The United States and Canada observe this agreement today.)

Rush-Bagot agreement

The Rush-Bagot agreement amounted to more than simple arms limitation. The Great Lakes became what we would call today a demilitarized zone. And similar agreements have been concluded in recent years in other places especially in regard to nuclear weapons. Twelve nations, including the United States and the USSR, signed an agreement in 1959

weapons-
free zones

making the Antarctic continent a weapons-free zone, and that agreement is considered successful and is still in force. In similar fashion, the outer-space treaty of 1967 and the seabed treaty of 1971 preserved outer space and the bottom of the ocean as zones permanently free of "weapons of mass destruction." But perhaps the most important recent example of this kind of agreement is the Treaty of Tlatelolco, which established all of Latin America as "nuclear-free."

Several attempts were made early in this century to limit arms in another way: that is, to set limits on the conduct of warfare, to make it somehow more humane, or—better said—less inhumane. Most of these sought to restrain the use in war of new technologies that science and industry were then creating.

ASIDE———————————————————————————

The first Hague Conference was summoned by Czar Nicholas II in 1899 to stave off the arms race and was framed as a "Convention with Respect to the Laws and Customs of War on Land." It essentially established rules for the conduct of warfare. The Convention in 1907 increased the scope of those agreed-upon restraints.

Hague
Convention

In 1899 the Hague Convention prohibited dumdum bullets, soft-nose bullets that expand on impact and produce larger, more ragged wounds than conventional bullets. Also banned (in 1907) were poison gas and the launching of projectiles and other explosives from balloons. Regrettably, these agreements lacked means of enforcement and quickly became casualties of World War I. Mutual self-restraint is most difficult to preserve under the best of circumstances. In war, especially one like World War I, where both sides were desperate for anything that might break the stalemate, it is virtually impossible.

A good example of the difficulties in enforcing selective arms limitations, and one that has almost entirely been forgotten (because it failed so miserably), was the effort to regulate the use of bomber planes by restricting them to military targets. Early in this century, long before the bomber became a major weapon of war, the Hague Convention tried to prohibit explicitly the bombardment of undefended towns.

We are so used to seeing newsclips of the London Blitz and the Allied bombing of Germany and Japan (as well as of North Vietnam) that it is hard to try to imagine what aerial bombing signified when it first became possible. But when destruction from airplanes was first contemplated it horrified contemporary sensibilities. The issue was not just the degree of damage, the shock of being hit from the air, but the vulnerability of innocent civilians, who in some past wars had been considered, formally at least, out of bounds.

The Hague Convention had already in 1899 adopted a formal prohibition of *artillery* bombardment of undefended cities. In 1907 the Convention extended that prohibition—in Article 25—to include balloons and airships. But the article was undermined almost at once. The imprecision of available means of bombardment, including the airplanes of the time, meant that many civilians were killed even when military installations were the intended targets. (In Pentagonese this is called "collateral damage.") Moreover, as war became more unrestrained, the boundaries further deteriorated. The Germans shelled Paris during the First World War and used Zeppelins to bomb London; thousands of innocent civilians were killed in Belgium and France as well.

In 1937, during the Spanish Civil War, the limits eroded further when the Germans bombed the Basque town of Guernica. It is by no means clear that, given the passions aroused, the European powers would have observed Article 25 even if technology had permitted more accuracy. (The Royal Air Force during World War II seems to have favored terror bombing of cities in the belief that it would undermine German morale and bring a quick end to the war.*) But with existing technology it was impossible to tell the difference between deliberate attacks on civilians and their inadvertent killing.

For example, the bombing of Rotterdam by the Germans in 1940 may have killed only 300 people, but the number reported in the contemporary press was considerably larger, and this may have provided the Allies a pretext for going after German cities in return. Similarly, in August 1940 a

Article 25

---

*Russell Weigley, *The American Way of War* (New York: The Macmillan Company, 1973), pages 354–59.

navigational error by a dozen German planes resulted in bombs being dropped on the center of London. The British, thinking it was deliberate, bombed Berlin for the first time the next night.*

These initial, and perhaps accidental, instances of city bombing led to rapid escalation. Almost everyone agrees today that the bombing of Dresden was an act of British retaliation and an unsuccessful attempt to depress German morale. But the point is that when, by 1945, Japanese cities were routinely and indiscriminately fire-bombed, no one felt a need to justify wholesale bombing of civilian populations anymore. Well before Hiroshima the distinction between military and civilian targeting had vanished.

Henry Kelly, an analyst with the congressional Office of Technology Assessment, draws two important conclusions from the shift in World War II from military targets to the bombing of civilians. First, he notes how tactics are dictated by available technology (the inability to aim precisely enough to avoid civilians); and second, how difficult it is for rational people to contain events once war has begun.† This point is not unrelated to current discussions of "limited nuclear war." It is doubtful such a war could be contained because once there were substantial civilian casualties the conflict would certainly escalate into an all-out nuclear exchange.

Before there were nuclear weapons, however, a special horror was associated with chemical and biological warfare. Even today, with the destructiveness of the hydrogen bomb reasonably well known, a special aversion to chemical and biological weapons continues to exist. But the limits on poison gas negotiated before World War I still failed to prevent its use in that war. Following the First World War, an agreement prohibiting chemical and bacteriological weapons was signed in Geneva in 1925. By the outbreak of World War II most major powers, with the exceptions of the United States and Japan, had signed it. (Japan signed it in 1970, the United States in 1975.)

In this instance the restraints were for the most part observed, although this was less because of the agreement

---

*Shirer, *The Rise and Fall of the Third Reich,* pages 774–78.
†Henry Kelly, at the American Physical Society, San Francisco, January 28, 1982.

than because of the fact that both sides had stockpiles of chemical agents and were ready to retaliate if the other side used them. In a sense, then, poison gas was one of the older deterrent weapons. Significantly, it was used in one verified instance after World War I, that by the Italians in Ethiopia, where there was no threat of retaliation. That case is similar to its alleged use by the Soviets in Afghanistan. Again, with no fear of retaliation, the Russians seem to have felt free to use chemical agents.

As for biological agents, these are not supposed even to be produced. Research, it is assumed, is going on in several countries. But production on a large scale was prohibited by the Biological Warfare Convention of 1972 which 111 nations, including the United States and the Soviet Union, signed. An accident in the Soviet city of Sverdlovsk in 1978, however, in which many people became sick and some died of an anthrax-like infection, has raised suspicions about Soviet activity in this area. The scale of the accident suggests that the Russians might be producing large amounts of some biological agents.*

CONTROLLING NUCLEAR ARMS

Beginning in 1946, the United States and various other countries within the newly formed United Nations tried in several ways to put the nuclear genie back into the bottle. Most notable was the Baruch Plan, proposed by the United States, which called for the international control of all forms of nuclear energy. But even if sincere, these efforts were doomed to failure. We already knew how to build atomic weapons and no international controls could take that knowledge from us. And the Soviets, not yet having mastered the technology, were not about to submit to any nuclear limitations until they, too, had acquired it.

So the 1950s are best remembered for sweeping comprehensive disarmament proposals and counterproposals, emanating first from the British and French and later from

---

*The United States is still discussing the incident with the Soviets in an attempt to find out precisely what happened.

the United States. It is not unfair to say that these (like their counterparts emanating from the Soviet Union at the time) seemed to the casual observer more to be aimed at world opinion than to be serious attempts to control nuclear arms. And no wonder. At the time, the Soviets were not in a position to bargain as equals; and they refused to be locked into a position of permanent inferiority with respect to nuclear arms.

From the beginning the United States was unwilling to accept any agreement that was not verified by "on-site" inspection (and which, incidentally, did not first deal with the reunification of Germany, an early example of "linkage"). In an effort to break this impasse, President Eisenhower offered **open skies** an "open skies" proposal in 1955 as a confidence-building measure prior to negotiating arms reductions. This would have permitted Soviet and American reconnaissance aircraft to overfly one another's territory for the purpose of verifying numbers and types of nuclear arms. Unfortunately, the Soviets viewed this as a ruse for gathering targeting data and rejected it. Years later, when satellite photography made it possible for both countries to watch one another's military activities without asking permission, the knotty problem of verification (of large nuclear delivery systems) was solved, at least for the time being.

Until 1961, then, U.S. arms control activity was pretty much *ad hoc*. Between 1946 and 1955 the subject was handled here by the Bureau of United Nations Affairs in the State Department, with a staff of four. However, in 1955, determined to make arms control more meaningful and potent, President Eisenhower named Harold Stassen—sometime candidate for President and a highly respected figure in national and international circles—his Disarmament Secretary. To give the position status and power, he gave Stassen cabinet rank and a staff of fifty. In 1958 the Disarmament Secretary and his staff were disbanded, and in 1961 a permanent bureaucracy whose sole mission was to work on arms control and disarmament was put in its place.

ASIDE————————————————————————

Disarmament and arms control discussions after World War II have not been limited to bilateral negotiations between the two superpowers. Indeed, the United Nations has supported much multilateral activity in the area. Interestingly, as reviewed by Alva Myrdal in her book *The Game of Disarmament* (New York: Pantheon, 1976, pages *69ff.*), when the UN Charter was first drafted in 1945 the question of disarmament was not made a "major task" or one of "immediate urgency." Nor did the Charter prescribe that the member nations should reduce their armaments or even that they should not increase them. Rather, restraints were placed only on the defeated nations. The Security Council had within its mandate the power to "establish systems for the regulation of armaments," but the Cold War and the employment of the veto rendered that body almost immediately powerless to do much of anything, so the General Assembly became the forum for discussion and resolutions on disarmament matters. It established subsidiary committees to work on different aspects of arms control.

By 1962 a multilateral disarmament committee, reporting to and instructed by the UN General Assembly, started to meet regularly in Geneva. First it was called the Eighteen-Nation Disarmament Committee. Later it was expanded as the Conference of the Committee on Disarmament. And it soon became the forum at which the atmospheric test ban treaty (see below in the text) was formulated.

ACDA

With the support of Senator Hubert Humphrey and President Kennedy, Congress passed legislation in 1961 creating the Arms Control and Disarmament Agency (ACDA) as an "independent agency"—not necessarily "free" but at least bureaucratically distinct—located physically in the State Department.

The 1961 legislation assigned ACDA three principal tasks: first, to negotiate and prepare to negotiate arms control agreements; second, to carry out research on arms control and disarmament issues; and finally, to educate the public on arms control. As a result of this mandate, ACDA from the beginning has been staffed largely by foreign-policy experts (diplomats), physicists, and weapons specialists; and its direction has come jointly from the President, the Congress, and the State Department. As part of the executive branch, ACDA cannot take positions—certainly not publicly—without the concurrence of the key foreign- and defense-policy-making agencies in the government. So although it is in the arms control business, so to speak, it has to work and coordinate with other agencies that are not: the State Department, the Defense Department (the Secretary of Defense and the Joint Chiefs of Staff), the CIA, and the President's National Security Council.

Thus, while the director of ACDA is supposed to be the President's principal advisor on arms control (and may also be our chief negotiator of arms control agreements), neither he nor the agency can openly criticize military or foreign policy decisions even when these decisions are inimical to the prospects for arms control.

So, to take one instance, the general public will never know if the Arms Control and Disarmament Agency found fault with President Carter's "countervailing strategy"—P.D. #59—announced in the summer of 1980. Conceivably, the agency might have had strong, negative opinions about our planning to fight a "limited nuclear war." And in fact, after leaving office, the former deputy director of ACDA did warn publicly of the danger of this policy.* But the point is that however strongly they might feel about it, there is no way short of resigning on principle that the director or his staff could have publicly disagreed with the President on that or any other military policy. And the same is true of the agency's role in the development of the military budget. When the budget is being discussed, the public might want to know what ACDA thinks about it. But the agency cannot hold a press conference, given its mandate, to explain the arms control implications of that budget. It is a member of the executive team.

Instead, ACDA is allowed and indeed encouraged to comment privately in advance of decisions that impinge on arms limitations. As part of the routine interagency review process through which all new policies are examined before being adopted, it may "concur" or "nonconcur" or suggest modifications. Thus, while being a member of the executive inhibits public pronouncements, it facilitates the agency's ability to influence Department of Defense and State De-

*Keeney and Panofsky, *op. cit.*, pages 287–304.

partment decisions and documents. But this influence, of course, is subject to the realities of bureaucratic politics. DOD, State, or the White House may at any time withhold significant information or "forget" to notify ACDA of a key meeting or of important information until the last minute, effectively undermining the agency's ability to function.

In 1975, in an effort to bring arms control considerations into the Pentagon's weapons acquisitions process, Congress enacted legislation requiring ACDA to prepare "arms control impact statements" on the model of environmental impact statements, analyzing consequences of selected weapons programs. (In 1976 it enacted a similar requirement with regard to sales of weapons to foreign countries.) The requirement has given ACDA an opportunity to review and comment on the arms control consequences of many major weapons programs, but beyond that, the requirement seems not to have had much impact. Still, even with this enlargement of its functions, some critics complain that the agency is too involved in bureaucratic politics and has not sufficiently built its own constituency (as, for example, the Civil Rights Commission has done).

This is not entirely ACDA's fault. While there is a constituency for arms control in this country, it has been (until the recent national initiatives for a "nuclear freeze") amazingly small. The Arms Control Association, partially funded by the Carnegie Endowment for International Peace, has a membership-subscriber list of less than 2,000 names (although the Association's publications may well reach several times that number). The Council for a Livable World is somewhat larger, with almost 20,000 members, but is hardly a giant. There are other groups that take some interest in arms control as a by-product of their major concerns. The Center for Defense Information, which focuses on the Congress and essentially monitors military programs and spending, is one. The Federation of American Scientists, which has an audience of scientists and is concerned mostly with nuclear weapons, is another. The Union of Concerned Scientists recently extended its primary focus on nuclear power to include nuclear weapons, which makes it a third. By and large, while these groups support arms control, they are not entirely satisfied with ACDA's role, and have expressed keen disappointment at the rate of progress and at the inability of recent agreements to slow the increase in the numbers and the quality of nuclear arms.

On the opposing side are other individuals and organizations that are explicitly skeptical of arms control as a means of gaining national security, and believe instead that a policy of military superiority over the Soviet Union is the more secure route to follow. Groups such as the American Security Council and the Heritage Foundation devoted considerable effort, in the period when SALT II was being debated in the Congress, to its defeat.

ASIDE———————————————————————————————

The Committee on the Present Danger also actively campaigned against SALT II, claiming the treaty had serious flaws but insisting nevertheless that they favor arms control in principle; but SALT II as written was unacceptable to them. One leader of the committee, Eugene Rostow, is now director of ACDA. Another key figure, Paul Nitze, served on the SALT I delegation and is now chief U.S. negotiator in the intermediate nuclear force talks in Europe. Having roundly criticized Carter administration arms control efforts, they now have the chance to do a better job.

THE TEST BANS

The 1962 Cuban missile crisis had a resounding impact on the first major nuclear arms control agreement, the atmospheric test ban treaty. Prior to 1962, as we have noted, efforts to limit armaments consisted of sweeping but impractical gestures; but after the Cuban missile fright, the two superpowers seemed more ready than before seriously to negotiate more limited and meaningful steps. The two most important agreements of the post-World War II period were signed in these years: the 1963 Treaty Banning Nuclear Weapons Tests in the Atmosphere, Outer Space, and Underwater; and SALT I.

Between 1945 and 1963, in a period of rapid development of both atomic and later hydrogen weapons, the United States, the Soviet Union, Great Britain, and France detonated together a total of 488 atomic and hydrogen bombs—

atmospheric
test ban
treaty

an average of more than 27 a year for eighteen years. Virtually all of these explosions were in the air.* And the tests produced fallout and other serious radiation hazards, some of which can still be detected today.

The intense emotion generated by the bomb tests in the atmosphere was a potent political force both here and abroad in the 1950s and 1960s. Opposition was led by mothers who read about the likelihood of strontium 90 (an isotope that attaches itself to calcium in bones) moving from the atmosphere onto the grass, through cows and into their children's milk. It is now well documented that it was these women who helped get the atmospheric test ban (also known as the partial test ban treaty) passed in 1963. While it has been called "the first and greatest environmental protection act in the world," the political lobbying for the test ban is notable for what it did not seek: more general limitations on nuclear weapons. And because of this narrow concern with nuclear fallout, a comparable public interest in a more general test ban was not forthcoming.

ASIDE————————————————————————————————————

> For some Europeans, the partial test ban treaty was not an arms control agreement at all, but only a "public health measure." Noting that the treaty did not lead immediately (or even fifteen years later) to a more comprehensive prohibition of underground nuclear tests as well, Swedish diplomat Alva Myrdal concludes that popular concern with radioactive fallout probably oversold the health aspect of the ban. The public was too easily satisfied, she writes, with the "ostrich-like" solution of driving the tests underground; and this did not contribute to the curtailment of nuclear weapons development.
>
> (See Alva Myrdal, *op. cit.*, page 95.)

——

Weapons testing provided (and still provides) us with most of our information on the effects of nuclear explosions. The standard reference work published by the U.S. government is lavishly illustrated with photographs taken at some

*SIPRI Yearbook, 1981, page 382.

of these experiments (and it provided us with the information, by the way, used in Chapter Two to describe their impact). Testing underground continued after the ban. But it turned out to be much more difficult to get agreement on a more comprehensive test ban treaty—one that would also prohibit underground testing—than had been imagined.

The reluctance has stemmed from the fact that the military and its weapons designers feel they need to be able to test a random sample of nuclear weapons from their stockpiles even if only once in a while, for, in addition to doing "proof tests" of new designs, they need to check reliability of older supplies. (For many people this is the reason why a test ban is so valuable. If there is uncertainty about the reliability of nuclear weapons, they are less likely to be used.) Since there is no place else to do it, the weapons labs don't want a comprehensive test ban which would prohibit all underground testing. So while the signatories to the atmospheric test ban treaty pledged to work toward a comprehensive ban, that treaty is unfinished and has been on hold since 1980.

ASIDE————————————————————————————

Another problem in achieving a comprehensive test ban has to do with the difficulty of verification. Nuclear explosions in the air are detected more easily than underground tests. An underground nuclear test is done as follows: A large hole is dug in the ground, and the bomb is set off inside it. Sometimes a rise and subsequent depression in the earth can be seen, but usually no radiation is vented. But these telltale signs are not adequate for verification. Instead, seismographs of the kind used to measure earthquakes are used to monitor underground testing, but some people worry that underground tests could be concealed if small enough and if detonated in the proper kind of soil. Others doubt such tests (less than 5 kilotons) would be of much value.

threshold
test ban
treaty

Between 1963 and 1977 some progress was made toward a more comprehensive test ban. In 1974 a "threshold test ban treaty" (TTBT) prohibiting underground nuclear explosions larger than 150 kilotons—about ten times larger than the Hiroshima bomb—was completed but not ratified. The threshold test ban treaty is important because it helped clear away some uncertainties about the two nations' nuclear testing programs. To facilitate verification, both sides agreed to exchange scientific information on weapons test programs: the number of tests, their location, and the geological characteristics of test sites (important for interpreting seismic data). The United States and the USSR also agreed to consult promptly if an explosion exceeds 150 kilotons, an important provision since scientists do occasionally miscalculate the yields of their designs. The TTBT is awaiting Senate action but both sides continue to honor its provisions.

Some progress was made during the Carter administration (by the United States, the Soviet Union, and the UK) on a more comprehensive test ban. While a number of issues remained, the hitherto highly controversial issue of verification has been resolved, at least in principle.

comprehensive test ban treaty

ASIDE———————————————————————————————

national technical means

As in SALT I and II, verification would be by something called "national technical means," i.e., satellites and other remote monitoring devices, supplemented in this instance by cooperative seismic monitoring. Among the measures under discussion were seismic data exchanges, the installation of high-quality seismic equipment on the territory of the parties involved, and on-site inspection of "suspicious events," i.e., suspected explosions.

This last is most significant since the Russians have refused to allow on-site inspections on their territory in the past.

SALT I

In hindsight, the decision to negotiate limitations on strategic (meaning long-range) nuclear weapons was inevitable, given the mutual vulnerability that the ballistic missile brought in its wake. But however sensible it now seems that we would want to discuss ceilings on the numbers and kinds of weapons aimed at one another, the first steps represented a real innovation in the way the two countries thought about their national security. As we will see, the success of the negotiations involved a commitment to stabilizing the arms race. As John Newhouse notes in his book on SALT I, *Cold Dawn,* "The talks were launched not from a common impulse to reduce armaments, but from a mutual need to solemnize the parity principle—or put differently, to establish an acceptance by each side of the other's ability to inflict unacceptable retribution in response to a nuclear attack."[*]

Curiously, the idea for strategic arms limitation began as early as 1964 in a proposal made by the United States to the Soviets for a "nuclear weapons freeze"—an old and a very new idea at the same time—on the number and characteristics of strategic nuclear offensive and defensive arms. At the time, verification, as we have seen, was still a major stumbling block; such a freeze could be violated in many ways, and because both sides had fewer weapons than they do today, even small violations might have had serious consequences for U.S. security.

And so the idea foundered.

Throughout the Johnson administration there were further feelers, especially after it became known here that the Russians might be building an extensive anti-ballistic missile system (code-named Galosh). Both the concept of quantitative ceilings on offensive weapons and the concern for anti-ballistic missile systems were but two sides of the same coin, namely the need to stabilize mutual deterrence.

Another development propelling both sides to the negotiating table on strategic arms limitation was the problem of military uncertainty. Trying to anticipate what the other side was going to do was getting to be a major dilemma. We knew the Soviets had mastered atomic and hydrogen weaponry; that they were willing to devote a large portion of their scientific manpower and gross national product to weapons; that while their technology was supposed to be inferior to ours, they had surprised us by testing an ICBM and putting up a space satellite before we could. What else might they be working on? We tried to find out and used our intelligence-gathering services to collect whatever information we could.

[*]John Newhouse, *Cold Dawn* (New York: Holt, Rinehart and Winston, 1973), page 2.

But conclusions drawn from these data were in many instances quite wrong. As we have noted, in the early 1950s we overestimated the size of the Russian bomber force that would eventually be built; in the late 1950s and early 1960s we again guessed wrong about the pace of Soviet intercontinental ballistic missile deployment. In the mid to late 1960s, however, our analysts underestimated the Soviets' commitment to improving the quality and quantity of their strategic weapons. The point is that either way—underestimating or overestimating—we were unsure of what we might have to contend with.

These uncertainties were compounded by our finding ourselves locked in a deadly competition with the Soviets without there being any rules of the game. Our game was to hang on to our lead; theirs to catch up. They were catching up. That much our intelligence could assure us of. But without rules to this game, the cost of meeting every possible future challenge—worst-case analysis in the absence of firm information—was beyond both nations' capacity. To make more efficient use of resources, then, both sides were almost compelled to set some boundaries so that neither would have to build and prepare for every contingency.

A third concern was that given the tension between the two nations as well as the irrevocable nature of the nuclear step, both wanted to prevent any accident or misunderstanding—warships, for example, interfering with one another on the high seas, colliding and bringing us by accident into armed conflict. This is the reason the "hot line" was established and why an agreement to avoid incidents at sea was signed. But the most important step, quite obviously, was to begin talking about the most dangerous arms of all: strategic nuclear weapons.

Strategic arms limitations talks (SALT) started out in 1968 with the two nations having somewhat different agendas. The Soviets, still somewhat lagging behind the United States in technology and in numbers of nuclear warheads, were looking for ways to limit *offensive* systems: intercontinental ballistic missiles, submarine-launched missiles, and bombers. The United States, meanwhile, was becoming concerned about Soviet efforts to develop *defensive* systems, in particular ABM or anti-ballistic missile systems. Initially, the

Soviets were antipathetic to the notion of limiting defense weapons since (as we have noted before) they have always been particularly oriented toward defense, and defense against missiles was just a logical extension for them of the anti-aircraft defenses they had already in place to protect themselves against American long-range bombers. The United States was mindful of all of this but feared at the same time that missile defenses would destabilize deterrence (see Chapter Four).

It took awhile for us to persuade the Soviets that it made sense to limit anti-ballistic defensive systems, but despite the delays caused by their invasion of Czechoslovakia in 1968, and our having started out with different and contradictory agendas, we did get a treaty signed by 1972, within roughly three years from the start of negotiations.

ABM Treaty   SALT I was notable both for what it achieved and for what it failed to achieve. The Anti-Ballistic Missile Treaty, which comprises one-half of SALT I, stands as one of the major landmarks of recent arms control efforts. As amended in 1974, it restricts both sides to a single ABM location comprising no more than 100 interceptors and 100 launchers. This means that there are to be no more anti-ballistic missiles at this site than there are anti-ballistic missile launchers. With but 100 interceptors in place, each side could technically (if everything worked perfectly) knock out only 100 incoming warheads, and this, given the fact that at the time we had 1,054 long-range land-based missiles and 656 submarine-launched missiles and they had about 1,600 ICBMs and 585 submarine-launched missiles, meant that we were essentially agreeing to have no real ABM at all.

interim agreement   The second half of SALT I was the Interim Agreement on Offensive Weapons. While the agreement was not a flat *freeze* on strategic nuclear weapons, in that it allowed certain replacements and substitutes, it certainly was moving in the direction of a freeze. We agreed to overall ceilings on the numbers of ICBM launchers and submarine-based missile launchers, basically restricting ourselves to our respective 1972 levels. But by focusing on missile launchers and not on missile warheads, the treaty failed to address the issue of MIRVs (multiple independently targetable reentry vehicles). MIRVing permitted both sides to multiply the destructive power of their existing missiles, despite the freeze on launchers. So the failure to address the MIRV issue represents a major missed opportunity in strategic arms limitation.

ASIDE————————————————————————————————————

Among the negotiating options under review by the U.S. arms control bureaucracy in late 1969 and early 1970, during its preparations for the second round of SALT I talks, was a proposed ban on MIRV testing. The United States had begun MIRV testing by then but the Soviets had not, so it's not at all clear that the Soviets would have accepted any proposal that denied them the opportunity to develop the same technology. Still, there was a chance. Within the U.S. government the issue was how such a ban on MIRV testing could be verified. According to John Newhouse's account in *Cold Dawn*, ACDA, State, and the CIA believed verification by remote devices ("national technical means") would be adequate. In the estimation of the CIA some cheating might be possible under such an arrangement but hardly enough to make it worthwhile. The proposal gradually worked its way through the bureaucratic review process, overcoming a number of obstacles, including review and clearance by the Verification Panel, the interagency group responsible for evaluating the verifiability of negotiating proposals. However, when it got to the highest level it was fatally altered. The National Security Council, presumably at the behest of President Nixon and National Security Advisor Henry Kissinger, saddled it with a requirement for on-site inspection and made it part of a much broader proposal. It was the kiss of death, a guarantee that the Soviets, for whom on-site inspection was anathema, would reject it.

(See Newhouse, *op. cit.,* pages 179–81.)

————————————————————————————————————

The result of this missed chance was that within only eight years the Soviets MIRVed a substantial number of their land-based missiles—about half—opening, as President Reagan was to call it, a "window of vulnerability" on our side.

The ABM portion of SALT I was meant to be a permanent agreement to be reviewed after five years (in 1977 and again in 1982). In fact, in the ten years that have elapsed since the treaty was signed, neither we nor the Soviets have constructed or expanded an ABM system. While there is talk today of our building an anti-ballistic missile system to protect our land-based missiles, and even some suggestions that we scrap the agreement altogether, so far the ABM portion of the treaty has been a success.

The other half of SALT I, the Interim Agreement on Offensive Weapons, however, was not to be permanent—hence the term "agreement," not "treaty"—but rather of five-year duration, meant to be replaced within that time by a more lasting, comprehensive arms limitation document. SALT I, then, was to prefigure SALT II, and SALT II was meant— had it been ratified—to lead to SALT III.

SALT II

As it turned out, negotiations for SALT II took much longer than expected (1972–79). Talks were begun by President Nixon, continued by President Ford, and concluded by President Carter. As we all know, while SALT II was signed by both Carter and Leonid I. Brezhnev, it was never formally ratified by either the U.S. Senate or the Supreme Soviet. Nevertheless, both sides have said they would do nothing to undermine it, provided the other side does the same, leaving the treaty in a somewhat uncertain status.

Seven years seems a long time to negotiate any treaty, but when we consider its intended scope and some of the obstacles it faced, the fact that it was completed at all stands as a major achievement. U.S. and Soviet forces are asymmetrical. This means that each side has a different mix of strategic nuclear weapons with distinct characteristics and capabilities. One consequence of this is that ceilings have to cover more than overall numbers of weapons. So in addition to limiting the number of launchers, as we did in SALT I, SALT II also limited the number of MIRVed warheads (on each missile) and provided ceilings on numbers of MIRV missiles and on launch-weights and throw-weights of missiles as well.

In some instances the only way bargains could be struck—and any negotiation involves bargaining and compromising—was by logrolling. We might accept a Soviet approach on one weapon or issue in order to get our point of view accepted on another, quite different kind of weapon. So, for example, the United States wanted an allowance of no fewer than 14 MIRVs on submarine-launched ballistic missiles, because that is the maximum number our Poseidon missiles are designed to carry; and the Soviets wanted no fewer than 10 MIRVs allowed on their SS-18 long-range land-based missiles because this is the largest number they had tested and deployed. The agreement, then, not surprisingly, banned testing and deployment of SLBMs with more than 14 MIRVs and ICBMs with more than 10. (It is provisions like these that trouble some observers both in the United States and abroad, because they see our SALT negotiations as not contributing toward reductions in armaments but rather making it easier for the superpowers to do what they want anyway.)

A related and very time-consuming issue was the need for precision in language. Pure translation posed lots of problems. The Russian word for security (*bezopasnost*) is somewhat different from the English equivalent. In Russian it means much more than mere "security"; it encompasses our notion of lack of danger, total safety.* Besides language, there was also the matter of political style. The Soviets were always willing to accept vaguely worded provisions in the form of general statements because they expected to "reinterpret" these later on, to suit their own purposes. So the U.S. negotiators, many of whom had been trained as lawyers, pressed for precision of language, even to the extent of having one 173-word-long sentence in the treaty. The definition of MIRV in the joint draft text, by itself, covered four pages. The resulting document (as published by the government) is 25 pages long and is replete with separate sections called "Agreed Statements" and "Common Understandings," aimed at achieving as much clarity as was possible.

Negotiations in Geneva were carried on during the seven-year period by an American delegation of six, led by a senior government official, for a time the director of ACDA,

---

* Newhouse, *op. cit.*, page 57.

supported by a staff of about twenty-five. All of the participating agencies also had Washington-based staffs working on SALT; so the total number of Americans involved in the effort was perhaps a hundred or more. If all those in the intelligence community working on verification-related issues are also included, the total was perhaps two or three times that.

Since the period we are describing overlapped three administrations (two Republican, one Democratic), the personnel at work in Geneva underwent a number of changes. Of the senior members of the U.S. delegation only two people, Ralph Earle, of ACDA, and General Edward Rowney, representing the Joint Chiefs of Staff, were there for most of the seven years. Three different people headed the U.S. delegation during the SALT II period: U. Alexis Johnson (1973–76), Paul Warnke (1977–78), and Ralph Earle (1978–79).

ASIDE——————————————————————————

The fact that a senior official was part of the U.S. delegation by no means implied that he would be in favor of the final treaty. General Rowney retired from the military shortly after the treaty was signed and actively campaigned against it. Rowney heads the U.S. delegation to START (strategic arms reduction talks), the successor to SALT. Rowney's position was that the U.S. arms negotiators were not tough enough. They could have gotten a better treaty, he argued, if they had been willing to hold out longer.

——————————————————————————————————

The Soviet delegation, in contrast, was far more consistent over the long period, not having to deal with national Presidential elections or changes in administrations at home. In fact, the head of the Soviet delegation for many years, Vladimir Semenov, came to be called "Iron Pants" by the American negotiators because of his lengthy service in that position.

One other contrast between the American and Soviet delegations was the kind of office equipment each country provided its Geneva staff. The Soviets were burdened with extremely outmoded office equipment. They had laboriously to produce their documents on manual typewriters and to use carbon paper, while the Americans already had word processors and automatic copying machines. The Russians often joked about the disparity in office technology available to the two negotiating teams and asked how the U.S. could possibly worry about Soviet military superiority, given their lag in office modernization.*

All the while U.S. representatives were negotiating with the Soviets in Geneva, a parallel set of "negotiations" was going on behind the scenes within the U.S. government among five different government agencies: ACDA, the Department of State, the Department of Defense and the Joint Chiefs of Staff (giving the Defense Department two votes, so to speak), the Central Intelligence Agency, and, of course, the President's National Security Council staff as coordinator. These groups met regularly during the period with SALT II as their only agenda item to set U.S. negotiating positions in Geneva, to work out responses to Soviet proposals, and, in general, to provide instructions and guidance to our negotiators on the scene.

It was to be expected that our top foreign policy and military people would be supervising, indeed determining at every step along the way what was going on in Geneva. More interesting is whether what was happening in Geneva was influencing in any way what was going on at home. Critics on the political Right worried about precisely this: that our participation in SALT II would prejudice decisions about long-term military strength and particularly that it might delay what they felt to be an urgent need to further modernize U.S. strategic forces. As they saw it, the cancellation of the B-1 was exactly what they feared: something given away and nothing got in return (although, as we have noted, the B-1 was canceled in 1977 for military reasons).

Vladivostok accords

Two years into the SALT II process, President Gerald Ford and Chairman Brezhnev met at Vladivostok, in Russia, to endorse a kind of framework for the treaty. At Vladivostok the principle of equal aggregate ceilings on launchers

*Strobe Talbott, *Endgame: The Inside Story of SALT II* (New York: Harper and Row, 1979), page 93.

was laid out, and for the first time the issue of MIRVs was addressed—although the proposed ceiling on MIRVs was higher than either country had on line at the time. The final agreement lowered these ceilings somewhat and set some additional limits on types of strategic systems. (See below.)

Nineteen seventy-four was a high point for détente. President Nixon had resigned and there was some domestic peace at home. And President Ford and his Secretary of State Henry Kissinger enjoyed playing a critical role in a historic moment of arms control negotiations. In addition to the public relations, however, the meeting provided a real breakthrough in the negotiations.

SALT II—PROVISIONS

One reason SALT II took so long to negotiate is that it is a very ambitious treaty in scope and sets several different kinds of limitations on virtually every category of strategic nuclear weapons: those currently deployed as well as on several types not yet built. It also establishes numerical and qualitative limits on land- and sea-based missiles, heavy bombers, MIRVs, and aircraft equipped with long-range cruise missiles; and on several other types of strategic weapons.

First—in the spirit of the Vladivostok accords—the treaty sets an overall ceiling of 2,400 on ICBMs, SLBMs, and heavy bombers; and endorses a later reduction (by 1981) of this total to 2,250. To reach this total, the Soviets would have had to dismantle some 250 strategic weapons systems and the United States would have been required only to take apart some old mothballed bombers.

Negotiating this reduced ceiling was particularly difficult. When the Carter administration took office in 1977, it inherited Vladivostok but decided to undertake a major review of the negotiations so far, having a more ambitious arms control agenda than had the previous Administration. After the review the Carter people decided to propose not just ceilings but even a series of reductions in nuclear weapons, in some cases as much as 20 percent or more, and did so in March 1977. They saw this as a way to advance the arms control process. But others were not so sanguine. They predicted that the Soviets would reject these reductions and that this might derail the SALT process altogether. The Soviets did reject the reductions initially, but the idea of reductions, if not the proposed numbers, was later incorporated into the treaty. Whether it was worth the extra time it took to negotiate these extra reductions is still being debated. Had the treaty been completed sooner, it might have come to the Senate floor before the foreign policy turmoil of 1979 and might have been successfully ratified. As it was, SALT II was one of the many casualties of the year of Iran and Afghanistan. A less ambitious treaty, ratified, could have provided the negotiators with a new arms control floor, so to speak, and permitted them to move promptly on to SALT III.

In addition to the overall ceilings, the treaty sets sublimits on all major categories of strategic weapons: ICBMs and MIRVed ICBMs, SLBMs and MIRVed SLBMs, heavy bombers, and cruise missiles as well.

MIRV Limits

A combined total of 1,320 cruise-missile–equipped bombers, MIRVed ICBMs, and SLBMs is permitted. The total number of MIRV missiles may not exceed 1,200. Within this limit neither side may have more than 820 ICBMs with MIRVs. In addition, there may be no more than 10 warheads on existing ICBMs. This puts a cap on the total number of warheads either side could build. So the immense Soviet SS-18 is permitted but 10 MIRVs, although it could easily carry 20 or 30.

In addition, each side is allowed to build and deploy one new type of ICBM, but it must be a "light" missile and, of course, may carry no more than 10 MIRVs. This provision was inserted to permit our building the MX. Submarine-launched missiles may have up to 14 MIRVs. One reason for permitting more warheads on SLBMs is that they are the most stabilizing of all deterrents by virtue of their invulnerability, while their relative inaccuracy means they can't threaten the other side's deterrent. Many American arms control specialists would encourage the Soviets to build more submarine-launched missiles instead of their present concentration on ICBMs, since their ICBMs both threaten U.S. land-based missiles and at the same time are themselves vulnerable. About half of all U.S. warheads are carried on submarines; for the Soviets the number is less than a third.

ICBM LIMITS

The construction of new ICBM launchers, or the relocation of existing ones, is banned. So is the conversion of launchers for medium-range ballistic missiles into ICBM launchers. To keep much larger missiles from being put in existing silos, the treaty specifies how much the silos' internal volume may be increased. To preclude reloading and refiring from launchers (a concern of some analysts), the testing, development, and deployment of rapid-reload systems is also banned; as is the storage of spare missiles near silos.

Furthermore, the Soviets may not increase the number of SS-18 "heavy" ICBMs beyond their present total of 308. This was a major source of contention. SALT II critics charged that our failure to reduce the number of SS-18s was a major flaw in the treaty, although it does limit the number of MIRVs this missile can carry.

Mobile ICBMs that could be moved around on trucks or trains were another source of concern. We succeeded in getting the Soviets to agree not to produce, test, or deploy their SS-16 mobile ICBMs or to build mobile launchers for heavy ICBMs. Since the SS-20 is simply the first two stages of the three-stage SS-16, we were concerned that the Soviets might try to convert their SS-20 intermediate-range missiles into long-range SS-16s, or launch SS-16s from SS-20 launchers. Both options are banned.

HEAVY BOMBER AND CRUISE MISSILE LIMITS

For the United States "heavy bombers" include the B-52 and the B-1. For the Soviets they are the Bear (Tu-95) and the Mya-4 Bison. In addition, any airplanes equipped to carry long-range cruise missiles (more than 600 km in range) are counted as heavy bombers. Moreover, should planes not initially counted later be equipped with long-range cruise missiles, they become heavy bombers for purposes of the treaty.

A major controversy in the United States involved the fact that this section did not include the Soviet Backfire bomber (Tu-26, or Tu-22m in the treaty). As we have seen, the Backfire is a medium-range, maritime attack aircraft (see pages 140–141). American medium-range F-111s stationed in Europe are similarly excluded from the treaty. However, we did get a commitment that the Soviets would not increase their production of Backfires beyond 30 aircraft per year.

More limits pertain to aircraft equipped to carry long-range cruise missiles. Existing aircraft (i.e., the B-52) may carry no more than 20 long-range cruise missiles each. New types designed for the mission may carry up to an average of 28. Finally, to facilitate verification, there is a requirement that existing or new airplanes equipped with cruise missiles must be distinguishable on the basis of "functionally related observable differences" (FRODs), in other words, observable features which tell whether they are equipped with cruise missiles.

OTHER LIMITS

In addition to those limits in the treaty, other provisions were included in a protocol which expired at the end of 1981. This was a temporary expedient since neither side was ready finally to settle these issues. The protocol banned deployment of sea- and land-based long-range cruise missiles. The parties also agreed not to deploy mobile ICBM launchers or test ICBMs from such launchers.

The last part of the treaty is a statement of principles and guidelines which were to form the basis for subsequent negotiations. SALT II, clearly, represents the most complex, comprehensive agreement on strategic arms limitations yet negotiated. It encompasses a wide range of different kinds of weapons and involves equally comprehensive verification requirements which twenty years before were unthinkable.

The SALT II Debate

The ratification debate was intense and fraught with many complications. One problem resulted from the Senate custom of holding concurrent hearings. Normally, the Foreign Relations Committee has responsibility for holding hearings and making a recommendation to the Senate. But in the tradition of senatorial courtesy, the Armed Services Committee was also invited to hold hearings on the "military implications" of SALT II. (The same was done for SALT I and the Panama Canal treaties.)

Because of the two-committee procedure, the process was prolonged, giving opponents more time to organize against it. They had two opportunities to testify and to get media coverage. Since more than a few Senators had to be convinced before the treaty could get to the floor, the President had to use his prestige and influence. With two committees meeting, moreover, no one could duck the issue.

During the 1979 hearings, SALT II raised considerable organized citizen interest. More than 25 organizations testified, more than 100 citizens were heard from. Senators, diplomats, military officers, religious leaders, scientists, professors, and *ad hoc* citizens groups all testified. On one side were people such as Phyllis Schlafly, representing the American Conservative Union in opposition to SALT; on the other Coretta Scott King, widow of Martin Luther King, speaking for the treaty. The Foreign Relations Committee hearings record runs to 1,500 pages.

On the other hand, as Senator Daniel P. Moynihan remembers, the man in the street was not very interested in SALT II. Moynihan got more mail during this period from constituents interested in preserving one endangered animal species than from people concerned about his vote on SALT II.*

Debate over ratification within the Senate was largely between those who supported the treaty and those on the political Right who saw a Soviet advantage. Critics on the Left were generally unenthusiastic because SALT did not go far

*The Washington Post, April 25, 1982, page A17.

enough in restricting nuclear weapons, but they played a lesser role.

The heart of the controversy held several issues, all of which provoked heated and emotional discussion. Verification was a key issue. Critics charged that parts of the treaty could not be verified by "national technical means," that is, remote sensing. Interestingly, one of the most respected critics, Paul Nitze, insisted that verification was not a problem. To his way of thinking, the treaty was so unbalanced in favor of the Soviets that there was little incentive for them to cheat; so there was little to worry about insofar as verification was concerned. The Soviets, Nitze insisted, were permitted to retain 308 SS-18 ICBMs for which the U.S. had no equivalent. Moreover, he noted, the Backfire bomber was not counted in the treaty despite its ability to reach the continental United States. Others argued that SALT II undermined deterrence by failing to limit Soviet weapons sufficiently, especially those that threatened U.S. ICBMs.

The Administration and other treaty supporters responded with a wide-ranging and spirited defense. Verification, though not flawless, was more than adequate to protect U.S. interests and detect any significant Soviet violations. Noting that it takes some 25 or so test launches to develop a new weapon, the Administration insisted that it would have ample opportunity to detect efforts at circumvention.

With respect to Soviet heavy missiles, it was noted that the United States had made explicit decisions in the past not to build them. We preferred instead smaller, more compact ICBMs and had no intention of building heavy missiles in the future. The one new ICBM the United States was planning to build, the MX, was permitted under the treaty and was more than a match for the SS-18 in destructive power. As for the Backfire, U.S. negotiators noted that the United States was free to develop an equivalent plane and that U.S. FB-111s were not counted although they are part of the Strategic Air Command. Moreover, F-111 medium-range bombers and other aircraft based in Europe were also excluded from the SALT aggregates. In addition, the Administration pointed out that it had obtained a binding commitment from the Soviets not to increase the Backfire's range or its rate of production beyond 30 per year.

Finally, the Administration denied that the treaty undermined deterrence. The United States retained a powerful retaliatory capability, despite some adverse trends. Moreover, they insisted, modernization of U.S. forces could go on under SALT. The treaty restricted the Soviets more than us, requiring them to dismantle 250 strategic systems. Even the chairman of the Joint Chiefs of Staff acknowledged that SALT II was a "small, but useful step."

In the last analysis, supporters and critics alike looked beyond SALT. Supporters felt that deeper cuts in nuclear weapons could be achieved only by first ratifying SALT II and then moving on. Critics, on the other hand, had a different agenda. They were as much concerned that SALT II would somehow lull the American public into neglecting what they believed were vitally needed improvements in U.S. nuclear forces.

The message was clear: politically active Americans were sharply divided on the issue and cared intensely about the outcome. Thus a vote either way would cost each Senator political support.

While the Foreign Relations Committee did vote in favor, the Armed Services Committee, led by SALT opponents John Tower (R.-Texas) and Henry Jackson (D.-Wash.), took the unusual step of issuing a report plus the unprecedented step of holding a vote, which went against the treaty. (Interestingly, seven SALT supporters on the committee did not vote against publishing the report, which was very damaging. Instead, they abstained in protest because the committee had no formal jurisdiction over the treaty.)

Divided, the Senate was stymied. To its relief the President withdrew the treaty in December 1979. The Soviet invasion of Afghanistan and a disclosure that some Soviet combat troops had been stationed in Cuba for some time fueled charges that the President was "soft" on the Russian threat. An election year was fast approaching and the Iranian hostage crisis together with Afghanistan created a climate that was not favorable to agreements with the Soviets. Above all, the natural constituency for SALT II was distracted. Social issues (the Equal Rights Amendment, school prayer, busing, abortion) and economic issues (interest rates, inflation, the threatened failure of the Chrysler Corporation) held center stage.

What happened was that a hostile constituency was already organized around the Panama Canal treaty of the previous year. And since SALT II had been signed (though not ratified), the kind of legislative compromising that might have won over a few Senators was impossible. The issue was highly charged because our "national security" was at stake. President Carter was not seen as particularly competent in matters military, or in foreign affairs in general for that matter. And while those who negotiated the treaty were skillful, they lacked Henry Kissinger's public flair.

But when all is said and done, it is a fact that few on either side could reasonably defend or attack the treaty based on an analysis of its contents. The military assumptions, the scenarios of what the military situation would be with the treaty contrasted to what it would be without it, the details as to the "threat" of new Soviet weaponry were all widely publicized. In fact, the case for the SALT II was well made and critics failed to do real damage. But it mattered little. The treaty became a test case of détente, being soft on the Russians, of American military preparedness. And the invasion of Afghanistan pushed all these issues to the fore. Thoughtful discussion of arms control as a vital part of national security appeared only in *The New York Times, The Washington Post, Foreign Affairs,* and the like. For the general public, knowledge of the treaty was so low that it wasn't even clear that many people knew what the *S* in SALT really meant.

In a situation where constituents are vocal and divided, politicians desperately look for a reprieve, an excuse not to decide. Many SALT supporters in and outside of the Administration believed that if it had been brought to the Senate floor, many wavering Senators would have felt compelled to support the President. The theory was never put to the test.

What is most interesting about the whole thing is that both the Soviet Union and the United States have said they will take no actions to undercut the terms of the treaty, despite the absence of formal ratification. Former Secretary of State Haig confirmed this in March 1981, as did President Reagan in his 1982 Memorial Day speech.*

Chronicle of Major Developments in Selected Areas of Foreign Affairs (January–September 1981), House Foreign Affairs Committee, page 2; also *The Washington Post,* June 1, 1982, page A1.

VERIFICATION

Without adequate verification, SALT and similar agreements would be unlikely because no one "trusts" the Russians. With sure systems of verification, arms control agreements can be taken out of the realm of trust. We can look at what they're doing and see for ourselves if they are in compliance.

Verification matters more to us than to the Soviet Union for the simple reason that it is already easy for the Soviets to keep tabs on American military activities. The United States puts large quantities of defense information into the public record in the normal course of presenting it to Congress. In fact, Soviet agents often collect published transcripts and send them home. In contrast, the Soviet Union is a closed society and most unwilling to share its military secrets.

What made verification a stumbling block in the early days was the inevitable requirement for on-site inspection. The Russians were reluctant, for reasons of their own, to allow foreign military personnel on their soil to observe their military installations. But, "remote sensing" can substantially compensate for lack of on-site inspection. Satellite photography is getting better all the time and both countries have a great deal of confidence in their capacity to monitor treaty compliance from space. In SALT these techniques are referred to as "national technical means," and both countries are explicitly prohibited from interfering with the "national technical means" of the other.

Since our negotiators feel free to discuss only those weapons that are verifiable from remote stations, there is constant interplay among negotiators, weapons analysts, and verification specialists. Verification specialists are asked questions like "If we were to negotiate the following kinds of limits, how could we verify compliance?" If a particular limitation cannot be verified with any degree of confidence (the production of missiles, for example, which usually takes place inside factories, or certain kinds of weapons testing that can be hidden in laboratories), then that limitation cannot be included in a treaty, regardless of how desirable it might be.

This is not as restrictive as it might appear because weapons are sometimes verifiable in not-so-obvious ways. Missile submarines are invisible when underwater, but they are produced in a few Soviet shipyards. So we can watch submarines being assembled steel plate by steel plate. The deciphering of space photographs has gone so far as to create specialists known as "crateologists," experts in identifying the kinds of equipment likely to be packed in certain kinds of shipping containers.

Of course, it is impossible to see inside a missile nose cone to count how many MIRVs are mounted. But we can monitor MIRV tests. So a "type rule" was included in SALT II. If a certain missile has been tested with a given number of MIRVs, the country counting the missile force assumes that all missiles of that type are equipped with MIRVs.

Because of verification requirements, neither SALT I nor SALT II could set limits on missile inventories per se. Missiles can be hidden anywhere. But missile silos cannot. Hence, the ceilings in the treaty are in terms of *silo launchers*. Lest if one country attempted to conceal the launcher with, say, a house built over it, it would be in violation of the treaty, which expressly prohibits interference with "national technical means." Besides, silos are comparatively large and visible and their construction requires many months. So it is unlikely that a silo could be built without satellite photographs picking it up.

Silos are presumed to be the functional equivalent of missiles ready to fire because the time required to reload a silo launcher after its missile has been set off is probably weeks or months in the case of the hot-launch method currently employed. The reason cold-launch technology (used in submarines, you will recall, but not yet in American land-based missiles), is of concern to the arms control community is that cold launch could permit a rapid reload of the silo— within a few days. It was for this reason that two provisions were included in SALT II: one prohibiting missile warehousing anywhere near silo launchers; the other forbidding the development of rapid reloading equipment.

Having gone so far as to forbid a technology for rapid reloading to be developed, it is interesting that the negotiators did not go one step further and specifically prohibit cold-launched missiles on land. One reason may be that the Soviets had missiles of this type already operational at the time the treaty was negotiated while the United States was developing its own cold-launched missile, the MX. The negotiators would say, however, that prohibiting rapid-reload equipment and warehousing made the cold launch issue moot.

For some people the fear that the Soviets might have thousands of spare missiles waiting to be reloaded in the midst of a nuclear exchange is very real. Bear in mind that even under the best of circumstances, it would take several days, not hours, for the silos to be reloaded.* It indicates that even with the advanced technology of verification available to both sides, distrust of the Soviet Union is pervasive.

THE CASE OF CRUISE MISSILES

Arms control can have the reverse effect: namely, to stimulate the development and production of new weapons that are not limited by an agreement. Arms controllers would argue that this is not necessarily all bad. Remember, their purpose is not to rid the world of nuclear weapons, but to find ways of guaranteeing security in a stable, predictable environment. Moreover, they would argue, the Soviets have pursued development of new weapons right up to the agreements' allowable limits.

The cruise missile is a good example of a situation in which not being included in an arms control treaty, namely SALT I, made the weapon a desirable option to be exploited. Since it is not clear that the cruise missile is going to contribute to stability, arms controllers expressed reservations about this new technology. Like MIRVing and mobile missiles, the cruise missile has a growing importance that was not dealt with in SALT.

The cruise missile may have been part of a deal between President Nixon and the military. In exchange for its willingness to accept a freeze on numbers of offensive missiles and an indefinite postponement of ABM, the Air Force was given a go-ahead to develop air-to-ground cruise missiles. Later, with the cruise missile in development, President Car-

*Soviet Military Power, page 56.

ter opted to go with it as a way to upgrade the B-52 and cancel the B-1. It has been of particular concern to the Soviets, because, being so small, it is extremely hard to detect on radar. Also, it's relatively cheap, so we can build a lot of them. Thus the Soviets will have to contend with a greater threat. For some, these qualities make it a valuable bargaining chip.

Meanwhile, if it were included in an arms limitation agreement, it would be hard to verify. Its size makes it easy to conceal and how could we be sure that both sides had complied with agreed-upon limits on range?

ASIDE

An attempt was made to come to an agreement on cruise missiles, and it found its way into the temporary SALT II protocol. The nations agreed that no cruise missile with a range beyond 600 km could be developed or tested. This figure was a compromise. The Soviets wanted a lower maximum range, we a higher one. We wanted to build cruise missiles with as great a range as possible so aircraft could launch them as far away from Soviet air defenses as possible. The Soviets, quite obviously, didn't want this. The 600-km limit was temporary, lasting to the end of 1981. The issue was left to be resolved by SALT III.

As in all aircraft, cruise missile range is a function of fuel and weight, which can vary, and depends on speed and altitude. Some altitudes are more favorable to jet engines than others. The range of cruise missiles is thus more variable than that of ballistic missiles. So verification of range would be difficult to monitor. Under SALT II such verification would have to be done at the time of cruise missile testing.

The Air Force is now deploying cruise missiles on bombers as well as on the ground in Europe beginning in 1983. The Navy expects to mount them on submarines and surface ships and perhaps even on its own aircraft. So from the point of view of arms control, cruise missile containment was a missed chance. Although it must be remembered—given the pattern of the past thirty years—that while the Soviets do not yet have cruise missiles as technologically sophisticated as ours, they do have large numbers of less modern ones and are sure to improve them in time.

One source of concern about anti-satellite weapons, incidentally, is that we depend so heavily on satellites for verification. Some satellites are designed to provide early warning of missile attacks but also are a means of verifying missile testing. So as space weapons become more widely available, their potential impact on verification technology may be severe.

In the final analysis, verification involves both technical and political judgments. Technical judgments are required in interpreting the photos and other data collected by national technical means. Political judgments, perhaps the most important, are required to determine how much verification is sufficient to protect U.S. security. The key word is sufficient. Verification does not have to be perfect, just good enough. And what is good enough depends in part on the agreed-upon numbers of weapons on both sides. If the ceilings are high—that is, pretty close to what both sides have now—small errors have a minor impact on the military balance. If the ceilings are low, then a small error, say of 10 or 15, could be serious.

If the parties agree to dismantle existing weapons—the Soviets, for example, were required to dismantle older submarines as well as some ICBM launchers as part of SALT I—then the task for the verifier is relatively easy. Just as we can monitor Soviet submarine construction by observing the few shipyards that produce them, so we can observe the process of dismantling or converting submarines when required. (By the way, the United States also recently dismantled some old Polaris submarines, although it was not compelled to do so since SALT II has not been ratified.) We assume the Soviets have been watching as well. Besides, they have the resources to count our ships all over the world, and we, of course, can do the same.

When the U.S.S. *Vinson*, our newest aircraft carrier, underwent sea trials in 1982, a Soviet reconnaissance plane was on hand to watch. When we test-fire Trident missiles from submerged submarines, Soviet intelligence-gathering ships are there. The United States observes Russian tests in similar fashion. Big items on both sides can simply not be kept under wraps.

DÉTENTE, LINKAGE, AND ARMS CONTROL

However imperfect, the major successes of arms control in recent years coincided with a situation described by foreign-affairs people as détente. Unfortunately, détente raised different expectations in the Soviet Union and here. Broadly stated, Americans tend to see détente as *linking* all spheres of international activity. Thus, if we are negotiating arms control agreements with the Russians, they should refrain from provocative actions elsewhere. The Soviets appear to have a very different understanding. For them it is narrowly construed as the easing of tension between us and them. By their logic, détente does not require them to behave differently elsewhere. Now, with this understood (and to be sure, the Russians are not naïve; they know full well we don't want them expanding their influence), we see why some Americans are determined to tie Soviet behavior in the third world (or Poland, for that matter) to détente. Even if our diplomats were willing to play by Soviet rules for the sake of continuing the arms control process, the apparent contradiction of negotiating while they are "misbehaving" somewhere else tends to make headlines. And this puts pressure on the President and his diplomats to respond.

Our response to this situation was to coin the term "linkage." This concept suggests that arms control negotiations cannot be isolated from what is going on elsewhere. However, as strong a proponent of linkage as President Reagan has shown willingness to "de-link" some activities, such as our sale of grain to the Soviet Union, while insisting on linking others, such as trade in high-technology items. **linkage**

There is no question but that the effect of linkage on the arms control process has been disruptive. After the Soviet invasion of Afghanistan, President Carter found it impossible to ratify SALT II. Even if linkage hadn't been invented by diplomats, a link was forged in the popular mind between the Soviet invasion of its neighbor and our willingness to trust them on arms control. Though arms controllers argued that SALT II was in our best interest whatever the Soviets were doing, the treaty went unratified.

INTERMEDIATE NUCLEAR FORCE TALKS (INF)

One of the exceptions to linkage for President Reagan is the intermediate nuclear force talks, to limit nuclear arms in Europe. Former Secretary of State Haig stated that because such talks are "advantageous" to the West, they are a permissible exception to the linkage policy. What are the "intermediate nuclear forces" to be addressed in these talks? While we shall have more to say about this issue in Chapter Eight, the essence of the argument is this: In 1979, NATO agreed to modernize its "theater nuclear weapons" by deploying 572 ground-launched cruise missiles and 108 Pershing II medium-range ballistic missiles. This was an attempt to counter Soviet deployment of the new SS-20 medium-range missile, a new, more accurate MIRVed missile, mobile to boot, that the Soviets are using to replace older SS-4s and SS-5s.

The Soviet SALT negotiators have always urged that American fighter-bombers based in Europe be included in the SALT talks because their location makes them "strategic" in function in that they can hit the Soviet Union. Indeed, because of their ambiguity they are sometimes called "Euro-strategic." But until 1981 the United States has refused to discuss Euro-strategic weapons within the context of SALT, arguing that they are tactical nuclear weapons. (Sometimes Euro-strategic weapons are called "forward-based systems.") Up to 1981 the Soviets had reluctantly accepted this view. But as part of the NATO modernization program, the United States promised the Europeans that we would begin negotiations to limit Euro-strategic arms if they would accept the new medium-range Pershing IIs and cruise missiles.

Another factor propelling us to the bargaining table is public opinion. A strong new antinuclear movement in several NATO countries threatens the nuclear modernization program. So to satisfy the NATO countries, who are risking political disaster by allowing nuclear arms on their soil, we began the talks. Indeed, President Reagan spoke on November 18, 1981, just before the talks were to begin, and pro-**zero option** posed a "zero option," the elimination of all Soviet SS-4s,

SS-5s, and SS-20s in exchange for our not emplacing Pershing IIs and cruise missiles in Europe.

However gratifying it is to the arms control community to have at least one level of nuclear arms under review, the fact is that the more threatening weapons are strategic. Europe is clearly within striking distance of such weapons. Resumption of the SALT talks (renamed by ACDA director Eugene Rostow the START, or strategic arms reduction talks) would appear to be a higher priority. Senior Reagan administration officials have said linkage would not be invoked in the case of START, and in fact, these talks did begin in June 1982.

FUTURE TRENDS

The divisions within the Administration as well as the failures of the Carter administration make clear that the consensus which shaped U.S. policies on nuclear weapons and arms control for some fifteen years no longer exists. That consensus embodied a good deal more than arms control. In fact, it constituted a comprehensive concept of how to preserve national security. Yet many within the Reagan administration achieved national prominence by challenging and demolishing that consensus. Some people argue that arms control has failed us these past ten years because there has been no absolute reduction in the number of nuclear warheads and delivery systems. We now face weapons that are even harder to verify (mobile missiles, cruise missiles) and more effective (MIRVs) than before. We are working on "hard-target capability," giving us the capacity to knock out the land-based missiles on either side; when serious arms control started, weapons were too inaccurate for that kind of scenario. SALT II, these critics contend, can hardly be called arms control since it permits the MX.

hard-target capability

The critics have a point. Arms control efforts have generally been well behind the curve of advancing weapons technology. As long as it takes to develop new weapons, it takes longer still to negotiate constraints. George Kennan captures the frustration when he writes:

> Can we not at long last cast off our preoccupation with sheer destruction—a preoccupation that is costing us

our prosperity and preempting the resources that should go to the solving of our great social problems, to the progress of our respective societies? Is it really impossible for us to cast off this sickness of blind military rivalry and to address ourselves at last, in all humility and in all seriousness, to setting our societies to right? *

Basically, Kennan feels it is time to "throw the experts out," to stop "incrementalizing," and just cut nuclear arms inventories by 50 percent. Others are calling for a "freeze" on the development and deployment of nuclear weapons, by means of a verifiable agreement between the United States and the Soviet Union. Such a freeze could be a dramatic and valuable first step toward reductions in nuclear weapons, although it's argued that without the incentive provided by U.S. weapons programs, the Soviets might be unwilling to negotiate reductions. Others push for a selective freeze on ICBMs rather than an across-the-board freeze. There are nuclear-freeze initiatives on the ballots of several states, as well as many cities and counties. It could well be an idea whose time has come.

Others, no less strongly committed to controlling nuclear weapons, say that if it's a freeze and reductions in such weapons that are desired, why not take the bird in the hand and ratify SALT II?† That treaty, as we have already noted, wouldn't just freeze Soviet weapons, it would actually reduce them, and among them, some of the most threatening Soviet weapons at that. And, of course, SALT II provides a basis for further reductions. We have already shifted gears on arms control with each of the last two changes of administration and made arms control one of "the most partisan of foreign policy issues." This might be just the right time to try to reestablish a nonpartisan arms control policy.‡

no first use   Another idea that has been around a long time, but is only just now getting public attention, is a pledge of "no first use" of nuclear weapons—either tactical or strategic. Current U.S. policy calls for the "first use" of tactical nuclear

---

* "On Nuclear War," *The New York Review of Books,* January 1982, pages 10–12.
† For example, Les Aspin in "Freeze? Why Not Just Okay SALT II?" *The Washington Post,* April 15, 1982, page A25.
‡ *Ibid.*

weapons in response to a Soviet conventional attack on Europe, but several former senior officials have now challenged that policy. Fearing escalation to general nuclear war, George Kennan, McGeorge Bundy, Robert McNamara, and Gerard Smith urge abandonment of the policy of first use, favoring instead expansion of NATO's conventional forces.* The idea harks back to a 1973 agreement, "Measures to Prevent Nuclear War." The United States and the Soviets agreed to "make their primary objective the lessening of the danger of nuclear war" and pledged to "practice restraint in their mutual relations." They also agreed to "consult with each other where danger of nuclear confrontation exists." Like the "measures to prevent nuclear war" agreement, the proposal for "no first use" is seen as a way of formalizing deterrence, namely, the underlying principle that nuclear weapons exist to not be used.

As Jonathan Schell has noted in *The Fate of the Earth,* "the only means in sight for getting rid of our knowledge of how to destroy ourselves would be to remove the knower." Barring such an eventuality, it is obvious that a renewed and reinvigorated arms control effort aimed at achieving verifiable reductions in nuclear weapons, stabilizing the nuclear weapons competition, and reducing the danger of their use is probably the most important contribution to national security that this or any administration could make.

---

*"Nuclear Weapons and the Atlantic Alliance," *Foreign Affairs,* Spring 1982, Vol. 60, pages 753–768.

8.

Defense Controversies in the 1980s

THUS FAR WE HAVE GAINED some fundamental understanding of why nations buy arms; indeed, that they seek to limit armaments for the same reason: their national security. In addition, we know that some of our weaponry exists for the basic purpose of never being used: strategic forces are deterrents, and if the day comes that they must strike their targets, they have failed us. Finally, we have learned that the way we purchase weapons is a bureaucratic pentathlon and that no one person or institution has final say; that these decisions are driven more than anything else by the "threat" and by technology, the urge to possess the "best," the latest thing.

But if technology is the medium, politics is the message. While defense debates involve arcane and impenetrable technical language alien to those outside the defense community, breaking the code is but one step. At their heart, defense debates are intensely political because the issues are rooted in varied conceptions of national security as well as different judgments of the nature of the threats we face. For the Reagan administration the first task of government is protection of the nation from external threat. Military strength is this administration's most favored means for achieving that security.

But there are many paths to military security. There is a diversity of weapons and strategies from which to choose. Individuals and organizations within the defense establishment tend to advocate their own favored solutions for self-serving reasons as much as conviction. As a result those who favor different solutions must fight for a hearing. Sometimes they are successful, sometimes not. Those outside the Pentagon, and especially those outside the defense community, have a particularly tough time introducing alternate points of view into the debate. And as we noted earlier, the "not invented here" syndrome is a powerful force; it applies to ideas as well as hardware.

The environment in which defense disputes are played is emotionally charged. After all, war, peace, and the survival of the Republic are at stake, not to mention billions of dollars and thousands of careers. In this climate information is rarely neutral and always a source of power to its possessor. This is one reason that officials make such a fuss over leaks by others but are often quite willing to leak information themselves if it bolsters their own point of view. Leaks are weapons in the bureaucratic battles that rage endlessly within the Pentagon and other government agencies. (*Aviation Week & Space Technology* is referred to as *Aviation Leak* because it reports secret information from Pentagon sources so frequently.) In April of 1982, for example, columnists Rowland Evans and Robert Novak, Jr., reported that U.S. intelligence analysts were worried that the Soviet Union had been secretly building and deploying SS-16 mobile ICBMs in violation of the unratified SALT II agreement. Within days another story appeared in *The Washington Post* quoting other unnamed "informed officials" who described previously published stories on the SS-16 as "mostly garbage." According to these officials, reports of violations were wrong; to support their position they cited a just-completed top-secret national intelligence estimate (NIE) which concluded there had been no violation of SALT II by the Soviets.* So even after we've broken the code, we must learn to read between the lines.

We should keep in mind that 80 to 90 cents of every defense dollar is spent on arms not part of our strategic retaliatory forces. These Army, Navy, and Air Force units are often referred to as "conventional," although some are commonly

*The Washington Post, April 9, 1982, page A2.

328 What Kinds of Guns Are They Buying for Your Butter?

equipped with "tactical" nuclear weapons of some sort. What makes them different is that they are mainly for fighting wars. True, they have a deterrent effect, but if push comes to shove they can be used to defend our interests. And there is no shortage of trouble spots on the globe: from the Middle East to Central America, Africa to Southeast Asia.

THE TROUBLED NORTH ATLANTIC ALLIANCE

EUROPE'S PROTESTERS STRAIN TRANSATLANTIC TIES
Another tumultuously busy weekend for Europe's anti-nuclear protesters underlines the need for greater American understanding of west European nuclear fears. . . . It is a NATO decision of 1979 that the demonstrators are trying to get reversed, to install U.S. cruise and Pershing II missiles in the European theater by 1983.
—*The Christian Science Monitor,* October 26, 1981, page 1

Throughout most of this century, Europe has been a major concern of American foreign-policy makers. Two world wars and the cold war have led us to station nearly half a million military men and women in and about the Continent. Essentially, our Army today camps where it stopped when the Germans surrendered in 1945, but now some people wonder if it's worth it. They doubt our allies are doing their "fair" share in our mutual defense and suggest that our troops should be brought home. But Europeans have doubts of their own.

The North Atlantic Treaty Organization (NATO) is our oldest continuing military alliance. Begun in 1949, it is unique in world history in that it is a military pact that exists in the absence of a war. (Historically, alliances formed in anticipation of war but always dissolved once it was over.) In 1979, NATO, prodded largely by West German Chancellor Helmut Schmidt, agreed on the need to maintain parity with the Soviets. To do this the alliance needed to respond in some way to the new nuclear weapons the Russians were deploying. Schmidt was worried about the impact of these weapons on what is called the Euro-strategic balance. The Soviet weapon of greatest concern (then as now) is the

SS-20, a mobile, intermediate-range ballistic missile (IRBM), **IRBM**
carrying three MIRV thermonuclear warheads and capable
of hitting targets anywhere in Europe. There are about 300
SS-20s now in place: 200 or more in the western USSR, and
75 in Asia, aimed at China.

It's not that the Soviets have had no such weapons before. In fact, they have had as many as 600 medium-range
SS-4 and SS-5 nuclear-tipped missiles since the mid-1960s.
What makes the newer SS-20s especially worrisome is their
accuracy combined with their multiple warheads. NATO
planners fear the Soviets could wipe out most of our theater
nuclear weapons (i.e., those whose range is limited to a theater of war, as in the European theater) in a first strike, leaving NATO no means with which to retaliate short of turning
to our central strategic forces (Minuteman, Poseidon and
Trident and our B-52s).

Therefore NATO agreed to modernize its own long-range
theater nuclear forces (LRTNF) by deploying 464 ground- **LRTNF**
launched cruise missiles (GLCM) and 108 Pershing II ballistic missiles in England, Germany, Italy, Belgium, and the
Netherlands. The missiles are to be provided and paid for by
the United States at a cost originally estimated to be about
$5 billion, but likely to be higher in the end. At the same
time, the alliance also agreed that it must seek to negotiate
an arms control agreement with the Soviets limiting these
forces, without specifying what form such limits might take.
As a third part of the policy decision, NATO agreed (apart
from any negotiations) to withdraw 1,572 older nuclear warheads that had been stationed in Europe for many years,
1,000 of these within a year of the LRTNF deployment decision and 572 more on a one-for-one basis as new weapons
begin to arrive in 1983. In fact, the 1,000 older warheads
have already been withdrawn.

Increasing talk of nuclear weapons and fighting a nuclear war in Europe have brought a long-simmering pot to a
slow boil. New fears were heaped on top of the old, and
many Europeans now demand that Europe be transformed
into a nuclear-free zone from the Atlantic to the Urals.

From the early 1950s on, the United States has relied on
threats to use our nuclear weapons to deter a Soviet conventional attack on Europe, to balance the superior numbers

of Soviet ground forces deployed there. As the Soviets gradually acquired their own nuclear forces, the likelihood that we would use nuclear retaliation began to decline. In other words, we lost credibility. Many Europeans wondered whether we would actually come to the defense of Europe if it meant all-out thermonuclear war. Would the United States be willing to sacrifice New York and Washington for Paris and Bonn?

The French had no doubts. De Gaulle did not believe the U.S. "nuclear umbrella" was reliable. He didn't expect the United States to be willing to risk such a sacrifice and therefore decided that France needed to build its own independent nuclear deterrent, the *force de frappe*. Today the French have a modest thermonuclear force, by U.S. and Soviet standards, but they have steadily improved and modernized its capabilities. It now consists of five ballistic-missile submarines, each with 16 single-warhead missiles, and 18 intermediate-range missiles in mountain silos.

In the 1960s the United States turned away from massive retaliation and increasingly toward the doctrine of "flexible response," a change that had important consequences for Europe. As massive retaliation ceased to be credible, the United States sought a variety of appropriate responses to a range of potential Soviet provocations and contingencies. But while NATO policy changed in the late 1960s, NATO weapons and operational planning changed very little until the mid-1970s. At that time U.S. Secretary of Defense James Schlesinger sought to give NATO a range of options, something other than massive retaliation, in the face of a Soviet attack on Europe. Mostly, this was done through improvements in U.S. strategic nuclear forces, especially by the deployment of MIRVs. This provided us with a large number of warheads, some of which could be aimed at targets in the European theater. In addition, Schlesinger pressed strongly for improvements in NATO's conventional, non-nuclear forces.

The peace treaty the Western allies concluded with the Federal Republic of Germany forbids the West Germans to have nuclear weapons. So the Germans, unlike the French, never had the option of an independent nuclear force of their own, which has led them to a different course. Obviously they have no wish to fight a war of any kind, nuclear or conventional, on their territory. Germany was devastated by World War II, and they do not wish to see this happen again. Thus for the Germans the problem has been how best to deter war in Europe, any kind of war. To do this they have counted on the fear that a war in Europe, even one that began conventionally, could escalate to all-out nuclear war. They, too, worry that the United States might not be willing to sacrifice New York for Bonn. American troops stationed in Germany and our nuclear weapons deployed there provide a "tripwire," a link that increases the risk that any war in Europe will immediately involve the United States. Once we were involved, the possibility of escalation to strategic nuclear war would become greater. Far from being bloodthirsty, the Germans believe this to be the best way to deter war. Escalation is by no means certain, but it's the uncertainty that makes an effective deterrent.

Growing Soviet strategic nuclear forces, as well as those weapons aimed at Europe, however, raised new worries for the Germans. Helmut Schmidt felt that the SS-20, for which the West did not have a precisely equivalent counter, might somehow break the potential chain of escalation that tied NATO forces in Europe to U.S. strategic nuclear weapons. He feared that the SS-20 might allow the Soviets to attack Europe knowing that NATO would have nothing comparable with which to retaliate. Parity, he believed, required matching Soviet forces at every level. Without comparable long-range theater nuclear forces, NATO feared the United States might be loath to retaliate against the Soviets, especially if it meant risking all-out nuclear war and the prospect of sacrificing Washington for Bonn.

The United States, Schmidt feared, would be self-deterred in such a situation. So the new cruise missiles and Pershing IIs are intended to provide a counter to Soviet SS-20s while keeping intact the chain of deterrence (and potential escalation), from conventional arms through short-range nuclear weapons (mostly artillery) to long-range theater nuclear forces and all the way to central strategic forces.

At the heart of the controversy is the old question of European confidence in the NATO alliance and European perceptions of U.S. resolve. While modernization of NATO's long-range theater nuclear forces has helped allay some Europeans' fears concerning the alliance, it has raised still others.

ASIDE————————————————————————————————

This is where the neutron bomb comes in. The idea of a tactical nuclear war in Europe—that is, the employment of nuclear weapons along and around a battlefront as opposed to their strategic use—lacks credibility because of the immense amount of collateral damage that would result from the use of even small ones. Because the neutron bomb has a reduced blast (see Chapter Two), its threatened employment is more credible; or so the theory goes.

————————————————————————————————

Discussions of nuclear weapons and of fighting a limited nuclear war in Europe have aroused the fears of many Europeans, especially (but not only) in some of the smaller countries such as the Netherlands. While for NATO planners these are technical issues concerning the most effective means of preserving deterrence, for many Europeans the discussion symbolizes much more fundamental concerns about the consequences of nuclear war. While the arms control aspect of the basic 1979 policy decision becomes a vital means of dealing with those concerns, it is not at all clear that negotiations will produce results quickly enough or on a scale sufficient to satisfy a growing antinuclear sentiment.

As the date for the initial deployment of these new weapons approaches, a ground swell of popular protest in Europe has arisen, putting enormous pressure on a number of European governments to renege on the commitment to allow these missiles on their soil. Essentially, this new "ban the bomb" movement is repudiating deterrence as a viable strategic doctrine for Europe. Its leaders maintain the hope that European nuclear disarmament will be a first step toward persuading the United States and the USSR to reduce their nuclear stockpiles.

It is against this backdrop that the negotiations between the United States and the Soviet Union called the INF (intermediate nuclear force) talks were begun in late November 1981 in Geneva, Switzerland. On November 18, shortly before the talks were to begin, President Reagan made a dramatic gesture, proposing to cancel deployment of the Pershing II and ground-launched cruise missiles if the Soviets would agree to dismantle all their SS-20s as well as the older SS-4s and SS-5s. Some suspect the President's proposal was aimed more at rhetorically disarming the popular European opposition to the new weapons than at physically disarming either the United States or the Soviets. Nevertheless, the talks continue, albeit with uncertain prospects. Plans for deployment of these two missiles have not been altered.

Both missiles (the ground-launched cruise missile and the Pershing II) incorporate some interesting innovations. Both can be rapidly moved to avoid being attacked on the ground by Soviet weapons. Both are considerably more accurate than currently available NATO systems. The ground-launched cruise missile employs a terrain contour matching (TerCoM) guidance system identical to that used by the air-launched cruise missile. It carries in its computer memory a three-dimensional map of the terrain over which it flies. At several points along the missile's almost treetop-level flight path, the missile takes a radar picture of the ground over which it is flying. This is compared to terrain maps stored in the guidance computer's memory. If the two don't match, necessary adjustments are made in the missile's course. The Pershing II uses a somewhat similar system, but only near the end of its flight. It's a ballistic missile, but as it approaches the target, a radar image of the area is compared with a map stored in the memory of the missile's guidance computer; then the path of the warhead is adjusted to hit the target precisely.

GLCM, Pershing II

The improved accuracy provided by this system has made possible the use of a more compact warhead, smaller both in size and explosive power. This in turn allows the missile to carry more fuel, which more than doubles its range compared to the older Pershing I (of which there are 108 now in Europe). The Pershing II and the GLCM have a range of about 1,000 miles, sufficient to hit targets inside the Soviet Union from western European launch sites, something the older Pershings now in place cannot do.

Ironically, it is the technical improvements in these nuclear weapons that have raised European fears that they will actually be used in war. The resulting popular uproar has

334 What Kinds of Guns Are They Buying for Your Butter?

put great pressure on several European governments and increased the strains in NATO. Domestically, President Reagan's proposed massive increases in defense spending, combined with the apparent shift in emphasis to a nuclear war-fighting doctrine, are creating a renewed American apprehension about nuclear weapons. It now appears that a significant push to ban the bomb (or at least a movement calling for a freeze on nuclear weapons) has become prominent here as well.

As noted in Chapter Seven, a new issue was added to this debate in April 1982, when four former senior government officials proposed that the United States renounce the option first use of the first use of nuclear weapons in the event of a European war. The former officials, McGeorge Bundy and Robert McNamara, who served in the Kennedy and Johnson administrations, George Kennan, former ambassador to the Soviet Union, and Gerard Smith, chief SALT negotiator under President Nixon, fear that deterrence will fail and the first step across the nuclear threshold would start a chain of escalation leading to full-scale atomic war. "I never met anyone who believed nuclear war could be limited," said McNamara in a press conference called to discuss their proposal.* They believe nuclear weapons must be kept in Europe to serve as a deterrent to first use by others but they favor avoiding their use as long as possible. They recommend strengthening conventional forces to enhance both deterrence and conventional defense to Europe, an essential requirement if "no first use" is to have any chance of becoming policy.

The proposal goes to the heart of NATO's dilemmas and is sure to be controversial for some time to come.

THE RAPID DEPLOYMENT FORCE

> The emphasis on getting troops to the Persian Gulf or other troublespots continues with more than $11 billion allocated to fixing C-5 transports, buying a new version of that plane and buying new KC 10A cargo/tanker aircraft in addition to increased conversion and chartering of vessels to pre-position equipment overseas.
> —*The Washington Post,* February 7, 1981, page A10

The Washington Post, April 8, 1982, page A12.

But there is much more to American security than just the nations of the alliance. How are we to deal with trouble spots outside Europe? Half a century ago the words "The Marines have landed and the situation is well in hand" embodied our projection of military power in obscure corners of the globe. Thus the Somozas came to power in Nicaragua. But the Marine Corps is a "light" force made up of well-trained and disciplined volunteers that has few tanks and not much heavy artillery. Its mission is to attack "across a hostile shore," relying on the shock of the assault to carry the day. Since in combat the Marine Corps routinely experiences heavy casualties, this kind of action can be sustained for a few days at best. For more extended engagements a "heavy" force (equipped with lots of armor and artillery) is needed.

Persian Gulf oil and continued access to it by ourselves and our allies have absorbed the attention of U.S. military planners for several years now. The focus has been the development of some way to move American heavy combat forces rapidly to that area, as well as to other parts of the Middle East, Korea, and other faraway parts of the globe.

Several developments in the past few years have pushed the question to the fore. The Soviet invasion of Afghanistan seems to place Soviet military forces physically closer to the Persian Gulf than ever before. More worrisome than direct Soviet intervention is the specter of internal unrest and turmoil in the countries of the region. No one can forget what happened when the Shah's regime collapsed and the Ayatollah Khomeini rose to power in Iran. And some people also worry about the long-term stability of the Saudi monarchy; they fret about the possibility that it could be overturned by an internally based but externally supported insurgency.

Still, despite several years of planning, the rapid deployment force (RDF) remains more a concept than a reality. A Marine general has been named commander of the RDF and a headquarters has been established, but there are as yet no forces to command. In a crisis situation existing military units would be brought together and merged into a unified force. Then the essential task would be to move them, by sea and air, to the trouble spot.

If speed is essential, we would have to rely on aircraft to move troops and equipment. But this is a logistical nightmare. Troops can be easily moved by air. However, heavy equipment such as tanks, armored personnel carriers, and artillery as well as all the ammunition and supplies that would be needed is difficult and expensive to move by air. It is possible to carry two M-1 tanks in a C-5A, but no ammunition or spare parts could go along. Even then, the giant transport couldn't take off on a hot day or from an airfield much above sea level and would still need aerial refueling as soon as it was airborne. So as a practical matter we can move but one tank at a time, and the round trip from the United States to the Middle East can easily consume 50,000 gallons of jet fuel.

Water is another major problem. The Army estimates that it would need an average of several hundred gallons per day per soldier if the RDF were operating in the Middle East. While each infantryman alone would require eight to ten gallons each day for drinking, cooking, and sanitation, much of our equipment uses a lot of water, too. For example, the engines of the B-52, KC-135, and AWACS require several hundred gallons of distilled water to increase their thrust on every takeoff. So RDF planners have to assume the likelihood that fuel, water, and equipment will be moved by sea. Several ships filled with heavy equipment, water, and munitions are already pre-positioned near the U.S. island base of Diego Garcia in the Indian Ocean.

Diego Garcia is but one base. We have signed agreements with nations on the rim of the Indian Ocean to permit us access to bases on their territory—Oman, Somalia, and Kenya. Even with these facilities the Navy would be hard pressed to sustain its own forces given the long supply lines. Don't forget we're talking about a part of the world that is 12,000 miles from home, but no more than 1,000 miles from the Soviet Union.

Also at issue is whether the Navy would be able to land its supplies and equipment to support the RDF. In fact, the entire concept has been based on the assumption that we will be going to the assistance of a friendly nation, which means we will be able to land our troops and equipment unopposed. By itself, the RDF is but a bureaucratic umbrella for a number of modular forces that could, if need be, include a Marine amphibious force in the event that landing on a hostile shore would be required. However, many of the supply vessels are basically container ships and cannot be brought anywhere near shore. They require modern port facilities and could not be easily unloaded in a hostile environment.

To make the RDF work will require the expansion of America's existing airlift capability. To this end, the Reagan administration is currently planning to buy 50 more C-5s, now called the C-5B (at $400 million apiece, including spares—a total contract of $8 billion), and 44 more KC-10 tanker transports at $30–$40 million each; and to take some freighters from U.S. cargo airlines, increase the floor strength of the planes (such as Boeing 747s and DC-10s), and then pay the airlines a subsidy for carrying all the extra weight around so the planes could be used in an emergency to ferry U.S. troops and equipment to world trouble spots. airlift capability

One reason for the emphasis on airlift capability is that the Saudis in particular, but other governments as well, have made it clear that they do not want any large, permanent U.S. military presence on their territory or, for that matter, anywhere else in the region. (The exception to this is the Israelis, who have indicated some willingness to let us use their bases.)

Suppose we had had a fully equipped and functioning RDF at the time our hostages were taken in Iran. Would it have made a difference? If we had been willing to make a quick decision to send several thousand ground troops to Iran during the period before Khomeini took control, the answer might be yes. But while we might have avoided the hostage taking, the invasion would probably have fanned the flames of anti-American feelings in the area. So we might have had to shoot our way 800 miles from the coast to Teheran and then fight our way out again.

A seemingly more realistic scenario might involve some unspecific threat to the Saudi oil fields—a civil war, a coup, who knows?—that jeopardized the supply of crude oil that the United States and especially our allies in Europe and the Far East have depended upon in the past. While we could certainly occupy the oil fields, there is some question whether American troops could keep the oil flowing. Presumably, large numbers of technicians and other trained

338 What Kinds of Guns Are They Buying for Your Butter?

personnel would also have to be brought in to do the job. And, of course, they'd have to be protected from guerrilla attack.

Korea has been mentioned as another possible spot for an RDF landing. Let's say the North Koreans invade again. We could have troops there within twenty-four hours to reinforce the 30,000 or so Americans already based there. But the new arrivals would have only limited amounts of ammunition: some light antitank weapons, mortars, and machine guns. Obviously the RDF would have a tough time, especially since it would take about three weeks for ships carrying tanks and other heavy equipment to arrive. Far more important than these ground troops would be U.S. air power, some of which is already based in the region.

In the fall of 1981 the RDF conducted a large joint exercise with Egypt called Operation Bright Star. Several thousand American troops with their equipment (including helicopters) were flown there, as were a couple of squadrons of U.S. tactical aircraft, plus an AWACS. Once there they took part in war games with Egyptian troops in the desert west of Cairo. The climax of the exercise was a spectacular display of aerial firepower by six B-52s which had flown 7,500 miles nonstop from bases in North Dakota, then dropped 40 tons of live bombs on mock targets in the desert, and flew home. Presumably, this exercise demonstrated to Libya that it would risk a major confrontation if it were to try to invade Egypt.

As we have said, the RDF is still just a concept. The Reagan administration would like to transform it into a crisis-intervention force-in-being of some 200,000 troops from all the services. Aside from the politically sensitive issue of just where we would intervene, the President faces some opposition from within the usually loyal ranks of pro-defense Congressmen. Senator John Tower (R.-Texas), for example, is chairman of the Senate Armed Services Committee and has his own ideas about the RDF. Since he thinks that most crisis-intervention situations will require an armed assault from the sea, he wants a slimmed-down force (about 70,000–80,000 troops) consisting exclusively of Marines. After all, amphibious assaults are the Marines' job. We will undoubtedly hear more about the RDF in the future as Senator Tower jousts with the Pentagon.

THE NAVAL DEBATE

IN POLICY SHIFT, PENTAGON SEEKS NAVAL SUPERIORITY
In a policy shift that could ultimately bring basic
changes in the deployment of U.S. miltary forces around
the world, including a reduction of forces in Europe, Pentagon officials have decided the United States should now
seek "maritime superiority" over the Soviet Union.
—The Washington Post, December 14, 1981, page 1

"Sea power" was a term coined by Alfred Thayer Mahan
in the late nineteenth century. The idea is simple: a nation
that controls the world's oceans can dominate the earth because it can use the sea for its commerce while denying it to
any enemy. It's not quite true, of course, since Mahan
focused on the rise of the British Empire at the expense of
the French and ignored the fact that it is possible to have a
massive land power—such as Russia or China—that has little need for a navy. Nonetheless, it is obvious that without a
powerful navy it would be impossible to sustain our RDF.
And German submarines taught us in two world wars that
we could not fight in Europe without a "bridge of ships"
across the Atlantic. So even if we don't consider our missile-
carrying submarines, America must have access to the
oceans if we are to be able to protect our interests abroad.

The heart of the Reagan administration's plan to
strengthen our military is the goal of expanding the U.S.
Navy from its present 450 ships to 600, and increasing our
global striking power by building two more nuclear-powered
aircraft carriers. To achieve this 600-ship goal, we will have
to buy 133 new ones at a total cost of $9.6 billion over the
next five years. Moreover, 100,000 to 150,000 more sailors
will be needed to man these additional ships. Not only is the
price of such an effort at issue, but so is the question of how
the money should be spent. In particular, we need to ask
just what kinds of ships should be built and what kinds of
missions make the most sense to plan for them.

At the end of World War II the United States had the
largest and most powerful fleet in the world. We ruled the
seas with a dominance unmatched even by the Royal Navy
at the height of its power. For thirty years following the war
we could rely on the large numbers of ships built during that

conflict. Of course, some new ships were constructed during that period, but not in numbers that came anywhere close to matching wartime production. By the early 1970s many of those World War II ships were reaching the end of their useful lives. Rather than try to keep them sailing with their resulting high maintenance costs, the Chief of Naval Operations, Admiral Elmo Zumwalt, decided to retire many of them so as to make money available for new ships. But available funds never quite matched Navy aspirations, at least not until after the 1980 election.

The Navy wants more ships because greater demands are being made on it. In the past it operated in the Atlantic, the Mediterranean, and the Pacific. It is now being required to operate not only in those areas but also in the Indian Ocean (near the Persian Gulf) because of the high priority now given to that region in U.S. defense planning. Moreover, it is the avowed goal of the Administration in the event of war with the Soviets to expand the war to areas of our own choosing as a way of exploiting Soviet geographic vulnerabilities. As a result the Navy's resources are being stretched rather thin.

The Soviet Navy is another source of concern. It has grown in recent years from a coastal defense force, with little or no capability for sustained operations far from its shores, to a modern fleet with the capacity to sail almost anywhere in the world. Although it lacks large aircraft carriers comparable to those at the heart of the U.S. fleet, it would rely on land-based aircraft and its ships are heavily armed with many different kinds of cruise missiles, many of which have nuclear warheads. The Soviets also have a lot of submarines. Overall, the Soviet Navy has more ships than the United States, although we retain the lead in tonnage because our ships are bigger on the average. In the event of war, we assume, the Soviet battle plan would be to try to sink as many of our ships as quickly as possible in an overwhelming coordinated missile attack from surface ships, land-based aircraft, and submarines. Former Secretary of Defense Harold Brown took this scenario quite seriously, and shortly before leaving office noted that one of his major worries was how to keep our Navy from being sunk by Soviet nuclear-armed cruise missiles.

The Navy worries about this, too. It is taking steps such as installing Phalanx (a rapid-fire anti-aircraft gun) on all our warships, better to defend our ships against such a Soviet cruise missile barrage, and also trying to spread our offensive striking power among more ships and aircraft. Since the Battle of the Coral Sea in 1942, the aircraft carrier with its complement of planes has been the primary offensive weapon of the U.S. Navy. But cruise missiles make it possible to give even small ships a powerful punch. The Navy is now equipping most of its frigates, destroyers, and cruisers as well as land-based patrol aircraft with anti-ship cruise missiles. It is even refurbishing two World War II behemoths, the battleships *New Jersey* and *Iowa,* which had been in mothballs. It is equipping these ships with modern cruise missiles and defensive guns and missiles, as well as modern electronics (radar, communications gear, etc.)

While some critics ridicule the idea, the Navy points out that these ships have armor plate more than a foot thick, which makes them capable of absorbing much more battle damage while still keeping their fighting power. These battleships also would carry six 16-inch guns (that's the diameter of the barrel) capable of hurling high-explosive projectiles weighing more than a ton at least 20 miles, perhaps 50 miles with modern rocket-assisted shells. These guns could bombard distant shore targets in support of Marine landings on hostile shores. Indeed, the *New Jersey* was temporarily taken out of mothballs during the Vietnam War for this purpose.

The Navy views preparation for conventional wars in third-world trouble spots and fighting the Soviet Navy all over the world as its most important mission. The Navy's goal is to be able to challenge the Soviet Navy in the eastern Mediterranean and North Atlantic near the Kola Peninsula and win. It calls the latter "offensive sea control." Yet critics **offensive** of shipbuilding priorities feel that it would make more sense **sea control** for the Navy to concentrate on building a larger number of smaller, cruise-missile–equipped ships instead of concentrating on a few very large and very expensive aircraft carriers ($2.5 billion to $3.5 billion each, depending on whether they are nuclear-powered). We have but 13 aircraft carriers and they make tempting targets. People such as Senator Gary

Hart (D.-Colo.) believe it is foolish to concentrate so many of our resources in so few ships.

The critics see other ways the Navy could plan its strat-

defensive sea control

egy. It could concentrate on what naval analysts call "defensive sea-control"; in other words, it could focus on protecting friendly forces on vital sea routes while denying the sea to our opponents. American interests require a steady flow of resources to the United States as well as supplies and reinforcements to our military forces fighting overseas. Defensive sea control would give this mission top priority. Were this the case, Navy shipbuilding requirements would be different from those at present, because while aircraft carriers can be used in this role, a less costly alternative would employ smaller ships equipped with cruise missiles, attack submarines, and land-based patrol planes.

The point is this: offensive sea control, which is Navy doctrine today, envisions a war at sea in which our fleet seeks out and sinks the Russian Navy. This commitment to "go in harm's way" requires a powerful striking force of aircraft carriers supported by cruisers, destroyers, and other escorts. The strategy demands a sizable escorting force because it is obvious that the enemy will throw everything they have at our carriers; moreover, defending against these attacks will be more difficult because it is likely we will be operating in hostile waters close to the enemy's bases.

Defensive sea control, on the other hand, sees the enemy making the first move. It doesn't eschew the carrier strike force, but reduces its emphasis. By stressing the protection of vital sea-lanes and other strategic points, the idea is to force a Soviet strike force to run the gauntlet made up of cruise-missile–armed frigates and patrol planes and (most importantly) our attack submarines. After this, it is assumed, the enemy fleet will be significantly weakened from battle casualties, and be, now far from home, relatively easy prey for our carrier strike forces.

Whether we choose to let the enemy come to us or decide to press home the attack at all costs, there is no denying that the United States is a maritime nation. We have thousands of miles of coastline and rely heavily on the world's oceans for trade and commerce. The issue is how best to assure the access to the seas that all agree is vital. Now that such staunch pro-Pentagon lawmakers as Senator John Stennis

(D.-Miss.) question whether we can afford a 600-ship fleet, the debate over the size, composition, doctrine, and strategy for the U.S. Navy is sure to be thorough, even intense.

CHEMICAL AND BIOLOGICAL WARFARE

CRUISE MISSILES MAY GET CHEMICAL WARHEADS
The Army is studying the feasibility of putting chemical warheads on ground-launched cruise missiles of the kind now scheduled to be based in Western Europe, according to recently released Congressional testimony.
—*The Washington Post,* January 16, 1982, page A5

While deterrent weapons cost us relatively little compared to what we spend on general-purpose forces, their terrifying destructive potential commands the major share of our attention. That's why they're deterrents. But not all deterrent weapons are thermonuclear. Poison gas was considered unspeakable long before the first atomic bomb was tested at Alamogordo.

Amid State Department charges (which the Russians deny) that the Soviet Union has been using chemical weapons in Afghanistan, the Reagan administration is calling for the production, after a thirteen-year moratorium, of new lethal nerve-gas weapons as a deterrent to the Soviets. But popular abhorrence of poison gas—it's actually not a gas but an aerosol—is still strong, and renewed production of chemical weapons could arouse considerable protest in the United States.

We stopped building chemical weapons in 1969 and in 1975 ratified the Geneva Protocol, renouncing their first use. However, some military officials today believe the Soviets have large stocks of such weapons, estimating that from 10 to 30 percent of all their artillery shells are so equipped. They are also alarmed by intelligence suggesting Soviet production of biological agents as well, anthrax in particular.

In fact, the Soviets regularly conduct military exercises which feature the use of chemical agents, and Soviet tanks, warships, and other armored vehicles are routinely equipped with special filters to protect their crews from the effects of chemical weapons.

344 What Kinds of Guns Are They Buying for Your Butter?

The Army Medical Research Institute of Infectious Diseases began operations at Fort Detrick, Maryland, in 1956. Here the military's main *defensive* investigations into potential biological warfare agents are performed through the study of a wide variety of infectious diseases, ranging from botulism and anthrax to exotic marine toxins. The military's *offensive* biological weapons program, established in 1943, was shut down in 1970 after President Nixon unilaterally renounced U.S. development of biological weapons.

One of the most recent activities of the Fort Detrick center is the investigation of a substance which is called "yellow rain" by refugees fleeing the battlegrounds of Laos and Cambodia. It causes blistering of the skin, convulsions, rapid heartbeat, bloody diarrhea, and vomiting. Some people even drown in their own blood. These reports long puzzled U.S. experts because the symptoms, especially the massive internal bleeding, didn't match any known chemical warfare agent. We now think that yellow rain is made up of toxins produced by a fungus that grows in poorly stored grains. The Army is taking seriously the possibility that the Soviets have developed the toxins as a weapon. As a result, the Fort Detrick laboratory is searching for antidotes while the Army's Chemical Systems Lab at the Edgewood Arsenal in Maryland is working on means to protect military personnel from them.*

binary weapons
In America today the procurement of so-called binary weapons is the major issue. Unlike existing bombs and shells, which have the deadly chemicals already mixed within them, binary weapons consist of two relatively safe chemicals, separated by an impermeable membrane inside the weapon's case. When it is fired or dropped, the membrane is broken and the two chemicals mix, forming the deadly poison. It is said that our existing stockpile of chemical weapons is beginning to deteriorate and for this reason binary weapons would be safer to have lying about for long periods of time.

We should stress that these weapons exist only within the framework of deterrence. Our only reason for buying them is to deter their use against us by the Soviets. In actual

*William Kucewicz, "U.S. Army Studies Yellow Rain Defenses," *The Wall Street Journal*, April 29, 1982, page 34.

fact, horrible though it may be in its effects on human beings, poison gas has never been a decisive weapon in war. World War I was the only conflict in which it saw widespread use on both sides. There the gas gave no real advantage to either side; indeed, the Great War illustrates a major problem in using the weapon: if both sides use it, any advantage is lost. In Yemen, as well as Afghanistan and Southeast Asia, where we have had some reports of its use, the weapon has not handed victory to those who used it.

Also, we should be aware that although the Soviets appear to be better prepared for chemical war-fighting because their major weapons systems are designed to operate in a chemical environment, the fact is that the protective clothing we issue our troops is far superior to theirs since it employs an advanced charcoal-impregnated fabric while theirs is the old-fashioned type of rubberized garment that traps body heat, making it almost impossible to fight in.

THE B-1

SENATORS ATTACK REAGAN B-1 PLAN
President Reagan's proposal to build 100 B-1 bombers at a cost of $40 billion came under sharp attack in the Senate today as the lawmakers debated a proposal to delete funds for the aircraft from the 1982 military appropriation bill.

But the B-1's critics conceded that they had little chance of winning at a time when Mr. Reagan was entering new arms talks with the Soviet Union and using a "full-court press" to promote his strategic weapons program on Capitol Hill.

—*The New York Times*, December 4, 1981, page 1

The question of what to do about replacing the B-52 has been around for almost as long as the B-52 itself, or so it sometimes seems. The Reagan administration's decision to build a modified B-1 (B-1B) as an interim strategic bomber until the new Stealth bomber is available in the early 1990s may put the issue to rest. But people thought the same in 1977, when President Carter decided to cancel the B-1 and rely on cruise missiles launched from some 170 of our newer B-52s.

Bombers, as we have learned, form the third leg of the strategic Triad and have a number of valuable characteristics. They can be launched at the first hint of an attack and, if it's all a mistake, come home. Any Soviet plan for a disarming first strike would have to nail the bomber force before it could take off. The Soviets' problem is that we would have about a twenty-five-minute warning of an ICBM launch, enough time to get most bombers airborne. It has been suggested that the Russians could destroy the bomber force by firing missiles in "depressed trajectories" from submarines off our shores. This would reduce our warning time to no more than seven minutes, not enough to launch more than a few bombers. But the Soviets have never tested their missiles in this way and such an attack would pose significant coordination problems for them. So our bombers, subordinate though their role may be, still present an unsolvable dilemma to anyone planning an attack on the United States.

Bombers have other uses as well. In Vietnam, B-52s dropped conventional bombs, first in raids on suspected Viet Cong bases in the jungles of South Vietnam and later in Operation Linebacker, the bombing of industrial targets in and around Hanoi in 1972. Bombers also could be used to bottle up the Soviet Navy in its ports by laying naval mines in various maritime "choke points" around the periphery of the Soviet Union. Or we might want to use them for muscle-flexing or flag-showing missions. Indeed, the British found their long-range bombers quite useful in their war with Argentina over the Falklands. After the assassination of Anwar Sadat in the fall of 1981, Operation Bright Star also demonstrated the value of long-range bombers.

Indeed, in acknowledgment of this flexibility, the Air Force dropped the term bomber and substituted long-range
LRCA combat aircraft (LRCA) a few years ago. Strategic missiles, in contrast, have no such flexibility. They sit and wait in their silos and tubes with the express purpose of never having to be launched.

Clearly, then, bombers make important contributions to the defense of the United States. But how much of their capability do we need? This is part of the controversy surrounding the procurement of the B-1.

When originally proposed ten years ago, each B-1 was to cost about $20 million. When President Carter canceled the program in 1977, the price was up to about $90 million. At the time of the B-1's resurrection under the Reagan administration, the Pentagon put its cost at about $200 million apiece, and congressional opponents and proponents alike privately agreed that the cost would be more like $300 million. In fiscal 1983, the Administration asked for $3.9 billion to build seven, or $553 million each. That is the price of one plane. Originally, the Air Force wanted 244 but now they will settle for 100.

ASIDE———————————————————————————

There is a lively ongoing dispute between the Pentagon and Congress's General Accounting Office over the B-1's actual cost. The GAO points out, for example, that the Air Force made no provision in the budget for enlarging the B-1's rear bomb bay to accommodate cruise missiles. If this isn't done during the plane's construction, it will be prohibitively expensive to do it later on. Moreover, the Pentagon's cost estimates had not, among other things, allowed for EMP (electromagnetic pulse) testing of the airframe, or for a system to allow the flight crew to disable their nuclear weapons in flight as a safety measure, or for the design of a system to make the fuel system inert in case of battle damage. The GAO also believed that another three-quarters of a billion dollars would have to be spent to certify the system's nuclear weapons and as much as $2 billion more for maintenance beyond the B-1's original delivery to its squadrons. The Air Force made no provision in the budget for equipping the plane with conventional weapons. Obviously, without the ability to carry cruise missiles or non-nuclear ordnance, much of the bomber's flexibility would be lost.

———————————————————————————————

Not only is the B-1's cost a subject of controversy, its effectiveness is a matter of intense debate as well, especially in the face of the revolutionary new Stealth technology expected to be available soon after B-1 becomes operational. Serious questions have been raised about the wisdom of spending so much money to build the B-1 only to use it as a penetrating bomber for a few years, then relegate it to the mission of cruise-missile carrier—a role for which it seems overqualified.

There is no question that the B-1B is superior to the B-52. It is much less visible to radar than the older plane and

it can take off more quickly than the B-52. It also has greater range and payload and is more resistant to nuclear effects.*
The issue is whether it makes sense to spend so much to build the B-1 as an interim plane, when the Stealth is only a few more years away.

In the 1980 election campaign there was a big brouhaha over the Carter administration's supposed leaking of data about a new supersecret Stealth bomber that would be virtually invisible to enemy radar. Critics of B-1 point out that a Stealth aircraft could be available by the early 1990s. Thus B-1 would serve as a first-line penetrating bomber for just a few years.

While the details of Stealth technology are secret, we know that several different means are combined to achieve the effect. Radar countermeasures have been around almost as long as radar itself. Combat aircraft today are routinely equipped with a variety of devices that "jam" or "spoof" enemy radar, making it look as though there are more of you than there are, or that you are somewhere else, or heading in a different direction at a different speed or altitude. In Vietnam, F-4 and F-105 aircraft, called Wild Weasels, tracked North Vietnamese radars and then launched special missiles that homed in on the radar signals and destroyed the enemy's radar site. In addition, we had Ravens, small planes packed with electronic gear, which flew around spoofing North Vietnamese radar and gathering electronic intelligence. Today's B-52s carry a lot of this kind of equipment.

In addition to the electronic gadgetry, Stealth technology also employs radar-absorbing material (a type of plastic) to cover its reflecting surfaces. But more significant is the fact that the aircraft is designed to give it a lower radar "signature" than even the B-1. In addition to burying its engines in the fuselage (as is done to some degree with the B-1), it uses complex compound curves in its wings and other surfaces to deny radar waves a flat surface off which to bounce. Control surfaces are kept small by using a computer system to maintain stability instead of the high-profile stabilizers common

margin notes: **jamming, spoofing**

margin notes: **lowering the radar signature**

---

*John Correll, "Speed, Flexibility and Global Reach," *Sea Power*, April 1982, page 95.

to conventional aircraft design. Indeed, a major problem has turned out to be the weapons the plane will carry; enemy radar can detect them as they hang under the aircraft even though it cannot pick up the plane itself. So we will need to design "stealthy" missiles and bombs as well.

The B-1 issue was further complicated by a proposal to re-engine the B-52s at a fraction of the cost of building the B-1. Late in 1981, Pratt & Whitney (a division of United Technologies, formerly headed by General Alexander Haig) offered to remove the B-52's present engines and replace them with new fuel-efficient turbofan engines designed for Boeing's latest airliner, the 757. This would result in saving 120 million gallons of fuel per year, worth $6.4 billion over twenty years. The fuel savings would be so great that a B-52 flying on a long-range cruise-missile carrier mission that normally would require two in-flight refuelings would need none at all. The new engines would give so much more power that the plane would need 1,500 feet less runway to take off, so it could operate from more airfields.

How the B-1 issue will finally turn out is not yet clear, but two prominent Republicans, former President Gerald Ford and Congressman John J. Rhodes of Arizona (former House minority leader), are against it. Ford, still proudly proclaiming himself a "hawk," has urged that purchase be delayed to reduce the budget deficit. Rhodes, once a supporter, believes the plane should be canceled and funds concentrated on development of the Stealth.* No doubt President Reagan has some more convincing to do.

MX—A MISSILE IN SEARCH OF A HOME

In many ways the controversial MX has become a missile in search of a hole in the ground. Its wanderings are a bit of a political embarrassment to the Reagan administration. After castigating the Carter administration's MX program during the 1980 campaign, the Reagan team has had four different notions of where to put the MX over the past thirteen months, without settling on a satisfactory long-term answer.

—*The New York Times*, February 23, 1982, page A18

*The Washington Post, April 7, 1982, page A3.

The MX controversy is not one issue but (at least) two. The more visible issue centers around the missile's "basing mode," i.e., how and where it will be deployed, which we discussed in earlier chapters. The other issue, less visible but perhaps more important, centers around the missile itself and its potential uses. Both raise troubling questions.

The various MX mobile-basing schemes (see the sketches on pages 352–356) all had in common one principal objective: to enhance deterrence by providing "survivability" for our land-based missiles. As the accuracy and number of Soviet MIRV warheads have increased, our land-based missiles seem to be in jeopardy. Some analysts worry that the Soviets could destroy most of our land-based missiles and then be in a position to deter us from retaliating with our surviving submarine-based missiles and bombers by threatening to destroy our cities with their remaining forces.

This "window of vulnerability" scenario assumes that our ICBMs are not launched while they are under attack. If they were, the Soviet missiles would hit empty silos. The "launch under attack" option is always available, but most people feel it is too dangerous, because once both sides adopt it, the risk of reacting too quickly to imperfect (and perhaps faulty) information is increased. To get around this problem, the Eyring Research Institute in Provo, Utah, has proposed that the MIRV bus on some MXs be modified so that it can be placed into a low earth orbit. Then these missiles could be launched, like our bombers, upon warning of an attack. Were it a mistake, the warheads could be rendered inert by remote control and commanded to land in some safe area (such as Kwajalein, an atoll in the Pacific) or be picked up in orbit by the space shuttle. If we had this capability, it is argued, the Russians would be deterred from a disarming first strike.*

The first objection to this idea focuses on the fact that we have a treaty that forbids "weapons of mass destruction" in space. Beyond that, its orbit would decay in ninety minutes, so all we'd really be buying is an hour or so to think things over. A far more serious problem would involve the security of the data links between the missile and ground control.

---

*Clarence Robinson, "USAF Restudying Orbital Basing of MX," *Aviation Week & Space Technology*, April 12, 1982, page 83.

One of the major advantages of ballistic missiles is their self-contained guidance. Once they're launched, they're gone. But an orbiting system would need direction from the ground; thus it would be possible for an enemy to jam it or to feed it false information. While we can expect to hear more about this idea in the future, it seems likely that the major outcome will be to increase the legitimacy of the idea of launch under attack.

While the "dense pack" basing mode has been selected by the Reagan administration (as of May 1982), the basing issue is still uncertain. When, under intense pressure from western legislators in whose states the MX was to have been based, Reagan abandoned the multiple protective shelter (MPS) or "shell game" basing scheme, he was left with the dilemma of what to do with the new missile. The Administration had planned as an interim measure to put about 40 MXs in Minuteman silos while other basing was studied. But in April 1982 the Senate voted to withhold funding until a more satisfactory basing scheme could be devised. Senator John Tower (R.-Tex.) led the fight in the Armed Services Committee, supported by Senator Gary Hart (D.-Colo.). Tower worries that putting MX in Minuteman silos would do nothing to remedy the "window of vulnerability" which President Reagan made so much of during the 1980 election campaign.

dense pack *(margin note)*

ASIDE

Some critics raise fundamental questions about the "window of vulnerability" itself and the scenarios that justify the need for an elaborate and expensive new weapons system. Herbert Scoville, Jr., wonders whether the Soviets could in a real war achieve the accuracies (CEPs of about 800 feet) they get in tests. Moreover, he notes, missile reliability is such a severe problem that he doubts they could launch thousands of missiles without serious snags. But one of the most vexing problems is "warhead fratricide." This is the distinct possibility that the first explosions in the attack would destroy those warheads coming in after. Scoville, a former government official with long experience in matters relating to nuclear weapons, feels that fratricide would probably not allow more than two warheads to be fired at any one target in a short time.

warhead fratricide *(margin note)*

(See *MX: Prescription for Disaster,* page 123.)

ICBM BASING OPTIONS

LAUNCH UNDER ATTACK (LUA)

Positive Features:
- Low Cost
- Near term
- Public interface*
- Environmental impact*
- Cost*

* = no change from present operations

Negative Features:
- Vulnerable to attacks on warning and C³ systems
- Requires warning
- No endurance
- Extremely short decision time
- Catastrophic false alarm problem

Description:
- Launch Minuteman force when early warning systems assess attack in progress

ORBITAL BASED

Positive Features:
- Low cost

Negative Features:
- Vulnerable to attack in orbit
- Requires warning
- Accuracy insufficient for hard targets
- False alarm means loss of capability
- Orbital weapons violate space treaty

Description:
- New booster in Minuteman silos
- On warning, launch weapons into orbit
- On command, deorbit to attack or recover

SHALLOW UNDERWATER MISSILE (SUM)

Positive Features:
- Minimal public interface
- Minimal environmental impact

Negative Features:
- Same survivability mode as Trident but probably inferior
- Advanced technology subsystems
- Early 90's for earliest IOC (with new submarines)

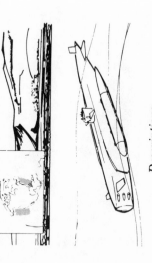

Description:
- Fasten two or more M-X encapsulated missiles to submarines that patrol off U.S. coast

WIDE BODY JET (W.B.J.)

Positive Features:
- None

Negative Features:
- Requires warning
- Endurance limited to hours
- High cost, particularly for airborne alert

Description:
- Launch missiles from C-5 or 747 class aircraft
- Aircraft operate on ground alert like bombers
- Option for continuous airborne operations

(Courtesy of the U.S. Department of Defense.)

COVERED TRENCH

Positive Features:
- Independent survivability mode
- Long endurance
- Automated operation

Negative Features:
- Removal of cover plus vehicle immobilization by light precursor attack
- Implanted sensors could localize missiles (decoys not feasible)
- Large public exclusion area

Description:
- Unmanned transporter/launcher travels randomly in a trench that is covered with a concealing fabric

HYBRID TRENCH

Positive Features:
- Independent survivability mode
- Excellent security
- Automated operation

Negative Features:
- Implanted sensors could localize missiles (decoys not feasible)
- Large public exclusion area

Description:
- Shallow buried tunnels with M-X missile on unmanned transporter
- Transporter randomly moves to locations in tunnel that have been selectively hardened

HARD ROCK SILO

Description:
- Build silos in granite outcroppings in western U.S.
- Design goal is to achieve highest possible hardness with surface-flush silo launchers

Positive Features:
- Distinct survivability mode
- Long endurance

Negative Features:
- Defeated by evolutionary accuracy improvements

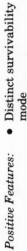

Description:
- Base missiles in horizontal shelters or vertical silos at the foot of south-facing mesa or mountain cliff
- Mountain/mesa shields missile from Soviet ICBM attack arriving from north

SOUTH SIDE BASING

Positive Features:
- Distinct survivability mode
- Long endurance
- Low cost

Negative Features:
- Vulnerable to responsive threats (low β R/Vs, SLBMs, MaRVs)
- Limited suitable deployment area
- Environmental impact, since sites in national parks

(Courtesy of the U.S. Department of Defense.)

COMMERCIAL RAIL

Positive Features:
• Independent survivability mode
• Long endurance possible

Negative Features:
• Enemy might trail trains
• Public interface problems of nuclear weapons on commercial railroads
• Poor security

Description:
• Special trains move ICBMs over existing commercial railroads
• Trains move randomly and park to launch

MINUTEMAN/MPS

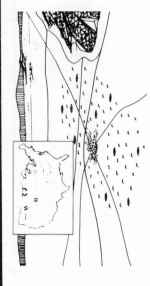

Positive Features:
• Independent survivability mode
• Long endurance

Negative Features:
• None

Description:
• Construct additional vertical silos in existing Minuteman silo fields
• Use Minuteman or new missile that is randomly shuffled between silos

But survivable basing is but half the MX story. MX is not just a basing scheme but a new weapon with at least 10 warheads per missile, more accurate and more powerful (in terms of total megatonnage combined with its "hard target kill" capability) than any of its predecessors. The plan is to put .335-megaton Mark 12A warheads on the MX, the same as on some of our Minuteman IIIs; but the Air Force is looking into a larger half-megaton warhead as well.

The fundamental point is that 200 (or even 40) MX missiles added to the force would increase our capacity to threaten Soviet ICBMs much as theirs threaten ours. Minuteman begins to do this, but the Air Force points out that there are not enough Minuteman III warheads to target two for each of the Soviets' 1,400 ICBMs. In the view of Pentagon planners, MX would provide those added numbers, giving us a "flexible second strike capability" consistent with a doctrine that emphasizes the fighting of a nuclear war; limited, as much as possible, to missile silos and military targets.

flexible second strike

Much of the real controversy centers on this point. Supporters argue that they do not want to fight a nuclear war, but the only way to make deterrence truly credible is to prepare for it. Critics maintain that it is impossible to limit a war to missile silos without causing immense destruction and millions of civilian casualties. (Recall how efforts early in World War II to avoid bombing undefended cities quickly broke down in the heat of war.) They also worry that MX's counter-silo capability could increase the danger of nuclear war because MX deployment might make the Soviets fear an American first strike against their ICBMs. In fact, Scoville believes such missiles only make sense in a first strike, and he notes that the Soviets depend on ICBMs for deterrence to a much greater degree than we. They have some 75 percent of their strategic capability concentrated in land-based missiles, while we have more than half our warheads on submarines.* The danger is that in a crisis or confrontation the Soviets might feel that they had to use their ICBMs quickly lest they lose them.

The controversies surrounding MX underline once again the difficulties in attempting to achieve security through

* Scoville, *op. cit.*, pages 140–141.

weaponry alone. Without arms control that in some way sets boundaries on the extent of the threat posed by the other side, the demands on U.S. military capabilities become very extensive indeed, and our ability to meet those demands increasingly difficult and costly. You can see that the scenarios and counter-scenarios get quite involved, but apart from knowledge of the systems' technical capabilities, there is no real expertise. Who is to say that one scenario is more plausible than another? Since there is no experience on which to draw, no one really knows if any nation's leader would actually push the button. Indeed, after a time the whole discussion comes to resemble a mass therapy session in which participants trot out their own worst fears and nightmares.

ABM, ASAT, AND THE WAR IN SPACE

> Strategic nuclear defense systems—ballistic missile and air defense . . . will receive increased emphasis through the 1980's. . . . The U.S. and the USSR are seeking ways to mitigate each other's growing offensive nuclear weapons force as new intercontinental and submarine-launched ballistic missiles with greater yield and higher accuracy are added.
>
> —*Aviation Week & Space Technology,*
> March 8, 1982, page 27

One MX basing mode proposed by the Air Force is "dense pack" (dubbed "duncepack" by Washington wags), a scheme that would place 200–300 missiles in an area no more than 20 miles square.* One advantage to this is the Air Force could use an existing air base instead of taking over large tracts of land for the multiple-basing schemes. The plan involves some deception in that there would be 10 silos for each missile to move among. The silos would be hardened to 5,000 psi, and the Air Force argues that even a massed attack on the pack would involve the incoming warheads in so much fratricide that many missiles would survive. But what is most significant about this is that plans include an ABM system to protect the missiles.

Aviation Week & Space Technology, March 29, 1982, page 21.

Thus comes the wheel full circle. Top Defense Department officials now call ballistic-missile defense "the hottest game in town."* In the late 1950s we developed and then abandoned the Nike X anti-ballistic missile while the Russians went ahead and built a similar primitive system around Moscow called Galosh. We also developed and began construction on the Safeguard system in the early 1970s, but the ABM treaty of 1972 effectively put an end to it. (This was, you will recall, the major achievement of SALT I.) Both nations realized that if each built ABM systems and then beefed up their ICBM forces to overcome the other's defenses, there would be no net gain in either side's security.

Under the treaty, research into and development of ABM technology are permitted and in fact have gone forward on both sides. We tested ballistic-missile defense (BMD) interceptors as late as 1975, and have continued to investigate other technologies, including exoatmospheric (outside the atmosphere—in space) interceptors, special radars, and non-nuclear means to destroy incoming warheads.

Several different potential BMD systems are currently under consideration. One, called LoADS, or low-altitude defense system, could possibly become operational by the late 1980s and would use small nuclear warheads to destroy incoming warheads in the atmosphere. The development of non-nuclear means to do the same job is being pressed, but is years away.†   **LoADS**

Another type of ABM under review—in this case designed to defend silo-based missiles—is the "layered" system. A two-tiered concept, it would supplement the LoAD system with longer-range interceptors armed with multiple non-nuclear warheads and designed to intercept attacking missile warheads outside the atmosphere. One estimate places the cost of building a layered system to defend 1,000 silos against a 5,000-warhead attack at $10 billion to $12 billion, but it could not be built until the 1990s.‡ Moreover, without some upper limit on the number of warheads in the   **layered defense**

---

*Aviation Week & Space Technology, March 8, 1982, page 27.
†FY 1980 Arms Control Impact Statements. U.S. Congress, 1979, pages 72–73.
‡Jonathan Medalia, "Antiballistic Missiles," Issue Brief IB 81003 (Washington D.C.: Library of Congress, Congressional Research Service, 1981), page 8.

Soviet force (via some sort of arms control agreement), the size and cost of the system would have to grow as the Soviets added more warheads. Otherwise, the system simply could be overwhelmed.

Both of these systems would rely on interceptor missiles launched from the ground with nuclear or thermonuclear warheads. Indeed, this field is where the first major research on electromagnetic pulse was undertaken and is the origin of the neutron bomb as well (it was developed for use with the Safeguard system in the late 1960s). But it was this use of nuclear weapons, among other things, that spurred past opposition to ABM. What was the benefit, many people asked, of trying to stop enemy missiles if in so doing you blanketed the skies of America with nuclear detonations of your own?

Also on the drawing boards are plans for systems that would launch a "swarm" of small, very high-speed rockets that would destroy an incoming warhead on impact. This concept is directed at "site defense" of a silo; it would use a simple "range-only" radar, and its missiles would climb to 5,000–10,000 feet in less than a second and a half.* Presumably, even if the enemy warhead were detonated by the impact, it would be far enough away for the targeted silo to survive.

ASAT (ANTI-SATELLITE WEAPONS)

As well as in land-based ballistic-missile defenses, there is growing interest in weapons based on space satellites. We should keep in mind that space satellites have become an integral part of our military system. We use them for reconnaisance (satellites beam television pictures back to earth or parachute film packages that aircraft pick up in midair) and to relay communications of all kinds. We are now orbiting systems for navigation purposes, too, both for ships at sea and planes in the sky. And in the future, satellites may be used to aim ballistic missiles more accurately. There is, fi-

---

Aviation Week & Space Technology, "Low Cost ABM Rockets Given Emphasis," March 1, 1982, pages 74–75.

nally, a growing commercial utilization of space satellites, primarily in relaying television programs and business communications, as well as in an infant commercial use of space photography for detecting mineral resources and evaluating agricultural conditions. Thus it's obvious that we're so dependent on our satellites that any threat to them leaves us with a serious vulnerability.

The Russians have already demonstrated one primitive anti-satellite weapon, what we referred to earlier as a sort of "space hand grenade." It is designed to be maneuvered into position near a target satellite and exploded. Our current version is to be tested in the spring of 1983. The United States had an operational anti-satellite system based on Johnston Island in the Pacific from 1964 to 1975, when it was dismantled. Our newest system will use a miniature homing vehicle launched from an F-15 via a two-stage rocket. Unlike the Russians', our system operates on kinetic energy—that is, after being boosted into space, the vehicle simply collides with the target satellite. In one sense this capability will operate as a deterrent, since if the Soviets were to knock out our satellites, we could knock out theirs.

What's interesting here is that an anti-satellite weapon could be adapted as an anti-ballistic missile as well, and vice versa. After all, if you are going to knock down a satellite in a low earth orbit (and thus far all proposed systems work only in lower orbits), at the instant of intercept the physics is essentially the same as hitting a warhead. The difference, obviously, is that you have but one chance to hit a missile warhead, and there would likely be hundreds or thousands to deal with in an all-out nuclear exchange. But in the case of anti-satellite warfare, we would probably shoot down just one at a time, and if we missed, we could always await its next orbit. Still, the basic technology remains much the same.

For example, in a study called High Frontier the Heritage Foundation proposed that the United States take the miniature homing vehicle being developed for our anti-satellite system and put 40–45 of them on satellites orbiting 300 miles up (this is a low orbit; a high orbit is 20,000 to 30,000 miles). The study claimed that about 450 such platforms, evenly spaced, would guarantee enough interceptor missiles in place over the Soviet Union to shoot down Soviet ballistic missiles.* This proposal is similar to Project Bambi, a ballistic-missile boost intercept, explored twenty years ago but abandoned because the technology of the day was not up to the task.

BEAM WEAPONS

Most people are far more excited by the potential of a totally new kind of weapon called "directed-energy" or "beam" weapons. Indeed, directed-energy weapons may represent the same kind of quantum leap in weapons development that nuclear explosives meant thirty-five years ago.

Beam weapons are of two kinds: laser, or "coherent," light; and particle beams. Their importance from a military standpoint is that they can deliver very large amounts of energy almost instantaneously to very small spots on a target without destroying anything else. In a world of massive chemical and nuclear explosives, these weapons are analogous to sniper fire.

Laser and particle beam technology have been around for some time. The laser, as we know it, is used as a "controlled burn-knife" in eye and other surgery. The particle accelerator has been used in nuclear physics research since World War II. What is new is the weaponizing of both concepts. The laser has emerged as a heat weapon that can deliver a beam of light whose waves vibrate in unison—not unlike the ray gun of science fiction. The particle beam weapon is simply an accelerator that sends a stream of subatomic particles, a sort of machine gun firing subatomic "bullets" almost as fast as the speed of light. There is no maneuvering away—no escape from—such weapons.

The reason the military is so excited about them is that they could be used to attack ballistic missiles in flight during their boost phase; or attack enemy satellites in orbit. And—though they are less efficient in the earth's atmosphere than in outer space—they might even be used from the ground to attack enemy aircraft and satellites as they pass overhead.

The amount of energy required for directed-energy weap-

* Philip J. Klass, "Missile Defense Key to Technology," *Aviation Week & Space Technology*, April 19, 1982, page 79.

ons may be a constraint, for their effectiveness depends on how much energy is pumped in. Kosta Tsipis, of MIT, has calculated that a typical laser weapon in space would require three-quarters of a ton of fuel to shoot down one missile in flight; and between 700 and 750 tons—or twenty space-shuttle loads—to shoot down 1,000.*

The Pentagon has already spent about $1.6 billion on laser weapons development, and Congress has urged the Air Force to pursue a coherent program with specific milestones and objectives. In April 1982 the Deputy Air Force Chief of Staff for weapons research and acquisition said, "It wouldn't surprise me to see the Russians put an effective laser weapon in space in the next five to ten years." He added that while this type of weapon might be able to "blind" an un-shielded satellite in a low earth orbit, it wouldn't affect our military satellites having shiny surfaces or other forms of protective shielding, and would be useless against our ballistic missiles. The Soviets' main goal, according to the general, would be propaganda, not military use, and he hoped "we will all be able to keep it in perspective" and not think "the sky is falling."†

As a matter of fact, the scientific community is deeply divided on the feasibility of beam weapons. One article in *Science* notes that the detonation of a single moderate-size (one- to 3-megaton) nuclear weapon in space could by itself cause an electromagnetic pulse sufficiently intense to disrupt and damage most satellites within thousands of miles. It would be as if the delicate computer elements that lie at the heart of a satellite were suddenly hit by a bolt of lightning.‡ Yet, at the same time, another report in *Aviation Week & Space Technology* tells of an underground test conducted in 1980 called Huron King, in which a satellite was exposed to the EMP levels expected from such a blast. Researchers found that "satellite-hardening techniques currently used are even more effective than originally predicted."§

---

* Kosta Tsipis, "Laser Weapons," *Scientific American,* December 1981, pages 51 *ff.* See also a special technical survey in two parts on beam weapons in *Aviation Week & Space Technology,* July 23 and August 4, 1980.
† *Wall Street Journal,* April 23, 1982, page 8.
‡ William Broad, "The Fatal Flaw in the Concept of Space War," *Science,* March 12, 1982, pages 1372–1374.
§ William B. Scott, "Radiation Hardening Found Effective," *Aviation Week & Space Technology,* March 15, 1982, page 71.

Moreover, even while beam weapons are being debated, people are thinking about countermeasures. One idea is to insulate the missile booster to absorb the beam's energy. Another is to coat the missile with a shiny surface to reflect it away. Warheads are already well protected with ablative, heat-absorbing materials that protect them during reentry; so a laser, which relies on heat to destroy the target, would have to contend with this. Another way to protect the target would be to make it spin so that the beam weapon's energy would be dispersed over a greater area, meaning the beam would have to have much more power to be effective. Other countermeasures include the secretion of some liquid film to cover the missile, which the beam would have to burn through; or the deployment of smoke rockets or decoys to mask the target.

The targeting system for beam weapons presents difficulties, too. If the weapon were designed to disable a missile, rather than destroy it, how would we know when this had occurred? It is important, because the weapon would in all probability need to be rapidly shifted to another target. Particle beams have a significant theoretical advantage over lasers since they work by penetrating the target with a barrage of subatomic particles rather than simply depositing heat energy on the target's surface. But used as a weapon, they have special problems. They travel somewhat more slowly than light, so it would be necessary to lead the target a bit. But the kind of particle beams that would work in space are invisible. So how does the system assess its shooting? In age-old artillery practice, a target is "bracketed." That is, one shot goes over, the next one is corrected and goes under, and so on until the shots are "walked" to the target. But it won't work if you can't *see* where the shot falls. So some sort of tracer element would have to be added to the beam, further complicating its development.

Another problem with beam weapons is that it is necessary to score a *hit* to get a kill. As we have seen, other weapons can score kills with a near-miss, either through shrapnel, blast effect, or EMP. But the targeting of a beam weapon would have to be perfect in order for it to work. The Air Force is working on a detection and tracking system, called Talon Gold, which uses a "staring mosaic sensor," an array of thousands of small infrared sensors linked to a computer much the way the rods and cones in the human eye interface with our brain. The Air Force is creating, in short, a kind of eye, which will allow us to "teach" the system to recognize ballistic-missile warheads and other targets.

In addition to tracking, a directed-energy system must be able to aim the beam at the target through some sort of mirror and lens system. But the biggest problem with all directed-energy weapons is to find a power source for them. Many people doubt that it will be possible to supply sufficient chemical energy to operate such systems in a war environment. As a result, some speculate that we would need a nuclear or even a thermonuclear reactor on the satellite.

Space Shuttle

Finally, we should keep in mind that when we contemplate war in space the United States has a significant edge that most people don't recognize—the space shuttle. The shuttle's payload bay is the size of a railroad boxcar, and it is not difficult to envision a variety of weaponry that could be mounted in it, whether as exotic as directed-energy weapons or as simple as radar-guided guns and missiles. The shuttle is designed to service satellites in orbit but could also snatch an enemy satellite as it flew by. The advantages of a manned space plane in a war situation are obvious. Though the shuttle's capabilities do not as yet figure much in our military's calculations (at least not in what is made available for public consumption), the Russians are quite concerned.

In recognition of the growing importance of space in national security policy, a separate Space Command within the Air Force was established to begin operations the first of September 1982. The new command will operate from its base in Colorado Springs, Colorado, and be responsible for all military satellites and space shuttle operations as well as anti-satellite weaponry. In addition, the command will be in charge of all new military spacecraft and any orbiting directed-energy weapons that we develop in the future.

Clearly, the space shuttle, laser beams, and anti-satellite weapons, as well as MX missiles and, to a lesser extent, the B-1 are all examples of high-technology, state-of-the-art design: high tech for short.

THE HIGH-TECH DEBATE

CHEAPER JETS SHOOT DOWN CLAIMS FOR NEW MODELS
In the shimmering blue skies north of [Las Vegas] . . . the
Navy's admirals and the Air Force's four-star generals received a nasty surprise. Their "magic airplanes" let them
down. The proud "air superiority fighter," F-15s and F-14s,
costing upward of $30 million apiece, had been fought to a
draw by a comparatively crude $4 million airplane, the F-5,
that Northrop Corporation builds for export to small
countries.
                    —*Chicago Tribune,* December 7, 1981, page 1

The news story refers to the ACEVAL/AIMVAL war
games held over the Nevada desert that we discussed earlier.
These exercises, designed to provide a basis for systematic
evaluation of air combat—weapons, tactics, and training—
have fueled an intense dispute over what constitutes *quality*
in weapons. The questions are simple: What wins battles?
What kinds of weapons are most effective in combat? Everyone would agree that if American soldiers are to fight, they
should be equipped with the best, the highest-quality weapons money can buy. But what constitutes the best? Most
Americans subscribe to the notion that "You get what you
pay for"; that the more expensive a weapon is, the better it
is. If it can do more—fly higher or drive faster—it must be
better. The Pentagon, too, is inclined in this direction. But
this conventional wisdom is increasingly being challenged
by "defense reformers," some of them Pentagon officials or
former Pentagon officials, some in Congress. These critics
look at the history of weapons and warfare and find lots of
examples of weapons that were cheap and successful, "winners," and others that were expensive and unsuccessful,
"losers." They want to persuade the Pentagon to identify and
buy the cheap winners and not the expensive losers.
    The reformers have also organized a loose congressional
caucus with more than 50 members to further their goals.
An article in *Aviation Week & Space Technology* summarizes
their concerns this way:

> They see a world in which our complex submarines, a
> few in number due to their cost, are overwhelmed by
> the enemy's in quantity; in which the last thing a U.S.
> fighter pilot sees is the computer terminal he was
> reaching for when destroyed by an enemy aircraft us-
> ing vacuum-tube electronics; in which sophisticated
> ground weapons go unused because of the high educa-
> tional levels needed to operate them.*

The caucus members have not gone unnoticed in Pentagon circles. One Air Force officer even accused them of
being "Luddites," but the reformers are unlikely to be deterred by name calling. Their political diversity—the caucus
includes conservative Republicans and liberal Democrats—
suggests that their point of view has broad appeal, at least
outside the Pentagon.

Air combat is one area of particular interest to the reformers; their views on the subject run sharply counter to established Pentagon practice. To begin with, the reformers
emphasize the importance of small planes because they are
harder to see. Since World War I and the Red Baron, experience has shown that surprise is the key to winning. The vast
majority of pilots shot down never saw their attacker. Other
things being equal, it is easier to spot larger planes than
smaller ones. Given the speeds involved, there are but two to
three seconds between a speck on the horizon and an enemy
on your tail. The problem is exacerbated by such things as
engine smoke. The engines of some of our fighters tend to
emit a trail of smoke which is often seen before the plane
itself. The F-4 is the worst offender. (Some of the "best" Soviet planes, MiG-23s, for example, have the same problem.)

But beyond visibility, a major problem with big, complex
fighters is their cost. A large F-15 can usually beat a smaller
F-5 in a one-on-one dogfight. But we could buy five F-5s for
the price of one F-15. No one claims that an F-15 could beat
five F-5s at once. In fact, the Nevada exercises demonstrated that the technical advantages one plane might have
over another disappear quickly when more than two planes

*Alton Marsh, "Military Reform Caucus Seeks Target," *Aviation Week & Space
Technology,* March 29, 1982, page 55.

are involved. The confusion of mass combat cancels out qualitative superiority. Yet it seems likely that any European war would see just this kind of melee. Worse yet, complex planes have more things that can go wrong, so they spend more time in the shop. As a result, we not only can buy fewer, but those we have are down for maintenance more often. We can afford to buy only a few hundred fighters per year, barely enough to replace those that wear out or that are lost in accidents.

Since the Air Force and Navy cannot afford many of these planes, the Pentagon, like most bureaucracies, has compromised over the issue. It has decided to buy a mix of complex and less complex weapons. For every F-15 the Air Force now buys, it will also buy two F-16s. But now even some of the supposedly less complex systems, such as the F-16 and the Navy's F-18, are growing more complex and costly. So the issue is not likely to disappear quickly.

ASIDE————————————————————————————————

A good example of the tendency for inexpensive simple systems to grow in complexity and cost is the F-16 fighter. The Air Force has a "multinational staged improvement program" (MSIP) for the plane. It plans to add the new advanced medium-range air-to-air missile (AMRAAM), which will allow it to shoot beyond visual range. Also to be added is a night/bad-weather bombing system called Lantrin. These changes will require new radar and computers as well as better radios and jamming equipment, and a whole new cockpit for the aircraft. This should push the price up another $5 million apiece.

(See "Costly Change in F-16 Gear Drawing Fire," in *Wall Street Journal*, April 12, 1982, pages 25 and 34.)

————————————————————————————————

The high purchase price of complex weapons is not their only cost. It's one thing to buy a piece of equipment and quite another to keep it running. In fact, the expense of what the Pentagon calls "operations and maintenance" is high and climbing. For every hour of operation, high-tech weapons systems require many more hours of maintenance and repair by dozens of skilled technicians. You may think you have the same problem with your car, but it's no contest. One naval officer put it this way:

> Expensive airplanes are complex airplanes, and com-
> plex airplanes, over the past ten to fifteen years, have
> been the bane of our existence. The costs of keeping a
> stable of these complex machines in fighting trim is as-
> tronomical—in terms of people. Our maintenance and
> support people have repeatedly fallen behind the heavy
> demands. . . . The Navy supply system . . . has rarely
> been able to stay apace with the spare parts for the so-
> phisticated systems.*

Murphy's Law (which states that if anything can go
wrong, it will) is also at work. In fact, things often go wrong
with complex weapons. In 1979, for example, the F-15 was
able to fly on average about one half-hour between component failure. There is a simple rule: as weapons increase in
complexity, their reliability declines. To be fair, it should be
noted that in 1979 the F-15 was comparatively new, and if
there is anything less reliable than a complex, sophisticated
weapon, it is a *new* complex, sophisticated weapon. It takes
time to get the bugs out. The reliability of the F-15 has improved with time, but not as much as many would wish.

Indeed, improvements in the F-15's reliability are in large
measure a tribute to the men who fly them. The plane has
been plagued with all sorts of engine problems, the most dis-
concerting of which has been a tendency to stall on takeoff.
But the pilots are so used to this that they have learned to
restart the bad engine (it has two) while continuing their
takeoff roll. Fighter pilots are the cream of the Air Force, and
F-15 pilots are the cream of the cream. So determined are
they to avoid losing an expensive aircraft, they have been
known to fly home with one engine dead and the other on
fire rather than bail out.

Yet as the maintenance needed to keep modern weapons
working has increased, funds for maintenance and spare
parts have lagged. When the Pentagon finds itself with more
money to spend, it often prefers to buy new weapons and
equipment rather than pay more for such unglamorous
items as maintenance or spare parts. The Reagan administration has devoted more resources to improving mainte-

*Quoted in Mary Kaldor's *The Baroque Arsenal* (New York: Hill and Wang, 1981),
pages 25–26.

nance and readiness, but what happens when the cost of all
the new weapons programs initiated in the past year or two
begins to rise, as surely it will? Congress has begun to balk
at approving increases in defense spending. And when Congress cuts the defense budget, operations and maintenance
are often cut first since this usually produces the largest
short-run savings.

As the cost of purchasing and maintaining modern military hardware rises, the number of weapons the Pentagon
can buy goes down. Available funds never seem to match
optimistic expectations. As a result, the projections used to
estimate program costs tend to shrink. So when the number
of units we can buy declines, the efficiencies that come with
mass production decline. Result: the price of each unit rises.
It's a vicious circle. Complexity pushes up costs; since ex-
penses go up faster than available funds, production runs
decline, which pushes unit costs up further still, leaving the
Pentagon with even fewer weapons. Yet, at the same time,
these weapons are less reliable because of their complexity,
which results in still fewer being available for service, and
those that are have higher maintenance costs. Thus, the
"curve of unilateral disarmament."

Defenders of the big, complex fighters point out that they
can operate in weather that would ground a 747. Moreover,
they criticize the western desert exercises as "jail-cell tests"
because the sophisticated planes weren't allowed to use their
radar. This is the nub of the argument. A complex fighter's
primary asset is its ability to track and shoot enemy aircraft
beyond visual range, allowing the United States to defeat enemies with more numerous weapons.

Harold Brown, Secretary of Defense under President Carter, told a national magazine in 1980, "Given our disadvan-
tages in numbers, our technology is what will save us."* He
went on to say, in his last annual report as Secretary, that
our technological advantages in certain military fields make
it unnecessary for us to match the Soviets gun for gun, tank
for tank, missile for missile.†

But Brown's views are increasingly challenged by the defense reformers. They point to the high costs, the main-

---

Business Week, August 11, 1980, page 81.
† FY 82 *Annual Report,* Department of Defense, pages 28–29.

tenance problems, the decline in numbers of available weapons. Above all, they look at the results of exercises such as ACEVAL/AIMVAL and question whether the high-tech systems will produce the payoffs in battle that their proponents claim. They feel that the F-15's long-range radar would be useless in a real war; that all previous air combat experience indicates that beyond visual range capability is irrelevant because the rules of engagement dictate that you must make positive identification of an enemy before you start shooting. Otherwise you're as likely to be blasting friends as downing foes. More significantly, they point out that radar functions as a beacon as well as a searchlight. Anyone can pick up radar emissions, the best example being the "fuzz buster" some motorists use to warn them of police radar. They ask, "If you and a bunch of other people carrying pistols and flashlights are in a dark room, who's going to turn on the first flashlight?"

The high-tech debate is not just about airplanes. The M-1 tank, for example, raises basic questions about the role of armored forces in combat. Should tanks slug it out with enemy armor in mass tank warfare? This mission demands thick armor and big guns, but speed is somewhat less important than agility. Or should tanks fight like cavalry, slashing through weak spots in enemy lines and dashing deep to attack the enemy's rear, disrupt communication and supply with the goal of cutting off the enemy's main force? Such a role demands speed most of all, with armor and big guns secondary. Fact is, the M-1 Abrams can do both. It's capable of going 45 miles per hour but weighs more than 60 tons, so big that our largest cargo planes can, as a practical measure, carry no more than one at a time. And they cost more than $2 million apiece.

If this weren't bad enough, the Army recently discovered that a common type of armor-piercing weaponry is quite capable of punching through the tank's armor. These kinetic-energy rounds are comprised of small, pencil-thin bolts of very dense metal which are fired at a very high velocity and which carry so much energy that they can punch their way through any known armor. So the Army may go back to the drawing board. It is studying a plan to eliminate the turret entirely, putting in its place an automatic cannon, and to make up for the lost space by reducing the four-man crew to three.

ASIDE——

Weapons analyst Pierre Sprey believes the older M-60 tank is a "cheap winner" and the new M-1 Abrams less effective even than the older model. Because of its poor reliability, the M-1 must stop more often and has one-third less range than the M-60. He believes the M-60's machine gun effectiveness—vital for protecting a tank against infantry with wire-guided antitank missiles—is superior to that of the M-1; and he judges the M-60's kill rate against multiple tanks at the most likely combat ranges to be superior because of slightly faster loading, greater ammunition capacity, and equivalent accuracy, using simple aiming devices. On mobility and crew survival he finds the differences less sharp; but most important, he notes that we could buy three times more M-60s than M-1s for the same amount of money, and because the M-60 is more reliable, there might be a 6-to-1 advantage of M-60s available at any moment to fight.

(See Pierre Sprey's "Comparing the Effectiveness of Current Tanks," unpublished paper, 1982.)

——

WHAT IS QUALITY?

While it is foolish to ignore state-of-the-art technology in making weapons procurement policy, it is clear that the slavish pursuit of the last word may have become self-defeating. The point to keep in mind is that our problems stem less from the pursuit of technology per se than they result from an attempt to create omnicompetent weapons. The best becomes enemy of the good as the impulse to add just one more feature to a design takes its toll. Complexity drives costs up and maintenance availability down. Inevitably, the last few percent in performance improvement ends up doubling the cost of the entire system.

Clearly, the essence of the problem lies in the definition of quality. We all want top-quality weapons, but we must realize that quality is not solely defined by performance. Rather, performance is a valid indicator only in relation to cost. And of course cost affects the quantity we can afford, which in turn largely determines the system's effectiveness. After all, the best weapon in the world is useless if you can't afford to buy it.

Buying a larger quantity of simple, less expensive weapons, whether they be ships, planes, or tanks, might be a sounder policy. An aircraft carrier, an M-1 tank, and MX missiles in a dense pack all have one fundamental characteristic: they are high-value targets. It is reasonable to expect the enemy to make a maximum effort to knock them out. And we know from the experience of modern warfare that this results in an awesome quantity of incoming warheads. No system can survive a saturation attack. That's why we call such targets "warhead sponges."

If we are to survive, we must make the warhead sponge effect work for us: our warheads, their sponge. There are modern weapons—and some not so modern—that show great promise in that they are relatively effective in relationship to their price. Among these are cruise missiles, remote-piloted vehicles, and naval mines.

CRUISE MISSILES

The cruise missile is a simple but effective high-tech system, although it isn't particularly fast (no more than 500 or 600 miles per hour). But it has great flexibility and its miniaturized terrain-following guidance system is a product of modern technology that relies on the precision of earth maps made by space satellites. Its turbofan engine is not much larger than a lawnmower engine, weighs about 100 pounds, and puts out 200 to 400 pounds of thrust. The engine can be modified and adapted to a variety of missiles that have different missions. Similarly, warheads can be changed to fit the task. The missile need not be limited to the TerCoM guidance system either. We might want to adapt one of the many inertial guidance systems that are available today, so the missile would be less vulnerable to jamming or spoofing. Also under consideration is a laser tracking system in which the missile would follow a beam from a space satellite, aircraft, or ground spotter/designator to the target.

The point is that it is a modular system which makes the cruise missile the epitome of flexibility. Moreover, it can be launched from the back of a truck, a ship, a submarine, or a plane. The Navy has planned to mount a few hundred on renovated World War II battleships, but our small, inexpensive Oliver Hazard Perry class frigates would do just as well.

Keep in mind that these frigates, as well as most Navy ships, carry helicopters that could also mount the missile. Some B-52s are now carrying cruise missiles, and Navy P-3 patrol planes are also armed with an earlier, short-range version called the Harpoon. We could modify any one of a number of commercial airliners to do the same job since they could avoid the battle zone while launching their weapons.

The essential point: keep it simple. The cruise missile is not invulnerable and can fall victim to enemy counter-measures. It can be shot down, for instance. But you have to find it first. Of course, the same qualities that make it elusive make it hard to verify by national technical means. So, however attractive it might be militarily, the cruise missile would complicate arms control verification.

REMOTELY PILOTED VEHICLES (RPVs)

Earlier we noted how reluctant the Air Force was to pursue ballistic-missile development in the 1950s. The same was true of cruise-missile development in the 1970s. Today a comparable issue involves the remotely piloted vehicle (RPV). This is a small robot aircraft which was originally developed as a practice target for fighters and anti-aircraft batteries to shoot at. RPVs are similar to cruise missiles in that they are pilotless airplanes, but different in that they are under radio control from an operator in another plane or on the ground.

Today there are no operational RPVs in our military. Of the 986 that were built, just 33 are left in storage. (Israel is the only nation that has any operating now and it has used RPVs to good effect, using them to spot Syrian anti-aircraft batteries and reveal their radar frequencies so that other planes can knock them out.) Yet between 1964 and 1975 the Strategic Air Command flew 3,435 RPV missions in and around Vietnam (some were over China, with whom relations were none too cordial at the time). These missions included photo reconnaissance, radar decoying and jamming, and the dropping of propaganda leaflets.

There are obvious advantages to RPVs. Cheaper, since they are smaller, they don't need the complex life-support systems and safety redundancy of manned aircraft. Also, they can be sent on missions that would be too dangerous for regular planes. (And there are no potential prisoners of war either, a point of some significance when we remember the twilight days of our Vietnam involvement when the status of POWs was the only significant issue.) In experiments in the United States, RPVs were tested as bombers, carrying early-model television-guided Maverick missiles linked to the remote operator. This experiment was so encouraging that it led to some work on developing them for air-to-air combat, the fighter mission. Since there's no human aboard, the aircraft can turn much more sharply, pulling Gs that would disable a man. And since most dogfights are turning contests in which the plane that can outturn its opponent and get a clear shot wins, the RPV would seem to be a formidable threat.

In the 1970s the Air Force studied the best way to train RPV remote operators. They compared the performance of trained pilots with nonpilots. The nonpilots were better. The Air Force dropped the project. It's hard to blame them; pilots occupy the apex of the Air Force's status pyramid and it's rare to find someone who wants to be replaced by a machine. Fortunately, the Army is less susceptible to such internal pressure and is pursuing its own RPV development, although its budget has suffered some cuts. Its system, the Lockheed Aquila, is a small propeller-driven Fiberglas aircraft that is very quiet and has a low radar signature. It's launched from rails on the back of a truck and recovered in a net. It is designed to carry a television camera and a laser target designator. With the TV and the laser target spotter, it's supposed to give artillery a good chance of a hit on the first shot.

Dr. Edward Teller feels that "the development of unmanned systems . . . presents the only possibility for the United States to close the military gap between ourselves and the Soviet Union in the foreseeable future." He told reporters that "the unmanned vehicle today is a technology akin to the importance of radar and computers in 1935."* Clearly, the RPV concept has much potential. It remains to be seen if it will flower in the Pentagon environment.

*Armed Forces Journal, February 1982, page 38.

NAVAL MINES

Naval mines have been around for more than a century. The Russians were the first to sink major warships with them, during the Crimean War. In the U.S. Civil War, twice as many ships were sunk by mines as by gunfire. This pattern was repeated in the Russo-Japanese War of 1904–1905, in which the Russians lost several major ships to them. During World War I mine warfare techniques were perfected. Fields of 3,000–4,000 were laid to keep ships out of certain areas, and they were sprinkled along well-traveled sea-lanes to make passage difficult as well. The Germans sank more than 900 Allied ships with mines, while we destroyed 150 of their warships, including 48 submarines, the same way. (Only 30 German submarines were dispatched by depth charges in World War I.)

In World War II mines sank nearly 2,700 ships, an average of one for every 37 mines laid. Many were dropped from aircraft, an idea predating World War I, and in this way the Danube River and the Kiel and Suez canals were closed to shipping. In the last five months of the war, the Army Air Corps dropped some 12,000 mines around the Japanese home islands. They lost 16 B-29s in the process but caused the destruction of 431 ships and damaged another 239. As it turned out, mines sank Japanese shipping for an average cost of but $6.00 a ton; to do the same damage with submarine-launched torpedoes cost $55.00.*

A typical naval mine weighs about half a ton, which means a submarine can carry two to each torpedo. They come in several varieties, the simplest being a floating bomb that was common a century ago but today is useful only to terrorists. The obvious problem is that it could just as easily blow up a friendly ship as an enemy's; indeed, this is always a problem in mine warfare since most of them can't tell friend from foe. In actual practice, the simpler type of mine either lies on the bottom or is moored there and floats at the end of a cable. In the First and Second World Wars, many were triggered by contact with the victim, but models that

---

*M. MacBain, "Mines: The Forgotten Weapon," *Sea Power*, April–May 1980, pages 37–41.

were detonated by a ship's magnetic field or the change in water pressure as a ship passed by were developed, too, Today's inventories also include acoustic types that are set off by the sound of a ship; moreover, these assorted triggering mechanisms can be combined into one weapon.

Most older type mines are limited to shallow water, about 100 feet deep, since their basic effect is to break a ship's keel and frames with the pressure from the explosion. (This is why it would be more difficult than it might appear from looking at a map to mine the 300-foot-deep Straits of Hormuz.) Once laid, mines are very difficult to get rid of. The moored variety are "swept" by small ships, called minesweepers or "mine counter measure" (MCM) ships, to cut them from their anchors. When they float to the surface, they are destroyed by gunfire. Bottom mines must be located by sonar and then retrieved or destroyed. The Pentagon is working on new sonars that can detect both the moored and bottom types over relatively wide areas.

This is dangerous work. Many MCM ships are made of wood so that they won't be magnetic (a new British model is of Fiberglas), but they still get blown up from time to time. The U.S. Navy prefers to sweep with a sophisticated helicopter-towed "sled" which has a variety of devices to simulate large ships and will detonate the mines without danger to the sweeping crew.* Still, the Reagan administration plans to buy more than a dozen new minesweepers that can deploy overseas as well as a larger quantity of smaller ships, called minehunters (MSH), designed to locate enemy mines in American harbors.

Both the United States and the Soviet Union have also developed deepwater, mobile mines. These are much more sophisticated weapons, which fire homing torpedos at their targets. The Soviet models are designated Cluster Bay and Cluster Gulf, while the U.S. Navy has CAPTOR, now with the Atlantic Fleet.† The Pentagon asked for 500 of these in its 1983 budget, enough to begin deployment in the Pacific as well. CAPTOR has an acoustic sensor linked to an onboard computer that stores the sound signatures of various ships. It can be programmed to shoot at specific targets

---

*Dunnigan, op. cit., pages 142–47.
†Norman Polmar, "Ships That Wait," Proceedings, April 1982, page 125.

(usually Soviet nuclear submarines) or, say, every third ship that passes. Also, the Navy is working on a new submarine-launched mobile mine (SLMM), which would let the submarine stay in safer waters while depositing the mine where it would do the most damage to the enemy. The SLMM uses a mine warhead combined with the back part of a regular torpedo for propulsion and guidance.

The basic problem with mine warfare policy is that the weapon lacks a "union" in the Navy. The Mine Warfare Command routinely suffers from a shortage of skilled personnel because it is not considered a career-enhancing technical specialty.* Like the cruise missile and RPV, it lacks glamour. You simply plant it in the water and go away. It does its work in your absence. No glory there.

CONCLUSION

It is certain that in the 1980s we can expect to see an array of complex, contentious disputes arising over American defense policy and military procurement. These will range from big ships versus smaller ships, complex versus simpler aircraft, the size of the Navy, the provisioning of the Rapid Deployment Force, and the feasibility of putting beam weapons into space and deploying advanced robot aircraft, to the value of arms control, and disputes over the appropriateness of particular foreign commitments and foreign policy. If we ordinary citizens are to play any role in these debates, we must have a clear conceptual framework within which to assess these weapons and policy decisions. Otherwise, as Congress and the bureaucrats sometimes are, we shall be overwhelmed with competing minutiae.

There are a number of challenging questions ordinary people can pose, even without extensive technical expertise. First and foremost, we have to assure ourselves that the experts' reading of the threat is reasonable and that their preferred military response is appropriate and adequate for the immediate and anticipated tasks. Second, we must weigh military expansion and weapons modernization against other uses of our national resources. National security, even as de-

*Deborah Kyle, "Mine Warfare," *Armed Forces Journal,* April 1982, page 72.

fined by the military, incorporates more than mere military preparedness; it includes a healthy economy, strong alliances, and the like. Third, we must bear in mind that advanced weapons, especially the thermonuclear variety, do not always provide security in direct proportion to their size, numbers, and cost.

In terms of conventional weapons, numbers matter very much. Yet we have the right to know what purpose (mission) a particular new weapon system will perform. And, in that context, we must examine the assumptions (scenarios) that have been used to justify the weapon and its mission. Moreover, as we analyze the military budget, we should consider the possibility that some proposed weapon systems are being promoted because they give an advantage to one faction within the defense establishment over another, rather than because they benefit our national interest.

We must also insist that the weapons we buy will work when needed: in the mud, so to speak. For example, will nervous, underskilled soldiers be able to manage and maintain state-of-the-art technology in the midst of battle? Are there easier, cheaper, entirely different ways of achieving comparable military preparedness? And what kinds of battles (and where) are we talking about?

In a democracy, these are our questions to ask, our decisions ultimately to make.

Afterword

SOME OF YOU MAY BE disappointed that, after laying out the sources and structures of American defense policy today, we have recommended neither a single, comprehensive approach to the defense of the United States nor a particular level of military spending. It's not that knowledge has rendered us impotent or that having explored the processes by which defense decisions are made we have no stomach for debate. Rather, in writing this book, we intended to address one particular issue: the knowledge gap. We don't want to tell you what to think, but what to think about.

The late author and political activist Paul Goodman once observed that America would never have to impose censorship, because the amount of information available on any one topic is so great that any critic trying to pin down an issue will simply be overwhelmed by it all. This is certainly true of defense policy. *Aviation Week & Space Technology* alone comprises about a hundred fact-filled pages every week. *Aerospace Daily* is but one of many daily newsletters. Each year Congress produces thousands of pages of testimony on defense matters. Yet it is said that no more than 50 of its 535 members are truly masters of it all. Books abound as well, although the general reader is often unaware of them. The point is, if there is a knowledge gap, it's not because of too little information. Indeed, it may be that there is too much.

Superabundance poses problems. We feel paralyzed in the face of so much material that lacks a natural beginning, middle, and end. Moreover, it's difficult to discern from among all this just what is important and what is not. While newspapers often present arresting bits of information, rarely do they combine them into a clear and comprehensive whole. So the public turns to editorials and journals of opinion which do the reverse: They select information to buttress a particular point of view, and naïve readers are not told what has been left out nor are they made privy to the process by which the conclusions were arrived at in the first place.*

As they are presented to us, then, the issues of defense, weaponry, and military spending provide a series of topographical features that become a landscape only if we have a map. It was to draw that map—not just to add to the profusion of material—that we conceived and wrote this book.

So what kinds of guns are they buying for your butter?

The weapons a nation builds—indeed, the way it prepares to fight its wars—reveal something about its character, values, and style. During World War I British officers often went into battle armed with nothing more than a swagger stick or, at most, a holstered revolver. The job of gentlemen officers, it was thought, was to lead and inspire, but not to kill. Killing was for ordinary soldiers, a division of labor that clearly reflected the British class structure of the time.†

In World War II the Soviet Army granted no home leave to its troops, from the beginning of the war until its end. True, the threat to the motherland was very real; but the practice of granting no leave speaks more to the nature of Soviet society and to the Russians' view of the relationship between the citizen and the state than to the seriousness of the crisis.‡

The Israeli Army, in turn, reflects the egalitarian ethos of Israeli society. It relies on the skill and motivation of citizen-soldiers as well as the initiative and aggressiveness of its small-unit commanders to conduct fast-moving, mobile war-

---

*Derek Bok, Harvard Commencement Address, June 10, 1982, quoting Walter Lippmann.
†John Keegan, *The Face of Battle* (New York: Viking Press, 1976), pages 315–16.
‡*Ibid.*

382   *What Kinds of Guns Are They Buying for Your Butter?*

fare. It is a style of fighting well-suited to the Israeli character and values, yet alien to their Arab neighbors. Elsewhere in the Middle East, initiative is discouraged in soldiers, while educated people view working with their hands (so vital to the development of modern military skills) as degrading. These social differences, quite as much as the quality and quantity of its weapons, account for Israel's military superiority.

Weapons, too, reflect the societies that produce them. One of the best German tanks of World War II was the Panzer IV. It represented not only the high state of German technology, engineering skill, and precision workmanship, but the *Blitzkrieg* style of war as well. The best Russian tank of the period, the T-34, was equally typical of Soviet values. The T-34 was simply designed and easily manufactured, but eminently reliable (particularly well-adapted to the Russian winter) and cheap. Moreover, being easy to operate and maintain, it could be manned by technically unsophisticated crews. If the Russians could not always outsmart or out-maneuver the Germans, they could certainly overwhelm them and frequently, in fact, did just that. Despite their simplicity, the T-34's generally prevailed over the Panzers. They worked when they had to and were available in greater numbers.*

And what does our weaponry and style of warfare say about us? As we have already noted, we often build weapons that are on the frontiers of their technology: complex, sophisticated, and expensive. Despite the defense reform movement, the Pentagon maintains (although there are some notable exceptions) that the superior quality of our sophisticated weaponry will allow us to overcome Soviet numerical superiority. Interestingly, this reliance on technology is relatively new, by and large a post-World War II phenomenon. In the past we relied instead on large quantities of dependable but conservatively designed weapons that could be operated by quickly trained troops.† But the impact of technologies such as radar and nuclear weapons in the Second World War led many American defense specialists to

---

*Thanks to Pierre Sprey for this comparison.
† Robert Perry, "The Interaction of Technology and Doctrine in the U.S. Air Force," unpublished paper #P-6281 (The Rand Corporation, January 1979), page 4.

view technological innovation as the decisive factor in victory.

Beyond our fascination with technology, Americans tend to approach military matters with the same can-do optimism we bring to other endeavors. We believe there is nothing we cannot achieve if we invest the time, effort, and resources. (One reason the Vietnam War was so traumatic is that we couldn't win despite our optimism and best efforts.) We are a society that places a high value on the lives of our soldiers and we would rather expend equipment and matériel, however costly, than lives. In Vietnam our lavish use of exotic weapons, airpower, and firepower reflected this and contributed mightily to the dollar cost of the war. Given the choice, we prefer capital-intensive to labor-intensive warfare.

Moreover, we believe where possible in comfort at the front. In Vietnam, ice cream, cold beer and pizza were routinely helicoptered to troops in the bush. Whether it is because soldiers, too, write to their Congressmen or because it's impossible to sustain morale and fighting effectiveness without it, we design and build weapons with an eye toward the creature comfort of their crews. This partly accounts for the larger size and higher cost of our warships and tanks, for example, in comparison to those of the Soviets, who give physical comfort a much lower priority.

Of course, to conclude that our defense decisions are influenced by our political and social values does not mean that these choices are preordained. In one sense, we get the weapons we deserve: the product of our infatuation with gadgets, our optimism, and our extravagance. But in another sense we may not be getting the weapons we need.

Several years before it became controversial there was a Pentagon briefing on MX. Even then, many shortcomings with the plan were evident, and the audience—mostly skeptical businessmen—was quick to point them out. The Air Force major in charge was more than candid in admitting the problems, but his optimism was irrepressible. Every difficulty raised was dismissed with the assertion, "We're working that problem." And implicit was his expectation that, in time, they would all be solved.

Technologists and bureaucrats alike tend to think of their work as a series of problems, all of which have unique, identifiable solutions. If we just "work a problem" long and hard enough, it will be solved. But, as we have noted throughout this book, solutions—even the right ones—have consequences, some anticipated and some unknown, which may themselves provoke new problems. Often there are no good solutions at all, and as a result, decision-making commonly involves finding that option which entails the least undesirable outcome.

But such choices are not "solutions" in the mathematical sense of the word. There is often no one "right" answer, although those with a commitment to a particular solution might have us believe there is. This practice obscures the fact that choices are being made. Indeed, many of the issues we described in our chapter on current controversies are not problems in the strictest sense of that word, but rather dilemmas. And while we ordinary citizens may feel we have no special skill for solving military problems, we have every right to examine critically all available options and participate actively in the debate.

That's what democracy is all about.

Appendix I

Map of Nuclear Weapons Locations in the United States

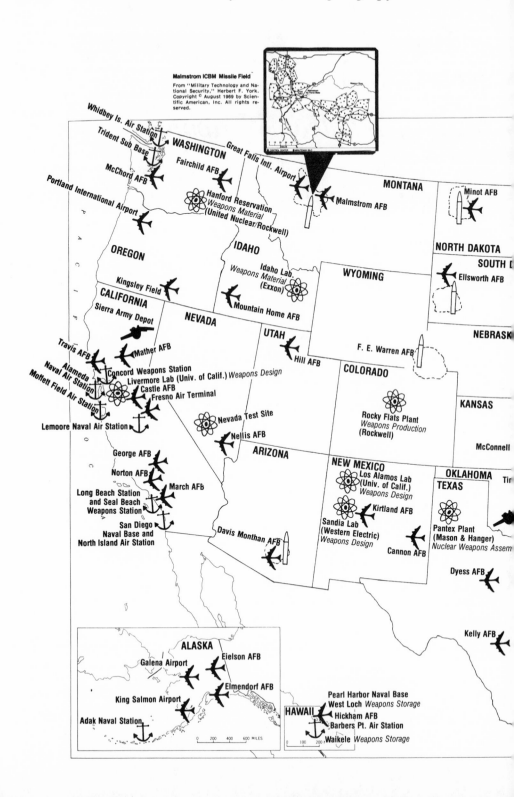

Malmstrom ICBM Missile Field

From "Military Technology and National Security," Herbert F. York. Copyright © August 1969 by Scientific American, Inc. All rights reserved.

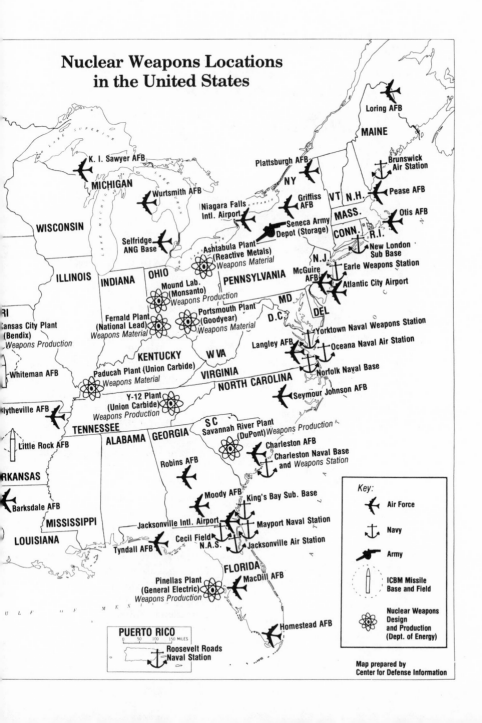

Nuclear Weapons Locations in the United States

Loring AFB

MAINE

K. I. Sawyer AFB

Plattsburgh AFB

Brunswick Air Station

MICHIGAN

Wurtsmith AFB

NY

Pease AFB

Griffiss AFB

VT

N.H.

Niagara Falls Intl. Airport

Otis AFB

MASS.

Selfridge ANG Base

Seneca Army Depot (Storage)

CONN.

R.I.

WISCONSIN

New London Sub Base

Ashtabula Plant (Reactive Metals) Weapons Material

N.J.

Earle Weapons Station

ILLINOIS

INDIANA

OHIO

PENNSYLVANIA

McGuire AFB

Atlantic City Airport

Mound Lab. (Monsanto) Weapons Production

MD

DEL

RI

Fernald Plant (National Lead) Weapons Material

Portsmouth Plant (Goodyear) Weapons Material

D.C.

Kansas City Plant (Bendix) Weapons Production

Yorktown Naval Weapons Station

KENTUCKY

W VA

Langley AFB

Oceana Naval Air Station

Whiteman AFB

Paducah Plant (Union Carbide) Weapons Material

VIRGINIA

NORTH CAROLINA

Norfolk Naval Base

Blytheville AFB

Y-12 Plant (Union Carbide) Weapons Production

Seymour Johnson AFB

TENNESSEE

ALABAMA

GEORGIA

SC

Savannah River Plant (DuPont) Weapons Production

Little Rock AFB

Charleston AFB

ARKANSAS

Robins AFB

Charleston Naval Base and Weapons Station

Barksdale AFB

Moody AFB

King's Bay Sub. Base

MISSISSIPPI

LOUISIANA

Jacksonville Intl. Airport

Mayport Naval Station

Cecil Field N.A.S.

Jacksonville Air Station

Tyndall AFB

FLORIDA

Pinellas Plant (General Electric) Weapons Production

MacDill AFB

GULF OF MEXICO

Homestead AFB

Key:

✈ Air Force

⚓ Navy

Army

ICBM Missile Base and Field

⚛ Nuclear Weapons Design and Production (Dept. of Energy)

PUERTO RICO

0 50 100 150 MILES

Roosevelt Roads Naval Station

Map prepared by
Center for Defense Information

Appendix II

Top U.S. Defense Contractors

Company	Major Work
1. General Dynamics Corporation	F-16 and F-111 aircraft. Stinger and RIM-66 missiles. Close-in weapon system (Phalanx). Nuclear submarines.
2. McDonnell Douglas Corporation	F-15 Eagle, F-4 Phantom, F-18 fighter aircraft, and KC-10 cargo aircraft. Harpoon, Tomahawk, and Dragon missiles.
3. United Technologies Corporation	F-100, TF-30, TF-33, and J-56 turbofan and turbojet engines. UH-60 and CH-53 Sea Stallion helicopters.
4. Boeing Company	Airborne warning and control system (AWACS). Tomahawk, ShoRAD, Minuteman, and Roland missile systems. Radio and TV equipment for the Advanced Airborne Command Post. Airframe structural components.
5. General Electric Company	Nuclear submarines. F-18 fighter aircraft engines. UH-60 helicopter engines. Minuteman missile. Miscellaneous electronics and communications equipment.

6. Lockheed Corporation	Trident, Polaris, and Standard ARM missiles.
	P-3 Orion, C-141 Starlifter, C-5 Galaxy, and C-130 Hercules aircraft.
	Space vehicles.
	Amphibious assault ships.
7. Hughes Aircraft Company	TOW, ShoRAD, Phoenix, Roland, and Trident missile systems.
	Radar equipment and guided missile systems for A-6 Intruder, F-14 Tomcat, and F-15 Eagle aircraft.
	Research and development for electronics and communications equipment.
8. Raytheon Company	Hawk, Patriot, Sparrow, and Trident missile systems.
	Electronic countermeasures.
	Underwater sound equipment.
	Miscellaneous electronics and communications equipment.
9. Tenneco, Inc.	Aircraft carriers and subchasers.
	Maintenance and repair of ships.
	Warehouse trucks and tractors.
10. Grumman Corporation	F-14 Tomcat, E-2 Hawkeye, E-6 Prowler, and A-6 Intruder aircraft.
	Electronic countermeasures for F-111 aircraft.
	Modification of aircraft equipment.
11. Northrop Corporation	F-5 Freedom Fighter aircraft.
	Guided-missile launchers and remote-control systems for the Hawk missile.
	Electronic countermeasures and miscellaneous aircraft accessories.
	Research and development for missile and space systems.
12. Motor Oil Hellas	Petroleum.

Working Vocabulary*

ABM—Anti-ballistic missile. A system of missiles and radars capable of defending against a ballistic missile attack by destroying incoming offensive missiles. The defensive missiles may be armed with either nuclear or non-nuclear warheads.

ACTIVE DEFENSE—The protection of civil and military targets through the use of defensive weapons such as surface-to-air missiles, ABMs, and anti-aircraft guns. (Also see *Passive defense*.)

AIMING ERROR—See *CEP*.

AIR BLAST—The force released from the explosion of a nuclear weapon in the form of a shock wave traveling through the air.

AIRBURST—Detonation of a warhead above the ground. In conventional artillery practice, this spreads destructive shrapnel over a larger area. With respect to nuclear weapons, this kind of detonation causes the greatest amount of destruction to unprotected ground structures. The ideal height for a nuclear airburst is the radius of the fireball; that is, it depends on the size of the weapon. Although most destructive, this kind of burst results in less radioactive fallout than surface or subsurface bursts.

---

*In the preparation of this section, some use has been made of other glossaries and lists of terms prepared by government and military agencies. Among these are *Glossary of Terms* (October 1975), Interservice Nuclear Weapons School, Kirtland Air Force Base, New Mexico; and *SALT Lexicon,* U.S. Arms Control and Disarmament Agency, Washington, D.C., revised ed.

Particular thanks are offered to Harry W. Thomas, Major, U.S. Army, for permission to draw from the glossary of terms from his M.A. thesis, entitled "Launch Under Attack: A Strategy to Enhance Deterrence" (1980), pages 75–99.

AIR-TO-AIR MISSILE—A missile fired from an airplane designed to shoot down other airplanes.

AIR-TO-SURFACE MISSILE—A missile launched from an airplane against a target on land or sea.

ALCM—Air-launched cruise missile. See *Cruise missile.*

ASSURED DESTRUCTION—The ability to inflict unacceptable damage upon an aggressor after suffering from his initial attack.

ASW—Antisubmarine warfare. The detection, identification, tracking, and destruction of hostile submarines.

ATB—Advanced technology bomber. Another term for *Stealth.*

ATOMIC BOMB (or WEAPON)—A nuclear weapon utilizing fission energy only.

ATOMIC ENERGY—Energy released in nuclear reactions. Of particular interest is the energy released when a neutron splits an atom's nucleus into smaller pieces (fission) or when two nuclei are joined together under millions of degrees of heat (fusion). "Atomic energy" is really a misnomer. It is more correctly called "nuclear energy."

ATTRITION—The loss of men and equipment in war through hostile action as well as breakdowns and simple wearing-out. In doctrine, it refers to a strategy that seeks to defeat the enemy by wearing him out. When employed by both sides, attrition becomes very costly in terms of men and matériel. The First World War is a classic example of attrition warfare.

AWACS—Airborne warning and control system. A large aircraft which carries a complex radar and computer system. It can track and store in its memory hundreds of targets over thousands of square miles. It is used to detect enemy aircraft and to direct fighter planes against enemy attackers, as well as to guide bombers to targets in enemy-held areas.

BACKFIRE—The NATO designation of the Soviet Tu-22M or Tu-26 bomber, a modern twin-engine variable-geometry aircraft that is currently being deployed with Soviet naval and theater forces as a replacement for older medium bombers. Its characteristics blur the line between strategic, heavy bombers and the smaller, medium variety. Some people maintain that under certain flight conditions the Backfire could have an intercontinental capability.

BACKGROUND RADIATION—Radiation arising from cosmic rays and other forms of natural radioactivity always present in the environment.

BALANCE OF TERROR—Buzz word describing two antagonists who each possess the capability of destroying the other with nuclear weapons. In effect, the populations of both nations are held hostage as one cannot expect to destroy the other without being destroyed in turn. This is not the so-called balance of power.

BALLISTIC MISSILE—A missile that moves, after a period of powered flight, on a free-falling trajectory under the influence of gravity. The range of ballistic missiles varies from a few miles to more than 6,000 miles.

BEAM WEAPONS—Weapons that employ directed-energy beams consisting of either laser light or subatomic particles to destroy targets. See *Laser*.

BINARY NERVE GAS—A toxic gas created by the mixture of two relatively harmless chemicals. Because its two components are nontoxic until they are combined, binary gas can be stored and handled more easily than other toxic gas.

BLAST PRESSURE—The force of a shock wave in air at a given distance from the source of detonation. Sometimes called dynamic pressure or overpressure.

BMD—Ballistic-missile defense. A system designed to destroy enemy ballistic-missile warheads before they reach their targets. Included, in addition to ABMs, are radars and tracking and guidance computers. BMD could also use beam weapons. See *ABM* and *Beam weapons*.

BMEWS—Ballistic-missile early-warning system. Large radar sets based in Greenland, Alaska, and England that are designed to detect and track Soviet ballistic missiles attacking the United States.

BROKEN ARROW—Code words used to identify and report an accident involving a nuclear weapon or warhead.

BUS—The part of a MIRVed missile's payload that carries the reentry vehicles. Each reentry vehicle carries a nuclear or thermonuclear weapon. The bus also carries guidance systems, and maneuvering devices for altering the ballistic flight path so that the reentry vehicles can be dispensed, in turn, toward different targets. Also called post-boost vehicle (PBV).

BUYING-IN—A technique whereby defense contractors use a low bid, sometimes even to the point of losing money in order to win a contract. Once the contract is in hand it can be altered or amended to recover the earlier loss. See also *Cost-plus* and *Sole-source*.

CEP—Circular error probable. Sometimes referred to as "aiming error," a measure of ballistic-missile accuracy. It is expressed in a linear measurement, fractions of a mile, meters, or yards, and is the radius of a circle around the target within which 50 percent of a given type of missile warheads will land. The measurement is significant because as the CEP gets smaller,

an enemy warhead is more likely to damage or destroy a hard
target such as a missile silo.

CHOBHAM ARMOR—A type of tank armor, developed by the Military
Vehicles and Engineering Establishment at Chobham, England, to defeat shaped-charge ammunition. It consists of several layers of different materials including metal, plastics, and
other materials designed to dissipate the intense heat of the
explosion. Also called layered armor.

CIVIL DEFENSE—Measures such as shelters, evacuation plans, and
dispersion for protecting civilian populations and industry
from nuclear attack. See also *Passive defense*.

COLD LAUNCH—A technique for ejecting a missile from its
launcher by means of compressed gases so as to avoid damage
to the launcher caused by the heat of the missile's rocket
motors.

COLLATERAL DAMAGE—Death and destruction to people and property incidental to the destruction of a target. In effect, such
casualties are "accidental."

COMBAT RADIUS—A measure of an aircraft's capability, the distance an airplane can fly and still return to its base without
refueling. This is not a fixed distance, but rather it may vary
depending on whether the plane is flying at high or low altitude, carrying a heavy or light load, and flying fast or slow.

COMMAND, CONTROL, AND COMMUNICATIONS (C^3) or COMMAND,
CONTROL, COMMUNICATIONS, and INTELLIGENCE (C^3I)—The
"nerves" of military operations, that is, information processing
systems used to detect, assess, and respond to actual and potential military and political crisis situations or conflicts. C^3I
includes systems which manage matériel and manpower, including nuclear and conventional weapons, during crises and
conflicts as well as during peacetime.

CONTAINMENT—U.S. policy toward the Soviet Union formulated
by George Kennan in the late 1940s. Basically, the policy
urged that the U.S. resist Soviet expansionism by means of
steady counterpressure, rather than overthrow or "roll back"
Communism, until such time as the government of the Soviet
Union changes.

CONUS—Continental United States. The military's term for U.S.
territory, including the adjacent territorial waters.

CONVENTIONAL WEAPONS—Usually applied to non-nuclear weapons, i.e., those that kill or destroy through explosive force, bullets, and shrapnel. The term does not apply to poison gas or
other chemical weapons, but does include incendiaries.

CONVERTIBLE WEAPON—See *Dual-capable system*.

COST-PLUS—A common type of Pentagon contract wherein the producer is guaranteed an agreed-upon profit margin *plus* all costs. This contract does not motivate the producer to be economical. Since the profit is often a percentage of the costs, the higher the costs, the higher, in absolute dollars, the profit.

COUNTERFORCE—The use of strategic weaponry, bombers, and missiles, to destroy enemy missiles, bombers, and other military forces. This generally requires greater accuracy than countervalue targeting, since many military targets (although by no means all) are very well protected and relatively small.

COUNTERVALUE—The use of strategic weapons to destroy enemy urban, industrial, agricultural, and transportation capabilities. This is the essence of strategic war. Some proponents of deterrence theory hold that by threatening a potential aggressor with destruction of his society, nuclear attack on the United States can be prevented. Its implementation generally requires less accurate thermonuclear weaponry.

CREDIBILITY—The essence of deterrence; for it to work, the potential enemy must believe that you possess the will to carry out your threats. If there is no credibility, there can be no deterrence.

CRUISE MISSILE—A small pilotless plane powered by a jet engine and equipped with its own guidance system. It may carry conventional explosives, nuclear warheads, or a chemical weapon, and may be launched from airplanes, ships, submarines, or from the ground. See also *ALCM, GLCM,* and *SLCM.*

DAMAGE LIMITATION—A strategy proposed by Robert McNamara in the early 1960s that sought to limit the damage to the United States in a thermonuclear war. It would have included "active defense measures" such as an ABM system, as well as "passive measures" such as civil defense. It was abandoned because the American people had no stomach for civil defense, and it became clear upon further analysis that the basic result would be a buildup of enemy capabilities to overwhelm the damage-limiting measures. The policy was succeeded by the *assured destruction* doctrine.

DEPLOYMENT—The distribution of a weapon to units for use in combat. The final stage in the weapons acquisition process.

DEPRESSED TRAJECTORY—A ballistic-missile trajectory significantly lower than usual. The advantage of depressed trajectory is that it makes it harder for the defender to detect the warhead with radar. The disadvantage is that it is much less accurate, since the warheads spend so much more time in the atmosphere. Technically, any ballistic missile can be fired in a depressed trajectory. (We have tested Minuteman in this firing mode.) But the usual scenario envisions Soviet SLBMs firing in a depressed trajectory from off the American coast in order to reduce our warning time to no more than a few minutes.

DIRECTED ENERGY—See *Beam weapons*.

DIRTY WEAPON—One that produces a relatively large amount of radioactive fallout.

DOCTRINE—Doctrine is a set of general principles used to guide the planning and conduct of military operations. While tactical doctrine is voluminous and is based on extensive wartime experience, strategic doctrine is almost all theoretical and based upon simulation.

DSARC—Defense Systems Acquisition Review Council. A committee within the Defense Department that reviews and evaluates weapons systems at various stages of their development. A post-McNamara reform, again an effort to control the weapons procurement process.

DUAL-CAPABLE SYSTEM—A weapon capable of carrying nuclear or conventional explosives.

DYAD—A strategic force structure that would have two "legs," most probably submarine-launched missiles and bombers. This is in contrast to the Triad, which includes land-based long-range missiles as well.

ELECTRONIC COUNTERMEASURES—Referred to as ECM. See *Electronic warfare*.

ELECTRONIC WARFARE—The use of electronic devices to confuse enemy radar, communications, and missile guidance systems. ECM refers to electronic countermeasures. ECCM refers to electronic counter-countermeasures. ELINT refers to electronic intelligence gathering.

ELF—Extremely low frequency. A special radio system using very long radio waves (measured in hundreds of meters) that can travel through the earth and water, thus making it possible to communicate directly with submarines at sea.

EMP—Electromagnetic pulse. One effect of a nuclear detonation, that is, a broad-band radio pulse of significant power and range. The phenomenon is not well understood, since atmospheric testing of nuclear weapons has been prohibited by treaty. EMP is capable of destroying all kinds of electronic circuitry, thus posing a threat to unprotected weaponry and computers. It could, for example, wipe clean all computer memories that are in range of the burst.

ENHANCED-RADIATION WARHEAD—Commonly referred to as the neutron bomb, it is in fact a missile warhead or artillery shell that produces somewhat more radiation and somewhat less blast than a standard nuclear weapon.

FAIL-SAFE—Doctrine which in theory prevents the accidental or unintentional use of nuclear weapons. The system is designed so that if there is a failure of some sort, the system will not work. For example, bombers on an attack mission do not proceed beyond a certain point unless they receive positive orders to do so; if no orders are forthcoming, they return to base rather than continue the attack.

FALLOUT—Radioactive particles made up of contaminated debris from a nuclear explosion that precipitate out of the mushroom cloud. Early (or local) fallout is defined arbitrarily as those particles which fall to earth within twenty-four hours of the explosion. Delayed (or worldwide) fallout consists of smaller particles that ascend into the upper atmosphere and are carried all over the earth by the wind. Delayed fallout will be brought to earth mainly by rain and snow over extended periods of time ranging to many years.

FBS—Forward-based systems. Medium-range U.S. nuclear delivery systems—usually aircraft—based in third countries or on aircraft carriers and capable of attacking targets in the Soviet Union.

FERRET—When used as a verb, to monitor enemy electronic intelligence. As an adjective, it describes a type of equipment, whether satellite, aircraft, or ship, which gathers electronic intelligence. (The *Pueblo,* for example, was on a ferret mission off North Korea when it was captured.) Related to *Wild Weasel.*

FIREPOWER—The volume of bombshells and bullets directed against an enemy on a battlefield. In doctrine the idea is to overwhelm the enemy with a large volume of fire. The term is related to the concept of attrition in warfare and is often contrasted with maneuver warfare.

FIRESTORM—An immense fire caused by intensive bombing of an urban area. First observed in World War II, when Hamburg was subject to mass incendiary raids by U.S. and British forces, the fire can easily cover several square miles with flames two miles high. The draft of the fire can create winds of several hundred miles per hour and the intense heat will destroy all structures and will suffocate people, even in deep bunkers. Only densely populated areas are subject to firestorm because of the necessary "fuel loading." So postwar

American communities dispersed in a suburban style are unlikely to experience the phenomenon in war.

FIRST STRIKE—An initial attack with nuclear weapons. In a *disarming first strike* the attacker attempts to destroy the adversary's nuclear forces before they can be used in retaliation. A
preemptive first strike is one in which a nation launches an
attack first on the presumption that the adversary is about to
attack. Not to be confused with *First use*.

FIRST USE—Distinguished from *First strike* in that it assumes
nonstrategic deployment of nuclear weapons. The common
scenario is that we would use tactical nuclear weapons to stop
a mass Soviet conventional attack in western Europe.

FISSION (NUCLEAR REACTION)—The splitting of a heavy nucleus
into smaller nuclei, accompanied by the release of energy and
one or more neutrons.

FISSION PRODUCTS—A general term for the complex mixture of
radioactive substances produced as a result of nuclear fission.

FLEXIBLE RESPONSE—A strategy devoted to meeting aggression at
the appropriate level of intensity with the capability of escalating that commitment as required.

FLEXIBLE STRATEGIC RESPONSE—Like flexible response, this plan
is designed to meet strategic nuclear threats at the level at
which they are offered. The notion first appeared in the late
1960s. It is designed to provide a limited alternative to a Soviet
limited strike rather than have our only response capability be
an all-out nuclear war or nothing. Flexible strategic response
became doctrine under President Carter with P.D. #59.

FLY-OFF—A means of choosing among competitive aircraft designs by testing them side by side. Following the contest, the
Pentagon then can choose the best system. There are also
"shoot-offs" and even "compute-offs" for various contracts.

FRACTIONATION—Putting more than one warhead on a missile.
See *MIRV* or *MRV*.

FRATRICIDE—A situation in which one nuclear warhead destroys
another. This is thought to be a problem where several warheads are directed at the same or closely spaced targets. The
first warhead to explode can damage other warheads in the
vicinity because of electromagnetic pulse; or the first warhead
detonation can cause a cloud of dirt and debris that will damage or deflect succeeding warheads. Since we have never had
multiple tests of warheads, no one knows for sure just how
serious the fratricide effect would be.

FUSION (THERMONUCLEAR REACTION)—A nuclear reaction in
which light nuclei join together (or fuse) to form a heavier

nucleus, accompanied by the release of great amounts of energy and fast neutrons. Fusion takes place only under extreme heat and is the source of the energy released by stars.

GAMMA RAYS—High-energy, short-wavelength electromagnetic radiation originating in the nucleus of an unstable atom. Gamma radiation frequently accompanies alpha and beta emissions, and always accompanies fission. It is very penetrating and is best shielded against by dense materials such as lead. Gamma rays are different from X rays, which originate outside the nucleus of an atom.

GASEOUS DIFFUSION—A method for separating isotopes of the same element, and the most common method used to separate U-235 from U-238 to make a bomb. It requires large plants and enormous amounts of electricity.

GLCM—Ground-launched cruise missile (pronounced glickum). A cruise missile designed to be fired from a ground-based launcher.

GROUND ZERO—The point on the surface of the earth at or directly below a nuclear explosion.

HALF-LIFE—The time required for the radioactivity in any given substance to decay to half its initial strength.

HARDENING—The process by which a facility or an object is modified or designed to be protected from attack. Usually this is accomplished by the liberal use of concrete and steel, but the term can also refer to the shielding of delicate electronic parts from an electromagnetic pulse.

HARD TARGET—A facility that has been designed to resist attack; usually it is buried deep in the ground and protected by thick layers of reinforced concrete and steel. In addition, hard targets are mounted on large shock absorbers to absorb severe shock waves. Normally, these are military targets, although some bank vaults and corporate record-storage facilities could also be classified as hard targets.

H-BOMB—An abbreviation for hydrogen bomb.

HEAVY MISSILE—A large volume ICBM with particularly large throw-weight and, if accurate enough, capable of destroying fixed, hardened targets. For the United States the Titan II is a heavy missile. For the Soviets the SS-18 is a heavy missile.

HOWITZER—A type of artillery with a short barrel and low muzzle velocity, able to fire shells in high-arcing trajectories.

HYDROGEN BOMB (or WEAPON)—A thermonuclear weapon in which part of the explosive energy is obtained from nuclear fusion.

ICBM—Intercontinental ballistic missile. A land-based rocket-propelled vehicle capable of delivering a warhead in ranges in excess of 3,000 miles.

INERTIAL GUIDANCE SYSTEM—The basic guidance system used in ballistic missiles. It consists of several gyroscopes which are capable of detecting and correcting deviations from the intended velocity and/or course. Inertial guidance systems are also used by military and commercial aircraft for navigation and by submarines for the same purpose.

INTERIM AGREEMENT—The second half SALT I, formally entitled the "Interim Agreement between the United States of America and the Union of Soviet Socialist Republics on Certain Measures with Respect to the Limitations of Strategic Offensive Arms." This agreement comprises one of two agreements signed in Moscow on May 26, 1972. While the Interim Agreement formally expired on October 3, 1977, in September of that year the United States and the USSR stated separately that they did not plan to take any action inconsistent with the provision of the Interim Agreement pending conclusion of the SALT II negotiations.

IONIZING RADIATION—Any electromagnetic or particulate radiation capable of producing ions (i.e., charged particles) as it passes through matter. Generally, the kind of radiation that is hazardous to living substances because it changes their charged state and therefore their nature. Ionizing radiation is different from thermal radiation, which damages cells by heat. When the term radiation is used, ask whether ionizing or thermal radiation is intended.

IRBM—Intermediate-range ballistic missile. Usually a ballistic missile with a range of from 1,500 to 3,000 miles.

IRRADIATION—Exposure to radiation.

KILOTON—A unit of measurement of a weapon's yield; one kiloton is the amount of energy released from 1,000 tons of TNT.

LASER—Light amplified by stimulated emission of radiation. An intense beam of light produced by exciting certain materials with large amounts of electrical energy. Lasers are capable of burning holes in metal and/or destroying electronic components and as a result are believed to have the potential to revolutionize warfare, although laser weapons are still in the experimental stage.

LAUNCHER—The equipment that launches a missile. ICBM launchers are land-based and can be either fixed or mobile, while SLBM launchers are the missile "tubes" on a submarine. An air-launched ballistic-missile launcher is a carrier aircraft. Launchers for cruise missiles can be mounted on aircraft, ships, submarines, or vehicles. The significance of the term launcher is that both SALT I and SALT II limit each side's launchers rather than missiles.

LAUNCH ON WARNING—The idea of launching our missiles and bombers upon notification that an enemy attack has started, but before any enemy weapons actually hit.

LAUNCH UNDER ATTACK—Similar to *Launch on warning*, except that this policy assumes that we wait a little bit longer to retaliate. Both launch on warning and launch under attack are ways of avoiding destruction of our missiles by a Soviet attack but are thought to be dangerous because they rely on rapid response and could increase the danger of accidental nuclear war.

LAUNCH-WEIGHT—The weight of a fully loaded missile at the time of launch. This includes the rocket booster stages and the payload.

LIGHT ICBM—For the purposes of SALT II, ICBMs are divided into light and heavy categories according to their launch-weight (see above) and throw-weight (see below).

LRCA—Long-range combat aircraft. The new term for bomber. Large military aircraft capable of penetrating heavily defended enemy airspace and flying long distances, more than 2,500 miles.

LRTNF—Long-range theater nuclear forces. Nuclear weapons designed for deployment in Europe. U.S. Pershing II and GLCMs (scheduled for deployment in 1983) and the Soviet SS-4, -5, and -20 are the missiles presently deployed. These are now called intermediate-range nuclear forces.

MACH NUMBER—A measure of aircraft or missile speed. Mach 1 is the speed of sound, about 700 miles per hour at sea level. Mach 2 is two times the speed of sound, and so on.

MAD—Mutual assured destruction. A condition in which all sides possess an assured destruction capability.

MANEUVER WARFARE—A tactical doctrine which emphasizes outmaneuvering the enemy in such a way as to cut off his lines of communication and supply. The emphasis here is on surprise and deception and is in contrast to the doctrine emphasizing firepower and attrition.

MaRV—Maneuvering reentry vehicle. A nuclear warhead which can be maneuvered in flight to enable it to evade ABM defenses and/or strike its intended targets with greater accuracy. The United States has developed but not deployed the Mark 500 "Evader" warhead for its submarine-launch missiles.

MASSIVE RETALIATION—The doctrine that calls for countering aggression of any kind with threats of tremendous destructive retaliatory power; particularly, a nuclear response to any provocation deemed serious enough to warrant military action. The doctrine was set forth by Secretary of State John Foster Dulles in a speech on January 12, 1954.

MEGATON—A measure of the yield of a nuclear weapon equivalent to one million tons of TNT.

MINUTEMAN—A three-stage, solid-propellant, second-generation intercontinental ballistic missile. It is a simpler, smaller, lighter missile than earlier intercontinental ballistic missiles (e.g., Titans) and is designed for highly automated remote operation. There have been three models of Minuteman. Currently, the United States has 450 Minuteman IIs and 550 Minuteman IIIs.

MIRV—Multiple independently targeted reentry vehicle. A mechanism whereby separate targets can be hit by one missile. See *Bus*. Most modern ballistic missiles today are MIRVed, although we still have in our arsenal 52 Titan IIs and 450 Minuteman IIs having single warheads.

MIRV BUS—See *Bus*.

MORTAR—A type of lightweight artillery varying in weight from about 100 pounds to several hundred pounds and capable of hurling small shells (15 to 40 pounds in weight) two to four miles.

MRBM—Medium-range ballistic missile. Usually a ballistic missile with a range of 600 to 1,500 miles. The United States has no MRBMs. The Soviet SS-4 is an example of an MRBM.

MRV—Multiple reentry vehicle. Multiple warheads on a single missile that are *not* independently targetable. This mechanism increases the destructiveness of the weapon on impact, but does not allow for multiple targeting with a single missile. Both the United States and the USSR have had earlier versions of this type of warhead.

MUZZLE VELOCITY—The speed of a bullet or shell as it leaves the rifle or cannon tube from which it is fired. Usually measured in feet per second.

MX—Missile experimental. The follow-on ICBM system which the United States may deploy. Because of the mobile basing scheme originally associated with the big new missile, it has become extremely controversial and its mode of deployment is in question.

NATIONAL SECURITY ACT—A law passed in 1947 that created the Department of Defense, with the Air Force as a separate service within it, as well as establishing the National Security

Council and the Central Intelligence Agency. Since 1947 the law has been amended to give increased power to the office of the Secretary of Defense.

NATIONAL TECHNICAL MEANS (NTM)—The term used to describe a number of different devices and techniques for monitoring compliance with provisions of arms control agreements. NTM include reconnaissance satellites, aircraft equipped with radars and other sensors, and sea- and ground-based systems for collecting the signals sent by missile test flights. See *Telemetry*.

NAVSTAR—Navigation system using time and ranging. A global positioning system comprising 24 satellites to be "parked" in continuous orbits to provide near-continuous signals, which may be monitored by receivers on board ICBMs, for example. Four such signals, plus orbital details from satellites, will enable a missile to determine its position to within 20–30 feet and so correct altitude or velocity.

NEUTRON BOMB—See *Enhanced-radiation warhead*.

NOT INVENTED HERE—A slang term for a common bureaucratic mind-set that is unwilling to perceive any new development, concept, or idea that did not originate within the bureaucracy as having any merit.

NUCLEAR DELIVERY SYSTEM—A nuclear weapon, together with its means of propulsion and associated installations.

NUCLEAR PROLIFERATION—The acquisition of nuclear weapons by states not previously possessing them.

NUCLEAR YIELDS—The energy released in the detonation of a nuclear weapon, measured in kilotons or megatons of TNT equivalent. Yields are categorized as very low (less than one kiloton), low (1–10 kilotons), medium (10–15 kilotons), high (50 to 500 kilotons, or one-half megaton), very high (500 kilotons to the megaton range).

ON-SITE INSPECTION—A method of verifying compliance with arms control agreements whereby representatives of a designated organization, or of the parties to the agreement, are given direct access to view force deployments or weapon systems.

ORDER OF BATTLE—Inventories of weapons and equipment (aircraft, tanks, artillery, missiles, ships, and so on) by number of type and their deployment, as well as numbers and organization of military personnel, all of which comprise a nation's military forces.

OVERKILL—Destructive capabilities in excess of those adequate to destroy specific targets or groups of targets.

OVERPRESSURE—The transient pressure, usually expressed in pounds per square inch, exceeding ambient pressure. Generated by a shock or blast wave from an explosion, the peak overpressure is the maximum amount at a given location.

PARITY—A level of forces in which opposing nations possess approximately equal capabilities.

PASSIVE DEFENSE—The protection of civil and military targets without the use of weapon systems. For protecting populations this usually includes evacuation and shelters. Military targets can be passively defended by camouflage, hardening, dispersal, and similar techniques. See *Civil defense*.

PAYLOAD—Includes warheads and reentry vehicles as well as penetration aids carried by a ballistic missile. Unlike throw-weight, the payload does not include the post-boost vehicle or MIRV bus.

PENETRATION AIDS—Techniques and/or devices used to deceive an enemy's defenses, thus increasing the probability of a weapon's penetrating the defenses and reaching the target. The term usually refers to devices carried by ballistic missiles but may also refer to devices and techniques used by bombers and fighter-bombers.

PGM—Precision-guided munition. Any one of several different guided weapons designed to hit targets with high accuracy. See *Smart bomb*.

PLUTONIUM—A heavy man-made radioactive metallic element with the atomic number 94. Its most important isotope is fissionable plutonium 239, which is produced by neutron irradiation of U-238. It is used both to fuel reactors and to make weapons.

POINT DEFENSE—Defense of a limited geographic area, such as an ICBM silo, against attacking missiles.

POLARIS—First-generation submarine-launched ballistic missile. Called Polaris because it was designed to get a navigational fix on the North Star to reorient its trajectory before reentry. Also refers to the submarines that carried them. All Polaris submarines and missiles have been retired from service.

POSEIDON—Second-generation submarine-launched ballistic missile. Was first submarine missile capable of carrying MIRVs. Also refers to the submarines that carry them.

PPBS—Planning Programming Budgeting System. A system for planning defense budgets first used by Robert McNamara in the Department of Defense in the 1960s.

PREEMPTIVE STRIKE—An attack initiated in anticipation of an opponent's attack; intended to reduce or prevent the effect of that attack.

RADIATION—Radiation is used both to mean the process of radioactive emission and to refer to the stuff that is being emitted—the fast-moving nuclear particles that result when nuclei are split or fused.

R&D—Research and development. Research and development are the first stages in the process of designing and building a weapon system. Subsequent stages include testing, production, and deployment. Sometimes referred to as "RDT&E"—research, development, test, and evaluation.

RAPID RELOAD CAPACITY—see *Cold launch.*

REENTRY VEHICLE (RV)—That part of a ballistic missile which carries the nuclear warhead and is designed to reenter the earth's atmosphere at the terminal phase of the missile's flight.

REM—Roentgen equivalent man. A particular unit of radiation, measured by its effect on human tissue.

RIFLE—A long gun characterized by grooves machined on the inside of the barrel in a spiral pattern. The grooves are designed to impart spin to the bullet, thus increasing its accuracy. The grooves are called rifling.

ROENTGEN—A unit of gamma or X-ray radiation.

RPV—Remote-piloted vehicle. An unmanned airplane used for a variety of missions including reconnaissance, communications, electronic warfare, and bombing. It is distinguished from a cruise missile in that it is under continual control from a remote operator, and it is reusable in that it returns to base at the end of its mission.

RULES OF ENGAGEMENT—A part of tactical doctrine that dictates when and how a weapon will be employed. For example, the rules of engagement for air-to-air combat may vary according to whether one may shoot at an unidentified aircraft or one must know for sure it is an enemy. Also refers to the use of nuclear or conventional weapons.

RV—See *Reentry vehicle.*

SAC—Strategic Air Command. That part of the Air Force dedicated to strategic warfare, including bombers and ICBMs.

SALT II AGREEMENT—SALT II consists of three parts: a treaty which will last through 1985, a protocol which lasted through 1981 (that is, it has already expired), and a "Joint Statement of Principles and Basic Guidelines for Subsequent Negotiations on the Limitation of Strategic Arms." The protocol established temporary limitations on mobile ICBM launchers, ground and sea-launched cruise missiles, and aircraft carriers.

SAM—Surface-to-air missile. A missile fired from a ground launcher and designed to shoot down airplanes.

SECOND STRIKE—A retaliatory strike in response to an enemy first strike.

SENSORS—Devices used to detect objects or environmental conditions. Radars, infrared detectors, sonar, and seismographs are all examples of sensors.

SHAPED CHARGE—A type of ammunition designed to destroy armored vehicles, such as tanks, by focusing the energy of its explosion on a very small point, creating a jet of molten metal capable of penetrating conventional armor. See *Chobham armor*.

SHOCK WAVE—A shock wave is sometimes mistaken for a wall of rapidly moving air. Like wave action in a pond, however (after you have thrown in a stone), it is not the movement of the medium itself but the transmission of energy *through* water or air; in other words, an abrupt change of pressure in the medium. The effect is commonly caused by explosions, either nuclear or conventional, but is also experienced in earthquakes or when an aircraft "breaks the sound barrier." See *Air Blast*.

SLBM—Submarine-launched ballistic missile. A ballistic missile carried in and launched from a submarine. Also called a fleet ballistic missile.

SLCM—Sea-launched cruise missile.

SMART BOMB—Any one of several types of bombs made more effective by attaching to them guidance systems, wings, and fins. A type of precision-guided munition.

SOLE-SOURCE—A common type of military contract wherein there is no competitive bidding. Rather, the item or service is purchased from a single designated contractor or source.

SRBM—Short-range ballistic missile. A ballistic missile with a range of 600 miles or less. The U.S. Pershing, Lance, and Sergeant are examples of SRBMs.

STEALTH BOMBER—"Stealth" is the popularized term for a new type of aircraft that would be nearly invisible to enemy radar. The effect is achieved through the combination of electronic countermeasures technology, covering the airframe with a plastic material that absorbs radar waves, and, most importantly, shaping the aircraft in such a way as to eliminate flat surfaces and sharp angles off which radar waves reflect. Moreover, because the engines are buried within the body of the aircraft, their spinning turbine and compressor blades will not reflect radar energy as much as will externally mounted engines. The Carter administration revealed the development of such an aircraft in the 1980 election campaign, and Ronald

Reagan charged the Carter administration with leaking military secrets for political purposes. In fact, the technology is relatively well-known. It is simply a matter of putting it all together. The Stealth bomber is considered by many people to be a competitor with the B-1 bomber.

STRATEGIC—Relating to a nation's military potential, including its geographic location, resources, and economic and military strength, as in "strategic position." Thus, weapons of long range, capable of directly affecting a nation's war-fighting ability, are called strategic as opposed to the tactical weapons used on a battlefield.

STRATEGY—The art and science of developing and using political, economic, and military forces during peace or war to increase the chances of victory and lessen the chances of defeat.

SUBSURFACE BURST—The detonation of a nuclear weapon below the surface of land or water. On land this explosion would be used to hit a buried hard target. At sea it would be used against a submarine or to inundate low-lying coastal areas.

SURFACE BURST—The detonation of a warhead on the surface. It is less destructive to surrounding structures than an airburst, but effective against hard targets and results in more fallout, since more irradiated dirt and debris are drawn into the mushroom cloud.

SWING WING—Technically known as variable geometry, this is a kind of aircraft wing which can be swept back for high-speed flight or swept forward, out straight, for more efficient low-speed flight as well as for landing on an aircraft carrier or a short airfield. A difficult technology to master since it tends to shift the aircraft's center of gravity, thus causing stability problems. Its first successful application was on the F-111 (né TFX), and it has since been adopted for use on the F-14 and B-1, as well as on some European and Soviet designs.

TAC—Tactical Air Command. That part of the Air Force dedicated to tactical warfare, including small bombers, close air-support aircraft, and fighters.

TACTICAL—Relating to battlefield operations as distinguished from strategic operations. Tactical weapons or forces are those designed for combat with opposing military forces rather than for reaching the rear echelons of the opponent or the opponent's homeland.

TACTICS—Detailed methods and routines for employing military forces in combat, including the arrangement and maneuvering of units in relation to one another and to the enemy.

TELEMETRY—The transmission of electronic signals by missiles to earth. Monitoring these signals aids in evaluating a missile's performance and provides a way of verifying weapon tests undertaken by an adversary.

THEATER—A large area in which a war is being fought, as contrasted to intercontinental war. During World War II we called Europe the European theater, the Far East the Pacific theater. The term is also used in referring to weapons of "theater range"—that is, weapons to be used within a theater of war and not beyond it.

THERMONUCLEAR—An adjective referring to the process whereby high temperatures are used to cause the fusion of light nuclei, releasing great amounts of energy.

THROW-WEIGHT—The "useful weight" which is placed on a trajectory toward the target by the central boost phase of the missile. It includes reentry vehicle(s), warhead(s) and the post-boost vehicles used for independently targetable warheads and any penetration aids, and their release devices. Throw-weight is distinguished from payload in that the latter does not include the post-boost vehicle.

TITAN—Titan I was a liquid-fueled missile whose fuel was not storable, but the missile was based in an underground silo. An elevator lifted it to the surface after it was fueled but before it was fired. Titan II, a follow-on weapon, uses a storable liquid fuel which allows it to be based in and launched from an underground silo. We currently have 52 of these two-stage Titan II ICBMs. One of our oldest ICBMs still deployed, the Titan II carries the largest (9-megaton) thermonuclear warhead in our ICBM arsenal.

TNT—A common type of chemical explosive, trinitrotoluene.

TNT EQUIVALENCE—A basic measure of explosive power equal to some weight (tons, thousand tons, million tons) of TNT.

TRIAD—U.S. strategic forces which are composed of three parts: land-based intercontinental missiles, submarine-launched ballistic missiles, and long-range bombers.

TRIDENT—A nuclear-powered submarine carrying intercontinental ballistic missiles. The submarine carries 24 missiles, each of which can carry up to 14 warheads. The term is also used to refer to the missiles carried by this submarine, some of which are also carried by older Poseidon submarines. See *Poseidon, Polaris,* and *SLBM.*

TRIP WIRE—A force, deployed in front of a numerically superior army, that has as its basic function the triggering of a sizable commitment of countering forces. Thus, U.S. forces in Europe have sometimes been viewed as a trip wire. In the event of a Soviet attack on Europe, the presence of these forces would guarantee U.S. involvement in the war.

TURBOFAN—A jet engine that increases its thrust by sucking in air that is not used to support combustion but rather is ducted past the engine and ejected out the back along with the hot exhaust. This type of engine is more fuel-efficient at lower altitudes. So, for example, attack aircraft such as the A-7 and the A-10 have turbofan engines, since their missions dictate relatively low-level operations. Commercial airliners using engines of this type are referred to as "fan jets."

TURBOJET—A "pure" jet engine. Air is drawn into the front by the compressor, mixed with fuel, and then the mixture is ignited in a combustion chamber, so that it expands greatly. The pressure results in its being expelled with great force out the back of the engine, providing the thrust. In so doing, it turns a turbine (analogous to a waterwheel or windmill) which is linked to a shaft which drives the compressor. Thus these types of engines are sometimes generically referred to as turbine engines. This type of engine is most efficient at high altitudes.

TURBOPROP—A type of jet engine wherein all or most of the exhaust energy is used to spin a turbine. The turbines are linked to a shaft which drives a propeller. This is the most efficient kind of jet engine at low altitudes, but its speed is limited because the tips of an aircraft propeller cannot exceed the speed of sound. Thus is it used only on relatively low-speed aircraft such as the P-3 patrol plane. Turbine engines are also adapted for use in other vehicles such as tanks (the M-1) and warships (our newest generation of frigates and destroyers are turbine powered). In these applications they are commonly referred to as gas turbines to distinguish them from steam turbines, which have powered ships and produced electricity since the beginning of the century.

URANIUM—A heavy radioactive metal with the atomic number 92. One isotope, U-235, is the only readily fissionable atomic nucleus occurring in nature.

VARIABLE GEOMETRY—See *Swing wing.*

VERIFICATION—The process of determining the degree to which the parties to an agreement are complying with its provisions.

WAR-FIGHTING SCENARIO—A term commonly applied to situations in which nuclear weapons would actually be used in war. It is controversial because it implies that nuclear weapons, like conventional weapons, can be used in battle and that it would be possible for one side or the other to win such a war, a view rejected by many people.

WARHEAD—That part of a missile, bomb, torpedo, or other munition that contains the explosive or chemical or biological agent which is intended to do damage.

WARHEAD SPONGE—Any high-value target that because of its importance tends to attract a concentrated enemy attack.

WEAPONS OF MASS DESTRUCTION—In arms control parlance, these are weapons that are capable of a high order of destruction. Usually they are thought of as nuclear and thermonuclear, but they can also include chemical and biological agents.

WILD WEASEL—Modified fighter plane adapted to detect and attack enemy radar sites and anti-aircraft batteries. See *Ferret*.

YIELD—The total effective energy released in a nuclear or thermonuclear explosion, usually measured and described in terms of an equivalent amount of TNT.

Further Reading

FOR EVERY CHAPTER in this book—perhaps for every paragraph; certainly for every weapon and weapons system— there is at least one book, and often an entire collection of materials to read. In the history of weaponry and warfare there are general histories of wars, as well as histories of specific battles. And there are books about most major weapons, especially about ships, airplanes, tanks, and firearms. There is even a *Social History of the Machine Gun*. There are hundreds of books about airplanes. In addition to these weapons-oriented books, there are political science studies about specific military and foreign policies.

Beyond books, there is a library of specialized magazines. *Aviation Week & Space Technology* is one of the most widely read. This weekly newsmagazine includes so much up-to-the-minute information about technical aspects of weapons and about military decision-making that everyone who wants to keep up subscribes. Many libraries also carry it. *Foreign Affairs* is a key journal on foreign policy and strategic doctrine and it is read by most defense policy makers, as are *International Security* and *Foreign Policy*.

There are many kinds of military journals, at least one for each of the services. The *Air University Review* and *Army* are two such journals. Then there are the magazines published by civilians affiliated with each of the services: the Air Force Association publishes *Air Force Magazine*, the Army Association issues *Army Magazine*, and *Sea Power* is the

Navy League's counterpart. *Armed Forces Journal* is an independent periodical of long standing, about one hundred years old. There are also technical journals, many of which are published abroad, such as the *International Defense Review*. *Defense Electronics* appeals to an even more specialized audience, as does *Naval Aviation News* (for Naval Air reservists) and *Approach* for naval aviators (*All Hands* is for sailors). Military newspapers circulated within the military (but not owned by the federal government) also abound: *Army Times, Navy Times, Air Force Times,* and so on. There is also a variety of newsletters and journals published by private organizations that follow defense policy. Among these are *Defense Monitor* by the Center for Defense Information, the American Enterprise Institute's *Foreign Policy and Defense Review*, the American Security Council's *International Security Review*, and *Arms Control Today* from the Arms Control Association.

Rather than attempt an exhaustive bibliography, we have compiled a suggested reading and reference list for each chapter. The works included here are, in our view, readable, important, and useful.

CHAPTER ONE

Department of Defense, *Annual Report,* prepared by the Secretary of Defense, available through the Department of Defense and the U.S. Government Printing Office.

Kenneth Waltz, *Man, the State and War* (New York: Columbia University Press, 1965).

CHAPTER TWO

Bernard and Fawn Brodie, *From Crossbow to H-Bomb* (Bloomington: Indiana University Press, 1973).

Dr. Helen Caldicott, *Nuclear Madness* (New York: Bantam Books, 1980).

R. Ernest Dupuy and Trevor Dupuy, *The Encyclopedia of Military History* (New York: Harper & Row, 1970).

Charles Fair, *From the Jaws of Victory* (New York: Simon & Schuster, 1971).

John Keegan, *The Face of Battle* (New York: Viking Press, 1976).

George Quester, *Deterrence Before Hiroshima* (New York: John Wiley & Sons, 1966).

Martin Sherwin, *A World Destroyed* (New York: Alfred A. Knopf, 1975).

Barbara Tuchman, *The Guns of August* (New York: Macmillan, 1962).

Herbert York, *The Advisors: Oppenheimer, Teller, and the Super-bomb* (San Francisco: W. H. Freeman, 1975).

CHAPTER THREE

Thomas M. Coffey, *Decision Over Schweinfurt: The U.S. 8th Air Force Battle for Daylight Bombing* (New York: David McKay, 1977).

Wilbur H. Morrison, *Point of No Return: The Story of the Twentieth Air Force* (New York: Times Books, 1979).

Harvey Sapolski, *The Polaris System Development* (Cambridge, Mass.: Harvard University Press, 1972).

Herbert Scoville, Jr., *MX: Prescription for Disaster* (Cambridge, Mass.: MIT Press, 1981).

Russell Weigley, *The American Way of War* (New York: Macmillan, 1973).

Ernest Yanarella, *The Missile Defense Controversy* (Louisville: University of Kentucky Press, 1977).

CHAPTER FOUR

Graham Allison, *Essence of Decision* (Boston: Little, Brown, 1971).

Louis René Beres, *Apocalypse: Nuclear Catastrophe in World Politics* (Chicago: University of Chicago Press, 1982).

Bernard Brodie, *War and Politics* (New York: Macmillan, 1973).

Phillip Green, *Deadly Logic* (New York: Schocken Books, 1969).

Gregg Herken, *The Winning Weapon: The Atomic Bomb in the Cold War, 1945–1950* (New York: Random House, 1982).

Samuel Huntington, *The Common Defense* (New York: Columbia University Press, 1961).

Herman Kahn, *On Thermonuclear War* (Princeton, N.J.: Princeton University Press, 1961).

Henry Kissinger, *Nuclear Weapons and Foreign Policy* (New York: Harper & Brothers, 1957).

John Prados, *The Soviet Estimate: U.S. Intelligence Analysis and Russian Military Strength* (New York: Dial Press, 1982).

Jonathan Schell, *The Fate of the Earth* (New York: Alfred A. Knopf, 1982).

Thomas Schelling, *The Strategy of Conflict* (Cambridge, Mass.: Harvard University Press, 1960).

————, *Arms and Influence* (New Haven, Conn.: Yale University Press, 1966).

Daniel Yergin, *Shattered Peace* (New York: Houghton Mifflin, 1977).

CHAPTER FIVE

James H. Belote and William M. Belote, *Titans of the Seas: The Development and Operation of Japanese and American Carrier Task Forces During World War II* (New York: Harper & Row, 1975).

Robert Berman, *Soviet Air Power in Transition* (Washington, D.C.: The Brookings Institution, 1978).

Cincinnatus, *Self Destruction: The Disintegration and Decay of the United States Army During the Vietnam Era* (New York: W. W. Norton, 1981).

Department of Defense, *Soviet Military Power* (1981), published annually by the Department of Defense, Washington, D.C.

James F. Dunnigan, *How to Make War* (New York: William Morrow, 1982).

James Fallows, *National Defense* (New York: Random House, 1981).

General Sir John Hackett et al., *The Third World War* (New York: Macmillan, 1978).

Michael Maclear, *The Ten-Thousand-Day War: Vietnam, 1945–1975* (New York: St. Martin's Press, 1981).

The Yom Kippur War, by the Insight Team of *The London Sunday Times* (Garden City, N.Y.: Doubleday, 1974).

CHAPTER SIX

Gordon Adams, *The Iron Triangle* (New York: Council on Economic Priorities, 1981).

Robert Art, *The TFX Decision: McNamara and the Military* (Boston: Little, Brown, 1968).

The Boston Study Group, *The Price of Defense* (New York: Times Books, 1979).

Alain Enthoven and Wayne Smith, *How Much is Enough? Shaping the Defense Program, 1961–1969* (New York: Harper & Row, 1971).

J. Ronald Fox, *Arming America: How the U.S. Buys Weapons* (Cambridge, Mass.: Harvard University Press, 1974).

Jacques Gansler, *The Defense Industry* (Cambridge, Mass.: MIT Press, 1980).

Berkely Rice, *The C-5A Scandal* (New York: Houghton Mifflin, 1971).

Adam Yarmolinsky, *The Military Establishment* (New York: Harper & Row, 1971).

CHAPTER SEVEN

Hedley Bull, *The Control of the Arms Race* (New York: Praeger, 1965).

William Kincaid and Jeffrey Porro, *Negotiating Security* (New York and Washington, D.C.: The Carnegie Endowment for Peace, 1979).

Alva Myrdal, *The Game of Disarmament* (New York: Pantheon Books, 1978).

John Newhouse, *Cold Dawn* (New York: Holt, Rinehart & Winston, 1973).

Alan Platt and Lawrence Weiler, *Congress and Arms Control* (Boulder, Col.: Westview Press, 1978).

Strobe Talbott, *Endgame: The Inside Story of SALT II* (New York: Harper & Row, 1979).

U.S. Arms Control and Disarmament Agency, *Arms Control and Disarmament Agreements* (Washington, D.C., August 1980).

Lawrence Weiler and John Barton, eds., *International Arms Control: Issues and Agreements* (Stanford, Calif.: Stanford University Press, 1976).

CHAPTER EIGHT

Aviation Week & Space Technology
The Christian Science Monitor
The New York Times
The Wall Street Journal
The Washington Post

GENERAL REFERENCE WORKS

Ray Bonds, ed., *The U.S. War Machine* (New York: Crown Publishers, 1978).

Tom Gervasi, *Arsenal of Democracy II* (New York: Grove Press, 1981).

International Institute for Strategic Studies, *The Military Balance* (London, published annually).

Jane's All the World's Aircraft (New York: Franklin Watts, published annually).

Jane's Fighting Ships (New York: Franklin Watts, published annually).

Jane's Weapon Systems (New York: Franklin Watts, published annually).

Ruth Leger Sivard, *World Military and Social Expenditures* (Leesburg, Va.: World Priorities, 1980).

Stockholm International Peace Research Institute, *World Armaments and Disarmament Yearbook* (Cambridge, Mass.: MIT Press, published annually).

Acknowledgments

OUR FIRST DEBT, of course, is to one another. Four people, living far apart, not knowing one another very well before beginning this work, have shared an unusual and perhaps unique experience. Our mutual respect has been, in the course of this work, much increased by affection. And now, rereading our book for the last time, while we are able to pick out a particular phrase, a metaphor, and an idea that could be said to belong very personally to one of us, we can safely say that there is no single paragraph that was not the work of us all.

This is unusual in collaborative efforts. Normally, certain members of a research or writing team will be assigned to one or another topic, and while the coauthors might edit and even rework some of those sections, each part will be recognizably the product of one person's mind. Not so with this book. While it was tempting to divide up the task, we wanted most of all to experiment with the idea that the beginners' perspectives and needs should inform the manuscript throughout. As a result, these are so thoroughly interwoven with the experts' knowledge that in the process we have all become each other's students.

We originally met through colleagues who urged us to contact one another. These are Professors Margaret and Harold Feldman, lately retired from Ithaca College and Cornell University, respectively; and Myra Dinnerstein, Director of Women's Studies at the University of Arizona in Tucson.

We are particularly grateful to these, our friends. While we had neither formal institutional backing nor any foundation support, we have made use of the resources of the Center for Defense Information in Washington, whose staff helped us clarify many important factual matters. We are also indebted to the Department of Political Science at the University of Arizona, which facilitated the collaboration by appointing Sheila Tobias visiting scholar for the year.

The technical aspects of weapons design are based in science, and in the writing of these chapters we were aided by Carl Tomizuka of the Department of Physics at the University of Arizona, who provided a particular kind of expertise none of us could have mustered alone. Later we needed a more overall critical reading and called upon our colleagues Sanford Lakoff, of the University of California at San Diego; George Quester, of the University of Maryland and the National Defense University in Washington; Bernard Halloran, formerly with the Department of Defense and now with the U.S. Arms Control and Disarmament Agency; and David Johnson, of the Center for Defense Information. In addition, Lawrence Weiler, formerly with ACDA, and Wayne Glass of the Department of Defense read parts of the book. Each of these provided direction as well as criticism, and we thank them.

To achieve our purpose of demystifying a very complex and confusing subject, we needed not just expert readers but "naïve" readers as well. Lucy Knight of Durham, North Carolina, served in this capacity.

To Doug Mathews, our research assistant at the University of Arizona, we owe a special thanks for tirelessly searching out the detail that we wanted for the book; also to Marge Neufer, our chief typist, who because of the distances among us became our trusted Manuscript Manager as well. Assisting with typing were Carmen Suarez of the Arizona House of Representatives and Kathy Pulford of Tucson.

The Department of Defense helped immensely in allowing us to search their picture files and by providing prompt answers to many questions. And our editor at William Morrow, Maria Guarnaschelli, and our agent, Gloria Stern, never wavered in their commitment to and support of what we were trying to do.

Above all, we have debts to our respective families.

Nanette Warner, Peter Goudinoff's wife, gave up his company for many long weekends so that her husband could work on the book after the legislative session started up again in Phoenix. And though he is still too young to express an opinion, we are certain that by the end, Stephen Goudinoff, aged three, began to think things had gone just a little bit too far.

Last of all, we owe a special bouquet to Lauren Leader, aged seven, who not only permitted her parents to leave her in the cold Northeast when they came to work in Tucson this past winter, but pretended that she didn't even mind.

Tucson and Washington, D.C., August 1982

Index

A-10 airplane, 191–192
A-18 airplane, 218
ABM (anti-ballistic missile) system, 118–120, 358–360
  layered type of, 359
  LoADS as, 359
  mutual escalation from, 161
  opposition to, 120, 155
  perfection necessary in, 161
  provocative aspect of, 160–161
  testing of, 120
ABM treaty, 122, 160–161, 302–304
Abrams, Creighton W., 185–186
"accidental measures" agreement, 159
ACDA (Arms Control and Disarmament Agency), 293–296
  constraints on, 294–295
  function of, 293–294
ACE (armored combat earthmover), 187
ACEVAL/AIMVAL (air combat evaluation/air intercept missile evaluation), 215–216, 366–367
acoustic detectors, 52
acronyms, meanings of, 84–85
active defense, 117–120
Afghanistan, Soviet invasion of, 335
air blast, 63–65
aircraft carriers, 49, 226–228, 341–342
  vulnerability of, 341–342
Air Force, U.S.:
  creation of, 262
  Space Command of, 365
American Enterprise Institute, 29
American Security Council, 296
AMRAAM (advanced medium-range air-to-air missile), 368
anti-satellite weapons, 320, 361

antitank missiles, 189–191
  defenses against, 190–191
Apocalypse Now (Coppola), 203
Aquila (RPV), 375
AR-15 rifle, 178
Arab-Israeli conflicts:
  in 1967, 229
  in 1973, see Yom Kippur War
Arms and Influence (Schelling), 286
arms control, 286–287
  linkage in, 292
  non-nuclear, 287–291
  on-site inspection in, 292
  satellite verification for, 292, 299
  see also SALT I; SALT II; Strategic Arms Reduction Talks
Arms Control Association, 295
Army Chemical Systems Lab, 344
Army Medical Research Institute of Infectious Diseases, 344
arquebuses, 40
artillery, 35, 179–181
  guidance systems for, 179
artillery shells, 38–40, 179
ASAT (anti-satellite weapons), 360–362
assured destruction, 155–157
Atlas missile, 98
atmospheric tests, opposition to, 297
atomic bombs, 52–58
  see also nuclear weapons; thermonuclear weapons
Augustine, Norman, 238, 273
Aviation Week & Space Technology, 327, 358, 363, 366–367, 380
avionics, 94
AWACS (advanced warning and control system) airplane, 209, 223–225
  capabilities of, 224

B-1 bomber, 129–131, 345–349
    cost of, 130, 346–347
    design flaws of, 347
    radar profile of, 52, 129
    Stealth bomber as competition of, 348
B-17 bomber, 50, 88–89
B-24 bomber, 50
B-29 bomber, 50, 86, 89–91
B-36 bomber, 91–93
B-47 bomber, 93
B-50 bomber, 91
B-52 bomber, 93–94, 129, 131
    re-engining of, 349
B-70 bomber, 20–21
Backfire bomber, 140
Baruch Plan, 291
battleships, 225–226
beam weapons, 362–365
    defenses against, 363–364
    laser type, 362–364
    particle beam type, 362–364
    Talon Gold tracking system for, 364–365
    targeting problems of, 364–365
Bennett, Charles, 253
binary weapons, 344
biological agents, 291
Biological Warfare Convention, 291
blast, characteristics of, 62–65
BMD (ballistic missile defense) systems, 359
BMEWS (ballistic-missile early-warning system), 118
Boeing, 269
bombards, 33
bombers:
    advantages of, 115
    non-strategic uses for, 346
    vulnerability of, 114
    see also specific bombers
bombs:
    Hague Convention and, 288–289
    laser guidance of, 193–194
    shock wave from, 50
    types of, 50–61, 192–194, 195
    see also nuclear weapons; thermonuclear weapons
bow and arrow, 37
Braun, Wernher von, 76
Brezhnev, Leonid, 304, 307–308
brinkmanship, 142
Brodie, Bernard, 34
Brodie, Fawn, 34
Brookings Institution, 29
Brown, Harold, 265, 340, 370
budget authority, 281
bullets, caliber of, 40–41
Bundy, McGeorge, 325, 334
Burke, Kelly, 254
Burt, Richard, 30

C-5A transport (Galaxy), 197–199
    cost of, 197
    load/unload time savings of, 198
    specifications of, 197–198
C-5B transport, 199
C-141 Starlifter airplane, 196–197
caliber, 40–41
California Institute of Technology, 29
Camp David Agreement, 25
cannon, 38
    see also artillery
cannonballs, 38
capability analysis, 140–141
CAPTOR, 377–378
Carlucci, Frank, 256
Carter, Jimmy:
    B-1 bomber and, 129, 345
    cruise missile development under, 318–319
    neutron bomb and, 61
    SALT II under, 304, 321
catapult, 37–38
CBS-TV, 215
Center for Defense Information, 295
CEP (circular error probable), 98–99
chain mail armor, 33
chain reaction, 55–56
chain shot, 38–39
chemical weapons:
    binary type, 344
    defenses against, 344–345
    deterrent value of, 343–345
    see also poison gas
Chicago Tribune, 366
China, People's Republic of:
    missiles of, 135
    nuclear weapons of, 135
Christian Science Monitor, 328
Chrysler, 185, 244
Churchill, Winston, 138
CIA (Central Intelligence Agency), 25, 271
civil defense, 120–121, 155
Civil War, U.S., 35, 44–45
    breech-loading rifle in, 43
    increased firepower in, 43, 45
Clausewitz, Karl von, 235
Cluster Bay, 377
Cluster Gulf, 377
Cobra helicopter, 203
Cold Dawn (Newhouse), 300, 303
cold launch, 126
collateral damage, 289
COMINT (communications intelligence), 272
Command of the Air (Douhet), 88
Committee on the Present Danger, 296
Common Cause, 252–253
comprehensive test ban treaty, 298–299

Conference of the Committee on Disarmament, 293
conventional warfare, 176
Copperhead shell, 179
Coppola, Francis Ford, 203
Coral Sea, Battle of, aircraft carrier use in, 49, 226, 341
cost-benefit analysis, 241, 265–266
cost optimism, 257
Council for a Livable World, 295
Council on Economic Priorities, 237
counterbattery fire, 179
counterforce, 153
countervailing strategy, 170
countervalue strategy, 153
Crécy, Battle of, 34
critical mass, 57
crossbow, 35
cruise missile, 128–131, 166, 182, 318–319, 373–374
    attempts to limit deployment of, 319
    B-52 deployment of, 129, 131, 374
    naval deployment of, 373–374
    technology in, 128, 373
    verification of, 319
Cuban missile crisis:
    cooperation resulting from, 158
    effect on arms control of, 296
    Soviet motivation in, 100–101
Curie, Marie, 55
Curie, Pierre, 55
curve of unilateral disarmament, 370

Danforth, John, 251
defense community, 29–31, 245–248
    lobbying in, 248
    in Pentagon, 246
    prime contractors in, 247
    profits in, 248–250
    subcontractors in, 247
Defense Department, U.S.:
    budget for, 280–284
    cost-benefit analysis in, 265–267
    creation of, 260–261
    interservice rivalry in, 263
    military vs. civilian control in, 262–264
    "not invented here" syndrome at, 238
    see also defense strategy; weapons procurement
"Defense of the United States, The" (CBS), 215
defense science:
    defense policy and, 275
    laboratories for, 274–275
    management of laboratories for, 275
    military involvement in, 275–276
Defense Science Board, 276
Defense Secretary, bureaucratic problems of, 263–264

defense spending:
    budgetary confusion in, 280–284
    budget authority for, 281
    effect of "capability analysis" on, 140
    geographical distribution of, 251–252
    immutability of, 20–21
    international total of, 24
    multiyear contracts in, 284
    outlays for fiscal 1983 in, 281
    Soviet vs. U.S., 167
    space program as part of, 280–281
    total obligational authority in, 281
    see also Soviet Union; United States; weapons procurement
defense strategy:
    assured destruction in, 155–157
    cost-benefit analysis in, 152
    countervailance as, 170
    damage limitation as, 154–156
    defensive sea control as, 342
    deterrence in, 22, 138, 144, 163–164, 172–173
    effect of accuracy on, 168
    firepower in, 174–176
    flexible response as, 145–149
    flexible second strike in, 357
    game theory applied to, 151–152
    massive retaliation as, 142
    mobility in, 174–175, 195–196
    modeling in, 30–31
    offensive sea control as, 341–342
    targeting strategies in, 153–155
Defense Supply Agency, 264–265
defensive sea control, 342
de Gaulle, Charles, 330
destroyers, 231
détente, 159, 166, 321
deterrence, 22, 138, 144–173
    ABM undermining of, 160–161
    assurance necessary to, 163
    see also defense strategy; nuclear weapons
deuterium, thermonuclear weapons and, 59–60
DEW (distant early-warning) line, 117
DIA (Defense Intelligence Agency), 271
directed energy, 20
directed-energy weapons, see beam weapons
doomsday machine, 157
Douhet, Giulio, 88
Dresden, fire bombing of, 50–51, 66–67
DSARC (Defense Systems Acquisition Review Council), 278–279
Dulles, John Foster, 142
dumb bombs, 195

Eagleton, Thomas, 251
Earle, Ralph, 306

Economic Advancement Coalition, 251–252
EF-111 fighter, 213
Effects of Nuclear War, The (OTA), 66
Eilat, sinking of, 229
Einstein, Albert, 60
Eisenhower, Dwight D., 137, 141–142
  "open skies" proposal of, 292
ELINT (electronics intelligence), 272
EMP (electromagnetic pulse), 73–74
ERCs (emergency rocket communication system), 107
Evans, Rowland, 327
exploding shell, 39
Eyring Research Institute, 350

F-4 Phantom II fighter, 206–208
  specifications of, 207–208
  versatility of, 207
F-5 fighter, 213–216
F-14 fighter, 217–219, 270
F-15 fighter, 209–211, 270
  capabilities of, 210
  cost of, 210–211
F-16 fighter, 209, 211–212
  rise in complexity and cost of, 368
F-18 fighter, 218–219
F-86 Sabre jet fighter, 206
F-105 fighter-bomber, 268
F-106 Delta Dart interceptor, 93
F-111 (TFX) fighter, 212–213, 267–270
  fly-off for, 269
  McNamara's influence on, 268–270
fail-safe systems, 103–104
Falklands War (1982), 21
fallout, 69–73
Fallows, James, 178
Fate of the Earth (Schell), 325
Federation of American Scientists, 295
Fermi, Enrico, 54–56
Fetter, Steven, 73
field guns, *see* artillery
fire storms, 66–67
first strike, 150
fission, nuclear, 53–58
Flanders Field, 35
flexible response, 145–149
  C-5A capability in, 198
  Carter's reemphasis of, 170
  Communist subversion as impetus for, 147
  decomposition of threat in, 148
  domino theory as impetus for, 147
  Green Berets as instrument of, 148
Flying Tigers, 204
FMC Corporation, 201, 244
FMS (Foreign Military Sales), 214, 253
Ford, Gerald, 304, 307–308, 349
Foreign Affairs, 169

Forrestal, James, 263
fragmentation bombs, 50
France:
  missiles of, 135
  nuclear deterrent force in, 330
  nuclear weapons of, 135
  submarines of, 135
frigates, 231–233
fusion, nuclear, 60–62

Gabriel missile, 229
Galbraith, John Kenneth, 29
Gallup Poll, 24
Galosh (ABM system), 300, 359
Game of Disarmament, The (Myrdal), 293
game theory, 142–144
  minimax strategy in, 143
  nonzero-sum game in, 142–144
  prisoners' dilemma in, 143–144
  zero-sum game in, 142–143
Gansler, Jacques, 254
GAO (General Accounting Office), 347
Gavin, James, 120
Gelb, Leslie, 30
General Dynamics Corp., 211, 213, 218, 269
Geneva Protocol, 343
Georgetown University Center for Strategic and International Studies, 29
George Washington, U.S.S., 108–109
Germany, Federal Republic of, defense options of, 330–331
GLCM (ground-launched cruise missiles), 329, 333
Goodman, Paul, 380
Goodyear Aerospace, 250
grapeshot, 38
Great Britain:
  bombers of, 135
  nuclear weapons in, 135
  submarines of, 135
Green Berets, 148
Ground Observer Corps, 92
Grumman Corporation, 217–218, 243
Guernica, bombing of, 49, 289
Guernica (Picasso), 49
gunpowder, 38, 42
guns:
  loading of, 42–43
  shoulder firing of, 40

Hague Convention:
  Article 25 of, 289
  weapons prohibitions of, 288
Haig, Alexander, 28, 315, 322
Halberstam, David, 148
Hamburg, fire bombing of, 50–51, 66–67
hard silos, 102, 105

hard-target capability, 323
hard targets, 153
Harpoon missile, 229
Hart, Gary, 216, 341–342, 351
Harvard University, 29
Hawk missiles, 221–222
Hayden, Carl, 250
H-bombs, *see* hydrogen bombs;
    thermonuclear weapons
HE (high-explosive general-purpose)
    shells, 40
helicopters, 202–204
    arming of, 203–204
Heritage Foundation, 296, 361
Hersey, John, 139
High Frontier study, 361–362
Hilsman, Roger, 99
Hiroshima, atomic bombing of, 16, 57
Hiroshima (Hersey), 139
Hoover Institute (Stanford University),
    29
hot line, 158
Humphrey, George M., 141–142
Humphrey, Hubert H., 293
Hundred Years' War, 34
Huron King test, 363
Hurricane fighter, 51–52
hydrogen bombs, 58–60
    see also thermonuclear weapons

ICBM (intercontinental ballistic
    missile):
    advantage of, 115
    development of, 94–97
    guidance of, 96
    MIRVing of, 122–125
    reentry of, 96–97
    vulnerability of, 115
incendiary bombs, 50–51
India-Pakistan War (1971), 231
Industrial Revolution, 34–35, 44
INF (Intermediate Nuclear Force)
    talks, 322–323, 332–333
intelligence collection, methods of,
    272–273
interceptor planes, 92–93
Iran, U.S. arms sale to, 217–218
IRBM (intermediate-range ballistic
    missile), 329

Jackson, Henry, 251, 314
James I, king of England, 34
Japan, defense spending of, 24
jet bombers, 93–94
    see also bombers
Johnson, U. Alexis, 306
Johnson administration:
    ABM system in, 118–119
    arms control "feelers" from, 300
    Vietnam escalation in, 148–149

Joint Chiefs of Staff, 261–262
Joliot-Curie, Irène, 55
Jupiter missile, 98

Kahn, Herman, 150–151, 155
Kaiser, Henry J., 48
KC-135 tanker, 93
Keeny, Spurgeon, Jr., 169
Kelly, Henry, 290
Kennan, George, 27, 31, 323–325, 334
Kennedy, Edward M., 251
Kennedy, John F., 267–268, 293
    inaugural address of, 147
    "missile gap" of, 100, 145
Kennedy administration:
    Communist subversion as seen by,
        147
    flexible response policy in, 146–148
    Vietnam and, 147–148
Krushchev, Nikita, 99–101, 171
kinetic energy shells, 39
King, Coretta Scott, 312
Kissinger, Henry, 172, 308
knights, as weapons systems, 33
Korean War, 141

Lance missile, 181–182
lasers, 20, 362
layered defense system, 359–360
LeMay, Curtis, 89–91
linkage, 292, 321
LoADS (low-altitude defense system),
    359–360
Lockheed Aircraft, 21, 196–197, 243
longbow, 33–34
LOW (launch without warning), 169
low-frequency radio transmission, 113
LRCA (long-range combat aircraft), 346
LRTNF (long-range theater nuclear
    force), 329
LUA (launch under attack), 169

M-1 Abrams tank, 185–187, 371–372
    armor of, 186
    engine problems in, 187
    support vehicles for, 187
M-1 Garand rifle, 35, 177, 244
M-16 rifle, 177–179
    debate over, 178–179
    operation of, 177
M-60 tank, 184–185, 372
M-113 armored personnel carrier,
    199–201
McDonnell Douglas Corp., 207, 212,
    243
Mach, Ernest, 207
machine gun, 46
Mach numbers, 207
McNamara, Robert, 151–157, 170,
    264–270

McNamara, Robert (*cont.*)
  ABM system of, 118–119
  Defense Department reorganization
    by, 152, 241, 264–267
  F-111 (TFX) fighter and, 267–270
  M-16 rifle procurement by, 178
  national defense as viewed by, 267
  "no first use" policy urged by, 325,
    334
  Soviet strategy as seen by, 126
  strategic decisions of, 153–156
Mahan, Alfred Thayer, 339
Major Force Programs, 282
Manhattan Project, 53–58
MAP (Military Assistance Program),
  214
Marine Corps, U.S., mission of, 335
Mark 12A warhead, 125, 257
massive retaliation, 142
  logical flaw of, 146
  loss of faith in, 145
Maverick missile, 194
MCM (mine counter measure) ships,
  377
"Measures to Prevent Nuclear War,"
  325
megadeaths, 150
megatons, 61–62
Merkava tank, 185
Merritt, Jack, 237
Meyer, E. C., 202
Middle Ages, 33
Midway, Battle of, aircraft carrier use
  in, 49, 226, 341
MiG-15 fighter, 92
MiG-23 fighter, 209
MiG-25 fighter, 21, 209, 273
Milestone I, 278
Milestone II, 278
Milestone III, 279
Mill, John Stuart, 28–29
mines, 41–42, 376–378
  deactivation of, 377
  deployment of, 376–377
  mobile type of, 377–378
minimax strategy, 143
Minuteman missile, 104–107
Minuteman III missiles, 162
  modification of, 124–125
MIRVs (multiple, independently targetable reentry vehicles), 122–125
  operation of, 123
missile gap, 100, 145
missiles:
  accuracy of, 98–99, 167–168
  ballistic vs. nonballistic, 76
  defense against, 117–122
  development of, 74–77
  fail-safe systems for, 103–104
  fueling of, 97

  guided vs. nonguided, 76
  miniaturization in, 96
  reentry technology of, 96–97
  security for, 104
  silo basing of, 102, 105
  solid fuel for, 104–105
  submarine launching of, 107–114
  surface-to-surface, 181
  see also specific missiles
Mitsubishi, 222
mortars, 179
Mount St. Helens, eruption of, 63–64
Moynihan, Daniel P., 312
MRVs (multiple reentry vehicles), 122
MSH (minehunter), 377
muskets, 35
Muskie, Edmund S., 251
mutual assured destruction (MAD), 156
MX (missile experimental), 133–134,
  349–358
  ABM defense of, 358
  basing plans for, 133–134, 164–165,
    171, 350–351, 358
  "dense pack" basing of, 351, 358
  development of, 133
  effect of SALT II on, 164–165
  flexible second strike capability of,
    357
  MIRVs orbiting from, 350–351
  Reagan's basing plans for, 171, 349,
    351
Mya-4 Bison bomber, 92
Myrdal, Alva, 293

Nagasaki, atomic bombing of, 16, 57
napalm bombs, 51
National Defense, 178
National Security Act of 1947, 261–262
  amendments to, 262, 263
NATO (North Atlantic Treaty Organiza-
  tion), 27, 328–332
  artillery strength of, 183
  European confidence in, 331–332
  force modernization in, 329
  Soviet threat to, 329
Navy, U.S., expansion of, 339–341
neutron bomb, 60–61, 118, 332
  credibility of, 332
  effects of, 60–61
Newhouse, John, 300, 303
newspapers, defense coverage in, 30
Newsweek, 30, 197
New Yorker, 138
New York Times, 39, 216, 345, 349
Nicholas II, czar of Russia, 288
Nike X ABM, 359
Nimitz, U.S.S., 226–227
Nitze, Paul, 296, 313
Nixon, Richard:
  ABM decision of, 119

biological weapons renounced by, 344
cruise missile and, 318
SALT II and, 319
nonproliferation treaty, 158–159
nonzero-sum game, 143–144
NORAD, 238–239
Northrop Corporation, 213–214, 218
Novak, Robert, 327
NS-20 guidance system, 124–125
NSC (National Security Council), 139,
  303
NSC #68 (policy paper), 138–140
nth country problem, 158–159
nuclear fission, 55–56
nuclear reactors, cooling methods for,
  110
nuclear weapons:
  atomic bombs as, 52–58
  blast from, 62–63
  deterrence value of, 22, 138, 172–173
  effects of, 62–74
  EMP from, 73–74
  European opposition to, 332–334
  fallout from, 69–73
  freeze on, 324, 334
  heat released from, 65–66
  "no first use" policy for, 324, 334
  radiation from, 68
  relative power of, 16, 61–62
  Trinity test of, 53–54
  undergound testing of, 298–299
  see also thermonuclear weapons
Nunn, Sam, 251
Nunn Amendment, 252–253

offensive sea control, 341–342
Office of Technology Assessment
  (OTA), 66
on-site inspection, 292
On Thermonuclear War (Kahn), 150
"open skies" proposal, 292
Oppenheimer, Robert, 54
OSA (Office of Systems Analysis),
  265–266, 270
outer-space treaty (1967), 158, 288

P-3 Orion aircraft, 233–234
P-38 Lightning fighter, 205
P-39 Aircobra fighter, 204
P-40 Warhawk fighter, 204
P-47 Thunderbolt, 205–206
P-51 Mustang, 205
PALS (permissive action links), 176
Panofsky, Wolfgang, 169
particle beams, 362
passive defense, 120–121
Patton, George S., 47, 184
Pearl Harbor, Battle of, 49, 226
penetration aids, 107

Pentagon, see Defense Department,
  U.S.
Pershing missile, 182
Pershing II missile, 182, 333
Phalanx gun, 231
Phoenix missile, 220
Pickett, George E., 45
pike, 37
Pinetree Line, 117
poison gas, 47
  deterrent value of, 291
  use and prohibition of, 290–291
  see also chemical weapons
Polaris missile, 108–109
  warhead flaws in, 112
POM (Program Objective Memoranda),
  277
Poseidon missile, 111, 125, 162, 172
PPBS (Planning Programming Budget-
  ing System), 267
Pratt & Whitney, 349
Price, Melvin, 252
prisoners' dilemma, 143–144
Project Bambi, 362
Project on Military Procurement, 238
proximity fuse, 51

radar (radio detection and ranging),
  51–52
  jamming (spoofing) of, 348
  lowering "signature" in, 348
radiation, 55
  effects of, 68–73
  measurement of, 69
railroads, military significance of, 44
Rand Corporation, 29
R & D (Research and Development),
  236–237
Raytheon Company, 221, 222, 244
RDF (Rapid Deployment Force),
  334–338
  airlift capability of, 337
  logistical problems for, 335–337
  Navy support for, 336–337
  Operation Bright Star of, 338, 346
  viability of, 337–338
  water supply for, 336
Reagan administration:
  aircraft carrier proposals of, 227
  arms reduction proposals of, 332–333
  Milestone III decisions in, 279
  MX basing plans and, 134
  naval buildup in, 339
  neutron bomb and, 61
  projected defense budget of, 23
  SALT II as viewed by, 315
  zero option of, 322–323
Red Flag training program, 208
rems, 69
Rhodes, John J., 349

Rice, Berkeley, 197
Rickover, Hyman, 172
rifles, 40
  see also guns
Rivers, L. Mendel, 250
Rolls-Royce Merlin engine, 205
Roman infantry, invincibility of, 33
Rostow, Eugene, 296
Rowney, Edward, 306
RPV (remotely piloted vehicle),
  374–375
Rush-Bagot agreement, 287

SAC (Strategic Air Command):
  Eisenhower administration support
    for, 142
  formation of, 89–90
  political support for, 91
  resistance to missiles of, 95–96
Safeguard (ABM system), 119,
  161–162
Sagger antitank missile, 190
SALT I, 122–123, 159–162, 299–304
  ABM treaty in, 302–304
  antecedents of, 158–159, 300–301
  Interim Agreement on Offensive
    Weapons in, 302, 304
  MIRVing resulting from, 162, 303
  parity in, 162, 300
  U.S. vs. Soviet motivation for,
    301–302
SALT II, 15–16, 160, 162–165,
  304–320
  bargaining for, 304–305
  cruise missile limits in, 310–311
  definition refinements resulting from,
    163
  delegations for, 305–306
  effect on MX basing of, 164–165, 318
  heavy bomber limits in, 310–311
  ICBM limits in, 310
  launcher limits in, 317
  MIRV limits in, 309
  non-ratification of, 162, 304, 314
  overall ceilings in, 308–309
  Senate debate over, 312–315
  verification of, 313
SALT III, *see* START
SAM (surface-to-air missiles), 122,
  221–223
satellites:
  military uses for, 360
  reconnaissance with, 134
  warfare with, 134–135
Schell, Jonathan, 325
Schelling, Thomas, 286
Schlafly, Phyllis, 312
Schlesinger, James, 170, 330
Schmidt, Helmut, 328, 331
Science, 363

Scientific American, 73
Scoville, Herbert, Jr., 351, 357
seabed treaty, 159, 288
second-strike capability, 151
secular priests, 29
Semenov, Vladimir, 306
Senate, U.S.:
  Armed Services Committee of, 134,
    312, 314, 351
  Foreign Relations Committee of, 312,
    314
shaped charge, 39
shrapnel, 39
Sidewinder missile, 219–221
SIOP (Single Integrated Operating
  Plan), 264
Slaughterhouse-Five (Vonnegut), 67
SLBM (submarine-launched ballistic
  missile):
  advantage of, 115
  development of, 107–108
  disadvantage of, 115
  improvements to, 125
  see also Polaris missile; Poseidon mis-
    sile; Trident missile
SLMM (submarine launched mobile
  mine), 378
smart bombs, 192–194
Smith, Gerard, 325, 334
Smyth, H. D., 53
"sole-source" contracts, 254
solid rocket fuel, 104–105
sonar (sound navigation and ranging),
  49
Soviet Union:
  anti-satellite weapons of, 361
  arms limitation as attractive to, 165
  civil defense in, 121
  defense spending in, 25, 166–167
  détente and, 159, 166, 321
  global interests of, 27–28
  ICBM development in, 99–101,
    116–117
  mobile mines of, 377
  naval strength of, 340
  Persian Gulf oil and, 335
  submarine technology in, 116–117
  tank design in, 187–189
  total weaponry of, 136
  weapons buildup in, 126–127, 166
space shuttle, 365
Sparrow missile, 219
Spitfire fighter, 51–52
Sprey, Pierre, 237–238, 372
Springfield rifle, 35, 244
Spruance, Raymond, 231
Spruance class destroyers, 231
Sputnik, 95, 99–100, 145
  effect on U.S. missile system of, 145
  science education and, 145

SRAM (short-range attack missiles), 122
SS-9 missile, 116, 122
SS-11 missile, 115, 122
SS-13 missile, 116
SS-17 missile, 126–127
SS-18 missile, 126–127
SS-19 missile, 126–127
SS-20 missile, 329
START (Strategic Arms Reduction Talks), 160, 323
Stassen, Harold, 292
State Department, U.S.:
  Bureau of Intelligence and Research of, 271
  Bureau of United Nations Affairs of, 292
  defense community in, 29
state-of-the-art design, 259–260
Stealth bomber, 52, 131, 171, 347–349
  antiradar technology of, 348–349
Stennis, John, 252, 342–343
Stinger missiles, 222
Stirling bomber, 50, 89
Stoner, Eugene, 178
Strategic Bombing Survey, 89
Strategic Rocket Forces (Soviet), 95
strategic warfare:
  aerial bombing in, 87–89
  scorched earth policy in, 86–87
strategic weapons, 15–16
  see also nuclear weapons
submarines, 47–49, 108–114
  attack type, 233
  command and control of, 112–114
  communication with, 112–113
  design improvements for, 110–111
  different generations of, 111
  improved technology of, 110–111
  navigation in, 111–112
  nuclear powering of, 108
surface blast, 65
swords, 35

T-38 training plane, 213–214
T-62 tank, 185
T-72 tank, 185, 188, 273
T-80 tank, 188
tactical warfare, 86
Talon Gold tracking system, 364–365
tanks, 47–48, 84, 183–189
  designations of, 84
  Soviet vs. American design of, 187–189
targeting strategies, 153–155
Taylor, Maxwell, 145
telegraph, military significance of, 44
Teller, Edward, 59–60, 276, 375
TerCoM guidance system, 333, 373
test ban treaty, 158, 296, 298–299

Texas Instruments, Inc., 193
TFX fighter, see F-111 (TFX) fighter
thermonuclear weapons:
  development of, 59–61
  relative power of, 61–62
  workings of, 58–60
  see also nuclear weapons
Thinking about the Unthinkable (Kahn), 150
think tanks, 29
Thiokol Chemical Company, 105
Thor missile, 98
threshold test ban treaty, 298–299
throwweight, 95
Titan I missile, 98
Titan II missile, 101–104
Tlatelolco, Treaty of, 288
TNT (trinitrotoluene), 51
Tokyo, fire bombing of, 50–51, 66–67
Top Gun training program, 208
TOW (tube-launched, optically tracked) antitank missile, 189–191
  operation of, 189
Tower, John, 338, 351
Triad, 114
Trident missile, 112
Trident submarine, 19, 131
Trident II missile (D-5), 171
Trinity (nuclear test), 53–54
Truman, Harry S, 141
Tsipis, Kosta, 73, 363
Tu-4 bomber, 91
Tu-20 "Bear" bomber, 92

UH-1 Huey helicopter, 203
Union of Concerned Scientists, 295
United Nations, 24–25
  disarmament activity of, 292–293
United States:
  anti-satellite weapons of, 361
  civil defense in, 120, 155
  European confidence in, 330–332
  global interests of, 26
  military optimism of, 383–384
  mobile mines of, 377–378
  pilot training in, 208, 214
  in Saudi arms deal (1981), 209, 224
  total weaponry of, 135–136
uranium, enrichment of, 58
uranium 235, manufacturing of, 57
U.S. News and World Report, 30

V-1 missile, 74–75
V-2 missile, 74–75
verification:
  national technical means of, 299, 316
  "type rule" in, 317
Vietnam War, 148–149
  bombing in, 149
  mutual escalation in, 148–149

Vietnam War *(cont.)*
  television coverage of, 149
  U.S. military deterioration from, 149
Vinci, Leonardo da, 44
Vladivostok accords, 307–308
Vonnegut, Kurt, 67

Wall Street Journal, 30
warhead fratricide, 351
"warhead sponge" effect, 373
Warnke, Paul, 306
Warsaw Pact, 27
  artillery strength of, 183
warships, 35–36, 44, 225–234
  designations of, 83–84
Washington Post, 239, 327, 334, 339,
    343
weapons:
  cost breakdowns for, 283
  designations of, 78–85
  development of, 243–244
  evaluation of, 278–280
  government production of, 244–245
  maintenance costs of, 368–370
  Murphy's Law and, 369
  public understanding of, 15–18
  quality vs. quantity debate over,
    366–368, 372–373
  as societal reflection, 382
  see also weapons procurement;
    specific weapons
weapons-free zones, 288
weapons procurement:
  "buying in," 249
  Congressional involvement in,
    252–253
  contractors' problems in, 283–284
  cost optimism in, 257
  cost overruns in, 256–260
  "cost plus" procedure in, 249
  curve of unilateral disarmament in,
    370
  design changes and, 255–256
  evaluation standards in, 257
  inflation in, 255
  known unknowns in, 259
  maintenance limitations on, 370

mission definition and, 266
  multiyear contracts in, 284
  performance evaluation in, 242–243
  politics in, 243, 251–253
  programming in, 277
  service cooperation in, 270–271
  "sole source" contracts in, 254
  state-of-the-art design in, 259–260
  "threat" analysis for, 271–274
  unknown unknowns in, 259–260
  see also defense spending
Weinberger, Caspar, 21
Westmoreland, William, 148, 178
Whitney, Eli, 244
window of vulnerability, 168, 350–351
  MX response to, 171, 351
  reality of, 351
  Soviet MIRVing and, 303
"wish lists," 277
Wohlstetter, Albert, 150–151
World War I, 35, 46–47
  mine use in, 376
  weapons introduced in, 46–47
World War II:
  atomic bombs in, 53–58
  bombing of civilians in, 289–290
  fire raids in, 50–51, 66–67
  mine use in, 376
  naval weapons in, 49, 225–226, 341
  Soviet memories of, 25–26
  weapons introduced in, 48–53
  weapons production in, 245

YAH-64 helicopter, 204
"yellow rain," 344
Yom Kippur War (1973):
  C-5A use in, 199
  Egyptian artillery in, 182–183
  Israeli tanks in, 183–184, 188–189
  naval warfare in, 229
  spending for, 21
Ypres, Third Battle of, 46

zero option, 322–323
zero-sum game, 142–143
Zumwalt, Elmo, 340

About the Authors

SHEILA TOBIAS is a pioneer in women's studies who has developed a reputation for demystifying complex information. With her 1978 book, *Overcoming Math Anxiety,* she launched a nationwide effort to persuade people who found themselves frightened by and alienated from mathematics to give the subject one more chance. She has been a lecturer in history, a women's studies scholar, and an administrator at a number of universities, and is currently a visiting scholar at the University of Arizona in Tucson.

PETER GOUDINOFF is a member of the Political Science Department at the University of Arizona and a three-term Representative in the Arizona House of Representatives. He has been teaching National Security Policy for ten years. Educated in political science, with a doctorate from Ohio State University, he has also been an aviation cadet in the U.S. Navy. He is a member of the Navy League, the U.S. Naval Institute, the Air Force Association, and the Inter-University Consortium on Armed Forces and Society.

STEFAN LEADER is a national security affairs consultant and has held positions with the U.S. Arms Control and Disarmament Agency and the Center for Defense Information in Washington. He specializes in U.S. and NATO defense budgets, weapons systems, the U.S.–Soviet military balance, and arms negotiations. He has taught at Ithaca College and been associated with the Cornell University Peace Studies Program. Educated at Hofstra University, with a doctorate in political science from the State University of New York, he is the author of many articles on national defense and foreign policy.

SHELAH GILBERT LEADER is a policy analyst and teaches at The American University. Educated at Hofstra University, she holds a doctorate in political science from the State University of New York. She has specialized in the political role of the military, as well as public policy and its special impact on women. She has held positions with the U.S. Department of Health and Human Services and the National Commission on the Observance of International Women's Year.